THE HORRIBLE PEACE

A VOLUME IN THE SERIES

VETERANS

EDITED BY

Brian Matthew Jordan and J. Ross Dancy

THE HORRIBLE PEACE

BRITISH VETERANS
AND THE
END OF THE NAPOLEONIC WARS

—◄◉►—

EVAN WILSON

University of Massachusetts Press
Amherst and Boston

Copyright © 2023 by University of Massachusetts Press
All rights reserved
Printed in the United States of America

ISBN 978-1-62534-733-6 (paper); 734-3 (hardcover)

Designed by Sally Nichols
Set in ITC New Baskerville
Printed and bound by Books International, Inc.

Cover design by Sally Nichols
Cover art by Joseph Mallord William Turner, 1775–1851.
War. The Exile and the Rock Limpet. Exhibited 1842. Photo © Tate.

Library of Congress Cataloging-in-Publication Data
Names: Wilson, Evan, 1984–author.
Title: The horrible peace : British veterans and the end of the Napoleonic
Wars / Evan Wilson.
Other titles: British veterans and the end of the Napoleonic Wars
Description: Amherst : University of Massachusetts Press, [2023] | Series:
Veterans | Includes bibliographical references and index.
Identifiers: LCCN 2022045061 (print) | LCCN 2022045062 (ebook) | ISBN
9781625347336 (paperback) | ISBN 9781625347343 (hardcover) | ISBN
9781685750251 (ebook)
Subjects: LCSH: Great Britain—History, Military—19th century. |
Napoleonic Wars, 1800–1815—Veterans. | Napoleonic Wars,
1800–1815—Peace. | Napoleonic Wars, 1800–1815—Participation, British.
| Veterans—Great Britain—History—19th century. | Great Britain—Armed
Forces—History—19th century.
Classification: LCC DA68 .W55 2023 (print) | LCC DA68 (ebook) | DDC
355.00941—dc23/eng/20220930
LC record available at https://lccn.loc.gov/2022045061
LC ebook record available at https://lccn.loc.gov/2022045062

British Library Cataloguing-in-Publication Data
A catalog record for this book is available from the British Library.

An earlier version of chapter 6 appeared in *Navies in Multipolar Worlds: From the Age of
Sail to the Present*, edited by Paul Kennedy and Evan Wilson (London: Routledge, 2020),
62–81. Portions of chapter 12 are slated to appear in *Soldiers in Peace-Making: The Role
of the Military at the End of War, 1800–Present*, edited by Beatrice de Graaf, Thomas
Vaisset, and Frédéric Dessberg (London: Bloomsbury Academic, 2023). I am grateful to
Routledge and Bloomsbury Academic for permission to republish that material here.

FOR ERIN, AGAIN

Contents

Figures and Tables

FIGURES

TABLES

Preface

The idea for this book came out of a conversation with Roger Knight as I was finishing up my first book on British naval officers. He pointed out that there did not exist a history of demobilization, and so I set about writing one. Ironically, we know more about the demobilization of naval officers than about most other members of the armed forces. It was only natural, then, that I broadened my interests to include army officers as well as ordinary soldiers and sailors.

Having identified the groups to study, I sketched out the questions that I thought were worth asking about them. Those questions were informed by my professional experience during the research and writing process. My first book studied naval officers to address questions in British social history; similarly, this book examines the relationship between members of the military and society. I have also become more interested in strategic issues. Shortly after my conversation with Roger Knight, Paul Kennedy hired me to set up a naval and maritime studies initiative at International Security Studies at Yale, and I am currently employed by the U.S. Naval War College. Thus, questions of naval strategy, past and present, permeate my professional life, and they shape the analysis that follows as well.

My historical education has made me uncomfortable with drawing out "lessons of history," however. Historians are always more likely to see differences in the past—it is a foreign country; they do things differently there—than to see similarities. As a result, most of this book is about Britain from 1812 to circa 1825 and not about the challenges facing the U.S. Navy or the world today. Perhaps, however, it might be useful to preview where I think interested readers might look for contemporary relevance. My professional and personal background as an American employed by the military necessarily informs the thoughts that follow, but they are entirely my own and not those of the U.S. government, U.S. Navy, or U.S. Naval War College. The same disclaimer applies to the rest of the book.

There are several areas in which contemporary U.S. strategy could be informed by a closer look at the end of the Napoleonic Wars.[1] This book suggests a few novel conclusions. Command of the sea underpinned Britain's victory over Napoleonic France, but the pressure to demobilize caused Britain to relinquish its command precipitously in key areas. Command of the sea in fact requires constant maintenance. When that is not possible or when that requirement is forgotten, it opens windows of opportunities for enemies to take advantage. Napoleon's return from Elba forms a key moment in the book for this reason. It was a tactical and operational naval failure caused by neglecting that most basic of requirements for sea control: presence. But it was also a strategic and diplomatic failure caused by miscommunication within the government. Large sectors of American professional military education seek to improve communication between branches of the military and between the military and the rest of the government; the Elban affair is an example of the consequences of poor coordination.

The chaotic end to the wars is also an example of the challenges of war termination. A war is not over until the defeated side accepts defeat. The Allied Army of Occupation reflected the lessons learned from Napoleon's first abdication. Recent books have contrasted its success with the failure of the Versailles settlement in 1919 and with the failure of U.S. nation-building efforts in Iraq and Afghanistan. This book suggests some other areas for further research on questions of war termination that might prove fruitful. To give one example, there were actors in both the United States and Britain who were dissatisfied with the status quo ante bellum settlement of the War of 1812, and therefore the chance that war would resume after 1815 was high. Yet the British lacked the capacity to deter American aggression. Instead, Britain turned to diplomacy to de-escalate tensions with a rising power. The Rush-Bagot Treaty was the world's first arms control agreement, and perhaps there is scope for a similar approach with potentially hostile rising powers today.

The second half of this book follows veterans home from the wars. Transitioning from military to civilian life is never easy. Today, the U.S. Military's Transition Assistance Program (TAP) attempts to mitigate some of the challenges facing veterans. Its materials, distributed to all those beginning the process of leaving the military, explicitly reference past demobilizations: "At the end of past conflicts, leaders like George Washington and Jonathan Wainwright challenged those who served under them to assume the mantle of leadership and become an integral part of their communities." A recent addition to the TAP materials is a cover letter signed by all the service chiefs, which warns, "Today's veterans will be challenged to find meaningful purpose in their post-military careers and to tackle reintegration with the same degree of skill and motivation with which they took on their wartime missions."[2] That the military is aware of the problems that veterans will face is admirable, and it is better if veterans approach their postservice lives with a realistic understanding of the effort required to succeed. But the military has also helped to create this problem. Many recruiting campaigns emphasize the skills that recruits can learn in military service. In fact, just as with soldiers after 1815, it is not always clear how those skills will translate to the labor market. These are enduring issues.

The cover letter from the service chiefs is intended "to help establish a positive narrative around this generation of veterans and inspire them to continued service to our great Nation."[3] The clear implication is that there is not currently a positive narrative around this generation of veterans. Indeed, the letter was written and signed by the service chiefs just three weeks after the January 6, 2021, attempted coup at the U.S. Capitol. Veterans were overrepresented among the rioters: 20 percent of those charged were veterans, even though they make up just 7 percent of the U.S. population. Some were still on active service in some capacity when they participated. Social media posts indicate that one of the driving factors behind their participation in the attack was a sense that they no longer recognized the country they had served.[4] That is not to excuse their actions but rather to highlight the ways in which military service can dislocate veterans from civilians. This book shows that the same was true for many soldiers and sailors in 1815. It is yet another example of the shadows long wars cast into the peace.

Other contemporary resonances are highlighted in the text, and hopefully readers will identify more on their own. I am deeply grateful to my colleagues at the Naval War College for encouraging me to connect my research to contemporary affairs. I am solely responsible for the content of the book, for better and for worse, but I acknowledge the support of the many dozens of individuals who helped me bring it to these pages, and not just in Newport. While working at Yale, I benefitted immensely from exposure not only to leading historians but also to political scientists. Foremost among them was Nuno Monteiro, who sadly and unexpectedly passed away in 2021. When he took over the directorship of International Security Studies, he did not immediately fire his strange naval historian deputy, for which I will forever be grateful. Instead, he took me under his wing. That is not to say that he is at all responsible for the product that you are about to read. In fact, he would be baffled by many of the questions this book asks and by my purpose in answering them. Nevertheless, he was a wonderful mentor, and he is sorely missed.

I am in debt to those friends and colleagues who read or heard portions of this project in various stages of preparation and in various contexts. Many provided feedback, for which I am thankful, and I hope they will forgive me if I forget to mention them here. I thank in particular Sam Cavell, Lindsay Cohn, Eliza Gheorghe, Beatrice de Graaf, Chris Green, Christine Haynes, John Kuehn, Alicia Maggard, John Maurer the Elder, John Maurer the Younger, Kevin McCranie, Jamie McGrath, Nick Prime, Jakob Seerup, Veysel Simsek, Jan Stöckmann, and Ryan Wadle. Sara Caputo took time out from her busy publishing schedule to help me with the chapter on sailors on strike. Luke Reynolds made sure this naval historian did not commit too many army-related faux pas. All that remain are my fault, not his.

I am fortunate to be embedded in a network of experts who are always willing to talk about best practices or point me toward a useful resource. I owe them a significant debt of gratitude. James Davey produces cutting-edge scholarship that is readable—the dream of all historians. Geoff Till is the model of the kind of professor I aspire to be: hardworking but never too busy to make time for others. Craig Symonds enlivened my first few years in Newport and pushed me in all the right directions. I hope to live up to his expectations. Nicholas Rodger generously provided me with excerpts from the great work, and that was the least of the support that he has given me over the years. He sets the standard in the field, and I count myself lucky to continue to benefit from his expertise. Brian Jordan and especially J Dancy helped me frame this project and find it a home at UMass. There, Matt Becker and his team have exhibited the kind of flexibility and professionalism that all authors seek. Thank you, all.

Finally, there are a few people without whom this project would not exist. Second books are hard, I have learned. They demand more of an author's network and family than doctoral dissertations, even though this time around I was supposed to know what I was doing. It never feels sufficient to acknowledge the support of this group in a few sentences, but I hope that they are all aware how deeply grateful I am to them.

Paul Kennedy mentored me as a young undergraduate and hired me after my postdoc when nobody else would. I owe my career to him. Roger Knight told me I should write this book, and he has supported me throughout the research and writing process. He is a wonderful scholar who showed me that it was possible for a naval historian to learn how to speak army, and that it is essential for us to do so. John Hattendorf continues to be the guiding light of the Naval War College. He showed me how to speak U.S. Navy, shared his wonderful library with me, and encouraged me in all things. Both John and Roger read major drafts of this book, and I cannot thank them enough.

My family has been a constant source of strength. My father is the best writer I know, and I hope that this book does not embarrass the family name. He read a draft and encouraged me to make it more accessible (yes, it used to be even worse!). Much of it was written during the pandemic. I know how hard it was to do that, but that challenge was nothing compared to being married to me while I did that. My amazing wife Erin not only endured those hardships but also gave birth to our two children, Vera and Henry. On top of that, she read drafts and asked all the right questions. There is no one else to whom I could possibly dedicate this book.

Note on Conventions

There is a Royal Navy; there is no Royal Army. Therefore, this book should capitalize *Navy* and not capitalize *army*. But that would be tiresome and distracting. While fully acknowledging that the Royal Navy was and is proud to carry that title, this book keeps both *navy* and *army* lowercase, emphasizing the similarities between the two services rather than their differences. One reform-minded politician, writing in the 1860s, explained that in 1819, "The term Radical, used as a substantive, had not come into use, but was commonly applied as an epithet."[1] This book capitalizes "Radical" throughout, but doing so does not imply the existence of a defined political party. The original spelling of all quotations has been kept except in rare cases when it would impede understanding. All such cases are noted in the endnotes. The endnotes contain mostly shortened entries aimed at pointing interested readers toward the bibliography.

THE HORRIBLE PEACE

INTRODUCTION

"England Expects every Man to do his Duty," read the handbill. In this case, the duty required was not fighting the Combined Fleet off Cape Trafalgar in October 1805, but rather attending a public meeting at the Loyal Volunteer pub in December 1816. Attendance was needed, the handbill went on to say, because of the state of the country: "Four Millions in Distress!! Four Millions Embarrassed!!! One Million-and-half fear Distress!!! Half-a-Million Live in splendid Luxury!!! . . . Death now would be a relief to Millions—Arrogance, Folly, and Crimes—have brought affairs to this dread Crisis. Firmness and Integrity can only save the Country!!!" At an earlier meeting on November 15, attendees had written a petition calling for parliamentary reform and delivered it to the Home Secretary, Henry Addington, Viscount Sidmouth. Now they were to hear the answer.[1]

The day of the meeting, December 2, the organizers arrived at the pub at noon, and already it was packed. Henry Hunt, one of the speakers, was initially unable to get in the door. Eventually the meeting was called to order and the enthusiastic crowd settled down. As expected, the news about the petition was disappointing: Sidmouth had done what Hunt had requested and passed it on to the prince regent, but it had failed to have any discernable impact. Hunt made a point of prefacing the bad news by requesting that the attendees be "orderly and peaceable," and he said, to get ahead of

1

events, that anyone who rioted was likely to be an informer from Sidmouth's Home Office. But he recognized the crowd's frustration with the widespread unemployment, starvation, and misery, and with the government's apparent unwillingness to take any action. One source of untapped government funds, claimed Hunt, was prize money that the Admiralty was illegally withholding from deserving sailors. He asked the crowd if they would rather have "a penny of their own earning, or a pennyworth of soup given to them in charity?" They responded, "A penny of our own earning!" and "No soup!" and "Damn soup!" Hunt said he was not opposed to charity, except when it came from "a nest of Bankers and Contractors, who had got rich by the war which had brought the nation into its present distressed state." Finally, Hunt helped organize another petition calling for parliamentary reform, this time to be presented in Parliament by two Radical MPs, Sir Francis Burdett and the former naval officer Thomas, Lord Cochrane.[2]

The meeting broke up at half past three in the afternoon, and it was then that events began to spiral out of control. Spillover from the pub had flooded Spa Fields, the nearby open area northwest of the City of London, and the crowd was joined by thousands of others who had seen the advertisement or heard about the meeting through word of mouth. There were perhaps ten thousand people in total, and they were increasingly restless, brought to higher pitch of frustration by speakers standing on wagons and reading from the handbill. All that was needed was a spark, and it was provided by a band of sailors who showed up carrying a tricolored flag. They were well aware that this would provoke a response, and so they also carried a banner saying, "Be not afraid of the Soldiers, for the Soldiers are our Brothers."[i] It is difficult to piece together what happened next, but most sources agree that bands of rioters broke into three shops that sold guns and ammunition. They shot at least one bystander and stabbed another while destroying property on their way south. One group headed southeast across the City to the Tower of London, presumably in the hopes of recreating the storming of the Bastille, but they were not followed by the central mass.

---

i   Alternatively reported as "The Brave Soldiers are Our Friends" and "The Brave Soldiers are out; Brothers, treat them kindly."

Meanwhile, the authorities countermobilized and armed themselves. Businesses in the City and on the Strand had closed early in the afternoon in anticipation of trouble, so there were plenty of volunteers around to be sworn in as constables. The lord mayor stationed two hundred soldiers from the Life Guards at the Bank of England, another detachment at the Stock Exchange, and the Ninth Light Infantry at Mansion House. As the rioters moved south into Holborn, they lost cohesion, broke into smaller detachments, and lost momentum. The troops at the Tower of London had little trouble with their mob. The Life Guards dispersed the last band at Temple Bar, although in the process a guardsman was seriously wounded. All night, London was in the hands of the military, as soldiers patrolled the streets.[3]

The tricolor flag was indeed a provocative symbol—a treasonous symbol, even—in a country that had just fought that flag and the ideas it represented for almost a quarter of a century. The sailors who brought it anticipated that the lord mayor would react by sending in soldiers both because they knew the authorities would take the threat seriously and because that was what always seemed to happen. Indeed, there were plenty of soldiers available to send because large portions of the army had come home following Napoleon's final defeat a year earlier. In other words, we cannot understand what happened during the Spa Fields riots of December 1816 without understanding the context of demobilization from the wars that had just ended. This book aims to provide that context by extending the story back into the wars and forward through the postwar decade. The question that animates its analysis is broad and simple: What happened when soldiers and sailors came home from the Napoleonic Wars?

That question has not attracted much attention from historians, which is in many ways understandable.[4] For historians interested in strategy, operations, and military administration, few battles in world history provide a cleaner dividing line than Waterloo: before, there was Napoleon; after, there was the Pax Britannica. Those appear to be two different subjects, best tackled by two different books (or more usually, two different historians).[5] Historians interested in the domestic unrest that characterized the Regency (c. 1811–20) have naturally written across the 1815 dividing line, but in most cases, soldiers and sailors appear only in the margins.[6] This book connects the military and naval history of the climax of the wars with the domestic unrest of the postwar period. To understand *when* soldiers and sailors came home, we need to examine the strategy that allowed them to be released. To understand *what happened* when they were released, we need to examine the role they played in shaping British society in the postwar decade. Those are the two parts of this book; connecting them is its goal.

Reframing the end of the wars in this way transforms a story of British triumph over Napoleon into a less happy affair, as the Spa Fields riots suggest. A few months before the riots, *The Times* wondered how Britain would celebrate the one-year anniversary of Waterloo. "The nation will have but little occasion to rejoice in the peace," warned an editorial. "After a long and sanguinary war, and many a glorious victory achieved by British valour, [what if] a most destructive peace broke out at home, by which the hopes of the nation, which had expected relief and repose after its innumerable sufferings, were cruelly frustrated, and the people was sunk into a still lower abyss of misery and ruin?" The editorial concluded with the original Latin passage from Tacitus's second chapter of *The Histories*, which translates as "the history on which I am entering is that of a period rich in disasters, terrible with battles, torn by civil struggles, *horrible even in peace!*"[7, ii]

The idea that peace might be horrible sounds strange to us. After all, war is hell, so peace must necessarily be better. That logic is sound, but it is also conditioned by our own expectations for great-power war. In the shadow of mushroom clouds over Hiroshima and Nagasaki, we cannot imagine great-power war as anything but horrifically destructive. Even a nonnuclear great-power war would be unimaginably devastating. It is tempting to project that perspective back two centuries, to assume that in 1815 Europeans universally rejoiced in the long-awaited peace.

We should resist that temptation. In fact, great-power war in an era before mass bombing of civilian targets and nuclear weapons was not so obviously catastrophic, especially for inhabitants of an island nation. Large French armies never did manage to march on British soil, which spared many Britons from direct experience

---

ii Tacitus was writing about Rome in the aftermath of Nero's death in 68 CE. The text reads, "Opus aggredior opimum casibus, atrox proeliis, *ipsa etiam pace savum!*" The emphasis is in the *Times*' original, and the Latin differs slightly from modern reproductions of *The Histories*.

of war's horrors. War was a constant presence in this period—a twenty-five-year-old at Spa Fields in 1816 would not have known a world without global war—and it shaped the lives of millions of Britons through mobilizations, food shortages, and invasion fears. But the combat, the destruction, and the death were overseas. Even if the war shaped much of daily life, it could be treated as a source of curiosity. War shapes the plots of Jane Austen's novels, which were all written during or immediately after the wars, but it does so as a background rumble.[8] The Reverend John Stonard, safe in his parsonage, complained about the peace in 1814, "Surely there never will be any more news as long as we live. The Papers will be as dull as a ledger and Politics as insipid as the white of an egg."[9]

Samuel Taylor Coleridge tackled this contradiction head-on in his 1798 poem *Fears in Solitude*: "Secure from actual warfare, we have lov'd / To swell the war-whoop, passionate for war!" The British were "thankless" for peace, which had been "long-preserv'd by fleets and perilous seas." With no enemy armies in their fields and cities, Britons were ignorant of war's "ghastlier workings (famine or blue plague, / Battle, or siege, or flight through wintry snows,) / We, this whole people, have been clamorous / For war and bloodshed, animating sports, / The which we pay for, as a thing to talk of / Spectators and not combatants!" War to the British was nothing more, accused Coleridge, than the "best amusement for our morning meal!"[10]

The British cheered for war because they were insulated from its horrors and because it created lucrative opportunities. As Edmund Burke put it, commerce could "be united with, and made to flourish by war."[11] The British state existed to fund and fight wars, and wars compounded the benefits of its investments. The positive feedback loop created by regular wars waged away from British shores helps explain Coleridge's sense that war, to most Britons, was something to pay for, profit from, and cheer on. It was not obvious that the end of the wars would be the harbinger of a better world.

At the same time, as Coleridge well knew, war was also disruptive, costly, and risky. Britons might have been shielded from the worst of war's deprivations, but they were fully aware of war's capriciousness. All wars, even successful ones, caused credit crises, depressed foreign trade, and increased prices. Four million Europeans, or 2.5 percent of the population, died during the French Revolutionary

(1792–1801) and Napoleonic (1803–15) Wars. British casualties totaled about three hundred thousand soldiers and sailors, and the death rate increased over time so that by the last few years of the wars, twenty-five thousand men were dying each year. All told, Britain lost as many men in these wars, as a percentage of its population, as it did in the First World War.[12] Indeed, until 1914, they were simply called the Great Wars. Although Britons in 1815 had fewer reasons to fear great-power war than we do, we should not let their occasional enthusiasm for war blind us to war's horrors. Nor is it the goal of this book, which examines the difficulties of peace, to glorify war.

In fact, the Great Wars were a watershed in the modern conception of the value of peace. The endemic warfare of eighteenth-century Europe seemed to many enlightened Europeans and Americans to be irrational and wasteful, and some intellectuals wondered if human society could rationally move beyond war. Benjamin Franklin wrote to Sir Joseph Banks at the end of the American Revolutionary War in 1783: "I join with you most cordially in rejoicing at the Return of Peace. I hope it will be lasting, and that Mankind will at Length . . . have Reason and Sense enough to settle their Differences without cutting Throats: *For in my Opinion there never was a good War, or a bad Peace.*" Contra Burke, Franklin did not think the marriage of commerce and war was productive. He wondered what amazing achievements might be possible if governments devoted their military budgets toward infrastructure, with the goal of "rendering England a compleat Paradise." Instead, he complained, funds were spent "bringing Misery into thousands of Families, and destroying the Lives of so many Thousands of working People who might have perform'd the useful Labour."[13]

Thomas Paine agreed, and in the second part of his best-selling *The Rights of Man* (1792), he itemized the peace dividend that republican governments could expect. The root of the problem, he argued, was the nature of monarchical government: "All the monarchical governments are military. War is their trade, plunder and revenue their objects."[14] Paine's predicted peace did not materialize, of course, and so in 1795, as war once again raged in Europe, James Madison approached the question from the opposite direction. The system of government was not the problem but rather war itself: "War is the parent of armies; from these proceed debts and taxes; and armies, and debts, and taxes are the known instruments for bringing the many under the domination of the few. In war, too, the discretionary power of the Executive is extended; its influence in dealing out offices, honors, and emoluments is multiplied."[15] The same year, Immanuel Kant published *To Perpetual Peace*, and he too identified the debt as one of the major dangers of war because it contributed to making war endemic. To break the cycle, Kant argued, governments needed to "establish" peace. It was not enough simply to stop war; it was necessary to work tirelessly to create conditions for peace to take root.[16]

This book follows Madison and Kant in studying war and peace by emphasizing not just the conduct of wars but also the challenges wars create in their aftermath. What happened when soldiers and sailors came home is that Britons struggled to establish and maintain peace, both at home and abroad. They struggled strategically because there were still threats to peace after 1815, but the debt burden overwhelmed the budget. They struggled politically because the taxes needed to service the debt were unpopular. They struggled because there were competing ideas about the government's role in society. They struggled because it was not clear if there was a peace dividend, and if so, how it should be divided. Ultimately, they struggled because transitioning from war to peace is difficult, even in a victorious country.

Because the transition is difficult, we should not be surprised to find even those who suffered most in war—soldiers and sailors—to be ambivalent about the arrival of peace. Demobilization meant difficult separations from units and messes that had formed familial bonds. Returning home forced veterans to confront the common afflictions of veteranhood: (re)creating a home away from military service; finding meaning and purpose in civilian life; and learning skills relevant to civilian employment. Following Napoleon's first abdication in 1814, one soldier commented, "I believe it is common to human nature to forget hardships, privations, and fatigues . . . soon after they have ceased, and are succeeded by the common comforts of life. This may account, in some measure, for the assertions which I have heard made by a few zealots and fire-eaters, who . . . have declared that they were quite inconsolable when the armistice was concluded, and the prospect of no longer being targets for French bullets stared them in the face."[17]

Facing French bullets provided opportunities for officers to make their names and possibly their fortunes. In the face of the threat from revolutionary ideologies, the British state was eager to reward acts of heroism, and some men dramatically improved their social standing through promotions and honors. In both services, pay was relatively low compared to similar professions, but prize money and honors provided opportunities to earn vast fortunes. On the other hand, soldiers and sailors were not spectators to war, and for them, war was not amusing. The horrors of combat are well-known—not only the mutilations and deaths but the lingering effects of trauma. The greatest killer was disease, Coleridge's "blue plague." The army suffered eight times as many deaths from disease as in battle in the Great Wars—usually yellow fever for those in the tropics and typhus for those in filthy encampments.[18]

All these things can be true: War is terrible. War causes immense suffering. War is wasteful. War also provides opportunities for social mobility, profit, invention, and investment. Those contradictions linger for years after the war ends, and in doing so they shape societies' attempts to establish a lasting peace. The Great Wars' high profits were followed by a credit and agricultural crisis. Opportunities for promotion and advancement dried up. Diseases continued to ravage regiments in the tropics. Battles in the streets over the future of the country replaced battles in foreign fields. Any history of the Napoleonic Wars that stops in 1815 is incomplete. What this book shows is how difficult it was for Britain to transition from war to peace after more than two decades of war on the grandest and most destructive scale then known.

It is true, and it is important to acknowledge, that Britain in 1815 was on the verge of its greatest century. For the next three generations, Britons had more opportunities and enjoyed more wealth than any other people on the planet. Britain's lead in industrialization was matched only by the growth of its empire. Under Queen Victoria, no war comparable to the Great Wars scarred Europe, and the government was not overthrown in a bloody revolt. Britain was economically better off than most of the rest of the world in 1815. Nevertheless, that was not obvious to those living through demobilization, which was characterized by uncertainty and turmoil.

A climate catastrophe set the stage for the chaos of the postwar decade. In April 1815, as Napoleon was gathering his army around him for one last campaign, Mount Tambora in the East Indies erupted. It remains the second-largest volcanic event in recorded history.[iii] It exploded with the force of thirty-three billion tons of TNT, or about two million times the force of the bomb dropped on Hiroshima. Harvests failed around the world in 1816, the "year without a summer." Mary Shelley wrote *Frankenstein* while sheltering from the unseasonable weather on Lake Geneva, but she and her party were privileged. It has been estimated that two hundred thousand Europeans died that year.[iv] In Ireland, typhus followed on the heels of the starvation, and cholera outbreaks in Southeast Asia soon spread to Europe.[19]

It is commonplace to look to the peace settlement of 1815 as a model for contemporary international relations.[20] Yet a closer examination of the decade after 1815 reveals that the Pax Britannica seemed anything but assured after Waterloo, a battle that had only happened because the previous 1814 peace settlement had collapsed. Carl von Clausewitz, a veteran of the Great Wars, echoed Kant in worrying about the durability of any peace settlement. Writing in the 1820s, he argued that "even the ultimate outcome of a war is not always to be regarded as final."[21] Defeated states assumed they could recover their losses in the next war. Why would 1815 be any different? Just a few years after Waterloo, the Duke of Wellington survived a serious assassination attempt by a Bonapartist in France. He was in Paris commanding the 150,000-strong Allied Army of Occupation, which was put in place to avoid a repeat of the Waterloo campaign. Elsewhere, wars erupted in India, Burma, and Ceylon. Peace with the United States seemed unlikely to last. The public debt was as large relative to the size of the economy as at any point in British history, and interest payments crippled budgets. The navy's exhausted ships

---

iii Tambora's 1815 eruption has long been thought to be the largest volcanic event in recorded history, but recent evidence strongly suggests that the 1257 eruption of Mount Rinjani, just a hundred miles west of Tambora, put twice as much sulfate in the atmosphere as Tambora did in 1815. Both eruptions were more powerful than the other famous Indonesian volcanic eruption, that of Krakatoa in 1883. See Lavigne et al., "Source of the Great A.D. 1257 Mystery Eruption Unveiled." Scientists and historians are also finding close links between other explosive volcanic eruptions and societal upheaval, wars, and famines throughout the ancient world. See the Yale Nile Initiative at https://www.yalenileinitiative.org/.

iv So many livestock and horses died that Baron Karl von Drais invented the predecessor of the bicycle, the *Laufsmaschine*, in 1817, as a substitute for the horse. The "running machine" looked like the balance bikes used by children today.

overwhelmed the dockyards, which were suffering from drastic budget cuts. With few ships and sailors to man them, British trade was
exposed to the depredations of pirates.

Domestically, the situation was even more unsettled. Spa Fields was
by no means unique. Sailors had shut down the ports of Newcastle
and Sunderland in 1815, and across the first five years after Waterloo,
strikes and riots disrupted cities from Birmingham to Glasgow. Ministers responded by suspending habeas corpus and passing legislation
making meetings of more than fifty people illegal. With no other
effective tools available to them, they aggressively deployed soldiers
to suppress riots. At the same time, veteran soldiers trained protestors
to instill discipline and fight back. In 1819, Henry Hunt was back in
the news when he was the featured speaker at a meeting in St. Peter's
Fields in Manchester. This time, there were fifty thousand attendees,
but when the authorities overreacted to their disciplined marching,
the ensuing battle of "Peterloo" resulted in hundreds of casualties. The
very name of the battle, much like the use of Nelson's signal to adver-
tise the Spa Fields meetings, emphasizes the ways in which Britons
saw their world in postwar terms. Those who were calling for reform
believed that the war for the future of Britain was only just beginning.

The postwar period cannot be understood without looking back to
the last few years of the Great Wars, nor can it be understood without
placing veterans of those wars at the center of the story. That is the key
takeaway from the process of writing this book. It began life as a political and military examination of demobilization, but it soon became
clear that to tell the story properly, it needed to connect strategic and
domestic questions. Doing so provided an opportunity to revise and
extend the existing scholarship on the period. A full accounting of all
that is new about *The Horrible Peace* is not possible here, but two examples, one from each direction, can serve as proofs of concept.

John Ikenberry's influential interpretation of British foreign policy
in the postwar years is that the secretary of state for foreign affairs,
Robert Stewart, Viscount Castlereagh, chose a path of "strategic
restraint." Despite Britain's position as the leading power in Europe
in 1815, Castlereagh did not attempt to exploit this position to the
fullest. Instead, he made concessions "to signal restraint and facili-
tate agreement on the wider and agreed-upon institutional arrangements for the management of the postwar order. British policy also
reflected the incentives that a leading state has to secure an order

with a measure of legitimacy, and it was willing to place some modest limits on its power to achieve this end." Those limits involved participating in European collective security arrangements—the Congress System.[22] Henry Kissinger has argued that it was Castlereagh's devotion to this model of European governance that explains his unpopularity: "Castlereagh was out of tune not only with his contemporaries but with the entire thrust of modern British foreign policy. He left no legacy; no British statesman has used Castlereagh as a model."[23]

What this book shows, however, is that such interpretations are incomplete because they do not account for the domestic context or the actual state of Britain's military forces. Ikenberry's advocacy for strategic restraint may be a useful model for today's United States, but Britain in 1815 did not act with restraint solely to establish a legitimate postwar order. In fact, Britain was not able to dictate the terms of the 1815 settlement. Neither the army nor the navy was as powerful as has been supposed, and the domestic pressure to relieve the tax burden after two decades of war constrained the paths available to ministers. Furthermore, Castlereagh was unpopular not just because of his enthusiasm for a proto–European Union but also because he was seen as the mouthpiece of an unrepresentative government that was doing nothing to relieve extreme suffering amid the chaos of demobilization.

The strategic situation at the end of the wars shaped the domestic experience of demobilization in ways that have not been fully appreciated. Soldiers and sailors did not come home the day after Waterloo in one undifferentiated mass of veterans. Instead, sailors came home first because the strategic situation allowed the navy to demobilize first. Some arrived as early as 1812, and naval demobilization continued through 1816. Sailors were theoretically well positioned to find work in the postwar period because they had a marketable skill. The arrival of a hundred thousand sailors flooded the labor market, however, so sailors had to negotiate disputes with the government and shipowners from a weak position. Soldiers tended not to have marketable skills, but they were also more likely to remain in service on lifetime enlistments. Many thousands of soldiers never came home but instead redeployed to garrison the empire; others came home but remained in service as a domestic police force. Another large group had to wait until after the breakup of the Army of Occupation in 1818 to separate from their units. We cannot understand what happened when soldiers and sailors came home if we do not understand the strategic constraints and responsibilities of each service.

Uncovering how and when each service brought men home proved to be surprisingly difficult. For the navy, the list books that helpfully told ministers where every ship in the navy was in any given month stopped two years short of the end of the wars, the clerks apparently overwhelmed by the scale of the navy's global operations. When the list books resumed, the wars had been over for more than five years. Nevertheless, there are archival sources that allow a patient historian to reconstruct the patterns of deployment for both ships and regiments. They form the spine of the chapters that answer the question of *when* soldiers and sailors came home.

As helpful as it was to trace the patterns of deployment, it quickly became clear that the missing voice in the postwar period was that of the veteran soldier and sailor. Recovering that voice proved more difficult than originally imagined. Soldiers and sailors published memoirs in astonishing quantities in the decades after 1815. It can seem as if every participant in the Battle of Waterloo wrote his own account, and it might actually be the case that every literate person who encountered Napoleon from his surrender until his death wrote about the experience. Yet while these memoirs provide colorful accounts of the experience of war, they are often less helpful about the transition to peace. One, for example, states merely that the author "returned safely to the home I left in 1806—."[24] Nothing more is said. One of the primary goals of the research for this book, then, was to find memoirs that contained more than an em dash on the postwar period. Both officers and men published such works, and many are used in the text that follow. Officers were more likely to leave behind—and archives are more likely to contain—additional manuscript sources with coverage of the postwar period.[v] These diaries, letters, and memoirs form the heart of the chapters that answer the question of *what happened* when soldiers and sailors came home.

This bifurcated methodology requires handling sources on both sides with equal care. Government records that purport to tell a comprehensive and authoritative story of who went where when are not

---

v   Although even here there are some surprising gaps. The Navy Records Society's three
     volumes of the papers of Sir Thomas Byam Martin, the comptroller of the Navy Board
     in the postwar years, are blank from 1816 to 1822.

always as comprehensive and authoritative as historians would like. The missing seven years in the navy's list books is one example, but there are others as well. During the postwar protests, it was in the government's interest to paint its agents in the best possible light and the Radical protestors in the worst. On the other side, memoirs written by those who experienced the chaos of demobilization are processed records of the past, shaped by the time and place in which they were written. Importantly, that time and place was often very different than the time and place that the memoirist was remembering—and that is to say nothing of the challenges that all of us face in remembering events long ago. A more complete description of the challenges posed by memoirs as sources can be found at the beginning of chapter 9, but here we can say that there are two ways in which this book deals with these challenges. The first barely needs mentioning: historians should always treat their sources critically. Even soldiers' and sailors' letters home, which might superficially appear to be straightforward firsthand accounts of events, do not always offer an honest picture of the emotional state of the author because servicemen often sought to avoid worrying their families. The second, however, is to triangulate sources with other contemporaneous records. Newspapers, financial records, letter books, and older historiographies can often provide information about sources or events that are otherwise hidden. Interested readers can find a full list in the bibliography.

The variety of veterans' experiences pulls this book in several directions, but at its heart, it examines the messy legacy of the Great Wars in the country that supposedly benefitted most from them. To return to *The Times*' prescient editorial of 1816, this book shows how even a victorious nation could worry that its people would be "sunk into a still lower abyss of misery and ruin." It describes "a period rich in disasters," including global climate changes and pandemics. It narrates years that were "terrible with battles," even though the Vienna settlement is usually depicted as auguring the longest period of peace in European history. It witnesses the fabric of society being "torn by civil struggles," including most famously at Peterloo. It concludes by following veterans, many of whom were frustrated by these challenges, away from postwar Britain, into and beyond the empire.

Part I

—◀◉▶—

DEMOBILIZATION
AND
BRITISH STRATEGY

When did soldiers and sailors come home? The answer to that question depended on the strategic situation as ministers sought to bring the war in Europe to a victorious conclusion while simultaneously grappling with a new war across the Atlantic. The first two chapters set the scene by surveying the state of Britain and its armed forces in 1812. Chapters 3, 4, and 5 narrate the events of 1812–15 with a focus on the role that demobilization played in shaping British strategy. Stretched to the limit of its material and manpower capacities, Britain needed to bring soldiers and sailors home as quickly as possible without jeopardizing the outcome of the wars. Chapters 6 and 7 survey the strategic implications of the dramatic reduction in the two services and question just how powerful Britain was in the decade after 1815.

CHAPTER 1

The Government at the Beginning of the End

We now know that the Napoleonic Wars began to end just when Britain's strategic situation seemed to have reached its nadir, in the late spring of 1812. There had been other seasons in the Great Wars full of bad news—the winter of 1805, with Austerlitz coming on the heels of Nelson's death, for example, or the spring of 1797, when the Great Mutinies paralyzed the fleet—but the events of May and June 1812 rival any of those periods. On May 11, a disgruntled merchant named John Bellingham shot and killed the prime minister, Spencer Perceval, in the lobby of the House of Commons. On June 18, the United States declared war on Britain, and on June 24, Napoleon's multinational Grande Armée, the largest army ever assembled in Europe to date, crossed the Neman River into Russia. Leaderless Britain now had to fight a new opponent in a remote theater while Napoleon seemed poised to win yet another continent-spanning victory. Yet less than two years later, Napoleon abdicated for the first time.

Few wars have had a more roller-coaster ending than the Napoleonic Wars, which means that it can be challenging to determine when demobilization could begin. Before we can answer that question, however, we should survey the state of the British government and armed forces in 1812. This chapter focuses on the former. Who were the men responsible for bringing the war to a successful conclusion and then bringing soldiers and sailors home? They had to balance the strategic imperatives of global warfare with financial realities, but they also faced several domestic challenges. What were their priorities, and what shaped their perspectives?

This book is about veterans, and that usually refers to soldiers, sailors, and their officers who participated in combat operations. It is important to keep in mind, however, that all of Britain's political elite were in some sense veterans of the wars. Their entire professional lives had been shaped by the wars, and the youngest members, like Robert Peel (born in 1788), knew nothing but war. They took several lessons from this experience, not least of which being the danger of revolutionary ideology. Not only had the French Revolution resulted in the overthrow of the established political and social order, but it had also launched two decades of wars. Revolution and war were inextricably linked in ministers' minds. The new prime minister, Robert Jenkinson, Second Earl Liverpool, had been present at the storming of the Bastille, and nothing scared ministers more than a British sequel.

The fight against Radicalism had been most acute during the 1790s, as the French example had spawned corresponding societies and networks of men and women calling for an overturning of the social and political order. While there were moderate and extreme varieties of Radicals, we can say broadly that they hoped to encourage popular participation in politics, expand the right to vote, and reform Parliament to represent them more fairly. Some of these networks had been out in the open, and periodically the government had cracked down on free speech and the right to assemble. These efforts had been barely successful in the 1790s, and the overt threat from Radicalism had receded in the first decade of the new century. But ministers knew, thanks to domestic intelligence efforts, that there were other groups with violent intentions operating in the shadows. By 1812, some of the corresponding societies were back up and running, and Radical speakers like Major John Cartwright were attracting large crowds on tours of the manufacturing districts. The government's greatest fear was an alliance between Radical intelligentsia and an insurrectionary working class, and it was looking likely that this decade would see a resurgence of Radical activity, both violent and nonviolent, at all levels of society. Could Britain finally end the wars while simultaneously maintaining its ancien régime government?

To stave off revolution, the British elite had for the last century increasingly sought to bind the nation together in shared opposition to the French Catholic enemy. English, Scottish, and Welsh men and women began to see themselves as increasingly British, loyal (ministers hoped) members of a state and an empire centered on the monarchy and Parliament in London. If the end of the wars with France removed that binding agent, would British society hold? At the same time, local identities and local government remained essential components of the British nation. Much of the legislation that Parliament passed to deal with social problems was done through acts targeted at specific localities to address specific concerns, which were brought to Parliament's attention in the first place by local authorities. Most Britons experienced their government through their parish, which was responsible for poor relief, and Liverpool and his ministers governed through local authorities like the justices of the peace. Could the government in Westminster continue to rely on these authorities? What political steps might be necessary to shore up support among the country elite?[1]

The United Kingdom's population in 1812 was about eighteen million, but it was in the process of growing rapidly—in fact, the decade from 1811 to 1821 saw the fastest rate of population growth in British history. The largest single occupational group remained agricultural laborers, but there were also signs of increasing industrialization.[2] Much of the population growth was centered on northern manufacturing districts, none of which was fairly represented in Parliament. Doomsayers like Thomas Malthus predicted that the number of poor people would soon exceed Britain's capacity to feed them, resulting in mass starvation. Increased agricultural productivity eventually proved Malthus wrong, but that was not obvious to ministers at the time. Similarly, the introduction of steam technology showed promise for many industries, especially textiles, but followers of "Ned Ludd" engaged in the destruction of mechanized looms, known as frame-breaking, and other protests across the northern districts that threatened to spill over into a broader insurrection—precisely what the ministry feared most. How would these fundamental changes to the nature of towns, the countryside, and the economy alter the political and social landscape?

In confronting these and other questions, Liverpool and his ministers considered themselves to be aggressive reformers, but not of the political system that gave them their power—that smacked of the revolutionary ideology they were fighting. They did not sympathize with the Luddites, of course, and there was no thought of reforming Parliament during a war. Instead, they focused their efforts on finding efficiencies in government to fund and fight the wars most effectively and then to return Britain to peacetime normality, at which point it would be essential to begin preparing for the next great European conflagration. After all, that was what their great hero William Pitt the Younger had done in the 1780s. There were deep contradictions here. War was simultaneously endemic to European life, an abnormality that needed to be removed from the operations of the state, and an inevitability that demanded preparation. Much of the story in the following chapters can be found in the tension between the demand for "normalcy," whatever that meant, and continuing security challenges, both at home and abroad. Could ministers balance these contradictory pressures?

Paramount in British thinking about security was Ireland. In 1801, the Acts of Union had brought Ireland formally into the United Kingdom of Great Britain and Ireland, but they had not resolved fundamental questions about the relationship. Ireland was an occupied territory in this period, and the extent to which Catholics could participate in British and Irish political life remained a divisive political issue. Pitt had resigned over it, and even a decade later, it was one of the issues that cut across political party lines. Strategically, Ireland remained Britain's vulnerable underbelly, and ministers constantly fretted—with good reason—about the possibility of an uprising supported by a foreign power. Both the army and navy devoted significant resources to its defense, building coastal signal stations and barracks for large bodies of troops. More ominously, ministers also began organizing and arming fencibles, yeomanry, militias, and other paramilitary organizations in the hopes that they would remain loyal in the event of a French landing. Would Ireland remain quiescent, or would rebellion flare up again?[3]

The British were armed as well—they were an "armed nation," in one historian's telling.[4] In France, the idea of arming the people manifested in the levée en masse of 1793; the British equivalent was an increasing reliance on auxiliary military organizations like the militia and volunteers. All told, Britain armed one in six men of military age—the highest percentage in Europe—bringing the total size of its armed forces to three times what it had been in the American Revolutionary War.[5] Arming the populace in the era of the French Revolution was a double-edged sword. While it meant that an invading army would likely meet with some resistance and it freed up regular forces to be deployed abroad, it also meant providing training and weapons to potential revolutionaries. The government continued to pass repressive legislation to stamp out revolutionary ideas before they took hold—a theme that we will follow into the postwar period. Would the government's strategy of arming civilians backfire?

Britain at the beginning of the end of the Napoleonic Wars, then, faced major questions on a range of fronts. It was an armed country led by a group of conservative elites who sought above all else to prevent insurrection. This fear caused them to overreact to Radical organizations and think proactively about how to defend against foreign interference. In general, however, their power to act domestically was limited because the machinery of the modern state was in its infancy. Instead, they relied on buy-in from local authorities to carry out their domestic agenda. Their most potent tools were the army, the navy, and the growing power of the British economy. The industrial takeoff was only just beginning, but the fundamentals of the British economy were strong.

George III knew little about the state of his country in 1812 as he was well into the terminal stages of his illness. He lingered until January 1820, but from 1811, his son, the future George IV, reigned as prince regent. Broadly unpopular, the prince regent's profligacy and scandal-prone private life made him a significant source of anxiety for his ministers. Those ministers, following the assassination of Perceval, were led by Liverpool. The government he formed in the wake of the assassination was widely assumed to be temporary, unable to muster the support in Parliament necessary to lead. It proved to be one of the most durable governments in British history, lasting until Liverpool resigned following a stroke fifteen years later.

Liverpool's later-nineteenth-century successor, Benjamin Disraeli, did more than any other to shape the historical perception of Liverpool, dismissing him as an "arch-mediocrity." In this view, which some historians have shared, Liverpool's government was a wartime coalition ill-suited to the challenges of peace. Its ideological goals were no more than to follow blindly in the footsteps of the great administrator Pitt, and it was lucky to have remained in office so long.[6] The problem with this interpretation is that luck is an unsatisfying explanation for how Liverpool managed to become the third-longest-tenured prime minister in British history, governing longer than not only Disraeli and other titans of Victorian Britain like Gladstone and Salisbury but also Churchill and Thatcher. It is true that Liverpool lacked charisma, and his administration was hampered by its lack of speaking talent in the Commons. But he was clearly an effective manager of an increasingly talented ministry. There were five former or future prime ministers who served in his cabinets, and his subtle management of their egos provided Britain with remarkable stability at the highest levels of government. He won four consecutive general elections (admittedly in an unreformed Parliament) in one of the most turbulent periods of British history.[7]

Liverpool certainly benefitted from a weak opposition that failed to exploit the divisions of the wartime coalition, either during or after the wars. In both the 1812 and 1818 general elections, it has been estimated that the ministry had a majority of more than two hundred in the Commons (400 to 196 and 411 to 198, respectively), with about fifty additional swing votes. Yet this overstates the rigidity of the parties. Technically, nearly all mainstream politicians in this period would have considered themselves Whigs, and it was common for politicians to vote both for and against the government: from 1815 to 1818, 233 MPs (more than a third of the Commons) did so. For the sake of simplicity, most historians overlay party allegiances to Parliament in this period, even if the MPs themselves would not have seen their political allegiances in that way. We generally refer to Liverpool and his reliable supporters as Tories, or sometimes "Liberal Tories."[8]

We refer to the opposition as Whigs. Thanks in part to their sympathy with some of the ideological undercurrents of the French Revolution, the Whigs were generally less enthusiastic about pursuing the wars aggressively. In the 1790s, faced with republican opponents, they had opposed the wars altogether; now, faced with Napoleon, they criticized the conduct of the wars. In theory, they also supported parliamentary reform. Yet they tended to come from the wealthiest families in the nation, and they did not seem capable of capitalizing on popular movements for reform. They were internally divided as well, as followers of the Grenville family left the Whigs in 1817, leaving an even weaker opposition in the Commons.[9]

To manage the business of government, Liverpool relied on informal meetings of his key ministers at his home, Fife House in Whitehall. Very little actual business was conducted by the full cabinet because there were members of his coalition government who had been brought in for their votes rather than their expertise or opinions. Liverpool's great strength as prime minister was keeping that coalition together while conducting the business of government in closed-door settings that left the opposition guessing as to his next steps.[10] What follows is a brief survey of some of the major figures of Liverpool's government as a way of introducing them and their worldview. There were certainly divisions and disagreements in the cabinet, but fundamentally the opposition was weak enough and the coalition strong enough that we can say that most ministers shared similar ideas about the nature of the state and its relationship to war, the economy, and society. Those ideas shaped the process and consequences of demobilization.

Most of Liverpool's government and most MPs came from Britain's social elite. About 25 percent of the House of Commons were sons of peers; 40 percent were large landowners who drew their income from rents; and 60 percent held establishment positions in the church, the armed forces, or the legal profession (many MPs fit into more than one category).[11] Their reactionary crackdown on the postwar unrest can be at least partially explained by their social background, but that is insufficient. Many of the leading members of the ministry had ascended rapidly through the social and professional ranks. Lord Eldon, the lord chancellor, was the son of a coal merchant in Newcastle, and while his father had eventually made a fortune, it was certainly new money. Robert Peel, the rising star of the administration, was the chief secretary for Ireland from August 1812. His father had made an enormous fortune in textile manufacturing, but like Eldon's, it was new money. George Canning, who in 1816 became president of the Board of Control and was a pivotal figure in the later years of Liverpool's tenure, came from very little money. His father was a failed lawyer, and his mother was an actress.[12]

Eldon, Peel, and Canning participate in our story at the margins; more important for our purposes are the three men most responsible for domestic, foreign, and economic policies. Sidmouth sat with Liverpool in the Lords, which made him unavailable for the defense of policy initiatives in the Commons, but he played a major role in the administration as home secretary from 1812 to 1822. He was an easy man to underestimate or misunderstand. Derided throughout his career by his social superiors as "the Doctor" because of his father's occupation (Sidmouth himself had trained as a lawyer), he had had an unlikely three-year tenure as prime minister following Pitt's resignation over Catholic emancipation in 1801. As home secretary, he bore the brunt of the responsibility for the government's response to the popular agitation and unrest that characterized the postwar years. He worked to infiltrate Radical organizations with spies and supported the passage of repressive legislation. Yet when the Radical Samuel Bamford met him in 1817, he was surprised to find that Sidmouth's "manner was affable, and much more encouraging to freedom of speech than I had expected."[13]

Liverpool and Castlereagh formed the key partnership in foreign policy. Castlereagh was Liverpool's most important deputy as he sat in the Commons and was generally regarded as the best debater available to the government. He commanded respect but not admiration: his speeches were notable for their length rather than their rhetorical flourishes. He was capable of warmth in private, but his public persona was reserved and distant. His visibility in the Commons combined with that reserve made him one of the most unpopular members of the administration, widely seen as responsible for the gulf between the government's policies and the actual state of the country. Percy Shelley pulled no punches in his 1819 poem, "The Masque of Anarchy": "I met Murder on the way— / He had a mask like Castlereagh—." He was not faultless in his approach to foreign policy, but few men can claim more responsibility for the durability of the peace settlement of 1815.[14]

Nicholas Vansittart was chancellor of the exchequer. While his administrative talents were adequate, he was a terrible speaker who could not be trusted to defend his own policies. His voice was "feeble and indistinct," and he has been described as a man of "unexceptional abilities." Yet it often fell to Vansittart to make the government's case in the Commons because Castlereagh was frequently away on the Continent handling negotiations with the European powers. Vansittart's survival as chancellor for a full decade requires some explanation, and the best that can be said is that he was a team player. When Liverpool formed the commission to begin returning Britain to the gold standard in 1819, he gave the chairmanship of the committee to Peel rather than Vansittart. Where others might have resigned in a huff, Vansittart persevered.[15]

Some of the most talented members of the ministry could be found in military and naval administration. At the Admiralty, Robert

Dundas, Second Viscount Melville, was a reserved Scotsman who had inherited a vast network of patronage and political power from his father, who had also been first lord earlier in the wars. The younger Melville was diligent and sensible. Liverpool called him "an excellent man of business,"[16] while Sir John Barrow, longtime second secretary to the Admiralty, claimed that Melville "never made an enemy, or lost a friend."[17] Melville took a personal interest in naval affairs despite having trained as a lawyer. The daily work of the Admiralty Board was handled by the secretary to the Admiralty, who from 1809 was the Irishman John Wilson Croker. His first passion was literary criticism, and he was known for his scathing essays in the *Quarterly Review*. However, he did not neglect his duties at the Admiralty, where he opened all incoming letters himself. Once in the House of Commons he referred to himself as a "servant of the Board," which caused a former first lord to quip that it was precisely the other way around.[18]

Naval administration was complicated by the presence of a second board. While the Admiralty Board was responsible for the deployment of the navy's forces, the Navy Board was responsible for civil administration, in particular the navy's dockyards and other shore-based infrastructure. It was essential that the two boards work closely together. The navy was lucky in that two successive comptrollers of the Navy Board were efficient administrators with solid reputations among their fellow officers. Rear-Admiral Sir Thomas Boulden Thompson had been with Nelson at the Battle of the Nile and subsequently wounded and imprisoned in France. From 1806 until his retirement in 1816, he helped steer four first lords of the Admiralty through the challenge of expanding the navy to its largest size in the age of sail. His replacement faced precisely the opposite challenge of shrinking it back. We will first meet Rear-Admiral Sir Thomas Byam Martin as the naval liaison to the Duke of Wellington, and as comptroller he forged a strong relationship with Croker and Melville. They consulted closely on all naval budgets and smoothed over many of the questions of political and financial control of naval affairs that derived from the confusing administrative structure. Unlike the army, the navy was represented formally in the cabinet by the first lord, which meant it was generally easier for Melville, Croker, Thompson, and then Byam Martin to synchronize their efforts at reform and reorganization.[19]

That is not to say that the army lacked representation at the highest level or that it was incapable of change. The commander in chief of the army was the second son of George III, Prince Frederick, the Duke of York. An experienced soldier and skilled administrator, he had been in his position for all but two years since 1795. Unlike many of his brothers, he had actual talent that made his opinions on military matters carry more than just royal weight, and he had a reputation as a hard worker who could function on little sleep.[20] The prestige of the Dukes of York and Wellington (who was brought into the government as master general of the ordnance in 1818) meant that the army was fully capable of advocating for itself, but the army's administrative structure made the navy's two boards look simple by comparison. Much of the confusion stemmed from there being two different secretary positions. The more senior was Henry Bathurst, Third Earl Bathurst, secretary of state for war and the colonies, who ably managed Wellington's campaigns, although his talents were obscured by his being a "barely articulate" speaker in Parliament.[21] The junior position, secretary at war, handled the pay and accounts of the army but neither sat in the cabinet or reported to the commander in chief. Instead, the secretary's job was simultaneously to represent the army in Parliament and monitor the army for Parliament. The incumbent from 1809 was Henry Temple, Third Viscount Palmerston, the future prime minister. Like Croker, Palmerston imposed himself on army administration and did not hesitate to pick fights, even with York.[22]

The men responsible for military administration deserve our attention not only because this is a book about demobilization but because that was the primary business of the government. Historians today refer to the British state in this period as a "fiscal-military state," or, for those so inclined, a "fiscal-naval state." While those are modern terms, they would not have confused Liverpool and his ministers. In most years in the eighteenth century, 85 percent of the budget was devoted to the military, and to the debt incurred by the military in times of war.[i] The ratio of current spending on the military to debt management depended on whether Britain was at war, but war-

---

i   As a point of comparison, today's U.S. government spends about 15 percent of the
     budget on defense and about 8 percent on interest on the debt, not all of which was
     incurred by military spending.

related spending dominated the budget in all years.[23] Consequently, the budgets of the army and the navy were at the heart of British political life. Parliament set the budgets of both services by passing "estimates" each year, and the introduction of those bills were occasions for some of the most consequential political debates of the period.

The fiscal-military state provided ministers with few levers to shape economic or social policy beyond the military. There was no state-run social insurance or health care, and the nascent economics profession was skeptical of deficit spending and government interventions in the economy. Across the eighteenth century, most funds not devoted to military spending or the debt supported the royal family (see Figure 1.1). A small remainder went toward development projects, including investments in infrastructure, education, religion, and science, but even some of these initiatives had military value: bridge building and public paving meant troops (as well as goods) could move around the country more quickly; harbor construction helped the navy and the merchant marine. The government funded prizes to incentivize inventions, and many had obvious military applications, such as the creation of an accurate chronometer to aid in the calculation of longitude. There were some exceptions to this military myopia, such as endowed chairs at Oxford and Cambridge, new churches, and sewer cleaning, but most spending was military or closely related.[24]

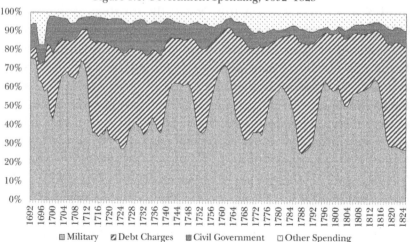

Figure 1.1: Government Spending, 1692–1825

The fiscal-military state had evolved across Europe over the eighteenth century as a result of endemic warfare among the great powers. Most states developed some version of a fiscal-military apparatus in which tax revenue was transformed primarily into military power. It was usually not possible for any state to ramp up its tax revenue fast enough to mobilize its forces at the beginning of a war, so all states relied to some degree on loans.[25] It was also politically easier, as Adam Smith explained. Peacetime revenues and expenses were usually close to balanced, so when war came, governments were both "unwilling and unable" to raise taxes to meet the cost of war. "They are unwilling," he wrote, "for fear of offending the people, who, by so great and so sudden an increase of taxes, would soon be disgusted with the war; and they are unable, from not well knowing what taxes would be sufficient to produce the revenue wanted. The facility of borrowing delivers them from the embarrassment which this fear and inability would otherwise occasion."[26] Whether they could sustain the interest payments on those loans and maintain the confidence of financial markets to continue to borrow were often the key questions that shaped the course of wars. For most fiscal-military states, the limit seemed to be about six to eight years of increased spending before collapse became imminent. The result was a pattern of wars lasting about that long, a resulting financial crisis, retrenchment, and then a return to war. Peace was often simply a pause between wars, a chance for each side to lick its wounds and prepare for the next round.

Each time Britain went to war, it was forced to raise roughly one-third of all its expenditures from loans; the question at the end of every war was how to pay down that debt. Thanks in part to the symbiotic relationship among the navy, merchants, and the financial system, Britain's fiscal-military state proved to be the most successful in Europe at managing this process. Over the course of the eighteenth century, the Bank of England had become the cornerstone of a well-organized system of long-term government borrowing. The City of London had grown ever larger, more influential, and more diverse in its activities. New partnership banks, insurance offices, and trading companies had emerged, providing a variety of investment vehicles for the busy brokers and merchants of the City. Combined, these new institutions provided a liquid financial market for the government, and the navy helped reassure investors that Britain was unlikely to be overrun by an invading army. That is not to say that it was immune from crises, but in comparison to its European rivals, it was resilient.[27]

The pattern of the debt growing in every war and stabilizing in every peace can be seen in Figure 1.2, as can the remarkable scale of the wars at the end of the century. In 1812, with no obvious end of the wars in sight and indeed a new war on the other side of the Atlantic, ministers were concerned with cobbling together resources to win the wars. Over the course of this book, we will see their focus shift to the challenge of every peace: getting on top of the debt problem without causing long-term damage to national power. Britain's record on this front was mixed, and the experiences of 1763, at the end of the Seven Years War, and 1783, at the end of the American Revolutionary War, were the recent history on which Liverpool and his ministers based their expectations for coming peace, whenever it arrived. After 1763, the pressure to fund the defense of Britain's newly won empire caused a political crisis in the thirteen colonies. After 1783, Pitt's savvy investments and a growing economy had laid the foundation for success in the next war. The crisis that ministers grappled with at the end of the Napoleonic Wars was similar to all previous crises in the sense that it confronted ministers with a large national debt, heated debates about taxes, and serious questions of international security. It was different

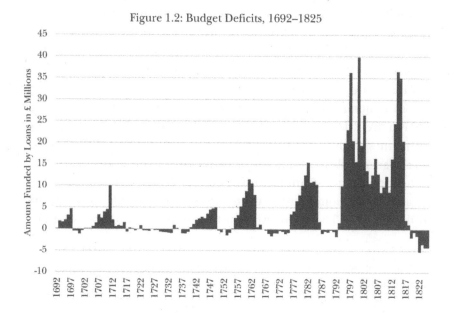

Figure 1.2: Budget Deficits, 1692–1825

mainly in scale: none of the eighteenth-century wars had lasted as long or demanded as much from the fiscal-military system as the Great Wars. The question that preoccupied ministers faced with this crisis was which path Britain would take: a managed financial crisis followed by recovery and reinvestment or economic collapse followed by a political or military crisis?[28]

There were several different proposals for tackling the debt floating in intellectual and political circles. Radicals like William Cobbett and some younger Whigs argued that the government should simply repudiate the debt. The economist David Ricardo proposed a massive new property tax to cover the interest payments. The Birmingham politician Thomas Attwood thought that the debt should be inflated away—that is, that the government should expand the money supply to make the debt less burdensome.[29] Yet despite their concern about the sustainability of the postwar budgets, ministers rejected each of these ideas out of hand. Britain's ability to raise money in wartime via loans underpinned its status as a great power, so there was no question of risking that to repudiate the debt. New taxes were, as we will see, politically impossible. And ministers identified the currency situation as a problem to be solved, not a tool to be used. In 1797, a small French force had landed in Wales, causing a run on the banks even though it quickly surrendered. In an atmosphere of panic and uncertainty, Pitt had made the momentous decision to take Britain off the gold standard: no longer did the Bank of England guarantee that its notes could be redeemed in gold. That was still the case in 1812, but ministers hoped to get Britain back on the gold standard as soon as possible.[30]

The desire to return to normalcy was pervasive, and normalcy meant limiting the government's role in the economy. There exists today a lively debate among historians about the role of wartime government spending in sparking Britain's industrial revolution. Most recent scholarship argues that it generally helped, especially in key industries like gun manufacturing, but the debate hinges on statistics created by economic historians that were not available to politicians at the time.[31, ii] They perceived wartime government borrowing and

---

ii   William Playfair published perhaps the world's first line graph of a time series in 1786 in his book *The Commercial and Political Atlas*. The subject in question was the expenditure of the navy.

spending as harmful abnormalities that crowded out private investment, and they believed that paper money was dangerously unreliable.
Only once the last vestiges of the wartime economy had been removed
would "normal" peacetime growth resume. They adopted this mind-
set largely on faith: they had few statistical measures available to them
to understand what was happening in the economy, and leading theorists like Adam Smith and David Ricardo were clear that they should
always seek to adopt a laissez-faire approach to the economy.[32]

All these components bounded Britain's political world in 1812
and in the decade that followed. How politicians addressed the
questions posed earlier depended on how they interpreted Britain's
recent historical experience, on the limited availability of economic
statistics, and on the economic policy consensus. There were many
good reasons to worry about a political crisis amid demobilization.
Slashing spending would damage industries dependent on government contracts and cause a collapse in the price of wheat, which was
currently being propped up by demand from the navy. How would
workers respond to widespread unemployment? How would landowners respond to deflation? Could Radicals capitalize on these clashes
to organize a mass movement for manhood suffrage, parliamentary
reform, or even more ambitious reforms? Would the army be able to
handle these domestic disturbances, or was it needed to police the
growing empire? What was the appropriate size and design of the fleet
in peacetime? Or were all these questions irrelevant because the only
thing that mattered was maintaining the government's credit by paying down the debt?

But before we get too carried away into the postwar period, we need
to restate an obvious but essential point: the financial crisis meant that
demobilization was badly needed, but it could not proceed so long
as threats to British security persisted. Up to 1812, Britain had persevered because its naval power gave it strategic depth, financial security,
and the ability to supply an increasingly effective army ashore. There
had been several false dawns since Britain entered the wars in 1793,
and even one brief peace. Ministers were understandably wary of making assumptions about the course of the wars, and the consequences
of mistakes were existential. It was essential to wait until victory was
assured before dismantling any part of Britain's strategic apparatus.
Paying off a seaworthy ship, for example, saved lots of money, so

ministers felt pressure to do so as soon as possible. On the other hand, paying off a ship meant letting the core driver of naval power—skilled sailors—disappear back into civilian life, possibly losing them to naval service forever. This tension—between the strategic need for the army and the navy to be at full strength and the financial exhaustion of two decades of war—shaped the patterns of demobilization. That is why we need to begin our story in 1812, not 1815, and why we need to understand the situation of the two services at that point in the wars.

CHAPTER 2

The Army and the Navy at the Beginning of the End

The army and the navy naturally had very different responsibilities, but they also shared some similar challenges. They both had to grapple with how much manpower could be spared for the American war without losing focus on Napoleon. They both had to identify their most essential contribution to British and Allied strategy and redouble their efforts on that front. They also had to deal with each other—an enduring challenge. In 1812, they were also on divergent trajectories. The army was in the process of becoming the best version of itself, with a greater influence on European affairs than at any time since at least the days of Marlborough a century before. Meanwhile, Nelson's great fleet victories were receding into memory, and the command of the sea that the navy had won was proving difficult to maintain.

British grand strategy began with the navy, so we should too. The navy had four roles to play in 1812. First and most important was the protection of trade. The fundamental principles of trade defense transcend technological eras: the British defended seaborne trade by organizing and escorting convoys, in much the same way they did in the two world wars. Commanders in chief carefully coordinated convoys in European waters and soon across the North Atlantic. It was a grinding, inglorious campaign, and only recently have historians begun to pay it the attention it deserves. The convoy system was ultimately successful, but as with the campaigns against the U-boats, there were dark days. The danger in 1812 came from privateers: over the course of that year, French privateers captured 475 British ships, most of which had been sailing independently.[1]

A second, related task was the blockading of French and Allied fleets in port. To calculate the distribution of forces, the Admiralty relied on intelligence on enemy readiness and sought to match the number of ships of the line in the blockading squadron with the number of ships of the line in port ready for sea. Trafalgar had not cured Napoleon of his enthusiasm for building ships of the line, and by 1812, there were about eighty in various states of readiness with a further thirty-five being built.[2] To prevent the escape of any of these squadrons, the navy deployed its ships of the line around western European waters in a C shape stretching from the Texel and the Scheldt estuary in the North Sea through the Channel to the Bay of Biscay, along the coasts of Spain and Portugal, and into the western Mediterranean.

These two defensive tasks took up the bulk of naval resources, as a closer look at deployments in Figure 2.1 suggests. About 70 percent of the navy's ships and men were deployed in Europe. The largest single fleet was in the Mediterranean because the largest enemy fleet was at Toulon—twenty-one French ships of the line by 1813, many of which appeared ready for sea. Sir Edward Pellew, the commander in chief of the Mediterranean from 1811, had nineteen ships of the line and numerous frigates to watch the Toulon fleet, attack French commerce, and raid the coasts of southern Europe. In the Bay of Biscay, French squadrons appeared eager to escape and required constant vigilance. In the North Sea and Channel, British squadrons monitored French ships of the line being built at Amsterdam, Antwerp, and, ominously, the newly opened port of Cherbourg in 1813. In the Baltic, Vice-Admiral Sir James Saumarez's large fleet escorted vital convoys past Danish gunboats, and his deft diplomacy maintained cordial relations with the Swedes even after Napoleon had forced them to declare war.[3]

This deployment pattern was just sufficient to meet the challenges of 1811 and early 1812. French fleets occasionally sortied and even escaped, but no great battle like Trafalgar called attention to the campaign. A squadron under Admiral Zacharie Allemand snuck out of Lorient on the night of March 8–9, 1812, and remained at large

Figure 2.1: Percentage of Naval Resources by Ships' Complements, 1811

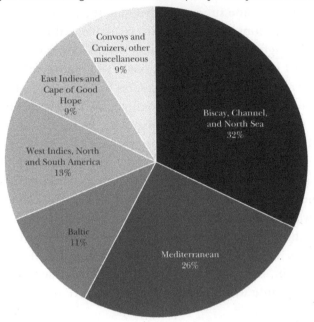

for three weeks before being forced into Brest. The Toulon fleet exercised its crews by leaving port periodically but always retreated when the British blockading squadrons appeared on the horizon. These were potentially serious threats, and countering them was stressful and draining, but in general, the navy rose to the challenge by supplying and deploying more ships and men than at any time in its history.[4]

In addition to its defensive responsibilities, the navy also took offensive action in both direct and supporting roles. The third major task was raiding the coastline of Napoleon's empire to tie down troops and incite local rebellions. In the Adriatic, for example, Captain William Hoste and later Rear-Admiral Thomas Fremantle raided French outposts along the coast, using local command of the sea to increase their mobility. Fremantle captured Fiume in 1813 and Trieste in 1814, demonstrating the potency of British amphibious power.[5] But even those successes would never be enough to damage Napoleon's empire seriously, and so the fourth and final task was the supply of British armies on the Continent. In 1812, that meant Wellington's armies in Portugal and Spain. Wellington famously told

Byam Martin, "If anyone wishes to know the history of this war, I will tell him our maritime superiority gives me the power of maintaining my communications while the enemy is unable to do so."[6]

That Wellington would admit as much must have caused wry shakes of the head from his naval colleagues. Wellington was a constant complainer, convinced that the navy was bilking him of the ships he needed to supply his troops. He even accused the navy of falsifying the rate at which ships under convoy were being captured. In fact, less than 1 percent of all ships in convoy were lost out of 13,427 ship voyages to the Iberian Peninsula, and those ships brought troops, military supplies, and bullion to pay the troops and pay for food. In 1811, the navy's supply lines to Lisbon had kept Wellington's army healthy while twenty-five thousand French soldiers died from disease and starvation on the other side of the lines of Torres Vedras. During the summer of 1812, the navy was busy along the Mediterranean coast of Spain, ferrying ten thousand British, Sicilian, and Spanish troops to Alicante to prevent the French from reinforcing the army facing Wellington.[7]

The navy's reputation rested in large part on the great fleet victories of 1794–1805, but every admiral who had been in command at those victories was now dead or retired: Howe, victor of the Glorious First of June in 1794, had died in 1799; St. Vincent, victor of the Battle of Cape St. Vincent in 1797, had last been active in 1806; Duncan, victor of Camperdown in 1797, had died in 1804; and of course Nelson had died at Trafalgar. Nelson had been by far the youngest of those admirals, so it was his generation that was now at the top of the naval hierarchy. Every generation has its stronger and weaker members, so we should not paint with too broad a brush here. Nevertheless, it is important to establish that the admirals of 1812 were many of the same men who had been involved in those great fleet victories. George Elphinstone, First Viscount Keith, commanded forces in the Channel in 1812, a role with which he was intimately familiar as he had been the admiral tasked with organizing Britain's invasion defense in 1803. Saumarez in the Baltic had been Nelson's second-in-command at the Nile in 1798, and Pellew in the Mediterranean was one of the greatest frigate commanders of his generation.

Below them, the naval officer corps was suffering from rampant unemployment. The increasing popularity of the navy as a career for upwardly mobile members of the middling sort meant that there were far more officers than could be employed at sea. There were roughly three officers for every command vacancy and more than two lieutenants for every billet. The question, then, was how the navy should go about choosing whom to employ. At the margins, elite social background and its associated political connections mattered, but we should not overstate it: there simply were far more officers than elite families. As a result, while the wars raged, the navy had the luxury of incorporating merit into its promotion process. We will see how that equation changed in peacetime, but in 1812, commanders in chief sought to surround themselves with subordinates who were competent and connected rather than incompetent but very well-connected.[8]

The Great Wars had lasted so long that they encompassed the entire careers of many officers in both services. Some senior post-captains in the navy had trained as midshipmen, been commissioned as lieutenants, and then been promoted twice, all since 1793. This is the generation that came under most intense scrutiny in the aftermath of the U.S. Navy's frigate victories in the War of 1812. Below them, many lieutenants had not yet been born when the Bastille fell. There seemed to be a sense among the younger generations that they needed to distinguish themselves quickly before the wars ended. That was unlikely to happen as the commander of a brig on convoy duty, yet that was the navy's primary responsibility during this period.[9]

It did not help officers that the ships they commanded were falling apart. Blockade and convoy duty forced ships to stay at sea for long periods, often far from friendly dockyards. Battered by the elements and occasionally by enemy action, the navy's ships in June 1812 were in an unhappy state. After the wars, Byam Martin claimed that rushed shipbuilding and the wear and tear of continuous service meant that at no time did the navy have "a really sound and desirable fleet."[10] That is not to diminish the remarkable accomplishment of British shipbuilding during the wars. From an existing fleet of one hundred ships of the line in 1793, the navy captured eighty-three enemy ships and built one hundred more, so that its effective deployed strength in 1812 was substantially greater than it had been two decades earlier.[11] Nevertheless, many of the newly built ships had been rushed, using green rather than seasoned timber. Not only did that make the ship less durable, but it also caused magazines and other essential supplies to become damp or spoil. The captain of the *Bulwark*, a seventy-four-gun ship of the line built in 1807, complained in December 1812 that not only was the green wood of his ship causing problems in his hold but also that there were rats "in such numbers, that the only remedy for extirpating them in my opinion will be by having recourse to suffocation by smoking."[12] The rats had eaten entire casks of beef, raisins, flour, and peas.

The men tasked with enduring such conditions were also a source of concern for the Admiralty. We do not yet have a quantitative study of naval manpower during the Napoleonic Wars, but qualitative evidence suggests that the outbreak of war with the United States pushed the manning system beyond the breaking point. While there were plenty of spare officers, there were never spare sailors. Melville complained in 1813 that six ships of the line and sixteen frigates plus many smaller vessels were "lying useless" because there were not enough men to man them.[13] A glance at the readily available quantitative evidence suggests that the system was operating at capacity from at least 1809. That was the first year in which there were at least 140,000 men in naval service, and it came on the heels of steady growth of between 10,000 and 30,000 men per year from 1803 onward. But after 1809, the number of men in the navy plateaued, never increasing or decreasing by more than a few thousand until 1814, even though the navy had ships in need of men. It did not seem to be possible to press or recruit any more men from Britain's pool of maritime labor.[14]

The army was also in the midst of a manpower crisis. The entire British military apparatus seems to have been teetering on the brink of catastrophe as the Napoleonic Wars reached their most critical years. The army had expanded even more dramatically than the navy, from a rump of 40,000 men in 1793 to a wartime peak in late 1813 of nearly 240,000. Unlike many other European states, Britain never resorted to widespread conscription: impressment targeted sailors, and army recruitment relied in part on a Rube Goldberg apparatus connected to the militia. The army, even more so than the navy, consumed men. In 1816, the Forty-Second Regiment of Foot calculated that it had had 13,127 officers and men belonging to it since 1797, but only three of its current members had been present during its campaign in Egypt in 1801. A regiment's theoretical strength was about 1,000 men, suggesting that the regiment had turned over thirteen times in nineteen years, although admittedly not all of the departures from the regiment were casualties. Nevertheless, about 200,000 soldiers deployed to the Peninsular War in the six years of heavy campaigning from 1808 to 1814, but the peak strength of Wellington's army never exceeded 73,000 men. The churn of campaigns plus the diseases endemic to armies placed enormous strains on the army's recruitment and retention systems. One estimate suggests the army needed to replace about 10 percent of its strength every year. Remarkably, from 1803 to 1815, every year but one (1807) it failed to do so: deaths plus discharges plus desertions consistently drained more men than could be replaced by new recruits. The Duke of York estimated that the army would be 10,500 men short of its requirements in 1813, which was in keeping with the average deficit across all the years of the Peninsular War.[15]

What of the soldiers and sailors themselves? Later chapters will delve into their experiences and amplify their voices, but here it is important to note some of the structures and demographics of the two groups of men. An individual sailor's experience of demobilization depended in part on where he was from and whether he was a skilled seaman. The navy divided its sailors into three categories: skilled sailors with experience at sea, who were rated as petty officers or able seamen; sailors with some experience at sea, rated ordinary; and landsmen. About half the lower deck was skilled, and the other half was divided evenly between ordinary seamen and landsmen. Unsurprisingly, the skilled sailors were the focus of the navy's recruiting efforts—they received the largest bounties and were the prime targets for press gangs. These men moved back and forth between the navy and merchant service as conditions allowed in wartime, and in peacetime, they were the core of the merchant marine.[16]

While maritime communities naturally made the largest contribution to the navy's manpower, there were plenty of sailors from land-locked counties. During the French Revolutionary Wars, 51 percent identified as English, 19 percent as Irish, 10 percent as Scottish, and 3 percent as Welsh, with the remainder made up by foreign-born men and men for whom we do not have data. Approximately a third of all soldiers in 1813 were born in Ireland, making the army substantially more Irish than the navy. Experience generally mattered more than skill in the army: a veteran sergeant was as valuable to the army as a petty officer was to the navy, but the sergeant did not have skills that transferred as easily to civilian life as the sailor did. In some ways, that did not matter, since sailors joined the navy for the duration of the war, whereas most soldiers enlisted for life (which usually meant twenty-one years, at which point they became eligible for a pension). Sailors expected to have to face a depressed postwar labor market; soldiers generally did not.[17]

Regiments functioned as lifelong communities for their officers and soldiers. They kept track of their own history and had their own uniforms and traditions, some of which originated a century or more in the past. Ships, in contrast, could be as tightly knit as any regiment, but for much shorter periods of time: few commissions lasted longer than two or three years before the exhausted ship needed to undergo substantial repairs. At the end of a commission, so long as the war still raged, the navy usually turned men over from the decommissioning ship to another in need of manpower. The men had no choice in the matter. Sometimes that allowed sailors to travel in sizeable groups from one ship to the next, but sometimes it also meant that close bonds between men were broken by the needs of the service. Nevertheless, both soldiers and sailors developed their most important relationships not with the ship or regiment but with what the navy called their mess: small groups of about four to eight men. These were their brothers-in-arms, and these were the men they risked their lives for in combat. On a daily basis, the mess or the squad made it possible to endure the hardships of campaigns.[18]

The army was increasingly aware of the privations that its soldiers had to endure, and so it slowly took steps to make itself a more hospitable home. In a nod to the importance of its Irish members, it allowed Catholics to attend Mass, and to ease problems of desertion, it discouraged extreme punishments. Both initiatives sought to address the manpower shortage. The long tradition of incorporating foreign manpower into the army also became even more pronounced. In addition to the King's German Legion, made up of Hanoverian soldiers, and the Portuguese forces already integrated into Wellington's army, other more unusual sources of manpower were tapped. The

Sixtieth Regiment gained two extra battalions made up of Channel Islanders and deserters from Napoleon's armies. Meanwhile, tackling the desertion problem resulted in several innovations: specific penal corps like the Royal African Corps and West Indian Rangers took in soldiers who had deserted from other regiments and forced them to serve in the most inhospitable climates; the York Light Infantry Volunteers, later renamed the York Chasseurs, were created from deserters deemed redeemable, often men who had simply wandered off from their recruiting party.[19]

These policies failed to close the manpower gap, but they also managed to prevent collapse—a considerable achievement. At the heart of this relative success story was the regimental system. The core organizing principle of the army was that regiments were self-contained ecosystems. Regiments recruited soldiers to enlist in them, not in the army more broadly, and they developed coherent identities. Transfers between regiments were relatively rare and required the permission of the Horse Guards (the term for the office of the commander in chief). Regiments were also responsible for maintaining their strength in the field in the face of the many drains on manpower already mentioned. It was difficult to do so when the regiment was on campaign, detached from its recruiting ground in Britain or Ireland. To overcome this problem, most regiments divided themselves into two or more battalions.[20] The first battalion was intended to be the primary deployed force, while the second battalion was designed to remain at home as a recruiting depot and recovery unit. It usually had less than half the manpower of the first battalion. Simultaneously, Wellington and other commanders developed rotation systems within theaters, so that units weakened by extended service could rotate to garrison duty while awaiting fresh recruits from home. The army also created units like the Tenth Royal Veteran Battalion, which served in North America for the duration of the War of 1812, as a place to send men no longer fit for frontline service.[21]

There were more than a hundred infantry regiments, led by officers of increasing quality. In many ways, army officers were similar to naval officers: professionals with defined careers drawn from the top quartile of British society. The major difference between the two services was how officers came by their commissions. Naval officers passed an examination for lieutenant and then, in most cases, were commissioned only if a billet as a lieutenant was available. Many army officers, in contrast, purchased their commissions at considerable expense. An ensign's commission in an unfashionable line regiment in 1800 cost at least £400, and prices generally went up as the number of the regiment went down. There were workarounds and regulations that gave those without ready access to such funds a career path, but that initial barrier to entry meant that army officers tended to come from slightly higher on the social ladder than naval officers. Another difference is that the sale of an army officer's commission had the benefit of providing a sizeable lump sum for retirement, whereas naval officers relied on inadequate half pay.[22]

Army officers tended to have slower and steadier promotions than naval officers. Most ensigns became lieutenants in two years, but then even officers who joined during the wars had to wait up to ten years for a vacant captaincy. Whereas a high-flying talented and connected naval officer could be a post-captain in his early twenties, it generally took army officers about eighteen years to reach field rank. Only about one officer in five made it that far. In contrast with the navy, unemployment was not a problem for army officers. There were roughly three thousand army officers on half pay during the wars, but that number stayed relatively steady as the size of the officer corps ballooned: in other words, half pay was more about disability than unemployment. From about three thousand total officers in 1793, there were about fifteen thousand in 1815, increasingly drawn from Ireland and Scotland.[23]

For the purposes of understanding the state of the two services in 1812, however, what matters is that the army's leadership was coming into its own in much the same way that the navy's had in Nelson's day. Sustained successful operations in Portugal and Spain had provided ample opportunities for senior officers to identify and promote talented subordinates. At the highest levels, Wellington's qualities are well-known, but his success depended on men like his quartermaster-general, Sir George Murray, who provided essential topographical intelligence and translated Wellington's vision into tactical reality. Generals Robert Craufurd and Sir Thomas Picton and Colonel John Colborne were the equal of any soldiers in Europe. Indeed, the reputation of the army as a whole was trending in a positive direction, reversing the traditional pattern in which the navy received the plaudits as the "wooden walls" that protected Britain while the army was mistrusted as a threat to domestic liberty. As the Peninsular War reached its climax, Wellington and his deputies were burnishing their reputations. One historian has concluded, "They led an army that was now the best the British Army was ever likely to be."[24]

Compared to its European rivals, British infantry had weaker cavalry and artillery support—not necessarily in terms of quality but simply quantity. On the other hand, no other European army could deploy to a remote theater and rely on the logistical support of the British navy to keep it in the field. What stands out about the state of the army in 1812 was how much of it was deployed abroad. In 1804, just a third of all soldiers had been abroad; by 1812, as Figure 2.2 shows, 70 percent were garrisoning the empire or engaged in active operations on foreign soil, and that figure increased to 76 percent

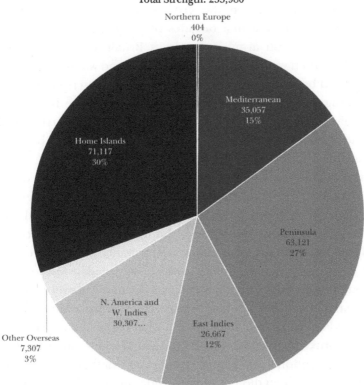

Figure 2.2: Army Deployments in July 1812
Total Strength: 233,980

Northern Europe
404
0%

Mediterranean
35,057
15%

Home Islands
71,117
30%

Peninsula
63,121
27%

N. America and
W. Indies
30,307...

East Indies
26,667
12%

Other Overseas
7,307
3%

the next year. Only three regiments had first battalions at home in December 1813.[25]

Historians have generally interpreted these data in one of two ways. One camp emphasizes how comparatively small the Peninsular War forces were relative to global deployments, while the other dismisses most troops not deployed to Iberia as strategically irrelevant, mainly imperial garrisons of uncertain fighting quality. Wellington was certainly and understandably in the latter camp. In August 1813, he reminded his superiors in London, "The British government or nation . . . forget that we have but one army"—namely, his.[26] It was not just Wellington, though. In 1808, George Canning had told Sir John Moore before sending him to Portugal that the thirty-two thousand men under his command were, "in fact, the British army."[27] The figure shows clearly that this was not true. The Peninsular War never accounted for much more than a quarter of all British manpower, and the largest single contingent was almost always in the British Isles.

Both Canning and Wellington well knew this, so to explain their comments we can turn to the great strategic theorist Sir Julian Corbett. Writing in the first decades of the twentieth century, he described the British army in Iberia as Britain's "disposal force." Although Corbett was more interested in how and where the disposal force should be deployed, we can infer from his description that he saw Wellington's army as the largest single part of the British land forces that could be safely sent abroad, and not just for garrison duty. To achieve its strategic ends, it needed to be not only large but effective, capable of influencing the outcome of the wars.[28]

Corbett's framing also helps explain the historical focus on the Peninsular War. The sixty thousand men under Wellington were not really the only British army, but they were its most powerful component. And the army did achieve the desired strategic effects by marching into France. Its impressive performance has given veterans of the Peninsular War an almost mythical status, akin to the sailors who fought at Trafalgar. Much as we know the name of everyone present at that battle, historians have been eager to learn as much as they can about Peninsular War veterans and what happened to them after that army broke up. In this book, Peninsular War veterans will receive significant attention for a different reason: *because* their army was broken up. Many of them did not fight at Waterloo, nor did they remain in garrisons in France. Instead, they were sent to North America, to India, and to the British Isles. More than any other part of the British army, they were the soldiers who came home.

Wellington's army broke up surprisingly quickly in 1814, but in general, what emerges from a comparison of the army and navy in this period is how inflexible the army's regimental system was when it was engaged in a campaign. Whereas the navy could quickly move ships of the line around the globe in response to changing circumstances, the army tended to be more static. The navy was also more willing to recombine crews by turning men over from one ship to another to maximize the effectiveness of their trained men. The regimental system, in contrast, forced commanders to think in terms of whole units. Wellington argued that a veteran soldier was worth two or more fresh recruits, much as an able seaman was worth much more than a landsman. Wellington therefore sought to keep his veteran troops in theater as long as possible, while the Horse Guards prioritized regimental and battalion integrity. When a battalion was so depleted as to be useless, it was usually rotated out rather than combined with other weaker battalions, unless they were in its own regiment. Regiments were not broken up to distribute veterans among green troops, whereas it was common for ships' crews to be distributed based on skill and experience. It was consequently more difficult for the army than the navy to manipulate its most fundamental structure in response to changing strategic circumstances.[29]

As we pick up the narrative of the Napoleonic Wars in 1812, we need to keep in mind the challenges that each service faced not only in bringing the wars to a successful conclusion but also in reconfiguring themselves for peace. Since the wars had multiple endings, the two challenges interacted with each other in unexpected ways. It was not as simple as declaring victory and bringing the soldiers and sailors home, nor was it simply a matter of military strategy: throughout the end of the wars, demobilization was the dominant political issue of the day because the only way that ministers could hope to get on top of the debt was to cut back military and naval spending.

CHAPTER 3

Victory in Europe, 1812–14

Both of the major events of June 1812—the American declaration of war and the invasion of Russia—owed their origins to decisions taken six years earlier, when Napoleon, frustrated at his inability to attack Britain directly, embargoed all British goods from the Continent, a policy that came to be known as the Continental System. The British responded with Orders in Council of their own that tightened the blockade of France and required neutral vessels to route through a British port before trading with the Continent. For the Americans, the British violation of neutral rights launched a five-year debate about the appropriate response, eventually culminating in the declaration of war. For the Russians, Napoleon's Continental System was also a casus belli. Forced to join it in the Treaty of Tilsit in 1807, they soon grew frustrated at the economic hardships it caused. Napoleon's invasion in 1812 surprised few observers, least of all the Russians, who had withdrawn from the Continental System in 1810 and begun preparing for war.[1]

British ministers thought one of these events was much more important than the other. The invasion of Russia looked likely to result in yet another transformative French victory, while the American war was an unfortunate misunderstanding. In the face of domestic pressure, ministers revoked the offending Orders in Council five days after the American declaration of war. The news traveled too slowly for either side to be aware of the other's actions, so it had no effect, but it indicates that Britain had no intention of opening another theater in the global war against France and its allies. So long as Napoleon remained in power, nothing else mattered, strategically.[2]

The British official best placed to respond to the Russia campaign was the naval commander in chief in the Baltic, Saumarez. Napoleon's invasion had further complicated an evolving strategic situation in that theater. France had forced Sweden to declare war on Britain in November 1810 as part of Napoleon's efforts to embargo British trade, but since an actual shooting war with Sweden would have been disastrous for British commerce in the Baltic, Saumarez had come to an understanding with the Swedes that the war would be "phoney." Throughout 1811, he had maintained this delicate balance and then, as usual, returned home to Guernsey when ice covered large sections of the Baltic. By the time he reentered the Baltic in May 1812, for his fifth consecutive summer deployed, he reaped the benefits of his careful diplomacy. In his absence, Franco-Swedish relations had collapsed, and in January, France occupied Swedish Pomerania. The ever-opportunistic Swedish crown prince, Jean Bernadotte, had been one of Napoleon's marshals, but now, in March, he switched sides, requesting an end to the formal state of war between Sweden and Britain. In addition to a possible alliance with the Swedes, the imminent French invasion of Russia also allowed British diplomats to negotiate a treaty with the Russians. A month after Napoleon's armies crossed into Russian territory, Britain, Sweden, and Russia were aligned against the French threat.[3, i]

As noted earlier, Napoleon's invasion initially appeared to make Britain's strategic situation substantially worse. Given his track record, the smart bet was that he would force Russia to come to even more punishing terms. Yet the Russian army left the field intact after the horrifically bloody Battle of Borodino in September, and even though Napoleon was able to occupy Moscow afterward, Tsar Alexander refused to come to the negotiating table. By October, when Saumarez went home early following the sudden death of his daughter, signs were beginning to appear that the Grande Armée might

---

i   They were not yet formally allied, as Bernadotte drove a hard bargain. Not until August 24, 1812, did Britain and Sweden sign a peace treaty, and Sweden did not declare war on France until December.

not have won the victory Europe expected. On November 8, news reached London that Napoleon had abandoned Moscow and was retreating back across central Europe. Few could believe the full scale of the disaster that had befallen Napoleon's forces—usually given as 100,000 serviceable men left from an original army of 600,000—but it was clear by the turn of the year that, finally, Britain and her Allies had an opportunity to strike back at Napoleon's Continental empire.[4]

An ideal solution would have been to deploy a British army quickly into northern Europe, both to bolster relations with the Allies and as a practical means of degrading Napoleon's forces. Yet the only disposal force was with Wellington in Iberia: when ministers looked at what was left over in Britain, they found only a few dozen depleted second battalions full of men not deemed fit to go to Spain. Nevertheless, they persisted. After scouring the country for troops, Bathurst sent Sir Thomas Graham, on sick leave from the Peninsular War, to attack Antwerp in December 1813 with what one historian has called "quite simply, a very bad army."[5] Of the nine battalions under his command, one was a single-battalion regiment, seven were second or third battalions, and one was a veteran battalion. Its actual effective strength was barely more than three thousand men. Britain's manpower reserves were tapped out, and Wellington was jealously hoarding manpower in Iberia. It was not possible or easy to reconfigure British army deployments to take advantage of the opportunity presented by Napoleon's folly.[6]

The navy proved capable of doing so, however. While Danish gunboats continued to pose a threat, it became clear by the end of 1812 that the new alignment with the Swedes and the Russians meant that shipping in the rest of the Baltic no longer required one of the navy's largest fleets. In response, the Admiralty withdrew many of the ships of the line, accounting for roughly sixty-five hundred men. Some went back to Britain to be discharged as their tired ships needed refitting. Saumarez, for example, never again saw significant active service. The same could be said for his flagship, the *Victory*, which was once again in need of a refit (she had been refitted after Trafalgar as well). After the ship's company was paid off in November 1812, the *Victory* was put into ordinary and then began a three-year refitting at Portsmouth, the results of which are still visible today.[7]

Had the United States not declared war, the return of the Baltic fleet may have solved, or at least substantially alleviated, the navy's manpower crisis in 1813. Instead, many of the men and ships were redistributed to cover operations on the other side of the Atlantic. Nevertheless, the drawdown in the Baltic coincident with Napoleon's disastrous retreat from Moscow marks the beginning of the end of the Napoleonic Wars. That is not to argue that anyone in November 1812 understood that the final descent had begun, or even that Napoleon's subsequent defeat was inevitable. Rumors of his retreat from Moscow seemed too good to be true, and he soon demonstrated a remarkable capacity for raising new armies. From this point forward, however, Britain and the Allies could shift—cautiously—to the offensive.

To launch the offensive against Napoleon while simultaneously fighting a war across the Atlantic, both services grew in 1813 to reach their wartime peaks. Already by far the largest maritime force in the world, the navy now had 147,047 men distributed over nearly 700 ships in commission. The army also gained a few thousand men from 1812, rising to 238,730 in July 1813. In that sense, the story told in this chapter sits awkwardly in a book about demobilization—the army and navy were mobilizing more resources, not fewer. But at the same time, some sailors had already gone home, which begins to answer the broader question about the timing of demobilization, and the overextension of British forces in 1812 and 1813 made the imperative to demobilize quickly in 1814 that much stronger. With campaigns in multiple theaters, each full of its own setbacks and advances, the roller-coaster ending of the Napoleonic Wars makes it impossible to tell a single-narrative story. Much like British ministers in the fall of 1812, all we can do is hold on tight for the ride.

The opening rounds in the War of 1812 demonstrated the fragility of the strategic situation. Once again, the army's inflexible regimental system and the primacy of the Peninsular War meant that there was little thought given to bolstering the land forces in North America. Ministers assumed that Canada was lost and that there was little they could do about it. Two battalions that had been sent out to relieve two already there were instead kept on as reinforcements, but it was not until the spring of 1813 that more substantial forces—in the form of three battalions from Bermuda—could be moved to Canada.[8]

The lack of army resources in the theater meant that the burden of fighting the United States initially fell on the navy. While the fledgling U.S. Navy boasted no ships of the line, it had built several heavy frigates, and they soon proved their worth. Carrying twenty-four-pound guns rather than the usual eighteen-pound guns, USS *Constitution* and her sisters substantially outgunned British frigates nominally of the same class. The war's first major battle, between the *Constitution* and HMS *Guerriere* on August 19, 1812, pitted a 754-pound American broadside against a 526-pound British broadside. After hours of maneuvering but just fifteen minutes of intense firing, the *Guerriere* surrendered. Two months later, the *United States* captured the *Macedonian* and towed her into Newport harbor. The *Constitution* also beat the *Java* on December 29. The three major frigate defeats dominated the headlines in Britain, and the U.S. Navy's sloops also won several victories while American privateers captured $2 million in prizes. George Canning said in the House of Commons that the "spell of invincibility of the British navy was broken."[9]

Not only did the frigate defeats damage the navy's public standing, but they also shaped deployments. The Admiralty issued secret instructions that no British frigate was to sail alone in American waters. That order further stretched the ships on station, as now tasks that normally would be done by one frigate had to be done by two. When USS *President* crossed the Atlantic in the spring of 1813, she preoccupied two British ships of the line and a frigate in an ultimately fruitless chase to Norway and back—one is reminded, perhaps, of the *Bismarck*. Melville told frigate captains that the American heavy frigates like the *President* were equivalent to ships of the line—in other words, if they did meet one while sailing alone, they were not expected to engage.[10]

By the end of 1812 it did indeed seem that the British navy had finally been stretched to the breaking point. With so many global responsibilities and an obvious need to focus on events in Europe, it simply did not have sufficient manpower or ships to deal with the crisis in North America. In the hopes of avoiding the conflict altogether, ministers waited until October to authorize general reprisals against U.S. forces, and the commander in chief was given the authority to negotiate a settlement, if possible. A few weeks into the war, British sailors in American service were encouraged to return to the Royal Navy. They would be forgiven any previous transgressions and welcomed back because the real enemy was "the tyranny and despotism of France."[11]

Yet the American war nevertheless intensified, and the resources already deployed to the North American and West Indies stations seemed wholly inadequate to the scale of the problem. American privateers swarmed into the West Indies, targeting the lucrative convoys—one convoy of fifty-one ships was estimated to be worth £5.5 million. Protecting that trade both secured the political support of the powerful planters and helped fund the subsidies that underpinned the fragile Allied coalition in Europe. In 1812, there were only five frigates and nine sloops on station, which could not prevent insurance rates from rising 10 percent in the first six months of the war. Halifax was home to just one small ship of the line, six frigates, and sixteen smaller vessels, which was hardly enough to organize the hundreds of convoys that would be needed to keep the Atlantic trade routes safe. All the while, vulnerable American merchantmen managed to find safe harbors in Europe or return to the United States relatively unmolested.[12]

In Canada, Lieutenant General Sir George Prévost commanded a little over seven thousand regulars—four line battalions, a veteran battalion, and some artillery—plus thousands of locally raised militia of uncertain quality and loyalty. With this mongrel force he was expected to defend an enormous territory from Halifax to Detroit. Few thought he would be successful at this, despite his considerable abilities as an administrator. His regulars had a frustrating tendency to desert, further complicating his mission. The temptation of abundant land in Canada and the United States proved to be too much for many, and the Americans did their best to exacerbate the problem by offering large enlistment bonuses. Fully 9 percent of the U.S. Army during the War of 1812 was born in Britain. Despite these challenges, however, the initial results for Prévost in Canada were good: in the summer of 1812 alone, superior British leadership defeated pathetic American leadership at Fort Mackinac, Fort Dearborn, and Detroit, and in the fall, there were additional British victories at Niagara, Lacolle Mills, and Frenchman's Creek.[13]

The good news on land was soon matched at sea by a commitment on the part of the Admiralty to take the American threat more seriously. Shortly after the war began, the Admiralty replaced the commander in chief at Halifax with Admiral Sir John Borlase Warren and gave him unified command of all vessels in North American waters from Nova Scotia and Halifax to Jamaica and the Leeward Islands, eighty-three ships in all. But Warren had only six of those ships free from escorting and other responsibilities to impose a blockade. In early January 1813, the Admiralty promised him substantial reinforcements—ten ships of the line, thirty frigates, and fifty sloops—although they qualified that promise by encouraging him to wrap up the conflict as quickly as possible so the ships could be transferred back to European waters. Here again we see the primacy of the European theater and the difficulty that the navy faced in stretching its resources beyond what had been deployed in June 1812.[14]

The reinforcements came from the drawdown in the Baltic. As noted earlier, most of the men and ships in the Baltic in 1812 were not discharged but rather redeployed, freeing up resources to be sent to North America and the Caribbean. It took about six months from the early reports of Napoleon's disaster for its strategic effects to be felt in the North American theater. Fifteen Russian ships of the line lent their services to the Allied efforts in the North Sea, which contributed to the domino effect of redeployed resources. What spare forces Britain had first appeared in the North Sea and then across the North Atlantic. The *Bellerophon,* which had been in the Baltic early in Saumarez's tenure, had spent 1812 blockading the Texel and Scheldt. In April 1813, with extra ships arriving in the North Sea, the *Bellerophon* escorted a convoy to Newfoundland, one of 366 such convoys that sailed to and from Europe that year. The *Bellerophon* was also one of ten ships of the line now on the North American station, along with thirty-eight frigates and fifty-two sloops. By the end of the year, there were nearly as many British sailors in North American waters as in the Mediterranean.[15]

The dramatic increase in the convoy system—16,228 ships were escorted in 1813 compared to 6,856 in 1812—was one of several ways that the release of the Baltic fleet transformed the British war effort against the United States in 1813. The Delaware and Chesapeake Bays could now be properly blockaded, devastating the customs-dependent revenue of the U.S. government. Taking advantage of the mobility provided by British naval superiority, Sir George Cockburn launched an aggressive and destructive campaign in the Chesapeake.

In June, Captain Philip Broke and the *Shannon* restored some of the navy's pride by capturing USS *Chesapeake* in a short, bloody duel. On hearing the news, the naval officer Graham Moore wrote in his diary, "Such a lesson will have the right effect on the Americans in bringing them to their senses, puffed up with arrogance and presumption as they are with their success in three very unequal actions they have had with our Frigates."[16] Further successes followed: the *United States* and the *Macedonian* were corralled and blockaded in New London, and the *Constellation* suffered the same fate in Hampton Roads. In case the larger American frigates escaped, three old seventy-four-gun ships of the line and three obsolete sixty-four-gun ships were cut down into "razees"—a cheaper and faster solution than building new heavy frigates, although that was begun as well.[17]

Yet for all these positive developments, there were reasons to be disappointed at the strategic situation in North America at the end of 1813. Operations on the Great Lakes saw mixed results. The arrival of the troops from Bermuda in the spring grew Prévost's force to about 13,700 men, but he remained on the defensive. Fighting near Niagara resulted in a draw, although eventually the British were able to push the Americans back and capture Fort Niagara at the end of the year. On Lake Erie, Master Commandant Oliver Hazard Perry defeated a British force in September, forcing the British army to withdraw from Detroit. Warren ended the year frustrated both with the quality of the reinforcements he had been sent—they were in a "wretched state," he told the Admiralty—and with the porousness of his blockade.[18] He estimated that there were no fewer than 600 American privateers ready for sea, and it was impossible to keep them all bottled up. So many escaped that they captured 435 British merchantmen in 1813, and not only in American waters: the next year, insurance rates for the Irish Sea rose to a wartime high of 13 percent as a result of their aggressiveness. With privateers in the navy's backyard, perhaps the handwringing over the frigate defeats in 1812 was warranted. William Cobbett wondered why the navy was making such a fuss about the *Shannon*: "There is more boasting about this defeat of one American frigate than there used to be about the defeat of whole fleets."[19]

It is common to focus on two wars in 1813, in North America and in Europe. But we should also be cognizant of the global nature of warfare in this period as the British Empire expanded. Ministers certainly had to be aware of global operations because they shaped the pattern of deployments and the resources available, and we need to be aware of them because most of the sailors and some of the soldiers deployed to other theaters came home after 1815. While the West Indies convoys were the navy's responsibility, the army also maintained sizeable garrisons on the islands to reassure the planters, and not only the West India Regiments that were raised locally. In 1813, fourteen battalions from line regiments were stationed in the theater. The navy also had a fairly large South American squadron of fifteen frigates and sloops on station to monitor the ongoing Spanish colonial revolutions.[20]

Across the Atlantic, the route to India required a sizeable presence at the Cape from both services. Its garrison consisted of battalions from three line regiments as well as the Twenty-First Light Cavalry, plus two ships of the line, five frigates, and a sloop. Only recently had the threats in the Indian Ocean receded: the navy in the East Indies, according to one recent account, was able to "rest on its much-deserved laurels" from about 1812.[21] Those laurels had been won by the belated capture of the French naval and privateer bases on Mauritius and Réunion in 1810 and the Dutch colony on Java in 1811, but the maintenance of those conquests drained manpower. The East Indies station consisted of one ship of the line and seventeen smaller vessels, and well into 1813 there were still four battalions stationed on Réunion and three on Java. The latter had been drawn from forces in India, where there were eighteen line regiments and various other establishments amounting to about twenty-seven thousand British men. That force was dwarfed by the East India Company Army, which had grown over the course of the war to number more than two hundred thousand soldiers raised on the subcontinent. The British Empire was increasingly reliant on foreign manpower, and not only in India. In the army, British- and Irish-born manpower had grown 25 percent since 1808, while foreign manpower had grown 61 percent. Many garrisons consisted of locally raised troops, from the Greek Light Infantry, raised in 1810, to the West India Regiments.[22]

That the services were operating globally affected the course of the war in Europe. One soldier in Canada was one soldier not in Spain. Liverpool had told Prévost at the beginning of the war that he should be prepared to withdraw from Canada so that Britain could "prosecute the contest with additional vigour in that quarter of the World, in which the Interests of the Country are, at the present moment, more immediately committed"—that is, Europe.[23] One historian has estimated that the army's operations in Canada cost Wellington three or four battalions of good infantry as well as two battalions of marines. While these forces are small compared to all the reinforcements sent to the Peninsular War in 1813, Wellington needed every able-bodied man he could find.[24]

Wellington's 1812 campaign in the Peninsular War had been bolstered by Napoleon's removal of 27,000 of his best troops from Spain to face the Russians, but at the beginning of the year, he was still outnumbered 262,000 to 60,000. The good news, from his perspective, was that French forces in Spain struggled to concentrate in one place to take advantage of their numerical superiority. Whenever they did, they faced immediate supply problems, but when they dispersed to find food and forage, they were easier targets for guerrillas. Nevertheless, it was a year of advances followed by setbacks. Victory at Salamanca in July was followed by the liberation of Madrid in August, which then had to be abandoned, as did Burgos after the siege in October. The winter of 1812–13 found Wellington back in Portugal searching for a way to launch a more sustainable offensive. His preferred solution was to blame the Spanish for his previous failures and demand control of Spanish forces. After visiting the Cortes of Cadiz in December and January, he got his wish.[25]

Wellington planned his 1813 campaign carefully and secretly, so that significant portions of his own army were surprised by his three-pronged advance along a northerly route in May. He redeemed the mistake at Burgos from the previous year, and he moved more rapidly through the difficult terrain of northern Spain than the French thought possible. In June, his Allied army of 57,000 British, 16,000 Portuguese, and 8,000 Spanish soldiers met 57,000 French soldiers at Vitoria in Basque Country. The result was a decisive Allied victory, although there were recriminations in the aftermath because a large body of French soldiers escaped to fight another day. One of the reasons the pursuit was not conducted with the enthusiasm one might have expected is that Joseph Bonaparte, soon-to-be-ex-King of Spain, abandoned fantastic quantities of treasure in the French retreat. Allied soldiers lost all discipline in looting the wagons.[26]

After Vitoria, it seemed as if the French position in Spain was finally imperiled. But the news from central Europe was less welcome: Napoleon had managed to raise a new army and defeat the Prussians and Russians twice in quick succession in May. On June 4, a few weeks before Vitoria, the Continental Allies signed an armistice with Napoleon, and Wellington and the British government grew increasingly concerned that it would lead to a separate peace, allowing Napoleon to turn his attention and his armies back to Spain.[ii] There was little that Wellington could do about those developments, but he decided it was prudent to abandon the light and quick operations that had been so successful up to Vitoria and proceed with more caution. In any case, he needed to realign his naval supply line from Lisbon to Passages, on the Biscay coast, and the French recovered from their defeat at Vitoria quickly. A hoped-for quick invasion of France was not possible. As summer turned to fall, Wellington's forces were fending off French counterattacks while besieging San Sebastian and Pamplona.[27]

The year 1813 was filled with doubt and uncertainty in international affairs: how badly had the retreat from Moscow damaged Napoleon's power? Could Russia and Prussia handle Napoleon? Would the Anglo-Portuguese-Spanish alliance hold together? The Portuguese seemed increasingly unenthusiastic about invading France—that was not what they had signed up for. Meanwhile Anglo-Spanish relations collapsed to such an extent that Wellington, without consulting London, threatened to withdraw his army from the theater. His petulance was embarrassing for Castlereagh, as it made it appear as if the British were looking for any excuse to back out of the agreement to keep land forces on the Continent. But separately, ministers had arrived in a similar place, although for very different reasons. They considered bringing the Peninsular War to a close so they could redeploy Wellington and most of his army. They suggested southern Italy, where a small British force based in Sicily was engaged in operations, or northern Europe. Wellington appears to have given the proposals

---

ii The language ministers used when discussing these fears is revealing. They fretted about a "Continental peace" as distinct from a "maritime peace." Only the latter would involve Britain. See George Jackson to Sir Charles Stewart, Reichenbach, August 2, 1813, in Webster, *British Diplomacy, 1813–1815*, 74.

some consideration, but eventually he rejected them and opted to stay put. It was clearly necessary to do something for the Continental Allies, however, both to reinforce Britain's commitment to the cause and to ensure they were capable of fielding armies, so the British treasury doled out more subsidies in 1813 than it had in the entirety of the French Revolutionary Wars.[28]

The other major challenge in 1813 was that the manpower crisis had intensified. The tap of volunteers to both services had slowed to a drip, while the Impress Service was operating (and had been operating for many years) at capacity. A typical incident occurred in Lynn in August, when a mob estimated to be five hundred strong attacked the regulating captain and his lieutenant because they had pressed two ordinary seamen out of a returning Greenland whaler. It was not the existence of the press gang that outraged the citizens but rather the gang's violation of an established norm: it was customary for whalers to be given a few days in port before the gang did its work. The Impress Service could operate only with the toleration of Britain's port towns, and any expansion of its operations met with firm resistance.[29]

To address the army's crisis, in November, Parliament passed a bill allowing militiamen to volunteer for service in Europe, providing for the transfer of twenty-six thousand men into the regular army by whole companies. Normally, the militia could only be employed at home, where it served several essential purposes including guarding prisoners of war and suppressing domestic disturbances like the Luddites. In the straitened circumstances of 1813, however, ministers could not afford to leave any manpower reserves untapped even though most generals, very much including Wellington, doubted whether the militia would be effective.[30]

By the end of the year, it looked like the militia might not be needed after all. The armistice that had caused Wellington to worry that the Allies would sign a separate peace collapsed. Austria finally joined the Allied coalition in August, only to be defeated immediately at Dresden at the end of the month. Better news arrived in October, when a massive Allied army finally inflicted a significant defeat on Napoleon's rebuilt Grande Armée at Leipzig in the Battle of the Nations. Even then, however, the most likely outcome seemed to be that Napoleon would agree to peace terms that would keep him on the throne of France. That might provide a brief respite, as it had during the Peace of Amiens in 1802, and perhaps that would be enough for Britain to focus its attention more fully on the threat from the United States. But as Graham Moore noted, Napoleon and peace seemed incompatible: "They must see that his ambition is insatiable and that he never can rest, nor let them, while he lives, unless he can succeed in subjugating the whole of Europe."[31]

Belatedly, the Allies came to the same conclusion and agreed not to allow Napoleon to remain on the French throne. That meant it was necessary to invade France. The first British troops crossed the border in the first week of October 1813. Wellington moved deliberately and cautiously. The French were clearly on the defensive, and Wellington worried that the presence of a British army on French soil would have unpredictable effects on the French population. The initial target was the city of Bayonne, and after forcing three rivers—the Bidassoa, Nivelle, and Nive—from October to December, British forces managed to surround the city before entering winter quarters. Once supplies from Spain had caught up, in February 1814, the campaign resumed, and Wellington attacked inland toward Orthez, where he defeated French forces under Marshal Soult on February 27.[32]

Yet even as Allied forces poured over the French borders in the north and the south, with Napoleon on his heels, neither service could let down its guard. British ships still ploughed the same stretch of water off Toulon, still stood in to Basque Roads to count the ships ready for sea, and still dully trimmed their sails so as not to outpace their convoys. Rumors of peace abounded, of course, particularly after Leipzig, but they were balanced even as late as March 1814 by rumors that Napoleon had inflicted major defeats on Allied armies yet again. Ministers could not allow themselves the luxury of planning in expectation of peace. The navy's budget for 1814 was unchanged from the previous year on the assumption that once again, naval forces would be stretched to the breaking point. In the hopes of keeping up naval manpower, the navy announced shortly *after* Leipzig that volunteers would continue to receive bounties through the next year. The wars seemed to be never-ending.[33]

And then, all of a sudden, they ended. On March 31, 1814, Tsar Alexander I led an Allied army into Paris, and on April 6, Napoleon abdicated. The pessimistic rumors had been false, and in fact

Napoleon had been heavily outnumbered since Leipzig. A few weeks earlier, in the south, Wellington had learned that Bordeaux, one of the largest cities in France, was prepared to declare for the Bourbons, so he sent forces north to the city while simultaneously attempting to draw Soult into battle by attacking Toulouse, to the east. Toulouse fell on April 10. The Treaty of Fontainebleau, signed on April 11, sent Napoleon into exile on Elba, and the Convention of Toulouse, signed April 18, ended the Peninsular War. The Bourbon Louis XVIII became head of state on May 30.

In Britain, the prince regent announced a Jubilee, extravagant celebrations erupted in Hyde Park, and Allied heads of state toured the country. Small towns joined in the fun. On June 17, in Bury St. Edmunds, four thousand people gathered as the bells rang all day, while in Devon, prisoners were let out on parole to participate in a parade through town. It seemed that nothing could dampen the mood. "The people appeared to be all raving drunk, all raving mad," wrote Cobbett. [34]

But the wars were not over, as the Americans rudely reminded the British. In late April, USS *Peacock* captured HMS *Epervier* off the Florida coast, and in June, USS *Wasp* captured and sank HMS *Reindeer* in the mouth of the Channel. Amidst the celebrations, the government had to get back to work. The question now became how to send thousands of men and ships home while simultaneously reinvigorating the war effort in North America.

CHAPTER 4

Demobilization and the War of 1812

For the navy, demobilization took priority over the War of 1812, at least initially. The Navy Board maintained a book called *Preparations for Peace*, which it regularly updated even when peace was only rumored. The book provided step-by-step instructions to clerks for how to cancel contracts and prepare the dockyards to receive the fleet. The board's preparedness meant that the first stage of demobilization involved the navy's infrastructure: the dockyards, signal and telegraph stations, hospitals, and other shore establishments. To receive those portions of the fleet deemed surplus to requirements, all of these had to be retooled in anticipation or closed down to save money. While some tired ships and men were demobilized following the withdrawal from the Baltic, the hundreds of orders that the Navy Board issued to the dockyards in April 1814 marked a dramatic acceleration of that process. The board ordered the yards to stop building ships and boats and to stop making new sails, anchors, blocks, and dozens of other essential items. They had to store what supplies they had on hand and send an inventory along with a list of all of their contractors to the board.[1] Some smaller shore establishments, such as the facilities at Yarmouth, were closed, while others, such as the hospital on Malta, were placed on "the lowest" peace establishment.[2] The Admiralty also decided to close the shutter telegraph lines that connected its offices in Whitehall with Portsmouth, Plymouth, Yarmouth, and Deal, as well as the coastal signal stations that had been installed to warn about French invasions. Ministers would soon come to regret their haste, especially regarding the telegraphs, but their enthusiasm for limiting expenses and drawing down shore-based infrastructure is understandable.[3]

The Admiralty announced in late April that all sailors who had served since 1804 would be discharged and that the crews of all ships paid off were "to be considered as disposable," meaning they would not be turned over to another ship. While some recruiting stations in central locations were kept open, such as the one on Tower Hill, many other rendezvous were closed and press gangs disbanded.[4] The result was a mass discharge of experienced sailors, leaving the remainder of the American war to be prosecuted by younger and (the Admiralty hoped) happier crews. About forty thousand sailors came home in June and especially in July, even though the war with the United States continued. They demobilized in the second phase—following the dockyards—and in contrast with soldiers, comparatively few of them were sent to North America.

But the American war could not be ignored, and the next phase of demobilization involved the reorganization of the fleet to meet ongoing challenges. First on the chopping block were ships being built. In the spring of 1814, there were no fewer than twenty-one ships of the line, twenty-three frigates, and sixteen smaller vessels being built or ordered, which is another indication of how long the navy maintained its strength even after the tide had turned against Napoleon. The Admiralty cancelled all but seven of the frigates and four of the smaller vessels. Since such ships did not take long to be built, they could be cancelled more easily than ships of the line. There was nothing to be done about HMS *Nelson*, for example, which with 120 guns was the largest ship ever built to that point in Britain; the *Nelson* launched in the middle of the 1814 demobilization, on July 4, with Melville escorting the Prussian Marshal Blücher and the Russian Count Platov to the ceremony.[5]

As the *Nelson* slid down the slipway, fifteen ships of the line and sixty-eight frigates and sloops arrived back in port from fleets in the Channel, the North Sea, and the Baltic. Twenty-five ships of the line and more than fifty smaller vessels joined them from the Mediterranean, leaving only five ships of the line on that station. All told, seventy ships of the line were put into ordinary over the course of 1814. The process was barely managed chaos, as new Admiralty instructions admitted: "As great hurry and confusion hath formerly arisen," they began, it was essential that each component of each ship be handled with care to preserve it for the next war.[6] Ships' masts and spars were removed, along with their guns and stores. Their holds were filled with extra iron ballast, and they were lined up in the dockyards of the Thames, Portsmouth, and Plymouth as a reserve force to be mobilized in the event of another war. Most of the ships put into ordinary in 1814 were the largest in the navy. First- and second-rate ships of the line— with ninety or more guns—were enormous manpower drains, requiring crews of nearly one thousand each. By the end of the year, not a single ship of that size remained in commission. Taking their place were the workhorses of the fleet, the seventy-four-gun third rates.[7]

Comparatively few frigates and sloops went into ordinary in 1814 because they were still needed for convoy duty, and not only to protect against American privateers. When the Navy Board had ordered the dockyards to prepare for the arrival of the fleet, they had made one exception: Deptford Yard was told to remain on a war footing and continue supplying frigates and sloops operating out of Leith.[8] The reason for this was the ongoing conflict in Scandinavia. The January 1814 peace settlement among Britain, Denmark, and Sweden had transferred Norway from Danish to Swedish control. Nobody bothered to ask the Norwegians whether they liked that idea, however, and soon they were at war with their proposed overlords. The Norwegians formed an independent navy consisting of what was left of Danish warships in Norway. Some Danish officers opted to stay in Norwegian service, and there were plenty of Norwegian sailors available. This navy, although small, did pose a real threat. Sweden asked Britain for assistance, so the squadron at Leith operated off the Norwegian coast throughout the summer of 1814.

There were other reasons to keep small ships in commission. Lloyd's had initially been confident in the prospects for peace, as its chairman said in March: "Our intercourse with the other Nations of Europe, which has been so long interrupted, is restored, by the returning relations of peace and amity."[9] The Admiralty shared Lloyd's optimism and suspended convoy service in the Mediterranean and the Baltic shortly after Napoleon's abdication. But the uncertain situation in Norway caused the Baltic merchants to demand the reinstatement of convoys less than a month later, to keep insurance rates down.[10] There were also questions about the durability of the peace settlement and the coherence of the Allied coalition. Reports reached North America in July 1814 that "there were great commotions on the continent and things were by no means settled in Europe."[11]

The same could of course be said about the ongoing war with the United States, which showed little signs of diminishing. What mattered at least as much as the military situation was the perception of the military situation, and here both sides felt the war to be slipping away. In the United States, this led to a serious discussion of secession among New England states, where the British blockade was strangling commercial activity; in Britain, it manifested itself in fretting about the state of the navy. Some of the concerns were vague: for example, an editorial on "the poverty of British naval leadership" cited as evidence the simple fact that Britain had not been able to end the war in America quickly and on favorable terms, as one would expect given the balance of forces. Pessimists forecasted the growth of American naval strength, expecting to see in the next couple of years an American ambassador disembarking at Portsmouth from a ninety-eight-gun first rate. Robert Fulton's experiments with steam vessels suggested a novel way for the U.S. Navy to break through the blockade, and Melville took reports of their capabilities seriously.[12] In fact, neither an American first rate nor a viable armed steamship were imminent threats, but other problems were: the persistence of the American privateer threat and the challenges of manning.

American privateers, fretted *The Naval Chronicle*, have "literally swept our seas, blockaded our ports, and cut up our Irish and coasting trade."[13] They might even have the temerity to enter the Clyde. Insurance rates rose to three or four times as much for British ships as for neutral ships, and Lloyd's sprang into action in response. The chairman met with the new French foreign minister in June 1814. While he failed to secure restitution for American prizes currently in French ports, he did convince the French to stop supporting American privateers going forward. As a result, the Americans resorted to pillaging and burning prizes rather than selling them. Lloyd's complained to the Admiralty about these "numerous and mortifying depredations," and blamed the cancellation of the convoy system. There seemed to be

privateers everywhere, even in the South Atlantic, so that Lloyd's recommended that all ships leaving the Cape of Good Hope be forced to
stop at St. Helena to wait for a convoy. But the biggest threat was much
closer to home. At Lloyd's general meeting in September 1814, the
committee told the subscribers that American privateers had "taken it
for granted, that a considerable relaxation in our Convoy system would
take place in consequence of the peace." They have stationed themselves in the "Chops of the Channel, where all the commerce of Great
Britain is concentrated into a narrow focus." The committee said that
the "most obvious measure of protection" was a large naval force stationed there, but convoys might be necessary again because of the "the
impunity as well as success with which [the privateers] have so long
continued their depredations."[14] That a large naval force was needed
at the western end of the Channel may have been obvious to Lloyd's,
but it was not obvious to the Admiralty, which had disbanded the Channel Fleet at the time of the meeting. There was only one ship of the
line in commission in home waters. The rapidity and thoroughness of
demobilization in European waters left British trade open to aggressive
American commanders.[15]

If the privateer threat were to be stopped, then, it needed to be
cut off at the source, in American waters. But the chaos of European
demobilization made it difficult for commanders on the spot to plan
operations. Which ships were coming and which ships were going?
Complicating matters was a major hurricane that had struck Halifax
in November 1813, severely damaging Warren's fleet. The Admiralty
responded by sending frigates to North America rather than ships of
the line, since the Americans did not yet have an operational ship of
the line on the Atlantic coast. Three of the razees intended to match
the American heavy frigates arrived in early 1814, and eleven frigates
followed. These forces were a small fraction of the available ships, given
the scale of European demobilization, and it is perhaps surprising that
the Admiralty did not commit more resources. The problem was that
the Admiralty's priorities were always in Europe first, and Warren was
never able to convince the Admiralty to alter its stance. He was replaced
in April 1814, and his unified command was broken up.[16]

The new commander in chief in North America, Sir Alexander
Cochrane, had only twenty-five ships free for blockade duty—a significant force, but not an overwhelming one. He complained to the

Admiralty that his force was being drawn down below the strength he needed to carry out his objectives. The Admiralty was not sympathetic, and it could point to the one hundred ships currently deployed to his station and a recent transfer of eleven hundred men and boys as evidence of the ample resources at his disposal. In response, Cochrane could rightfully complain about the ongoing manpower crisis—apparently even the men transferred were insufficient. The frigates that crossed the North Atlantic in the summer of 1814 frequently sailed undermanned, and when they arrived on station, they struggled to prevent desertion. The *Junon*, a thirty-eight-gun frigate, lost nearly one hundred men in two years on the North American station out of an original complement of 315; only six were casualties of war, while sixty-two died or were incapacitated by illness and twenty-nine deserted. Rumors crossed the Atlantic that the U.S. government was offering one hundred acres of land to entice British sailors to desert, but most attributed the high rate of desertion to higher pay in the U.S. Navy. The Admiralty's only solution to the problem was to order captains to punish less severely. The alternative was to deploy fewer ships with stronger crews, but instead they chose to maintain the navy's presence around the American coastline with a large number of undermanned ships. By December 1814, half of the navy's deployed ships were in North American or Caribbean waters.[17]

The same debate played out in the army. Of the cabinet, Castlereagh was the most reluctant to send troops to Canada. In response, Canadians themselves made a concerted effort to encourage the government in Britain to send help, emphasizing the role that the colony played in providing naval stores and protecting the West Indies. They also organized a charity drive to alleviate the suffering caused by the war. The funds were helpful, but so too was the act of raising awareness of their plight by soliciting donations from key players in London, from the Duke of Kent to Lloyd's to the Bank of England. Liverpool's government promised to send troops as soon as it could, which is to say once Napoleon had abdicated in April 1814. There were 19,477 officers and men in North America that month, and over the next eight months, nearly thirty thousand additional officers and men arrived in the theater. The result was that by January 1815, on the eve of the Waterloo campaign, there were more British troops in North America than in Europe.[18]

We should not take that argument too far, as large numbers of troops had returned to Britain and Ireland and could easily be sent across the Channel if needed; on the other hand, it is clear that the War of 1812 now merited the deployment of the disposal force. It also provided an opportunity to reorganize many regiments. Here we can see the army attempting to execute the same dance as the navy: demobilizing European forces and redeploying to increase the pressure on the Americans. Twenty-four second and third battalions were eliminated, and their men redistributed to their regiment's first battalion. That had the practical benefit of strengthening some of those regiments since the deployed battalions were often undermanned. It no longer seemed necessary to employ so many veteran battalions and foreign regiments, so many of them were disbanded in the aftermath of Napoleon's abdication. The artillery and cavalry were also reduced to save money.[19]

Tracking battalions over the course of 1814 is a challenge, but some patterns emerge. New troops arriving in North America came from three sources. As in 1813, a handful of battalions moved from the West Indies to Canada. The First Battalion of the Ninetieth Regiment of Foot (1/90th) moved from the Leeward Islands to Canada along with the Ninety-Seventh Foot, and two of the West India Regiments joined the campaign in the Gulf of Mexico. The second group arrived from other locations in Europe: two battalions and a company of artillery that had been campaigning in Italy; three battalions that had been on the east coast of Spain; and a regiment from Gibraltar. These were veterans of extensive campaigns but not part of Wellington's core. There were also cobbled-together reinforcements from the British Isles. A battalion of Channel Islanders, the 7/60th, went to Newfoundland.[20]

The largest single contingent came from Wellington's army, which provided sixteen battalions, or just under a quarter of its total infantry strength. Peninsular War veterans therefore amounted to half of the troops sent to North America in 1814. The rest of Wellington's army went home, with one significant exception: the King's German Legion moved to the Low Countries, where they joined the second-rate army under Sir Thomas Graham that we met in chapter 3. All told, the new force amounted to about thirty-three thousand men, but this was well short of the commitment that Britain had made, along with all the

Allies at Vienna, to keep seventy-five thousand men on the Continent until the final settlement with France. Moving troops to North America rather than Europe forced the British to make up the difference by paying £355,333 in subsidies to the Prussians.[21]

With the disbanding of the Peninsular army, we can at last begin to provide an answer as to when soldiers came home. Unlike the navy, there were no significant army demobilizations before Napoleon's abdication, but then over the course of 1814, 34,293 men were discharged and approximately another 30,000 remained in service but came back to Britain and Ireland. The latter group came home as whole battalions, most of which remained in service. To meet their transports, the infantry moved to the coast of Spain and France over the course of July and August. It took ships displacing 12,828 tons (equivalent to about five third-rate ships of the line) plus two hospital ships to handle the homeward-bound troops from Bordeaux alone. The cavalry rode through France, where more hired transports awaited them at Cherbourg, Calais, and Boulogne. Many transports made multiple voyages, especially across the Channel. By September, enough of the major movements had been completed that the Transport Board felt it was safe to discharge 20,000 tons of shipping. The summer of 1814 therefore saw the largest arrival of both soldiers and sailors—about 100,000 men in all, though half of the soldiers were still serving in their regiments.[22]

The men who did not go home but crossed the Atlantic were generally not happy about it. Desertions spiked. The overall rate grew from 2.6 percent in 1812 to 3.8 percent in 1814, but it was especially high among units from the Peninsular army that redeployed to North America. Many soldiers felt that they had not signed up to fight the Americans, and as their enlistment periods were close to expiring, they were well within their rights to withdraw their labor from the army. If the regiment came ashore in the British Isles before redeploying, it provided men with an opportunity to make a break for it. They lost their pensions by doing so, but nevertheless, the temptation of returning home after so long away caused many to risk it.[23]

The first of the depleted redeployed Peninsular battalions reached Quebec in June, and they were quickly under pressure from the U.S. Army, which had improved from its early embarrassments and was well aware of the imperative to attack before the bulk of the British reinforcements arrived. The primary theater was initially concentrated around Niagara, and the Americans won at Chippawa on July 5 before being halted at Lundy's Lane on July 25.[24]

Strategically and operationally, it now seemed as if the conflict in America was Britain's war to win, especially as the blockade had eviscerated the U.S. economy. With stalemate at Niagara and reinforcements arriving daily, the British chose to make one last push, launching three offensives in three different theaters. In the Chesapeake, Cochrane embarked on a major campaign aimed at Washington and Baltimore. In Canada, Prévost attacked in the east, aiming to move south along Lake Champlain. In the Gulf of Mexico, a joint expedition began organizing itself in Jamaica. The war-weary public in Britain, however, was less enthusiastic, and put increasing pressure on Liverpool's government to end the war. As the offensives got underway, both sides sent representatives to Ghent to begin negotiations, but Liverpool ordered his ministers to move slowly in the hopes that the reinforcements could now begin to tell.[25]

With the ships and men now at his disposal, Cochrane was more aggressive than Warren ever had been. He gave command of the naval forces once again to Cockburn, scourge of the Chesapeake, but now the land forces were commanded by Major General Robert Ross, recently arrived from the Peninsular War. The expedition defeated American forces at Bladensburg on August 24 and then burned public buildings in Washington, including the White House—so called because of the white coat of paint it subsequently needed to cover up the scorch marks. A follow-up attack on Baltimore was less successful, and Ross was killed in an ambush. The campaign in Canada also showed promise initially before stalling out. American military and naval forces on Lake Champlain prevented Prévost from getting past Plattsburgh on September 11. Prévost's reputation suffered in the aftermath, in part because it was generally thought that his army of Peninsular veterans was far superior to the U.S. forces he faced. It is true that six of his nine battalions were veterans of the Peninsular War, but they were weaker than has often been supposed, their ranks thinned by desertions.[26]

The reversals at Baltimore and Plattsburgh had far-reaching consequences. With peace in Europe, the war in America began to seem increasingly pointless. In response to news of Ross's death, Graham

Moore predicted, "This war with America has cost us and will cost us many a gallant fellow, and, in my opinion, it will be well for both sides when it terminates."[27] The same week as Plattsburgh, a group of merchants in Liverpool publicly censured the Admiralty because more than eight hundred vessels belonging to that city had been lost since 1812. Liverpool asked Wellington to go to North America and assume command, hoping that Wellington's reputation would reignite the public's appetite for the war. But Wellington refused, pointing out how difficult it would be to do more than Prévost had without naval superiority on the Lakes. A week after Wellington's refusal, Liverpool told his representatives at Ghent to seek peace.[28]

The Treaty of Ghent was finalized on Christmas Eve 1814 and ratified in February 1815. It reinforced the pointlessness of the war. None of the major causes of the conflict was resolved, with the exception of the now-obsolete Orders in Council. British sailors still served on American ships; the British navy still reserved the right to press sailors in times of war; Canada remained under British control. But it was clear in the aftermath of the burning of Washington and the increasing stringency of the British blockade that the Americans could not fight much longer, while the British public was clearly tired of the war. American privateers were not an existential threat to the British economy, but they were sufficiently annoying to bring pressure to bear on the government to seek peace. A return to the status quo ante bellum suited all parties, and a public relations campaign to declare the war a success began on both sides of the Atlantic.[29]

During the final phase of negotiations, the third British offensive of 1814 targeted the Gulf coast. Royal Marines had captured Pensacola in August, but General Andrew Jackson recaptured it in November. There, he learned that the British had organized an expedition aimed at New Orleans, so he rushed west to supervise the city's defenses. The British forces of sixty-five hundred regulars, one thousand marines, and one thousand West Indian troops sailed from Jamaica under Cochrane's command, but after forcing their way across Lake Borgne in December, they were soundly defeated by Jackson's prepared defenses on January 8, 1815. Major General Sir Edward Pakenham, Wellington's brother-in-law and, like Ross, a Peninsular veteran, was killed, and his troops suffered more than two thousand casualties against just seventy-one American killed and wounded. The American victory occurred before ratification, and therefore was not, as the popular myth would have it, a postwar battle. Had the U.S. Senate not ratified the treaty, the victory would have mattered for ongoing negotiations.[30]

Other battles, however, came closer to spilling over into the peace. The War of 1812 has been aptly described as "a civil war among fragments of the first British Empire not yet reconciled to the settlement of 1783."[31] Like a civil war, it ended bitterly, with combat continuing right up to when the treaty was to take effect. Following the defeat at New Orleans, British forces besieged Fort Bowyer, at the mouth of Mobile Bay, on February 8; news of peace arrived the day after the fort surrendered. At Cumberland Island, Georgia, Cockburn learned of the treaty from an American officer's newspaper on February 25, but he decided the report was untrustworthy. He continued loading goods that had been captured from the Americans on to his ships until March 1, when he was able to verify the news. American privateers at sea were even less likely to receive official word of peace, and merchants in Barbados warned the local British naval officer that their ships still needed protection in April. Sporadic fighting with British naval vessels continued into June.[32]

The end of the war was soon complicated by Napoleon's escape from Elba, but we can see in the spring of 1815 a significant number of sailors and soldiers returning home from North America. The navy withdrew twelve ships of the line, thirty frigates, and fifty sloops, accounting for about twenty-three thousand sailors. The majority of them arrived in April and May, just as the situation in Europe was collapsing. Of the army's fifty-six battalions deployed to North America in January 1815, thirty-three were ordered home immediately and three more joined them by the end of the year. Included in the initial group were all but two of the battalions originally from Wellington's Peninsular army. A few of these battalions quickly redeployed in the midst of Napoleon's return and were present at Waterloo, including the 1/4th (King's Own) Foot and 1/27th (Inniskilling) Foot. Others were clearly too worn down to be worth redeploying: three of the returning battalions were disbanded by the end of 1816, including the 3/27th, which had fought through the Peninsular War.[33]

British possessions in North America and the West Indies still needed protection, of course, and later chapters will examine the fragility of the peace inaugurated by the Treaty of Ghent. As the last soldiers and sailors trickled across the Atlantic in the autumn, the Admiralty set targets for the strength of the stations at Halifax and the West Indies. They would each have a ship of the line to serve as the flagship of a small squadron of four to six frigates and four to six sloops. It took about a year to get the details of which ship was going where sorted out, so that even as late as June 1816, there were still eleven frigates and fifteen sloops in northern waters and ten frigates and twelve sloops in the West Indies. In the end, the Admiralty decided not to deploy any ships of the line, presumably to save money and manpower, and the two stations settled into a peace-time deployment pattern of seven or eight frigates accompanied by eight to ten sloops. Naturally, the army left the West India Regiments in the Bahamas, Jamaica, and the Leeward Islands—about nine battalions all told. But they were not alone. There were twelve line battalions alongside them in the islands, as well as a smattering of miscellaneous units and a garrison battalion. Canada merited eleven line battalions and one cavalry regiment, along with four Royal Veteran battalions that were soon to be disbanded.[34]

By emphasizing the role that demobilization played in shaping the end of the War of 1812, we can better assess Britain's performance. In purely military-operational terms, its record was mixed. With half of its deployable resources in a secondary theater by 1814, the navy had to balance the need for economy with the desire to defeat the United States decisively. In most respects, the transatlantic balancing act was successful. The achievement of the summer of 1814 should be more widely recognized. While drawing down forces in Europe, the navy was able to enforce an effective blockade of key ports that brought the United States to the negotiating table. On the other hand, the blockade was not comprehensive, and the navy's inability to prevent swarms of American privateers from preying on British shipping was one of the most significant reasons why the war ended in stalemate. The Irish Sea should have been among the safest places for British ships, but instead it was yet another theater in the war at sea. As a result, merchants put intense pressure on the government to put an end to the conflict, even if it meant returning to the status quo ante bellum.

The army initially had a much more successful war against the Americans than the navy. As the navy was losing frigates, the army was defending Canada with a small force of uncertain quality. By exceeding expectations in 1812 and 1813, the army provided a strong foundation for the arrival of the seasoned Peninsular troops in 1814. The Peninsular veterans showed their quality, defending Niagara and burning Washington. But the reverses at Baltimore and Plattsburgh, combined with the privateer threat, meant that there was no appetite for a further increase in effort against the Americans. The catastrophe at New Orleans proved the pessimists correct, and as a result, Britain's War of 1812 ended with all three of its major joint offensives stalled or defeated.

Britain was manifestly capable of deploying far more military force to the American war than it did. It is worthwhile to ask why it did not do so. One possible answer is to argue that Britain sent sufficient forces relative to American capabilities. Half the navy's deployed ships plus a large and growing army of veteran troops should have overwhelmed American forces. On the other hand, most of the navy's ships of the line were being put into ordinary, not into Halifax, and most of Wellington's army stayed in Europe. There was clearly latent capacity, and the commanders engaged with the Americans knew it and claimed they needed to draw on it. The disputes between Warren and the Admiralty and Cochrane and the Admiralty, combined with Liverpool's desire to send Wellington to Canada, suggest that British forces were not, in fact, sufficient.

The fundamental problem was that British objectives in Europe—the complete overthrow of Napoleon's regime—were different from British objectives in America—forcing the United States to sue for peace on favorable terms. In the terminology of strategic theorists, the wars against Napoleon had unlimited objectives while the War of 1812 had limited objectives. That does not imply that the former was more brutal than the latter—all war is terrible—but rather that the political purposes of the wars were different. Just before the passage in which Clausewitz laid out his famous dictum, "War is nothing but the continuation of policy with other means," he made this point: "War can be of two kinds, in the sense that either the objective is to *overthrow the enemy*—to render him politically helpless or militarily impotent, thus forcing him to sign whatever peace we please; or *merely to occupy some of his frontier-districts* so that we can annex them or use them for bargaining at the peace negotiations."[35]

The War of 1812 was of the latter variety. The British were not hoping to restore the thirteen colonies, and it would follow that therefore they did not employ all the means available to them. Ministers were initially willing to give up on Canada entirely, and while that position evolved over the course of the war, it indicates the kind of value that ministers placed on the points in dispute. Yet even this distinction does not satisfactorily answer the question because it conflates means and ends. Corbett, for example, thought that even in a war limited by its political object, maximal means would be employed: "You may, and usually must, employ your whole force."[36] The limited nature of British objectives in the War of 1812 provides important context for explaining why the means the British employed were insufficient, but it is not a sufficient answer itself.[37]

There were three reasons why Britain did not deploy all its available forces to North America. The War of 1812 was a war limited by its political objectives fought in the context of an unlimited war. In 1812 and 1813, the strategic imperative of the war in Europe made North America a secondary theater. But even in 1814, uncertainty about the political settlement combined with the Allied agreement to keep large armies on the Continent meant that ministers could not take their eyes off Europe. There were also practical impediments to deploying forces to North America. Thousands of miles of coastline stretching from New Orleans to Boston would have required even more resources to patrol than the Admiralty gave, and the difficulties in manning ships on station exacerbated the problem.

The third reason reveals the importance of demobilization for our understanding of the War of 1812. The paramount domestic policy issue in 1814 was dismantling the military part of the fiscal-military state so that the fiscal crisis could be addressed. As other historians have shown, public opinion played an essential role in pressuring both the American and British governments to seek peace. To that we should add that the British public, while riled up about the depredations of the American frigates and privateers, was also exhausted from the last two decades of war with France. That exhaustion manifested itself in demands for financial retrenchment and peace. "The point on which we are at issue with the United States," argued the *Leeds Mercury* two weeks after Napoleon abdicated, "is not of the slightest importance in a time of peace."[38] In the face of newspaper

editorials and lobbying efforts from organizations like Lloyd's, ministers saw more political benefit in bringing soldiers, sailors, ships, and
equipment home than any strategic benefit that might be gained by
pursuing the American war to the fullest.

No war is fought with absolute exertion, as Clausewitz pointed
out. Not only are the objectives in war often limited, but both sides
are uncertain about their own capacity to wage war and about their
enemy's capacity. Willpower cannot be easily measured, and so there
are always uncertainties in war. How much does the enemy value the
object of the war? Will mobilizing more quickly cause your military
machinery to break?[39] What is unusual about the War of 1812 is that
Britain knew full well what its military capacities were because they
were already deployed and available, yet ministers chose to demobilize those forces instead or keep them in Europe in case of a renewal
of hostilities. As is often the case in a war with limited objectives, ministers found themselves caught in the middle between the commanders on the spot and broader political concerns. Warren, Cochrane,
and Prévost demanded more resources because they were engaged
in high-stakes active operations. While Napoleon still ruled, it was
simple enough to put them off by pointing to the importance of the
European war, but by 1814, the resources they said they needed were
increasingly and obviously available. Yet committing all the available
means to a war with limited objectives in a remote theater seemed too
politically costly.

CHAPTER 5

Demobilization and the Hundred Days

In the winter of 1814–15, Napoleon began preparing a daring return to France. At his disposal he had three hundred Corsican soldiers and 566 former members of his Imperial Guard and some small vessels that had been given to his kingdom to maintain communications with the mainland. The largest vessel was a brig, the aptly named *Inconstant*. He had to keep his plans from being discovered by the British resident on Elba, Colonel Neil Campbell, who was widely assumed to be acting as Napoleon's jailor. Elba was also periodically visited by a sloop, HMS *Partridge*, which the British commander in chief of the Mediterranean, Sir Charles Penrose, had left "upon the station in case of any extraordinary circumstances."[1] Penrose's fleet was a shadow of its former self. Most of the ships of the line had gone home, leaving him an enormous station to cover with a fraction of Exmouth's resources. In the aftermath of the demobilization of 1814, Napoleon—Europe's most dangerous man—saw his opportunity.

In February, Campbell went to the mainland to visit an occultist and his mistress, who was possibly Napoleon's agent. In Campbell's absence, Napoleon put his plan into action. He ordered the *Inconstant* to be repainted to look like a British vessel and began loading supplies for his small army. On February 23, the *Partridge* visited Elba and Commander John Miller Adye came ashore. Napoleon quickly ordered the *Inconstant* to put to sea and tried to cover up the obvious preparations for his expedition. Somehow, Adye noticed nothing amiss and returned to his ship. Three days later, Napoleon seized his opportunity, sailing with most of his troops for France. En route, his squadron again met the *Partridge*, and Napoleon must have feared the worst. But for a second time, Adye bungled it: he mistook the *Inconstant* for a French Royalist vessel known to be in the area and apparently did not see the other ships carrying the troops. Napoleon's flotilla later encountered the French Royalist vessel in question, but, ominously, the captain allowed Napoleon to continue to southern France, where he landed on March 1. Less than three weeks later, he entered Paris to cheering crowds.[2]

Those are the facts, but they do not capture the spirit of what happened. The British failed spectacularly. Unsurprisingly, British historians have not dwelt on this calamity. A recent exception describes the navy's actions in February as "laughably inept," but even that understates the significance of the failure by focusing on the officers on the spot.[3] Campbell and Adye certainly deserve a significant portion of the blame, but the true failure was much higher up the chain of command. Ministers knew about the threat posed by Napoleon, chose to ignore it, and deflected blame when confronted with their failure. Major John Henry Slessor expressed a widely shared opinion when he visited Paris in the spring of 1814. He wrote in his diary, "Adieu, Paris. I cannot think you will be long quiet. Your Army will soon get tired of peace, and Napoleon's party, more particularly the Military, will not easily forget their leader."[4] After Napoleon's refusal to accept Allied terms in the winter of 1813–14, no sensible observer thought he could be trusted to live peacefully in retirement. It was obvious that a sloop and a colonel were insufficient.

It was not only a British failure, of course: Tsar Alexander had led the negotiations with Napoleon following the Russian occupation of Paris, and it was largely his idea to give Elba to Napoleon. Once he had committed himself in public to this course of action, it proved impossible for the other Allies (especially the Austrians and Prussians, who sought more punitive terms) to convince him to go back on his word. Castlereagh was fully aware of the dangers of Elba, but in the frantic negotiations to settle affairs in the spring of 1814, he allowed the tsar to dictate the terms of the treaty and then failed to come up with an alternative. The Allied coalition was fragile, and it was important to act quickly to dispose of Napoleon without alienating the tsar. Yet of all the Allied powers, Britain was the only one capable of maintaining a blockade of Elba. While the decision to concede on the question of Napoleon's destination must be seen in the broader context of the other negotiations at Vienna, it was clear at the time that Elba was at best a half solution and at worst a disaster waiting to happen. Castlereagh compounded his error by issuing unclear orders to Campbell: while most observers assumed Campbell was Napoleon's jailor, in fact, his orders were to protect Napoleon from assassination plots. In the interest of expediency and coalition maintenance, Napoleon ended up close to France, unguarded by any Allied representative, in possession of a small navy, and sovereign of an island in a sea that had just been abandoned by his most powerful foe to save money.[5]

Later, when Liverpool was confronted in Parliament by critics who blamed the navy for allowing Napoleon's escape, he protested: it was "impracticable" to confine Napoleon to his "asylum." Despite that tacit admission that Elba under Napoleon was not like other sovereign states, Liverpool's defense rested on the idea that it was. The entire British fleet, he said, would not have been capable of searching even the "meanest fishing vessel" because "according to the law of nations," the right of search depended "upon the continuance of hostilities; but even pending war . . . nothing could excuse or justify the search of an armed ship."[6] Granting Napoleon a sovereign kingdom was clearly a major mistake, but it was disingenuous to hide behind the right to search vessels at sea. The British practice of doing just that to neutral American vessels was one of the precipitating causes of the War of 1812.

Liverpool also pleaded that the ships of the Mediterranean fleet had been sent home, using the passive voice even though his own ministers had given the orders. When the first Treaty of Paris was signed in the spring of 1814, there were seventy warships on station, including thirty ships of the line; by the end of the year, there were fewer than fifteen ships.[7] Few funds could be spared amid a looming budget crisis, but the cost of allowing Napoleon to escape far exceeded the cost of a reasonable security arrangement. Despite that, ministers prioritized demobilization first, the transfer of forces to North America second, and Napoleon's security third. When news of

Napoleon's escape reached London, the navy had to change course quickly. On March 10, the Navy Board suspended its cancellation orders to its contractors, and on March 21, the day after Napoleon entered Paris, the Admiralty announced "with great reluctance" that demobilization was suspended.[8] The result was a period of confusion and expense, all of which could have been prevented had Napoleon been properly secured.

Now that the navy had failed in its primary task of preventing Napoleon's escape, what was its purpose in this new yet old war? The general historical consensus is that there was "little to do," and the lack of naval operations during the Hundred Days does bear out that judgment.[9] Graham Moore did not expect that "this will be much of a Naval war, the game must be played on shore."[10] The Navy Board later assessed its response to Napoleon's escape by explaining that "the French were incapable of making efforts by sea" and that naval operations were "carried on, on a comparatively small scale, the French having sent out no Squadrons during its short continuance; and nothing occurred in the course of it, to add to the Record."[11] However, these descriptions undersell the frenetic preparations the navy made in the event it would be needed, as well as the actions it did take in response to the renewal of hostilities. To be clear: compared to the scale of operations over the previous two decades or even the previous three years in North America, the navy's combat role in the spring of 1815 was small. But this story is about the process of demobilization, and in that sense, Napoleon's escape made an already chaotic situation worse.

In terms of the fleet's deployments, Napoleon's return kept smaller ships in service that would otherwise have been demobilized. Nowhere is there a plan from an administrator laying out which ships were needed and which were not, so we cannot be precise about the numbers involved. Nevertheless, we can estimate based on the number of ships put into ordinary after Waterloo: presumably if they were not needed then, they were likely to have been demobilized sometime in 1815 had Napoleon not returned. Just over a hundred ships fit this criterion, about forty frigates and seventy sloops. Since there were no French fleets obviously ready for sea, it made sense for the Admiralty to rely primarily on small ships to continue convoying troops and keeping open lines of communication.[12]

Byam Martin traveled to meet Wellington in Belgium to ask what he needed to secure his lines of communication across the Channel. They had developed a positive working relationship during the closing stages of the Peninsular War. Initially, Wellington was confident that little naval assistance would be needed, telling Byam Martin that he did not anticipate acting on the defensive. As the situation evolved, however, Wellington's tune changed. Byam Martin helped prepare the defenses of Antwerp and Ostend to ensure that in the event of a disaster, Wellington's army could be removed.[13]

Across the Channel, the navy scrambled to halt and then reverse the reduction in the shore establishments. The dockyards were generally well stocked with stores except for rope, and in April, the Navy Board approved the rehiring of rope makers they had discharged only months before. From mid-April through the end of May, signal stations were reestablished all along the Channel coast as well as on the Channel Islands. The visual telegraph system that had been so unwisely dismantled had to be rebuilt to connect Whitehall with Deal, Portsmouth, and Plymouth; only the last two were opened before the end of the war, but just days before Waterloo, Parliament passed a bill allowing the government to acquire ground for signal and telegraph stations. Clearly the Admiralty wanted to avoid making the same mistake again, and in 1816, they began trials of a new telegraph system designed by Sir Home Popham.[14]

Much of the activity following Napoleon's return concerned the Mediterranean, the very region the navy had so precipitously abandoned in 1814. Pellew, now ennobled as Baron Exmouth, was reappointed to command, and as he scrambled to put together a fleet, the dockyards in Portsmouth and Plymouth sprang back into life. One of the Navy Board's first orders in March was to send one of its largest storeships to the Mediterranean filled with supplies for ships of the line. The cabinet's strategy was to arm those in France who did not welcome Napoleon's return, so Exmouth was given fifteen thousand muskets and told to do what he could in southern France until an expedition could be launched. The idea was to attack Naples first, then Genoa, and then Toulon. For a time, it appeared that a serious effort would be needed. HMS *Rivoli* intercepted and captured the French *Melpomène*, which was en route to Naples to retrieve Napoleon's mother.[15]

In the end, however, the Hundred Days was not a naval war. The Allies at Vienna had agreed to raise large armies throughout central Europe: an Austrian army of 200,000 on the Upper Rhine; a Russian army of 150,000 in the Middle Rhine; and a Prussian army of 120,000 in Belgium, joined by a British-led army that was supposed to be 100,000 men. The goal was to apply pressure against the outlaw Napoleon all along France's eastern borders. From the British perspective, the problem was that there simply were not 100,000 men available. Ministers were eager to be seen to be pulling their weight in the alliance, and not just by sending subsidies as they had done in 1814. With the end of the American war and the return of the greatest threat to European security, there was no longer any thought of half measures. Unfortunately, the army in Belgium consisted of the understrength battalions that had been scraped together for Sir Thomas Graham, about 36,000 soldiers in all. The challenge was not only to grow the force but also to increase its quality. Appointing Wellington was one obvious step. He claimed that he did not really need 100,000 men—40,000 would be fine, so long as he had 12,000 cavalry and 150 pieces of artillery. The latter in particular was unrealistic on such short notice, but it gives some sense of Wellington's awareness of how difficult it was going to be to find the men.[16]

The redeployment effort received a lucky boost when the excellent Fifty-Second Light Infantry, which was slated to be deployed to North America before Napoleon escaped, was twice turned back by bad weather and could therefore be transferred to Wellington. Four more experienced regiments soon joined it, plus some heavy artillery, by the end of March. After that, it got much more difficult. There was no time to lose, as Napoleon was rapidly assembling his own force of 250,000 men, or so the rumors had it. The closest troops were preferable to the best troops, so the Horse Guards stripped Britain and Ireland of soldiers. That was not without risk, as Castlereagh admitted to Wellington on April 13: "It will leave Ireland weak for the moment til the troops arrive from Canada, but they will be there before Paddy can prepare for mischief, and force in your hands at the outset is everything."[17] The Horse Guards also looked hopefully toward the remnants of the expedition to New Orleans, which was due to arrive in May, and they extended the enlistment periods of limited service troops.[18]

The frantic preparations in the spring of 1815 had global effects. Wellington tried to bolster his rag-tag army with Peninsular veterans from Portugal, but it was going to take too long to transfer them from Lisbon to cause the plan to be put in action. It was easier to organize transports from North America because many troops were already en route when Napoleon returned. Others were headed west and had to be intercepted and turned around, as was the case with at least one convoy of transports destined for Bermuda. At the heart of the reshuffling was Ostend. Transports arrived not only from across the Channel but also from Cork and even Bermuda and Halifax. They unloaded wherever they could, including directly onto the beaches. (Dunkirk, it should be noted, is only fifty kilometers southwest of Ostend.) The logistical achievement was considerable. For example, on June 1, forty horses in slings made it off ships in only ninety minutes. They were soon joined by forty-two thousand barrels of gunpowder that the government had purchased—an astonishing quantity as only 569 of them ended up being needed at Waterloo. Troops and supplies continued to arrive throughout July and into August.[19]

From the original core of about thirty-six thousand men, by June, Wellington had a more respectable army of about sixty-eight thousand. To call it British would be an exaggeration. Less than half of the army was normally part of the British army establishment: 36 percent of the troops were British, and the King's German Legion accounted for an additional 10 percent. A more apt description of Wellington's army is therefore European: 10 percent were Nassauers, 8 percent Brunswickers, 17 percent Hanoverian, 13 percent Dutch, and 6 percent Walloons and Flemish. Some of the British troops, like those from the Fifty-Second Light Infantry mentioned earlier, were seasoned, but many were not. Wellington sought to distribute the veteran battalions across his formations, although here again the rigidity of the regimental system hampered his efforts.[20] He was unimpressed with the result: "I have got an infamous army, very weak and ill-equipped and a very inexperienced Staff."[21] The staff problem was easier to address than the quality of the rank and file, so Wellington did his best to badger Bathurst and the Horse Guards into giving him officers he could trust.

Napoleon denied him the luxury of time. Operationally, that was his only option: there was little hope for France if the Allies mustered seven hundred thousand men along the entire eastern frontier. Better for Napoleon to move quickly and target one of the weaker armies in the hopes of winning a quick victory. In theory, defeating Wellington or Blücher or both would buy time for France to rearm, and the defeat of the British or Prussians might cause them to leave the alliance as had happened repeatedly in the recent past. Strategically, however, Napoleon had already lost. Not only had his intransigence in early 1814 convinced the Allies that he could not be allowed to remain on the throne of France, but by returning so quickly from Elba, he ensured that the Allied armies were still mostly mobilized. The British had withdrawn significant forces from Europe, but with the end of the American war, they were on their way back. The other Allies were still largely ready to fight with well-equipped and seasoned troops. Had Napoleon been more patient on Elba, perhaps the situation would have been different; on the other hand, had he been more patient, he would not have been Napoleon.

Napoleon left Paris on June 12 and joined his army two days later, hoping to drive a wedge between the two Allied armies that were encamped south of Brussels. The first clashes with the Prussians occurred the next day, and they fell back to Ligny to concentrate and give battle on ground that they had previously chosen. Although the Prussians left the field after heavy fighting on June 16, they were mostly in good order and capable of continuing the campaign. Meanwhile, Wellington's army was dispersed, and he was relatively slow to respond to Napoleon's advance. As the Prussians received the heaviest blows at Ligny, Marshal Ney's advance forces met Wellington's gathering army at Quatre Bras, a road junction about a dozen kilometers to the northwest. It was a bloody but indecisive engagement, and on June 17, both Allied armies retreated north toward Brussels. The next day, Napoleon seized his opportunity to defeat one of the Allied armies in detail. Wellington had chosen a strong but not obvious defensive position, with gently rolling hills behind two farm outposts—La Haye Sainte and Hougoumont. The fiercest fighting happened at the farmhouses, as just twenty-six hundred men defended Hougoumont, but the French threw 12,700 soldiers at it. The French attack was uncomplicated, but it nearly worked: late in the afternoon, after La Haye Sainte had fallen, Wellington's center was under real pressure. But just then, the Prussians began arriving from the east and the final charge of the Imperial Guard failed. The Allied armies advanced and the rout was on.[22]

And yet the war did not end. We should not be surprised since the wars had had so many endings already. Why would Napoleon's final defeat be any different? In the immediate aftermath of Waterloo, both Blücher and Wellington knew that they needed to advance on Paris, but Blücher seems to have placed a higher priority on getting there first than Wellington did. The Prussians advanced to the east of the Sambre River, plundering as they went; Wellington encouraged his troops to act as liberators rather than conquerors, which had some effect. On June 20, the Prussians fought an indecisive action with French forces under Marshal Grouchy, who had failed to join Napoleon at Waterloo. Over the course of the next week, both the British and Prussian armies encountered a string of fortresses lining the route to Paris. The Prussians bombarded some of them, while Wellington preferred to leave blockading forces in his wake. By June 29, the remnants of the French army began trickling into Paris, with Blücher close on its heels. He bypassed defenses to the north of the city and advanced from the south. Even after Wellington's arrival on July 1, however, neither commander was confident in an assault on the city's prepared defenses. But on July 3, the Prussians fought the last significant action of the Waterloo campaign southwest of the city at Issy—each side suffered more than a thousand casualties—and Paris surrendered later that day.

Meanwhile, Napoleon had fled to Rochefort in the hopes of escaping to the United States. He probably could have made it out of Rochefort and into the Bay of Biscay had he traveled lightly and quickly. There were three possible exits from Basque Roads, and for four days in early July, there was only one British ship, the *Bellerophon*, to guard them. Instead, he hesitated, and soon two frigates joined the seventy-four to watch all three channels. Whether he would have made it much farther than the harbor exit is unclear, as the commander in chief of the reconstituted Channel Fleet, Admiral Lord Keith, had set thirty ships the task of preventing Napoleon's escape. On July 15, after negotiating with Captain Frederick Lewis Maitland, Napoleon agreed to come on board the *Bellerophon*.[23]

Much has been made of the symbolism of this moment, of the former master of Europe surrendering to the one country that had

always stood up to him on board a ship in a navy that had so repeatedly thwarted his ambitions. In the broad sweep of the twenty-three
years of wars, that is a powerful representation of its course and consequences, but in the context of the Hundred Days, it overstates the
navy's role. If British strategy had not failed so comprehensively after
Napoleon's first abdication, the navy's—and indeed Britain's—role
in Napoleon's surrender would not be so well remembered. This
time, however, there would be no escape. Napoleon later claimed
that Maitland had promised him asylum in Britain, a charge Maitland denied. Instead, the cabinet decided not to turn him over to
the Bourbons but rather to maroon him as a prisoner on St. Helena,
thousands of miles from everywhere. It was a tacit admission of the
Elban error.

Even Napoleon's surrender and the fall of Paris did not end the
war. Some—but not all—of the delay can be attributed to how long
it took for news to travel. In the Mediterranean, Exmouth and three
thousand men under Sir Hudson Lowe executed a revised version of
their plans and took Genoa and Marseilles on July 10, a week after
Paris fell. On the day Napoleon boarded the *Bellerophon*, Captain
Frederick William Aylmer of HMS *Pactolus* led a squadron into the
Gironde, forcing the surrender of Bordeaux. Closer to Paris, many of
the fortresses that Wellington had left behind held on pointlessly into
August: Valenciennes surrendered August 4, Philippeville on August
10, and Rocroi on August 18. The fortress at Charlemont persevered
all the way to the end of November, foreshadowing the persistent
minority in France that would remain fervently attached to the Bonapartist cause in the postwar years.[24]

In the West Indies, communications delays caused confusion all
around. The French garrison on Guadeloupe began flying the tricolor flag in late June, and the British army and navy commanders
disputed how best to respond. The navy, led by Sir Philip Durham,
maintained that it was authorized to act only on the defensive, while
the army, led by another Scotsman, Sir James Leith, argued that
the tricolor was the enemy's flag—or at least Louis XVIII's enemy's
flag. Durham requested definitive news from Europe about whether
Napoleon was acting aggressively, thereby authorizing his use of
force, while Leith, operating under more loosely written orders from
Bathurst, demanded action. Eventually, six weeks after Waterloo,

Durham and Leith put aside their disputes long enough to launch a joint operation. In capturing the tricolor flag on Guadeloupe, Durham became the answer to a trivia question. In February 1793, he had captured a French privateer flying the tricolor flag—the first such flag captured by the British during the wars; the flag he captured at Guadeloupe in August 1815 was the last.[25]

The end of combat operations in 1815 provides an opportunity to summarize and assess the narrative of demobilization presented in the last few chapters. When did soldiers and sailors come home? The two services did not demobilize in the same way: the navy's discharge of sailors was not matched by a similar discharge of soldiers. Since many of the latter enlisted for life, we can identify three distinct groups of veterans returning to British shores: discharged sailors, discharged soldiers, and active-duty soldiers. We should not, however, be too precise in counting each group. On the naval side, for instance, a parliamentary study in the middle of the nineteenth century produced annual returns for the number of sailors in the navy. It says that from its peak in 1813, the navy discharged 111,851 men over the next three years. But that does not tell us when and why they came home, so it is better to follow the monthly movements of ships and estimate discharges based on their complements. Admittedly, that brings its own challenges, as ships often sailed undermanned in these years; nevertheless, it gives us a better insight into the patterns of arrivals than simply waving at 1814 and declaring that 47,523 sailors came home. On the army side, historians have done more research and, in some cases, provided precise numbers of discharges. For the purposes of this study, I have rounded numbers of soldiers to make them easier to compare with sailors.[26]

To summarize, then, there were four stages of demobilization. Stage 1 was the withdrawal of the Baltic fleet in late 1812; stage 2 followed Napoleon's abdication in the spring of 1814; stage 3 was the end of the War of 1812; and stage 4 followed Waterloo.

Stage 1: The navy demobilized first. In late 1812, the withdrawal of much of the Baltic fleet allowed the navy to discharge approximately sixty-five hundred men as their tired ships were paid off. The next year, however, both services grew to their wartime peaks, and operations consumed men on both sides of the Atlantic. But even that small demobilization from the Baltic helped the navy meet the challenge of more aggressively pursuing the War of 1812 by allowing ships to be redeployed from the Baltic to the North Sea and then to the North Atlantic convoy routes. The army was preoccupied with the final phase of the Peninsular War, and its manpower crisis meant that the forces deployed to the Low Countries under Sir Thomas Graham were inadequate to the task. Comparing the two services' experience of 1813 shows how close both were to exhausting their manpower resources, and how demobilization shaped strategy and operations.

Stage 2: Napoleon's abdication in the spring of 1814 initially had little effect on sailors, as the navy prepared its dockyards first. But beginning in June and accelerating in July, approximately 40,000 men were discharged in less than three months, mainly from ships of the line. This was the first large group of sailors to arrive. The army moved remarkably rapidly to break up Wellington's army, and while much of it returned to Britain, a substantial portion went to North America. In rough numbers, we can see that of the 60,000 soldiers who celebrated Napoleon's first abdication in France, about 15,000 went to North America, 25,000 were discharged, and 20,000 remained on active duty in Britain. Similarly, 15,000 troops in the Mediterranean also came home or were sent to North America in roughly the same proportion as Wellington's army.

The parts of Wellington's army that went to North America were joined by a motley assortment of available forces from the West Indies, Mediterranean, and Britain. As early as June 1814, the new arrivals were engaged in operations in Canada, and in August, there were sufficient forces to launch three almost simultaneous offensives on the northern, eastern, and southern frontiers of the United States. For the navy, many frigates and sloops remained in commission to pursue the American war and protect trade, so approximately 45,000 sailors spent the year between Napoleon's abdication and escape convoying ships and participating in joint operations.

Stage 3: When the American war ended in the spring of 1815, ten ships of the line, thirty frigates, and fifty sloops returned to British ports and discharged their sailors, accounting for about 23,000 men in all. The escape from Elba caused a flurry of naval activity that brought a few thousand men back into ships frantically recommissioned for service in the Mediterranean, but that process stopped after Waterloo. Soldiers instead bore the brunt of the campaign, and thousands who were destined to go home from garrisons in Europe or the campaigns in North America instead found themselves at Ostend. The haphazard construction of the army that fought at Waterloo threw the demobilization from the War of 1812 into chaos. Many of the units arriving home from Canada replaced garrisons in Britain and Ireland that had been sent to the Continent.

Stage 4: The final stage of demobilization occurred after Waterloo, when both services finally felt confident that peace had arrived. The peace settlement called for Britain to provide 30,000 troops for the Army of Occupation. Those troops that were deemed unfit or not needed for that responsibility left Paris in large numbers (equivalent to about twenty-five battalions) from November 1815 through January 1816, and the majority were back in Britain by April 1816.[27] The frigates and sloops that had remained in commission through the Hundred Days were finally paid off, accounting for about 31,000 men. By December, only 181 ships remained in commission, down from a peak of 551 in late 1813.[28] Missing from this broad narrative are about 18,000 sailors who trickled into port as their ships were paid off throughout the last two years of the wars.

The budgetary pressure to demobilize shaped British strategy and operations from 1812 and especially from 1814. How did each service meet the challenge of fighting and ending two wars? The last chapter discussed that question with regard to the War of 1812, but it is worth broadening the aperture to include the global wars of 1812–15. The navy was the foundation of Britain's war effort. Its role in the last few years of the Napoleonic Wars was as essential as it had been for the previous two decades, but it lacked the high-profile fleet battles that would have called both contemporary and historical attention to its significance. Instead, it endured a relentless campaign of convoy escorts, blockades, and troop movements. Stretched to the limit of its manpower reserves, it could not command the ocean as comprehensively as it wished. When it did come to public attention, it was for the wrong reasons: defeats at the hands of the upstart Americans. Those defeats have tended to obscure a more impressive story of perseverance and logistical accomplishments. The handful of French fleets that escaped the blockade did little substantive damage. British trade suffered at the hands of French and American privateers, but at the same time, the blockade of the American coast was the primary reason why the Americans came to the negotiating table. The Admiralty redeployed ships around the globe effectively and correctly judged when the largest ships of the line were no longer needed. The Navy Board kept the dockyards supplied and the small convoy escorts and frigates equipped, even if manning continued to be a challenge throughout. The Transport Board successfully organized troop convoys and other logistics. Joint operations were occasionally spectacularly successful.

The navy should shoulder a significant portion of the blame for Napoleon's escape from Elba. Putting him there was the original sin, but after that, the episode can only be understood in the context of demobilization. The Elban error was costly, both in the lives lost in the Waterloo campaign and in the financial blow to the British government. In 1816, during the first full year of demobilization, the government was able to cut £15.7 million from the budgets of the army, ordnance, and navy. If we assume that roughly the same savings would have been available in 1815 had Napoleon remained on Elba, we can calculate the cost of the campaign. Napoleon's return forced the government to keep the budget for the army the same from 1814 to 1815, and even increase the naval budget slightly. On top of that, Britain provided an initial £5 million, rising to £7 million, in subsidies to keep the Allied armies in the field. Thus, to save £15.7 million, ministers ended up spending that much plus an additional £7.3 million. Put another way, the £23 million cost of the Hundred Days was more than the annual budget of the navy at any point in the wars, even in 1814. Delaying the onset of full demobilization by a year also prevented ministers from using the savings to begin tackling the debt. Their enthusiasm for reduction blinded them to the obvious threat posed by Napoleon.[29]

The saga ended with Wellington and Blücher's great victory at Waterloo, so historians have forgotten the risk the navy ran by not securing Elba properly. Had it done so, there would have been no Waterloo and no meeting of Wellington and Napoleon on the battlefield. It is perhaps not surprising, then, that the army's reputation in this period eclipsed the navy's. It was not just Waterloo, but rather a culmination of years of successful campaigns. In 1812, the Peninsular

War had shown promise, but also risk: there really was only one army, one disposal force, and Wellington could not afford to lose it. His light and quick operations of 1813 were bold and successful, and while he was more cautious when invading France, the point is that he was invading France. This was the strategic opportunity that ministers had been looking for since 1793, and the army took full advantage of it.

Elsewhere, the army's achievements were less glorious. While the defense of Canada in 1812 owes something to British organization and leadership, it also owes something to American incompetence. The army was unable to capitalize fully on the steady pressure that the navy was able to build over 1813, despite the arrival of veteran troops in 1814. The return to the status quo at the end of the war left the army with a large territory that still needed protection—and then suddenly a new European war disrupted those plans. The creation of Wellington's army was a remarkable achievement, particularly given the poor quality of the original force deployed to the Low Countries and the chaos of ongoing demobilization on both sides of the Atlantic.

Few campaigns in world history have been studied in as much detail as the Waterloo campaign, with the result that it can sometimes appear as if no commander had any idea what he was doing. There were blunders aplenty, and tactically, it was neither Wellington's nor Napoleon's finest performance. But that is more a result of the fog and friction of war than a reflection of the quality of leadership. The context in which those operations were done is what mattered most. By creating and deploying a serviceable army in three months, funding yet another Allied coalition, and then winning a great victory on the Continent, Britain cemented its status as the leading power in Europe.

CHAPTER 6

The Navy after Napoleon

Our sword has prevailed on land; we are masters of the ocean from pole to pole; revered for knowledge, unrivalled for ingenuity; and, as the SEA by which we are girded round, the wealth of every country rolls into our ports.

Saxo, *A Hasty Sketch of the Origin, Nature,
and Progress of the British Constitution*
(1817), 25.

British power in 1815 is often compared with that of the United States in 1991, at the dawn of the "unipolar moment."[1] We read that in 1815, Britain was the "tutor of Europe" and held an "overwhelming preponderance" over the rest of the world.[2] Britain was "possibly the only power which could afford a major war at this time."[2] Henry Kissinger compared Britain in 1815 with the United States in 1945 and concluded evocatively that Britain was the "arbiter of Europe" and was powerful enough "to fashion a new interpretation of reality."[4] Many naval historians have followed Kissinger's lead. British sea power was "supreme in all its elements."[5] Britain was the "only global maritime power," "unchallenged" and facing "no effective threats."[6]

A smaller group of naval historians have come to a different conclusion. Despite Britain's apparent naval superiority, British power was not absolute. Jan Glete, the leading authority on shipbuilding, identified five great powers but only three great-power navies: Britain, followed by France and Russia. While France and Russia were weaker at sea than the British, he still considered them peer competitors.[6] Others have described British policy after 1815 as defensive and measured. One leading account argued that "Britain did not interfere on the continent except in peripheral (mainly Mediterranean) matters."[8] Another version borders on isolationism: "The British wanted nothing more than to be left alone to make money." So long as the Scheldt estuary was in nonthreatening hands, Britain could stand off from continental affairs.[9] These are not descriptions of a dominant superpower.

This chapter follows the latter group in questioning just how powerful the British navy was in 1815, but it goes further than they have in attempting to explain Britain's defensiveness—even passiveness—in the postwar decade. In places where British naval power had long been supreme, such as the coast of North America and the Caribbean, it finds ministers reluctant to deploy their supposedly world-beating weapon, the navy. The usual reasons given for this strategy are the policy preferences of Liverpool and Castlereagh. They sought peace and stability at all costs, both to establish the legitimacy of the postwar settlement and to provide breathing room to deal with domestic unrest.[10] Liverpool's stated policy was "Iniquissimam pacem justissimo bello antefero" ("I prefer the most unjust peace to the most just war") [Cicero]).[11] Castlereagh described British policy in similar terms in a letter to an ambassador in 1817: "The avowed and true Policy of Great Britain is, in the existing state of the World to appease controversy, and to secure if possible for all states a long interval of Repose."[12]

The preferences of Liverpool and Castlereagh are undoubtedly an important part of this story, as is the domestic political context. But there is an additional explanation that has not been explored before: the actual state of the Royal Navy in the immediate postwar period. It was dire. When ministers deployed naval forces in the postwar years, they were not wielding "Nelson's navy," nor were they even wielding the navy that had handled a two-front war from 1812 to 1815. The dockyards had just about managed to keep the fleet deployed in those years, but peace brought about a collapse in readiness. Questions about how the fleet would be manned in the event of another war persisted. Another war seemed likelier than not—after all, Napoleon's first abdication had lasted less than a year, and there were plenty of hot spots around the world that threatened to grow into another conflict. The alliance that had won on the Continent threatened to fracture. Would the navy be ready when the next war came?

We should not take this argument too far. Potentially, British naval power was comprehensively superior. Britain had a fleet of 609,000 tons displacement, France 268,000, and Russia 168,000. Put another way, the Royal Navy had 126 ships of the line (and another 88 in reserve), and the rest of the world combined had no more than 100. The overly ambitious American building program of 1816 called for nine ships of the line and twelve of their notorious heavy frigates (like USS *Constitution*, of a heavier armament and larger size than most British frigates). Such frigates were a threat, to be sure, but not an existential one. Trafalgar had damaged the Spanish navy more than it had damaged the French, so the Spanish resorted to purchasing some old Russian ships, which turned out to be useless. The Dutch remained weak, while the Swedes and the Danes could put perhaps only ten ships of the line each to sea. The Russian navy was growing, but it was divided between the Baltic and the Black Seas, while the French were in too dire financial straits to maintain their fleet. Gone were the days when the French fleet rivaled the size of the British, or when the combined French and Spanish fleets were larger than the British.[13]

To all outward appearances, Britain appeared capable of deploying the world's largest navy in response to threats. British policy makers began to speak about standards in this period. Castlereagh declared that the minimum acceptable size of the navy was equivalent to any two other powers.[14] In 1815, Britain effectively had a global standard. But in the postwar decade it proved to be surprisingly difficult to translate potential naval power into kinetic naval power. The British could not fashion "a new interpretation of reality"—in fact, reality rudely intervened, repeatedly, and weakened British power in the postwar years. We should be wary of putting British naval power on a pedestal. It faced challenges common to all navies, and it did not have a magic formula to meet them.

The fundamental reason why British naval power was weaker than has been widely assumed is that Liverpool and Vansittart slashed the navy's budget to the bone. There was no spare capacity in the ledger for naval administrators to turn to when crises erupted. Naval spending fell even relative to other government expenditures: from 16 percent of government expenditure in 1816 to a low of only 9 percent in 1823. It is true that Britain had 126 ships of the line while its closest competitors had a dozen or two at most. Yet those numbers were, to a certain extent, accounting fictions. After two decades of combat operations, the navy was full of worn-out ships—and worn-out ships are in many ways more of a burden than a source of strength. When the wars ended, the Admiralty systematically sorted its ships into three categories: those to be scrapped or sold, those to be retained, and those that needed to be built new. The target total number of ships of the line was reduced to one hundred, of which more than eighty would be laid up in ordinary in preparation for the next war.[15]

This massive reorganization proved far too optimistic, as the budget cuts hit the dockyards especially hard. Chatham Dockyard suffered a 50 percent reduction in its workforce in the years after 1815, and working hours were reduced for those still employed. Yet the demands on the dockyard grew larger. The process of demobilization saw 374 ships sold and 178 broken up, but building new ships at a rate sufficient to prepare Britain for a new war proved impossible. In January 1817, there were fifty-nine ships of the line supposedly fit for up to eight years' service; just one year later, there were only thirty-seven. It was often difficult to know the state of a ship until its planking was removed. Of eighteen frigates sent to refit in 1817, seven turned out to be beyond repair and were broken up. Those that had been built with green timber were particularly likely to be rotten. While they were barely capable of meeting the fleet's needs when the navy was fully mobilized, the overwhelmed dockyards could not handle the resulting crush of exhausted ships during and after demobilization.[16]

In relative terms, such setbacks were minor annoyances because Britain still boasted an overwhelming number of hulls, whatever their state. Nevertheless, there were signs that competitors were emerging. The remarkable arms race on the Great Lakes during and after the War of 1812 had produced a small fleet for both the Americans and the British. By 1819, however, Byam Martin worried that the British ships' "dilapidated state . . . made them entirely unprepared for any hostile movement on the part of the Americans."[17] Russia launched nearly as many ships as Britain did in the postwar decade—130,000 tons for Britain and 110,000 for Russia. In Britain, amidst the slips and drydocks crowded with ships in need of repair, little new building could be undertaken. As a result, the composition of the fleet remained relatively static in the postwar years. There were only eight British frigates of comparable size and armament to the heavy

American frigates in 1815, and the new frigates ordered in 1818 did not address this reality. Instead, the British continued to prioritize smaller frigates for use on a variety of imperial stations. Yet even here, the cuts were severe: no fewer than 168 fifth rates were sent to the breakers in 1814 and 1815. In 1820, only five years after Britain held a global standard, Byam Martin warned that it would be eight or nine years before the navy would meet even the desired two-power standard. In 1830, Britain finally had ninety serviceable ships of the line, but that was still ten fewer than had been hoped for in 1815.[18]

Manning, an ever-present concern for navies in the age of sail, was unsurprisingly also an issue in the decades after 1815. Could impressment continue to provide the core group of able seamen in the event of a new war? There was no shortage of opinions on the subject both within and outside the navy. Impressment had high domestic costs: it tended to cause port towns to riot, and it seemed fundamentally incompatible with claims that Britons enjoyed liberties unknown in other countries. Yet naval administrators were unanimous in arguing that impressment had to remain in place. There was no other proven method of securing enough skilled men for the navy. Both France and Spain had attempted to create registries of seamen, but impressment proved to be more flexible because it was used only in wartime and more adept at targeting the most valuable commodity for any navy, able seamen.[19]

Of more concern in the postwar decade were impressment's international costs. If the navy began pressing sailors again, it guaranteed war with the United States. James Madison wrote to James Monroe at the end of 1818, succinctly summarizing the problem: "Impressment and peace [with Britain], it must now be evident, are irreconcilable."[20] British leaders agreed, as Liverpool wrote to Castlereagh, "If satisfactory arrangement on [impressment] cannot be effected, I am persuaded we never shall be engaged in a maritime war with any Power without it leading to a war with the United States of America."[21] In the event of a new European war, continuing to press sailors guaranteed that the conflict would quickly spread across the North Atlantic once again.

Concern about a resumption of war with the United States was at the forefront of naval administrators' minds in the postwar period. In addition to the problem of impressment, other sources of tension included fishery rights, the arms race on the Great Lakes, and flare-ups in frontier territories. The fundamental problem remained that British and American interests were mismatched in terms of intensity. Unlike Britain, the United States was not exhausted from globe-spanning multidecade wars, and the problems in North America between the two countries were naturally closer to home for the United States. As a result, the United States could easily threaten war, safe in the knowledge that the war threshold in Britain was much higher.[22]

In addition to those political and financial considerations, however, Liverpool and Castlereagh were also constrained by the dilapidated state of British forces. On the Great Lakes, for example, the British position seemed likely to be overrun in the event of a new war. The defense of Canada's southern frontier posed severe logistical challenges. The border was long and poorly charted. As a result, communications always favored the Americans. It was possible, barely, to reach Montreal in a frigate, but from that point on, vessels had to be flat bottomed or built in situ. Much of the frontier was iced over from December until April, leaving only lengthy and expensive overland routes. To address these problems, the Admiralty sent a team of surveyors led by Captain William Fitzwilliam Owen. Focusing on the area around the Detroit River, Owen's team not only drew maps and took soundings, but they also scouted American defenses. Both tasks necessarily brought them into close contact with Americans, with predictable results. In September 1815, one of the surveyors was arrested and imprisoned in Detroit following a brawl; he was found guilty and fined $600. The Americans then seized the British schooner *Julia* for smuggling. These and other incidents came to the attention of John Quincy Adams, the American ambassador in London. He and Castlereagh met regularly to smooth tensions, although Adams remained deeply suspicious of Castlereagh's motives.[23]

The two countries managed to avoid war because of Castlereagh's restraint, but also because of his recognition of the weakness of the British position. Captain Sir James Yeo, the commander of British forces on the lakes during the war, told Melville in May 1815 that "the preservation of the province of Canada by means of a Naval force on the Lakes, will, in my opinion, be an endless, if not futile undertaking."[24] Castlereagh told Adams as much during one of their meetings, expressing a desire to keep only enough naval forces on the lakes as was necessary to prevent smuggling. That was a sharp retreat, as in the last months of the war, both sides were building enormous three-decked ships of the line on the lakes, with the American ships *Chippewa* and *New Orleans* slated to be the largest in the world. Castlereagh correctly guessed that the Americans were also interested in reducing the pace of this building. To pass the Navy Estimates in Parliament, however, the British government played up the threat of a resumption of war with the United States in late 1815, which caused Adams to worry that no permanent reduction of force was achievable on the lakes.[25]

In reality, however, the situation on the ground was deteriorating rapidly for the British. Sir Robert Hall, acting commissioner on the lakes, reported to Byam Martin in 1816 that the British presence on Lake Erie was in serious jeopardy: "If we do not possess a naval force equal to that of the Americans, we had much better abandon the navigation of Lake Erie with vessels bearing the King's colors." He argued that the lakes were "a Millstone round our necks and indeed the Colony is scarcely worth the Expence."[26] The Admiralty's response was to order the construction of corvettes on the lakes, but they gave secret instructions to the builders to ensure that the ships were "strong enough in Timber to have another Deck built over them on appearance of War."[27]

The convertible corvettes were never completed, however, because negotiations among Adams, Monroe, and Castlereagh resulted in the outlines of the world's first arms limitation agreement, the Rush-Bagot Treaty of 1818. British naval officers were furious, warning that if the two sides were limited to the same strength, the Americans would be at an advantage because they were better able to build and equip ships quickly in the event of a war; their American colleagues agreed. Eventually domestic politics overcame these objections, as the Admiralty realized that further cuts to the Navy Estimates were forthcoming. The arms limitation treaty was risky, but it eased the funding crisis. The state of the fleet on the lakes as well as the quality and quantity of the men available to man it declined rapidly in 1818 and 1819.[28]

The navy's weakness meant that, in the end, the defense of southern Canada fell to the army. The Rush-Bagot Treaty limited naval building, but it did not slow the construction of barrier fortresses along the frontier by both sides. Ironically, given their aversion to naval spending, the British ended up spending enormous sums over the next decade on a network of fortresses connecting Halifax, Quebec, Montreal, and Kingston. While these fortresses were perhaps useful in trading with and supporting Indigenous allies, naval officers were understandably frustrated at the shift away from the lakes. They saw the fortifications as inadequate and continued to warn that tensions on the lakes remained high. The commander in chief in Halifax, Sir David Milne, argued that the Rush-Bagot Treaty did little to prevent war. He predicted in November 1818—six months after the Senate had ratified the treaty—that war would break out before June 1819. In fact, the crisis was seven years off, and it would be sparked by a completely different dispute.[29]

That dispute was in Oregon, and it presented distinct challenges from the situation on the Great Lakes. Here, none of the three participants in the dispute benefited from the proximity of resources. The Americans had to traverse an entire continent or, like the British, sail around Cape Horn; the Russians had an even greater logistical challenge. Russian interest in the region dated to their arrival in Alta California in 1805 and their establishment of Fort Ross in San Francisco Bay in 1812. The explorer Otto von Kotzebue had crossed the North Pacific in 1816 and used Sitka, in present-day Alaska, as a base of operations. Tsar Nicholas I eventually proclaimed Russian territorial sovereignty down to 51 degrees north, near Vancouver Island. The lurking threat of Russian colonization spurred both the British and Americans to reinforce their establishments in Oregon. The American effort consisted mainly of John Jacob Astor's attempt to establish a colony at the mouth of the Columbia River. The British blockade of the American east coast in the War of 1812 had severed communications with Astoria, however, and the North West Company (headquartered in Montreal) had moved in to take control, renaming the settlement Fort George. That was the situation at the signing of the Treaty of Ghent, which was supposed to return Anglo-American relations to the status quo ante bellum. The long delays in communications to Oregon meant that for two years after the treaty, the North West Company remained in control of Fort George.[30]

The forces involved in this dispute were much smaller than those on the Great Lakes. During the war, the frigate HMS *Phoebe* and sloop HMS *Cherub* had tracked down and defeated USS *Essex* off Valparaiso, causing one historian to claim, rather preposterously: "By this single engagement, the Royal Navy gained command of the sea in the Pacific."[31] In fact, the Oregon question was as much about a vacuum of power as it was about the actions of military or naval forces. Here again we see a disconnect between the bombast employed by historians describing British naval power and British policy when presented with a crisis. If British naval superiority was "ubiquitous and all-pervading," and it "eliminated the threat of war for the half century beginning with Waterloo," then why did Britain agree to joint control over the Oregon territory in 1818, effectively ceding the initiative in the region to the Americans?[32]

The answer, once again, was both an unwillingness and an inability to project power in the postwar decade. In 1817, Castlereagh had a choice. The United States had failed to send a ship to take possession of Fort George because its ability to project naval power was similarly in tatters. It would have been simple enough for Castlereagh to encourage the North West Company to retain control of Fort George while pleading ignorance to the American ambassador; sending a frigate or two to reinforce their position would surely have won the day. But Castlereagh was so reluctant to risk war with the United States that instead he instructed the company to vacate the premises. When the United States eventually managed to send USS *Ontario*, a twenty-gun sloop, to take possession in late 1817, the British worried that the *Ontario*'s mission was in fact more aggressive than it appeared. The cabinet, however, decided to take Adams at his word, that the captain of the *Ontario* was instructed only to take possession of the fort peacefully. They ordered an eighteen-gun sloop to the region, not to contest the *Ontario* but rather to ensure that the *Ontario* was received peacefully and without any complications from the company. Castlereagh emphasized his peace-at-all-costs message by agreeing, as part of the Anglo-American Convention of 1818, that ownership of the Oregon Country would be jointly held. Unsurprisingly, this agreement solved nothing. While both sides agreed to grant freedom of navigation to the other, it ensured that the issue would fester for the next three decades, with notable crises in 1826 and 1844. Britain was barely capable of protecting its interests in Oregon and certainly not interested in asserting its superiority.[33]

Few incidents demonstrate more completely the British desire to avoid conflict than the response to Andrew Jackson's actions during the First Seminole War. At the end of 1817, Jackson invaded Spanish Florida to punish the Seminoles for harboring enslaved people who had escaped from plantations north of the border. In doing so, he demonstrated that Spain, preoccupied with the revolutions in South America, had no capacity to control Florida. In the Adams-Onís Treaty of 1819, Spain ceded Florida to the United States, which the British understandably interpreted as evidence of the American desire to conquer all of North America. Yet throughout the conflict, Castlereagh worked to defuse tensions, even though there was at least one good reason to consider a military response. During Jackson's campaign of extermination, he captured two British citizens. Alexander Arbuthnot, born in Scotland, had been in Florida since 1803, trading with the Seminoles and acting as a liaison and translator. Robert Ambrister had served in the Royal Navy as a midshipman, but as prospects for employment faded at the end of the wars, he sought his fortune instead in the Corps of Colonial Marines. Jackson accused Arbuthnot of sending a letter to warn the Seminoles of the approach of his terror campaign and Ambrister of aiding the enemy and commanding Seminole forces against the United States. Despite Arbuthnot's calm and rational defense, Jackson judicially executed both men on April 29, 1818.[34]

It might be reasonable to assume that Jackson acted without much thought for the wider political ramifications, focused as he was on suppressing Seminole power. In fact, Jackson was fully aware of his actions. He told the secretary of war John C. Calhoun that even if Arbuthnot and Ambrister were not "Authorized Agents of Great Britain," the British government was certainly aware of their dealings: "I hope the execution of these two unprincipled villains will prove an awfull example to the world, and convince the Government of Great Britain as well as her subjects that certain, if slow retribution awaits those uncristian wretches who by false promises delude and excite [an] Indian tribe to all the horrid deeds of savage war."[35] Jackson's deliberately provocative actions made headlines in Britain, once news arrived in the fall. Castlereagh asked for an explanation from Rush but ultimately took no further action. Historians have skated over Castlereagh's passivity, arguing that neither side wanted to jeopardize the delicate balance of the 1818 treaty.[36] When the full scope of British policy toward the United States is considered, however, the failure of British ministers to demand satisfaction for Jackson's outrageous executions fits the larger pattern of British passivity after 1815. War with the United States, it should be remembered, depended on the navy's ability to project power across the Atlantic, and its ability to do so had decreased substantially in the three years since Jackson's victory at New Orleans.

The threat of war with the United States was only one of several concerns for British ministers when they considered the Western Hemisphere. At least as pressing were the ongoing revolutions in Spanish and Portuguese colonies in Central and South America. British trade with Spanish America grew steadily during and after the Napoleonic Wars. Half of Britain's shipping tonnage in 1815 was employed on transatlantic routes, and while the United States was a major trading partner, most transatlantic trade was with the West Indies and Latin America. From 1804 to 1806, British merchants exported goods to Spanish America worth £1.1 million, which accounted for about 2 percent of total exports; twenty years later, exports were worth £5 million, or 13 percent of the total. Much of this trade violated Spanish law, but its potential for growth encouraged British merchants to try their luck in opening new markets. Ministers therefore had to pay attention to the situation in the crumbling Spanish empire.[37]

Doing so without alienating the Spanish proved difficult. During the second half of the Napoleonic Wars, the significance of the Spanish alliance trumped all other considerations, although that did not prevent an increase in illegal trade. After the wars, there was less of an imperative to keep the Spanish happy, but it was also dangerous to express outright support for revolutionary ideology that might spread back to Europe. Spain asked Britain to intervene to help suppress the revolts in 1815, but Castlereagh offered instead to mediate between Spain and her colonies, on the condition that Spain open the colonies to trade. The negotiations went nowhere, and so Castlereagh opted for a policy of apparent impartiality toward both the revolutionaries and the government of Ferdinand VII in Madrid. In choosing this course, he effectively delegated the problem of the Spanish American revolutions to the navy. He instructed the Admiralty to tell officers on the scene to avoid interfering in the revolutions, while simultaneously taking steps to protect British trade. It was up to the commanders to exercise their judgment about the best course of action. While this arrangement was in keeping with the usual practice of the navy's responsibilities in peacetime, Castlereagh's hands-off approach reflects his unwillingness to take risks to protect British trade.[38]

There is an interesting parallel to be drawn between the eruption of piracy following the Napoleonic Wars and the eruption of piracy following the War of Spanish Succession (1701–14). The latter is more famous—the so-called Golden Age of piracy in the Caribbean—but they share several similarities. In both cases, demobilized sailors were deprived of gainful employment in navies or as privateers and resorted instead to opportunistic captures of merchant shipping, which was now no longer protected by naval convoys. As in the first Golden Age, some pirates in the 1810s and 1820s became vastly rich and famous. The Lafitte brothers became de facto rulers of Barataria Bay, south of New Orleans. They deployed a large pirate navy and set up their own condemnation court in Galveston. Most pirates operated on a smaller scale, often out of hideaways in Florida. Some accounts claim that as many as twenty thousand American-born sailors were engaged in piracy in the postwar years around the Caribbean. Unlike the earlier Golden Age, however, the nineteenth-century pirates were joined by a confusing mix of privateers sponsored by the Spanish (whose naval presence was nonexistent) as well as the insurgent republics.[39]

While British and American merchants were rarely the focus of pirate and privateer activity, they suffered significant collateral damage. Insurgent privateers stopped hundreds of British ships in the postwar period. The worst years were 1817 and 1818, when, out of nearly one hundred interdictions, twenty-four British ships were plundered and four were captured. Some of the insurgent privateers were actually American, such as the *Ant*, which claimed to operate out of Buenos Aires but in fact had been fitted out in Baltimore. For British naval officers, distinguishing among insurgent, Spanish, and American privateers, not to mention pirates, proved difficult. There were too many ships to stop and search every one, and even when they did stop them, it was hard to produce firm evidence that they were operating beyond the law. Venezuela provided a list of authorized privateers to the British authorities, but it was far from comprehensive. British officers were frequently accused of violating their avowed neutrality in the rebellions. By placing responsibility for sorting out the complex politics of the Spanish empire in the hands of overworked naval officers, Castlereagh once again demonstrated his reluctance to use significant force to protect British interests.[40]

Unsurprisingly, British merchants complained vociferously about the inadequacy of the navy's response. In the summer of 1817, *The Times* published a letter from a Jamaica merchant claiming that the Caribbean was unsafe for all British shipping, while other merchant groups called for the reintroduction of convoys. Insurance rates rose after 1815 for the region, and the navy's occasional single-ship victories over small-scale pirates did little to reverse the trend.[41]

There was a brief lull in piratical activity in 1820 and 1821, but in 1822, attacks on British ships returned to the same levels as before. Cuban pirates proved to be a particularly difficult challenge. Spain had made a point of reinforcing its military forces there, sending more than forty thousand troops in an effort to keep it in the empire. Operating against Cuban-based pirates made it more likely that Britain would endanger its relationship with Spain, so Britain encouraged Spain to police its own waters, with little success. Meanwhile, ominously, the French began sending naval reconnaissance missions to the Caribbean to judge how vulnerable Spanish and British positions were in that region. What finally spurred the British to action, however, was the arrival of substantial U.S. naval forces. American traders had suffered at least as much if not more from piracy and privateering in the postwar years, so the U.S. Navy created the West Indies Squadron in 1822 and the "Mosquito Fleet" in 1823. British merchants complained to the Admiralty that the U.S. Navy was doing the Royal Navy's job. Diplomacy had failed, they argued, and Cuban piracy was too dangerous. Some merchants even accused British ministers of deliberately misleading the public into thinking that the navy was responding when in fact it was not.[42]

As a recent account summarizes, "No matter how dissatisfied some British merchants were with the government's responses to privateering and piracy, they were unable to compel statesmen to act in significantly different ways."[43] The Admiralty's response was indeed half-hearted, waiting until 1823 to increase deployments slightly and reintroduce convoys. Canning, Castlereagh's successor as foreign secretary, did take a tougher line against Spain, threatening to send a reprisal squadron to the Caribbean to end Spanish privateer attacks on British shipping.[44] Here we can finally see "gunboat diplomacy" in action, but it came only after persistent pressure from merchants and action from rival naval powers. It also came nearly a decade after the end of naval operations against Napoleon.

So far this account has ignored the most famous example of gunboat diplomacy in the postwar period, the August 1816 bombardment of Algiers. The triumphalist version of the bombardment is that Britain took upon itself the burden of suppressing the enslavement of white Christian Europeans by North Africans for the good of white Christian Europe. Exmouth's Anglo-Dutch fleet consisted of twenty-seven ships, including five ships of the line, and it did enough damage to force the Algerines to release eleven hundred enslaved people. It is not surprising that the expedition is often used to herald the arrival of the Pax Britannica.[45]

In fact, the story of Algiers is more complicated. Britain's motivations for launching the expedition were not obvious. As Graham Moore noted in his diary, it was not clear why Britain should bother since Britain had an existing treaty with the Dey: "Why are we to take the lead in an attack upon them? The quarrel not being ours? There can be no doubt of the justice of a general combination of all the European Powers to force them to a change in their mode of making war but I see no reason why the whole danger and expense should fall on the Country which has nothing, or next to nothing, to do with the question."[46] The answers to Moore's questions are that sending Exmouth was more about Britain discouraging the creation of rival naval alliances in Europe than it was about the suppression of the slave trade. The Treaty of Alcalá between the Spanish and Dutch was the first step in the creation of one such alliance, and there were plans to include the Danes, Swedes, Russians, Neapolitans, Piedmontese, and Portuguese. The British were also not alone in taking naval action in the region: in 1815, the United States had sent two squadrons, including one ship of the line, to the Mediterranean. Stephen Decatur won better terms from the Dey than the British had negotiated, sparking outcry in Britain that the Royal Navy had lost its edge.[47]

The equipping of Exmouth's fleet also proved to be more difficult than the triumphalist narrative would lead us to believe. As Moore recounted, the ships designated for the task had been with Exmouth in the Mediterranean, and they "were all ships which had not been paid off since the conclusion of the war and the crews of which had a right to be paid off, being composed chiefly of Prest men many of whom had been in the service for twenty years." With the Admiralty's backing, Exmouth offered them two months' extra pay if they would volunteer to go back to the Mediterranean, but "the Seamen said they had served a long time, it was now peace and they wished to be set at liberty." Out of four ships of the line, Exmouth was able to persuade only two dozen sailors and less than half of the marines to remain in the squadron. With no other options, "every disposable Seaman was taken from the ships in England"—i.e., turned over—to take their place. That was still insufficient, so Exmouth's officers scoured the pubs for men who had drunk their way through their wages. They eventually manned the fleet by keeping the offer of two months' extra pay, and it was only with that offer that they found enough men.[48]

Nor was the execution of the bombardment a smooth operation. When the fleet arrived off Algiers, it faced a formidable opponent. Algiers is dead on a lee shore with no nearby bases for support. Exmouth knew the scale of the task, so he deliberately did not declare his intention to attack until after he had carefully placed most of his ships out of the range of the Algerine batteries. His second-in-command, Sir David Milne, was less cautious, and his ship the *Impregnable* suffered fifty killed and one hundred sixty wounded, which was more than a quarter of the fleet's casualties. Exmouth was lucky that the Dey agreed to a flag of truce just as the fleet's ammunition was about to run out. The bombardment also had little long-term effect. There were no fewer than eight further attempts at gunboat diplomacy by European powers in the next fifteen years, including two by the British in 1819 and 1824. Both were ineffectual, and not until the French invasion of Algeria in 1830 did the threat finally die out.[49]

This chapter has only scratched the surface of the postwar naval world by focusing on the northern half of the Western Hemisphere. It did so in part because the most serious immediate postwar naval crises occurred in North America and the Caribbean, but also because we do not need a global tour to demonstrate Britain's unwillingness to start another conflict. Even the brief discussion of the Mediterranean underplays just how delicate the peace settlement of 1815 was, and how concerned the British were to make as few naval deployments as possible. In 1817, the Admiralty felt compelled to maintain a single ship of the line in the Mediterranean to match the U.S. Navy's, despite the expense—long gone were the days of two dozen ships of the line off Toulon. The next year, at the Congress of Aix-la-Chapelle, Russia proposed a maritime league to deal with Mediterranean piracy and slaving. The Congress System had been designed in part with issues like this in mind, yet great-power rivalry took precedence over collective action. Castlereagh worried that such a league would encourage the establishment of a permanent Russian presence in the Mediterranean and scuttled the plans. Instead, the delegates sent an envoy to the Dey of Algiers, with predictably no tangible results. Britain's unwillingness to flex its naval power allowed problems like Mediterranean corsairing and slaving to fester.[50]

A concerned Melville wrote in the summer of 1817, "Independently of the mere question of immediate danger, this country is placed in the eyes of the World in such a prominent situation that in many cases the appearance of letting down our Naval force too low . . . is as unwise and unsafe as the reality."[51] Yet British naval forces were repeatedly too low in the postwar years, unable to deal effectively with the challenge of the United States on the Great Lakes and in Oregon and with the depredations of pirates and privateers in the Caribbean. When the Navy Estimates were defeated in Parliament in 1818, Melville had to abandon plans to reinforce the South American station. Even as late as 1821, he recalled most of the ships from the Mediterranean in the interests of saving money.[52]

The standard account of the Pax Britannica begins in 1815 and emphasizes the enforcement power of the globe-spanning, victorious Royal Navy. What this chapter has shown is that in fact, the decade after 1815 was anything but peaceful and the Royal Navy was incapable of and unwilling to span the globe. For an island nation, naval power provides security, and for a global empire, naval power protects the sea lines of communication. Naval power is also expensive to maintain and limited in its ability to dictate terms to determined Continental powers. Castlereagh understood all this, and his reluctance to use naval power reflected not only his desire for peace but also his recognition that the navy was not yet ready to be the world's police officer. In later crises—the Opium Wars, Crimea—the navy played a central role, but in the first postwar decade, ministers frequently found themselves without powerful gunboats to deploy. The explanation lies in the challenges of maintaining readiness in the aftermath of a major war.

What if war had broken out in the decade after 1815? We should not take signs of British weakness too far. War-weary Europe was unlikely to be able to gather itself for another general war, even if ministers feared it might. British power was drained but probably still relatively greater than any single competitor; in naval terms, its reserves and infrastructure dwarfed all comers. War with the United States was much more likely than a general European war. While the War of 1812 had been a difficult struggle in the larger context of the Napoleonic Wars, it was likely that in the event of a new war, Britain could, if forced, muster enough naval forces to recover any losses sustained in the opening months, when the American advantage would be at its greatest. The U.S. Navy, for all its braggadocio and grand building plans, was an order of magnitude smaller than the Royal Navy. Yet what this chapter has shown is that the British cabinet's decision to ignore the many possible causes of war with the United States reflected not just war weariness but also short-term naval weakness.

CHAPTER 7

The Army after Napoleon

There were reasons to tout British naval strength in 1815 as well as reasons to question it, and the same applies to the British army. On the one hand, the army was at the peak of its powers after Waterloo. That victory cemented Britain's place as the leading power in Europe, demonstrating that British power was not just maritime but could play a direct role in shaping continental events. By ensuring that Britain, and especially Wellington, received credit for the final defeat of Napoleon, Britain entered the postwar period with the strongest possible negotiating position at the Congress of Vienna and its follow-on conferences. Wellington's supremacy made him the logical choice to lead the Allied Army of Occupation, which was tasked with pacifying northeastern France. The army's successes meant Castlereagh could meet Prince Metternich or Tsar Alexander as an equal or superior partner in shaping the postwar settlement.[1]

On the other hand, the army that had won at Waterloo had been cobbled together at the last minute, and the victory owed much to the arrival of the Prussians. True, the British had developed and deployed a world-class army in the Peninsular War, but the breakup of that force distributed British forces around the world, where they had not always met with success, as at New Orleans. The army was subject to the same fiscal constraints as the navy, and the postwar cutbacks undermined both the number of troops that could be deployed as well as the staff and logistical infrastructure that had contributed so much to Wellington's success. Tactically, the army stagnated in Wellington's long (and long-lasting) shadow as he "denied the possibility of improving a system tested by service in war."[2] The duke finally died a year before the outbreak of the Crimean War in 1853, and the army's performance in that conflict suggested that there had been significant room for improvement in the previous decades.

Bound up in this argument are questions of empire. While the empire was in many ways shaped by the needs of the navy—Gibraltar, Malta, the Cape, Mauritius, and Ceylon all sat athwart sea lines of communications—it was ruled by the army. Here again, however, we can tell two different stories. For some historians, the French Revolutionary and Napoleonic Wars witnessed a "massive expansion of British imperial power" that encompassed "huge new colonies." Driven by a "constructive authoritarian and ideological" imperialism, British ministers and their military governors used the postwar period to build on the conquests made during the wars.[3] For others, the opposite is true: "As for empire, British statesmen were at pains to avoid it."[4] In 1815, ministers kept the key naval bases but gave back colonies to the French and Dutch that otherwise might have entailed costly governance, like Java and some of the West Indian islands.

This chapter surveys the deployments of the army in the aftermath of Waterloo in an attempt to chart a middle path, both with respect to the army's strengths and weaknesses and with respect to its role in the empire. It is true that the British Empire grew substantially in the wars, and it is also true that after 1815, the army fought a series of wars that resulted in the further growth of the empire. Military governors, many of them veterans of the Napoleonic Wars, established autocratic regimes to quell internal dissent, and they acted aggressively to prevent external threats from growing. However, all this growth came despite drastic cuts to the Army Estimates, not because of a concerted effort on the part of ministers in London to expand the empire. Neither the army's leadership nor Liverpool's government prioritized the growth of the empire; instead, they consolidated their holdings in the West and East Indies, secured key maritime choke points, and ensured that French commercial recovery would not threaten these positions. That freed them to focus their attention on continental security through the strengthening of the new kingdom of the Netherlands and the maintenance of the mutual defense pact with Russia, Prussia, and Austria. By forgoing aggressive imperial adventures and working collaboratively on the continent, they also hoped to free up military forces for the suppression of dissent at home.[5]

The empire grew in the postwar decade because agents at the periphery drew on local resources to address local concerns, not because London sought aggressive expansion. In any case, there simply were no funds available for such an expansion. The financial pressure of the debt overhang exacerbated a political climate that was averse to government spending, which forced ministers to make difficult decisions about the army's deployments. Surveying which parts of the world ministers prioritized dovetails with the navy's story over the same period. Britain emerged from the Napoleonic Wars with an enhanced reputation and immense relative power, but it behaved defensively and cautiously. British soldiers were mainly employed as police forces, a common role for soldiers in any postwar period. They were dispersed into small detachments and called out to put down riots, but they spent most of their time in garrisons fighting off disease and apathy, not campaigning. Nevertheless, we can still see places where the dynamics of empire encouraged colonial governors to act aggressively against perceived threats.

Our global tour, summarized in Figure 7.1, begins in Britain, where the number of troops deployed in the aftermath of Napoleon's second defeat was more than double what it had been in 1792 on the eve of war. The Horse Guards was well aware of this growth, and it kept internal track of how much larger the force now was. There had been 12,979 rank and file in Britain in June 1792, one document noted; in 1818, there were 26,000. Yet in a secret memorandum written in August 1818, the Duke of York pointed out to Liverpool that such an increase was necessary, especially among the cavalry, which was harder to grow quickly in the event of war. Also, the cavalry was more useful "to ensure the protection and interior tranquility of the United Kingdom, than a much greater number of infantry." In any case, "it will not be judged as too large with a view to the general change which has taken place in these Kingdoms since that period."[6] The "general change" and the role of the military in suppressing domestic dissent is the subject of chapter 12, so for now, we will leave aside the soldiers who were deployed at home.

Figure 7.1: Army Deployments, 1816

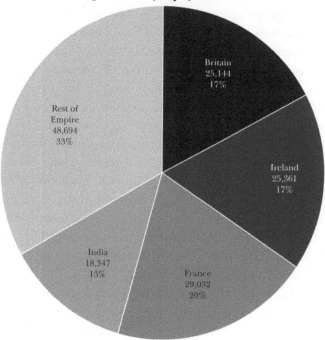

The next major priority was Ireland, or as one classic account put it, the next major priority was "the eternal trouble with Ireland."[7] Ireland was always at the forefront of British strategic thinking, and it is best understood as a colony. Even after the Union of 1801, its administration "remained distinctively colonial in both form and function."[8] To Irish nationalists, the British army was an army of occupation, no different from that currently pacifying France. But, however it is conceptualized, Ireland clearly merited both ministerial attention and boots on the ground. Regiments rotated through Ireland regularly, usually spending three to five years on station. Some endured multiple tours. The Eleventh Foot were in Ireland from 1814 to 1816 before spending five years at Gibraltar, at which point they rotated back to Ireland in 1821 for a six-year stay. The Seventh Hussars were part of the Army of Occupation until 1818 before deploying to Scotland (1819), Ireland (1820), England (1823), Scotland again (1826), and Ireland again (1828). No regiment was happy in Ireland, nor was the Horse Guards happy keeping any regiments in Ireland for long stretches, despite regular demands for more troops from Peel. In fact, there were more troops in Ireland in 1816 (25,361) than at any point in the postwar decade: by 1818 the Army Estimates had settled on 20,000 as the minimum acceptable number of regular troops for Ireland.[9]

The eruption of Mount Tambora in 1815 caused suffering in Ireland in 1816 that stands out for its intensity even in the context of Irish history. Persistent rain and cold temperatures caused the grain and potato crops to fail that summer. It was so wet that it was impossible to cut and dry turf for fuel. Widespread famine caused the worst typhus outbreak in eighty years. An estimated 1.5 million people got sick and about sixty-five thousand died between 1816 and 1819.[10] Peel recognized the distress in 1817, but he declined to act based on the long-standing conservative belief that the cure would be worse than the disease: "The Government might in case of *extreme necessity* administer relief by direct interference, but if half the population is in this state we cannot help trembling to think of the consequences of the first precedent."[11] By this logic, Peel concluded that it was better to hope charities would step in to take direct action to save lives rather than the government, which might have the insalubrious effect of making the people aware that the government was capable of providing relief now and in the future.

In such a climate and with such a government it is unsurprising to find that troops deployed to Ireland were busy. Following the famine and epidemic, the government learned of plans for a general rising in the spring of 1820. While that was infiltrated and suppressed, a year later, an agrarian movement in the west waged what one Peninsular veteran did not hesitate to call "the Rockite war."[12] It soon became clear that being deployed to Ireland was likely to be as challenging as any wartime campaign. Troop Sergeant William Dawes initially had high hopes for his regiment's deployment to Ireland in 1814: "Here we calculated upon reposing in quiet, and restoring to order and condition the wear and tear inseparable from the chequered and knocked-about existence of the last two years."[13] Instead, they were at the beck and call of the civil authorities, called out several times a week in detachments of ten to twelve men, usually late at night. Troops were spread thinly around the countryside in 441 detachments in 1816, from which nineteen hundred scouting parties had been created the previous year, according to Peel. They chased down highway robbers, protected civil authorities, and responded to riots and other disturbances. They were a police force in a colonial setting, otherwise known as a counterinsurgency force.[14]

Not coincidentally, this period also saw the creation of a regular armed police force, the first in the history of the British Isles. Called "Bobbies" or "Peelers" after their creator, the Royal Irish Constabulary somewhat eased the burden on the regular cavalry. Many of the chief constables appointed to it were former soldiers, and it operated as a paramilitary force alongside militia and yeomanry units.[15] Nevertheless, there remained plenty for the regulars to do. The Third Light Dragoons suppressed disturbances in Connaught in 1820, and the next year, after escorting George IV into Dublin, they were again called out into the countryside. In 1826, they returned to Ireland from England (where they had been deployed against the keelmen's strike in Sunderland—see chapter 11) and were again engaged in counterinsurgency operations in the countryside.[16] This was hot work. Rifleman William Surtees described the Rockite war in Limerick in 1821: "Here we were for a time actually shut up as in a besieged town; and no individual belonging to the army durst attempt to move out without a sufficient number being together, to deter the misguided peasantry from attacking us. Innumerable were the murders that were committed about this neighbourhood at this time."[17]

Being spread out into small detachments combined with the unsatisfying nature of the police work to erode readiness, create disciplinary problems, and damage morale. The Seventh Dragoon Guards spent so long separated into detachments in the countryside that when they were inspected as a regiment, they proved incapable of basic formation riding.[18] Dawes recalled, "The continuance and endurance of this vexatious and harassing life was becoming intolerable." Troops became increasingly angry at the lack of results, but "we were doomed to grin and bear it."[19] An artilleryman remembered what it was like to wear a British uniform in Ireland: "As soldiers we were hated and despised, insulted, and loaded with the foulest epithets,—in our different billets looked upon and received as if we had carried pestilence, robbery, and pillage with us."[20] The shared language between occupiers and occupied made life for the former more difficult than elsewhere in the empire because British soldiers in Ireland understood the epithets.

Officers also perceived Ireland as a dangerous place for their troops because discontented soldiers were more likely to desert. One major reason for this was that an increasing percentage of the army was Irish, so being close to home tempted many. At the same time, the army's shrinking size meant that the tempo of recruiting dropped, removing one of the safety valves that had traditionally helped Ireland endure periods of economic and agricultural collapse: men with no agricultural prospects could join the army. Neither of these trends, however, changes the fundamental point about Ireland's importance to British strategy after Napoleon's final defeat. By 1822, Palmerston estimated that Ireland's contingent of regular soldiers, militia, and yeomanry accounted for fully one quarter of the British army outside of India.[21]

In 1816, the largest single British army was in France with Wellington in the Army of Occupation. The day after Waterloo, Wellington wrote to his brother that his goal for Europe was to achieve a lasting peace and that he thought the best way to do that was to treat France as a friendly country. Over the course of the next weeks and months, however, it looked as if the first problem was going to be restoring some sense of order to France: Royalist supporters attacked Bonapartists in Marseille on the night of June 24, 1815, killing fifty and burning large sections of the city; Catholic reprisals against Protestants in the south went unpunished; and fifty to eighty thousand Bonapartist officials were dismissed. After the signing of the second Treaty of Paris in November, there was widespread pillaging.[22] As Liverpool reminded Castlereagh that autumn, "We ought never to lose sight for a moment of the consideration, that with whatever humanity and indulgence the French may have been treated by us, they hate us far more than any other nation."[23]

Liverpool's paranoia was shared by the Austrians and especially the Prussians, who advocated for punitive measures against the French. Wellington's more moderate approach was shared by Tsar Alexander and Castlereagh, and it was their faction that got the better of the argument. The treaty returned France to its 1790 borders, but the Army of Occupation set up camps in just seven northeastern departments. Behind them, the Allies embarked on a major building program of fortresses, called the Wellington Barrier, aimed at slowing any future French advances into the Low Countries, the protection of which was always the first British priority in any European war. To manage the occupation, the Allies innovated: they established the Allied Council that met regularly to coordinate day-to-day operations, and they developed a bureaucracy to handle a range of peacetime security practices including passports and secret police. What bound the alliance together, despite their differences, was a shared fear of war and of the revolutionary ideology that had led to war more than two decades before. They also vowed not to repeat the mistakes of 1814, and their enthusiasm for antirevolutionary security ensured that they did not.[24]

The turbulence that marred the six months after Waterloo finally abated in January 1816, and 30,000 British troops and 10,000 Hanoverians settled into their encampments in an area stretching from the Pas de Calais southeast toward Valenciennes. Wellington's headquarters were in Cambrai. With so many troops stationed just across the English Channel, the Duke of York agreed to cut the number of troops on the home establishment by 5,000 for 1816. Another added benefit was that the French were charged with paying for the cost of the occupation alongside an additional indemnity of 700 million francs, meaning that all told, the Army of Occupation saved the British government about £300,000 for its three years of existence.[25]

Making peace in France meant learning to live in enemy territory. Wellington insisted on strict discipline, particularly among the British troops. They were required to register with local authorities whenever they traveled through villages, submit daily reports, and abide by strict curfews. Soldiers lived with and among French farmers, and they helped gather the harvest in 1815 and 1816—their work in the latter year was especially helpful given the disastrous nature of the growing season. They were not stationary, however, as troops of cavalry and battalions of infantry moved around quite a bit during their time in France to accommodate redeployments and to help prevent disciplinary problems. They endured regular reviews from high-ranking officers and fought to stave off the general boredom of life in camp. Many soldiers married French wives, often without the permission of their regiment, and there was a rich cultural exchange between the two sides.[26]

There was also, naturally, trouble. The Prussians carried a deserved reputation for bad behavior, and although that made the British troops look saintly in comparison, there were plenty of incidents. Some of the approximately five thousand women brought to the Channel coast with the departing British troops in 1818 were there voluntarily, but many others were not—promised marriage under English law, they were instead abandoned, some of them pregnant, in France. British troops were also known for spreading rumors that Napoleon would return and for offering beggars money to shout "Vive L'Empereur!" in the hopes of causing a ruckus. Drunken misbehavior often led to theft, destruction of property, and assaults on French peasants. Each month saw courts martial held, and Wellington made clear that he expected punishments to be severe: flogging was the most common, but soldiers were also sentenced to solitary confinement, sent home, and in extreme cases, hanged.[27]

As the British prepared to depart in 1818, they left behind hundreds of deserters, many of whom undoubtedly had developed sincere attachments to French women. A further sixteen hundred soldiers were too ill to travel, so it took a few months to get them repatriated. They also left behind an economic crisis, as villages where they had been quartered no longer benefitted from soldiers' profligacy. Still, the French government was happy to see them go. In February 1817, the first reduction of the Army of Occupation took place, and after surviving a serious assassination attempt in February 1818, Wellington concluded that the occupation was beginning to cause more problems than it was solving. He and the other Allied leaders agreed to withdraw forces from France in October and November of that year, two years earlier than planned.[28]

It was the end of an era, and around Europe, genteel visitors took the opportunity to travel to Paris and the French countryside to see the army before it was broken up. Mary and Percy Shelley visited in 1817, and more than nineteen thousand other visitors could be found in Paris in 1818. Palmerston took advantage of his official trip to the Congress at Aix-la-Chappelle to see the Army of Occupation reviewed.[29] Graham Moore had no official reason to take his vacation in France, but he decided to make it a military-themed tour. After examining the naval facilities at Antwerp, he witnessed a review of fifty thousand British and Russian troops at Valenciennes in October 1818. Wellington kept a public table most nights, hosted a ball with the Russian and Prussian monarchs, and oversaw a mock siege of Valenciennes as part of the review. Moore was suitably impressed: "I have seen the last remains of a British Army. . . . I suppose there was never so fine a body of British Troops collected together, nor, for their numbers, in such high order for service."[30]

"The last remains of a British Army" refers to Moore's guess that it would be difficult to build such an army ever again because in the absence of a major European war, most of the army was distributed widely around the empire. Britain, Ireland, and France were clearly the top three strategic priorities, but tracing deployments elsewhere suggests how ministers conceived of the empire in the early nineteenth century. What stands out is how few troops were available: much as the navy struggled to meet its postwar commitments, so too did the army operate on a shoestring. We can also see how the army's deployments, and by extension the justification for the empire, were often shaped by naval needs.

Helpfully, in February 1816, the Duke of York compiled a memorandum on the proposed distribution of troops in the empire that also contained explanations for the size of each garrison. The memo began with Gibraltar, which was "of peculiar importance" for "commercial communications." It merited an establishment of four thousand troops, which was greater than it had been both during and before the wars. York justified the increase on the grounds that the larger the garrison, the lighter the duties, and "it never can be intended by the Government, nor desired by the Country, that the Troops should be subject to . . . harassing duties in time of Peace." Tell that to soldiers in Ireland. Nevertheless, while conditions for ordinary soldiers in imperial garrisons were bleak, York was famously a soldier's soldier by the standards of the time who often made a point of trying to manage his men's workload. The memo moved into the Mediterranean next to discuss Malta and the Ionian Islands. Malta had an establishment in 1816 of four thousand troops to guard the naval depot and arsenal, while a further three thousand troops were distributed among Britain's newest Mediterranean possessions to guard against the "jealousy of the Turkish Government."[31] What York did not say was that the troops were also necessary to enforce what one historian has called the "exclusive and despotic policy" of the British colonial government of Ionian Islands.[32]

Across the Atlantic, Upper and Lower Canada and Nova Scotia had a total of nine thousand troops. That number was unlikely to deter the aggressive neighbor to the south, but it was one of the largest detachments of troops outside the British Isles and India. York wrote that the major concerns in this theater were the "views and increasing power of the United States." Defending the thousand-mile frontier of the Canadian colonies was challenging, but York argued it was essential to do so because of Canada's "commercial importance, which occupies nearly a quarter of the whole merchant shipping of this country; thereby affording a principle [*sic*] nursery for seamen" and providing essential naval building supplies. York admitted that five thousand troops in the two Canadas would be insufficient in the event of a war, but they might form the "nucleus of an army fit to repel the sudden invasion which the proximity of the enemy may enable them to attempt." The hope was that the colony could draw on some of its available manpower (Canada had a population of 440,000 in 1815) in the form of colonial militias before reinforcements arrived. Similar concerns about American aggression applied to the one thousand troops allotted for the Bahamas and Bermuda (divided equally).[33] The latter was particularly important in the winter as a naval arsenal in place of Halifax, and "the jealousy and vigilance of the Americans would naturally be directed to it on the breaking out of a War." York noted that the garrison of five hundred was insufficient, but he did not see where any other troops might be found to supplement it.[34]

In the Caribbean, the largest single garrison was four thousand men in Jamaica. York justified its size in two ways. First, the Jamaica planters threatened to discontinue providing supplies to the garrison if it dropped below three thousand men; second, the troops were needed to enforce white supremacy. Jamaica had a large population that, "together with the disproportion between the White and Black Inhabitants not being less than 14 to 1, this force cannot be deemed an unreasonable amount for protecting a country nearly as extensive as Ireland. The disposition of the People of Colour in Jamaica to insurrection has frequently been manifest," the memo continued, which meant that it was essential to put down insurrections quickly with a "prompt application of force" so that they did not get any ideas about following "the example of independence held out in the Island

of St. Domingo [Haiti], which is so immediately to windward." The
Windward Islands merited nine thousand soldiers, and while York
thought that the inhabitants of those islands were less likely to follow
the "pernicious example" of Haiti, "yet a due precaution is necessary
to support the ascendancy of [an] inferior number of White Inhabitants and possessors of property, over a numerous class of people."
This was not an era in which white supremacy was clothed in euphe-
misms. The troops were there to reassure the white planters that they
were safe. York cited recent rebellions on St. Vincent and Grenada,
as well as the 1797 recommendation of Sir Ralph Abercromby, as
reasons for maintaining such a large establishment. Later that year,
his deployments were put to the test as troops deployed to suppress
a slave rebellion in Barbados. The slave trade had been abolished in
1807, but Britons still owned many thousands of humans.[35]

Finally, the memo turned its attention to the South Atlantic and
the Indian Ocean. St. Helena's garrison of twelve hundred had a
particular job that required no explanation, and York felt no need to
dwell on the navy's failure at Elba. There were one thousand troops
stationed in "Africa," which referred to forts along the West African
coast manned by penal battalions. Each fort of the Cape, Mauritius,
and Ceylon merited three thousand troops primarily for the protection of naval bases. In addition, Mauritius needed protection so
that it did not fall into the hands of enemy privateers in the event
of another war, while the Cape garrison was tasked with guarding
against "the constant apprehension of the Dutch settlers to violence
and insult from the [Xhosa], which render it necessary to detach
nearly 1,000 men into the interior."[36] A more accurate description
of the situation on the Cape would be that the settlers wanted a free
hand to exterminate the Xhosa while the governor, Lord Charles
Somerset, wanted to separate the two groups to avoid costly wars.
New South Wales had similar issues as its governor, the army officer
and Napoleonic War veteran Lachlan Macquarie, was in the process
of transforming it from a penal into a settler colony. It was soon to
become one of the largest colonies by land area, home to seventeen
million sheep in the 1820s, but in 1815 it had a human population
of less than fifteen thousand (of whom about 40 percent were freed
felons or nonfelons) and the smallest garrison of all, only eight hundred men.[37]

In all these imperial deployments, we can see two themes of this stage of the British Empire: naval needs came first, but the seeds of the enormous territorial empire of the later nineteenth century had been planted at the Cape and in New South Wales. Those seeds grew quickly: from 1815 to 1865, the empire grew on average by about one hundred thousand square miles per year—roughly equivalent to the state of Oregon—which was just slightly slower than the average annual growth rate from 1865 to 1914. Ministers in London may have wanted to resist adding to the empire's territories in the postwar decade, but frontier clashes between settlers and native inhabitants increased pressure on governors to wage wars of aggression. Even if that future was not yet clear, it was inarguable that the empire had grown in the previous two decades. As York pointed out in his memo, they could not use 1792 as a benchmark for postwar deployments. Whether or not they wanted it, ministers ruled over an empire that by 1820 contained about two hundred million people, or about 26 percent of the world's population, and it looked likely to grow even larger.[38]

Nevertheless, ministers insisted on cuts, much to York's dismay. Over the course of the summer of 1818, the Horse Guards prepared for the return of the Army of Occupation. Liverpool determined that Britain could not afford to maintain the troops that France had been paying for, so he demanded that York reduce the Army Estimates for 1819. York had already been expecting to lose about 20,000 men, but now he had to find 10,000 more to cut, from about 98,000 total rank and file to about 88,000, not including India. York prepared another series of memos aimed at stanching the fiscal bleeding. He suggested cutting the yeomanry and volunteers instead because they were easy to reconstitute whenever needed, while cavalry required much more training and equipment. Given the role of the yeomanry at Peterloo (see chapter 12), it is interesting to consider what might have happened if York's advice had been followed. It was not, however, and instead York was reduced to asking how the army could be deployed "in any manner adequate to give any real security to the whole of this vast Empire?" He argued that the best strategy would be to focus on securing "the main points, [rather] than to fritter away the force in attempting to afford a weak protection to the whole, and thereby leaving every point open to attack." Half of the cuts came from Britain

and Ireland because, as York explained, most of the foreign garrisons
were already so small that it was hard to find any spare capacity. The
other major cuts came in the Leeward Islands because he judged the
garrisons there to be already too weak to protect against "any serious
foreign attack." Better, York argued, to garrison just St. Lucia, which
boasted natural defenses, and the naval base at Antigua. In the end,
York was forced to eliminate ten regiments and enact an across-the-
board reduction in the established strength of all regiments. The
British commitment to the Army of Occupation was 30,000 men, and
it was not a coincidence that the end of the occupation reduced the
total size of the British army by 31,462 men.[39]

London's tightfistedness meant that the army had to meet its responsibilities with its existing forces. There was no spare capacity. Shifting
troops around the globe, as during the chaotic redeployments of 1814
and 1815, was no longer possible. The only colony spared some of the
postwar malaise was India. The regular troops on station were cut to
the bare minimum of less than twenty thousand, which, as usual, York
argued was insufficient "from the great disproportion of that force to
the extent of territory now under British Dominion."[40] Recall that as
recently as 1813, there had been twenty-seven thousand men allotted
to India. On the other hand, the massive East India Company ("the
Company") army more than compensated for that loss. Trained and
led by British officers, it was one of the largest European-style armies
in the world in 1815, and importantly, it was also paid for by extracting
resources from India. As a result, most of the army's active operations
in the postwar decade took place in the east.

India was a military empire acquired, initially, to deny its resources
to the French. Most governors were military men, including the
governor general from 1813 to 1822, Francis Rawdon, Lord Hastings, and he was deputized by other military men like Sir Thomas
Munro and Sir John Malcolm. Hastings argued that "the first duty
of the government was to fix the amount of military force necessary
for the maintenance of India."[41] Malcolm agreed: "Our government
of . . . [India] is essentially military and our means of preserving and
improving our possessions through the operation of our civil institutions depend on our wise and politic exercise of that military power
on which the whole foundation rests."[42] The withdrawal of the French
threat in 1815 did not change the character of the empire. Instead,

a new impetus for violent expansion emerged based on a multifaceted logic that no longer needed the threat of French incursions. Some of its components derived from James Mill's *History of British India* (1817), which set out to educate a new generation of officials on the opportunity they had to replace India's supposedly backward culture with modern laws and practices. Mill's "historical and cultural onslaught on Indian society" became the standard imperial handbook for the rest of the century, even though he had never been to India and did not speak any of its languages.[43, i] Another impetus for expansion came from a post-1815 decline in the economic profitability of the East India Company's trade, which encouraged the Company to demand more tribute payments and to search for new sources of revenue. Meanwhile, the military government's concern about "jacobinism"—a catch-all term for internal dissent—meant that there always seemed to be a reason to make an example of a local leader. Finally, perceived external threats on India's northern and eastern borders justified attack as a necessary form of defense. The army in India believed in aggressive deterrence both because it seemed to be the only way to maintain Britain's hold over the vast territory and because it provided opportunities for army officers to gain prize money and promotions.[44]

From 1814 to 1816, Company and regular forces were engaged in operations in Nepal against the Gorkhas. The war had started because of British interest in securing economic access to Tibet to offset some of the decline in trade in the south, and it was going poorly. An initial thrust into the mountains by thirty-five thousand men divided into four columns had been repulsed with significant losses—as an example, in one failed assault on a fort, the Thirteenth Bengal Native Infantry suffered 130 casualties. The most successful of the four columns had been led by Major General David Ochterlony, and it was his troops that eventually figured out how to be most effective in the mountains. When Ochterlony advanced on Kathmandu in March 1816, the Gorkhas sued for peace, accepting a British resident and renouncing some territorial claims.[45] It was an "arduous campaign," one of the participants later recalled, but it was not waged in self-defense. Rather, the British sought simply to bring "this artful and

---

i   Mill's eldest son was the philosopher John Stuart Mill.

warlike tribe to subjection."[46] Born in Boston to loyalist parents, Ochterlony was a colorful character in India, known for wearing turbans and smoking hookahs. Following the conquest of Nepal, he was awarded a baronetcy and later made British resident in Delhi. It was said that he had thirteen Indian wives who followed him around the city every evening on thirteen elephants.[47]

In 1817, war broke out in central India with the Maratha confederacy. The British had already fought the Marathas twice, and the Second Anglo-Maratha War (1803–5) is well-known as the conflict in which the future Duke of Wellington made his name. The third war grew out of concern on the part of the Marathas that the Company was using the uneasy peace to establish a monopoly of violence over the Indian subcontinent without engaging in outright war. Their concerns were justified, but their decision to risk it all by going to war accelerated the process. The governor of Bombay, Sir Evan Nepean, was another former member of the British military establishment, having held several positions in government including secretary to the Admiralty. He and Hastings set out to make this a short war by gathering the largest single British army ever seen in India, numbering 113,000 men with more than three hundred field pieces.[48]

The subsequent campaigns of 1817 and 1818 are notable for a few reasons. The Marathas fielded an army of about 180,000 men, which means that in terms of the number of troops involved, it was equal to many Napoleonic campaigns. Yet because the number of British-born regular troops was relatively small, it is not a conflict that has attracted similar historical attention. It should, both because it resulted in the consolidation of British control over central India and because it was remarkably bloody. At the Battle of Mahdipur in December 1817, Sir Thomas Hislop ordered a frontal assault on 5,000 trained Maratha infantry, which, while successful, cost 778 killed and wounded.[49] At the siege of Hathras, the British shelled the town with devastating effects, as one participant later recalled: "Many of their houses were on fire. The Congreve rocket is a most destructive instrument of death; its enormous shaking tail carries everything before it; and, when it explodes, it kills some yards round, and fires houses right and left."[50] Another major cause of death was cholera, and this war was the likely source for its first appearance in Europe.[51]

By the end of 1818, not only had the British finally defeated the Marathas, but they had also waged a brutal campaign of "agrarian pacification" against the Marathas' sometime allies, the *pindaris*.[52] These bands of mounted irregulars shared some similarities with pirates— remnants of the many armies that had roamed central India over the past decades, they raided settlements searching for subsistence.[53] One British officer described their tactics: "They will rest their horses on the Northern banks of the [Narmada]; cross the river in the evening, proceed 60 or 70 miles into the interior, commit their depredations, etc., before the dawn of day perhaps, and return to their home very comfortably."[54] Such anarchic behavior could not be countenanced by the Company, and so as the Maratha war wrapped up, its forces hunted the *pindaris* to extinction. Malcolm wrote to Wellington in July 1818 describing how the two campaigns had been linked: "At that period all the Maratha armies were completely destroyed. I had reduced all those plunderers [*pindaris*], who had disturbed this country for fifty years and taken and destroyed most of their strongholds."[55]

A similarly brutal campaign was being waged in Ceylon (Sri Lanka) from 1815 to 1818 against the Kingdom of Kandy, which controlled the central highlands of the island. Just four thousand British regulars had defeated Kandian forces in 1815 to secure the natural harbor at Trincomalee, but the situation then deteriorated quickly. By late 1817, there was a full-scale revolt against British rule. The army scrambled to bolster its forces, recruiting local regiments, Malays from Java, and Kaffirs from the African coast. Needless to say, there was no hope of reinforcements from Britain. In a brutal campaign, nearly 10 percent of the island's population of eight hundred thousand died of disease, famine, warfare, or summary executions by British forces. Entire villages were burned. The consequences for the Kandians far exceeded those of the British forces, but it is worth noting that British casualties were also high, with 40 percent of troops hospitalized after just three weeks of campaigning in the highlands.[56]

The pattern of British imperial aggrandizement in the period after 1815 should now be clear. Ministers in London, responsible for budgets and grand strategy, allotted small garrisons to guard naval choke points and arsenals while focusing most of their attention on pacification efforts in Britain, Ireland, and France. Many governors, like

Macquarie and Somerset, shared London's reluctance to engage in expansionary operations, but that was not the case in India. Because the Company's forces were both substantial and paid for on the subcontinent, London had little say in the conduct of operations. The establishment of Singapore in 1819 fits this imperial model well. Stamford Raffles was exactly the kind of headstrong adventurer who exploited the space between London and the empire for his own agenda. He did not found Singapore entirely on his own, as the governor of Bengal had requested a post on the other side of the Malacca Strait, and merchants were eager to exploit the Dutch islands. Once he had established it, moreover, he received support from ministers in London. But it was certainly his initiative and his willingness to operate as a free agent that resulted in the establishment of what eventually became the centerpiece of Britain's far eastern empire.[57]

The founding of Singapore resulted in a diplomatic crisis with the Dutch, which was eventually resolved by treaty in 1824. But many other peripheral issues resulted in bloody conflicts: violence was fundamental to the imperial project. One final illustration of the continuation of this pattern is the First Anglo-Burmese War of 1824–26. The proximate cause of the war was a dispute over the ownership of Shapuree Island, which lies off the mouth of the Naf River in the northeastern corner of the Bay of Bengal. The underlying cause, however, was a clash of expanding empires. The Burmese Kingdom was a significant regional power at its peak, and it had recently conquered the Kingdom of Arakan. The remnants of Arakanese forces had fled toward Company territory, and the Burmese pursued them across the Naf into what is today Bangladesh. The Company interpreted Burmese actions as a move to threaten Calcutta (Kolkata). In response, in May 1824 the British launched a joint expedition of naval, army, and Company forces numbering about ten thousand soldiers, split evenly between regulars and Company forces and under the command of the Peninsular veteran General Sir Archibald Campbell. It landed unopposed at Rangoon (Yangon) at the mouth of the Irrawaddy River, but the Burmese withdrew upriver, leaving the British stranded with no supplies as disease and starvation ravaged the men.[58]

Suddenly a war that was expected to be not more than a quick display of strength against the Burmese Empire looked likely to grow into something much more expensive, both in terms of men and materiel. Old diseases reared their heads: scurvy ravaged the troops at Rangoon because of the scorched-earth policy of the Burmese. Despite decades of evidence of the efficacy of fresh fruit and vegetables, Company surgeons attributed the outbreak to exposure to "impure air." To be fair to them, scurvy was not the only cause of death, as cholera once again demonstrated its lethality. Despite the losses to disease, the British fought off an assault by thirty thousand Burmese troops in October 1824 before managing to make their way north in difficult circumstances. They relied on Arakanese intelligence to capture the fortress of Mrauk U in 1825 before advancing on Ava in February 1826, bringing the war to an end.[59]

The First Anglo-Burmese War marks a turning point in Burmese history as well as a shift in the modus operandi of the British Empire. Recent nationalist military regimes in Burma have used 1824 as the cutoff date for determining Burmese borders, and therefore who belongs in Burma today and who does not. Britain did not formally annex Burma as a colony until 1853, but Britain had certainly invested in the conflict—by one account, it was the most expensive war in British Indian history.[60] The war also saw probably the second use of a steam vessel in combat.[ii] The *Diana* helped with the amphibious operations and, as one account put it, "inspired the [Burmese] with the greatest consternation, thirty [boats] were captured, having been previously abandoned by their crews, who, upon the approach of the steam-boat, threw themselves into the river, and were either drowned or swam ashore, apparently in an agony of terror."[61]

In addition to the dawn of the age of steam, another reason to use this war to bring to a close the story of the British army in the postwar period is that six new regiments were raised in Britain to fight it. Or rather, six new regiments were raised to help out in Ireland and the West Indies, where a slave revolt was once again threatening. But those new regiments meant that there were more troops available to send to the east. In 1825, following the initial setbacks of the Rangoon expedition, Palmerston asked for eight thousand more men to reinforce India, which in turn would free up troops to be sent to Burma. From this war onward, no longer can we describe British

---

ii The first was earlier in 1824, when HMS *Lightning* assisted with yet another bombardment of Algiers. See Gale, "Barbary's Slow Death," 145–46.

operations as being conducted amid shrinking resources. Similarly, by this time the navy was finally approaching its goal of one hundred deployable ships of the line.[62]

What did peace in 1815 mean? For the British army, it meant only the end of operations against peer competitors in Europe. It did not mean the end of operations, especially in the east, and it did not mean quiet, especially in Britain, Ireland, and France. Ministers used the end of the war in Europe to enact major cuts to the army that eroded its readiness, endangered its ability to meet a peer competitor if one emerged, and exacerbated the tendency toward a narrow outlook in which the only wars that mattered were those with Europeans (with exceptions made for the Turks and the Americans). Liverpool's stated policy of peace at all costs applied to the concert of Europe, but it did not apply to the empire.

Part II

———◄○►———

DEMOBILIZATION
AND
BRITISH SOCIETY

What happened when soldiers and sailors came home? Missing from part I was a detailed discussion of the politics of demobilization. Chapter 8 provides this discussion, which retroactively explains why the military and naval budgets were slashed so dramatically after 1814–15. But it also sets the stage for the story of returning veterans by discussing why Parliament did so little to help soldiers and sailors assimilate back into civilian society. Chapters 9 and 10 ask what it was like to be demobilized from the perspective of ordinary soldiers and sailors. Leaving the military was a complicated, emotional process; so too was homecoming. Sailors had a greater chance of continuing in their profession after leaving the navy, but they were thwarted by the depressed maritime labor market. Chapter 11 shows how they resorted to new techniques of organization and mass mobilization, with limited success. Chapter 12 looks at the domestic deployment of soldiers against postwar rioters as well as the role that veteran soldiers and sailors played in making those riots more disciplined. Officers' experiences of demobilization and the peace are the subject of chapter 13, and the final two chapters follow those veterans who, for a variety of reasons, did not come home.

CHAPTER 8

The Politics of Demobilization

Liverpool and his ministers believed, and their careers to date had shown, that Britain's success in the hypercompetitive European great-power system depended on its ability to tax efficiently, borrow cheaply, and transform that revenue into military power. It was perfectly reasonable for them to wonder in 1815 whether some limit had been reached and whether the strain was going to be too much. The wars had cost more than £1.6 billion, and the debt stood at £778 million. Using modern economic tools, we now know that the ratios of both public debt to GDP and public debt to income had never been higher, nor, indeed, have they ever been reached since—even in 1945. All Vansittart knew was that servicing the debt would cost £32 million in 1816, which, depending on how much revenue the government brought in, might account for half the budget. It did not seem likely that Britain's peacetime fiscal trajectory was sustainable.[1]

Since Vansittart lacked the kind of economic tools that we take for granted today, it is not surprising that he and his fellow cabinet members chose to take action to address one of the few areas of the economy on which they did have data. Newspapers regularly published prices of agricultural products. The ministerial view of the significance of the price of corn (a catchall term for wheat and other grains like barley and oats) began from the premise that one of the precipitating causes of the French Revolution had been

starvation among French peasants. While a laissez-faire approach
to the economy was preferred, ministers felt fully justified in intervening to prevent starvation in Britain. They also knew that one of
the consequences of Britain's entry into the French Revolutionary
Wars in 1793 had been to make the country a net importer of grain.
Britain had endured two major famines in that decade, and then,
following Trafalgar, Napoleon's Continental System had attempted
a reverse blockade of Britain by severing its connection to European
markets. Ministers connected these dots and concluded that they had
to provide a secure supply of foodstuffs, or even a strategic reserve, to
prevent revolution at home.[2]

In 1813, agricultural prices had dropped quickly, partly as a product of the onset of demobilization. Feeding Britain's sailors had
helped to keep agricultural prices high, but now the navy was beginning to sell off its surplus flour. Ministers assumed that the price was
likely to keep falling in the peace with the result that farmers and
landowners would be economically devastated. Many landowners
were more exposed to price fluctuations than they had been before
the wars because they had used the wartime boom to expand the area
of land under cultivation. They had enclosed open grazing areas at
unprecedented rates. Forty-three percent of all enclosure acts ever
passed were passed between 1793 and 1815, bringing three million acres, or 9 percent of the country's land, under cultivation for
the first time. If prices were allowed to fall too quickly, widespread
bankruptcies would jeopardize Britain's ability to feed itself. Foreign
wheat from the reopening of Europe might prove to be cheaper to
import, which would not only undercut the domestic market but also
expose Britain to the same kind of economic warfare that Napoleon
had attempted in the event war resumed.[3]

That is the background for the introduction of the Corn Law of
1815, which set the price at which imports of foreign wheat, barley,
oats, and other grains were allowed. It was not the first of its kind,
as there had been a recent version in 1804, but the new edition was
met with unprecedented animosity from the people who purchased,
rather than grew, wheat. London erupted in rioting against a bill
that kept food prices artificially high to benefit the landed interest.
For returning veterans, high food prices exacerbated the problems
of unemployment, and soldiers were deployed to suppress the riots.

Manufacturing towns organized petitioning campaigns against the bill: more than twenty-five thousand people signed three petitions in Newcastle, each of which was sixty yards long. But protests in pro-toindustrial towns were acceptable collateral damage to ministers because the price of bread was a lower priority than staving off famine and keeping prices stable.[4]

As it turned out, the Corn Law was unnecessary. Wheat prices exceeded the price set by the law on average from 1816 to 1819, but not because of the law. Rather, prices returned to wartime levels because harvests in Britain and on the Continent were so poor following the global climate catastrophe caused by the eruption of Mount Tambora. From Liverpool's perspective, however, the Corn Law appeared to be worth the political cost because it shored up his support among the landed classes for the coming fight about the debt. It demonstrated a commitment on the part of the ministry to ease the transition from war to peace for farmers and landowners. In fact, the political costs of the Corn Law were greater than Liverpool had estimated, sparking renewed calls for parliamentary reform because it was never more obvious that the landed elite were overrepresented.[5]

As the corn bill was becoming a law in the spring of 1815, Napoleon returned from Elba. Stopping and reversing the process of demobilization was expensive for all the Allies, but especially for Britain, as discussed in chapter 5. Vansittart worried that if the war lasted more than a year, British finances would finally collapse, with the government unable to meet the payments on the interest on the debt. A swift end to the campaign was needed, so Parliament risked exacerbating the financial situation by voting generous increases to the armed services' budgets. Their bet paid off at Waterloo, and the result was that Liverpool was relatively pleased with the financial situation in late 1815. Indeed, he was so confident that further funds were not needed that year that he declined to call MPs back to London in November, as was usual, and instead waited until February 1, 1816.[6]

The major issue at the start of the new session was how to service the debt. The government's proposal was to reintroduce the wartime income tax, technically called the property tax, which was levied on roughly the five hundred thousand wealthiest households.[7] The income tax was a relatively recent innovation in the fiscal-military apparatus, dating from the crisis years of 1797–99 when Pitt worried that the old ways of war finance were insufficient. It proved to be an essential component in Britain's war effort, and by the end of the wars, it was bringing in £14 million per year, or about a quarter of the government's annual expenditures. Taxing the wealthy directly was politically dangerous, but Pitt had argued, "In a war for the protection of property it was just and equitable that property should bear the burden."[8]

It was generally agreed that governments had the right to raise taxes in wartime—how else could the fiscal-military state function. But recall that war was seen as an abnormality, despite its endemic nature in this period, and ministers were expected on the conclusion of a war to return the country to normalcy as soon as possible. That meant removing taxes that had been explicitly labeled as wartime expedients. Liverpool and Vansittart well understood this expectation, so they came prepared in February with sizeable concessions. They proposed cutting the tax in half, to 5 percent, and making the collection of the tax less intrusive. The expected revenue of £12 million over the next two years would not be enough to cover the budget deficit, but it would be better than nothing.

Liverpool and Vansittart had made a misstep in April 1815 when they had let the tax lapse for the year—a decision difficult to understand in retrospect and one that allowed the Whigs to argue plausibly that the tax was justified only in wartime. Resistance to the tax forged an alliance between two constituencies normally at odds with each other: City merchants and country landowners. Although the landed classes bore a heavier brunt of the tax, the Whigs managed to get four hundred petitions against the tax put before Parliament including one from the City with twenty-two thousand signatures. As one historian has summarized, heavy peacetime taxation was not only "politically objectionable but morally wrong" because the wars had been fought to protect Britain from the kind of Continental despotism associated with heavy direct taxes.[9] Castlereagh was disgusted by the ignorance of these petitioners—did they not understand the severity of the budget crisis?—but despite his best efforts in the Commons, the tax was defeated. No fewer than 157 MPs who normally supported the government changed sides to vote against it. The voting public—meaning the professional classes plus the social elite—refused to continue to bear the burden of the wars despite the debt.[10]

Figure 8.1: Ratio of Public Net Debt to Total Net Income, 1754–1825

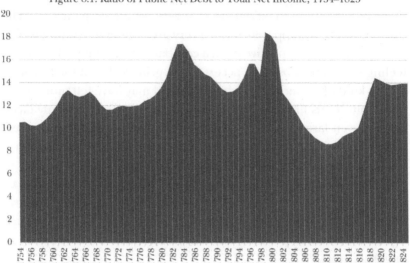

The significance of the income tax and the consequences of its defeat can be seen in Figure 8.1. From its introduction in 1799 (the highest peak), the ratio of debt to income fell precipitously as the new revenue poured in, reaching a level in 1810 not seen since before the Seven Years War. The challenge of the last years of the war is visible as well, as enormous subsidies to the Allies and war with the United States reversed the downward trend. By removing the tax in 1816, its opponents placed Britain back into the dire financial circumstances of the late 1790s, the same circumstances that had justified Pitt's introduction of the tax in the first place. Yet the sense among many establishment figures was that in peacetime, financial crises would pass so long as the government extricated itself from the economy. Graham Moore was among those who normally supported the government but was pleased to see the tax defeated. He wrote in his diary that "it was meant to be generally understood both in Parliament and in the Country that the Property Tax was merely a War Tax and that it should not be continued when the war ceased." There were widespread worries that the tax would be made permanent. Moore wrote, "I certainly think well of Vansittart, but I am not sorry to see his defeat on this occasion. It may force oeconomy upon our rulers. . . . The Income Tax was a most powerful Engine in the hands

of Government. It produced an immense sum with comparatively little trouble. It ought to be reserved for very great emergencies."[11] The
financial crisis was apparently not a very great emergency, which is an
understandable perspective from a combat veteran but perhaps not a
feeling shared by those with access to the grim reality of the budget.

The kind of austerity that Moore wanted may have felt morally justified, but it was financially disastrous. Vansittart was suddenly faced
with an even larger budget deficit than he had anticipated, approximately £20 million. With no other options, he resorted to short-term
loans, and once again, Britain's financial system proved willing to
loan the government money at favorable rates, this time with a £3
million loan from the Bank of England at only 3 percent interest.
But that was far from enough, making the defeat of the property tax,
in one estimation, "probably the sharpest reduction [in income] in
English history."[12]

The other revenue tools available to the government were indirect
taxes on consumption, listed as excise taxes in Table 8.1. Throughout the eighteenth century, these taxes had formed the spine of
Britain's revenue collection system, accounting for approximately
three-quarters of all revenue. The established pattern for dealing with a
postwar debt crisis was to convert short-term debt into long-term debt,
which was done by creating new indirect taxes and selling stocks linked
to those taxes. At the end of the War of Spanish Succession, for example, the government had introduced new duties on coffee, tea, books,
playing cards, calicoes, candles, coal, hackney coaches, linens, leather,
paper, parchment, soap, silks, and Irish salt. Each of these duties was
linked to government stocks, providing opportunities for further
investment from the City. Similarly, as the Seven Years War drew to a
close, the government issued £20 million in new government stock,
underwritten by substantial increases in the malt and beer excises.[13]

By removing the income tax from the government's ledger in 1816,
Parliament ensured that indirect taxation would become even more
important, but at this point there was no appetite for new taxes. Consumption taxes are generally regressive, since poor people spend a
higher percentage of their income on consumables than rich people.
In a nod to this issue, Parliament also decided to remove the malt
tax, which was estimated to bring in £2.7 million. Castlereagh told

the prince regent, "There being little hope of carrying the war malt tax through, your Royal Highness's Ministers thought it better to add two millions to the amount of the loan, than to perhaps make an ineffectual attempt to force this tax upon the agriculturalists and upon the poor, when the rich had delivered themselves from the property tax."[14] Yet as the list of duties from the War of Spanish Succession suggests, in fact most of the burden of consumption taxes fell on the middling sort and the wealthy because most consumption taxes—malt aside—were on luxury items. But whoever bore more of a brunt of the wartime tax regime, it was clear in early 1816 that there was no constituency eager to continue it. Only ministers faced with enormous budget shortfalls displayed any enthusiasm for taxes.[15]

The postwar political environment is best encapsulated by Sir William Curtis, who had made a vast fortune selling biscuits to the navy, standing up in Parliament to call for the demobilization of ninety thousand sailors so as to prevent the need for more wartime taxes.[16] It is little wonder that the army and the navy demobilized so quickly if even those who most profited from their largesse argued that they should be cut. It was the only way to achieve the desired goal of balancing the budget. The ministry's success in doing so stands out in Table 8.2: just two years after the end of the wars, the budget deficit was a manageable £2.1 million, and the budget was balanced thereafter.

8.1. Gross Public Income in £ Millions, 1812–20

Year	Total Gross Income	Customs	Excise	Stamps	Land and Assessed Taxes	Property and Income Tax	Post Office
1812	71	13	27.9	6	7.4	13.2	1.9
1813	70.3	14	25.9	6	7.5	13.1	2
1814	74.7	14.4	27.5	6.3	7.9	14.3	2.1
1815	77.9	14.8	29.5	6.5	8	14.5	2.2
1816	79.1	14.3	26.9	6.7	9.5	14.6	2.3
1817	69.2	11.9	23.2	6.8	7.3	11.8	2.2
1818	57.6	13.4	26.4	7.2	8.2	2.3	2.1
1819	59.5	13.9	26.5	7.2	8.2	0.6	2.1
1820	58.1	13	29.6	7	8.2	0.2	2.1

Source: Mitchell, *British Historical Statistics,* 581.

Table 8.2. Gross Public Expenditure in £ Millions, 1812–20

Year	Total Gross Expenditure	Debt Charges	Civil Government	Army and Ordnance	Navy	Budget Deficit
1812	87.3	24.6	5.2	33.8	19.6	16.3
1813	94.8	26.4	5.4	36.5	20.8	24.5
1814	111.1	27.3	5.3	49.6	22.5	36.4
1815	112.9	30	5.8	49.6	22.8	35
1816	99.5	32.2	6.1	39.6	16.8	20.4
1817	71.3	32.9	5.5	18	10.2	2.1
1818	58.7	31.5	5	11.1	6.6	0.9
1819	57.6	31.3	6	9.1	6.6	−1.9
1820	57.5	31.1	5.4	10.3	6.4	−0.6

Source: Mitchell, *British Historical Statistics*, 587.

It is likely that Liverpool and his ministers would have enforced stringent cutbacks even without the prodding of the opposition. Not only was the budget situation dire, but also the intellectual and political consensus was that deficit spending was harmful. Nevertheless, the Whigs played a significant role in spurring on the cuts at a faster rate, particularly in 1816. The realities of transitioning from war to peace put ministers in a difficult position as it was simply not possible to cut military budgets as deeply as they or the Whigs wanted. Shortly before the income tax defeat, Liverpool had tried to get the Army Estimates passed. While he and Vansittart anticipated trouble on the income tax, the Whigs' vociferous assault on the Army Estimates surprised them because in wartime, the estimates had rarely been controversial. The estimates were substantially reduced from 1815, but still large—larger even than the 1813 estimates. The Whigs introduced an amendment requiring the government to conduct "a careful revisal of our Establishments, Civil and Military, with a view to such an immediate reduction of the same as may be required by the principles of a rigid economy, and by a due regard for the Liberties of the Subject." Palmerston responded by arguing that the empire had grown since 1792 and the army needed to grow with it. Peel spoke about the importance of maintaining a strong military presence in Ireland. Subsequent speakers for the government mustered weaker arguments, however, and ministers found themselves on the defensive, arguing in favor of colonial commitments to justify a large standing army. Given the long-standing rhetorical trope in British politics about the dangers of a standing army, it was not a strong position to adopt.[17]

A more effective defense came from Castlereagh, who argued that the Army Estimates were bloated because 1816 was a transition year between war and peace. The government was taking all reasonable steps to reduce expenditure, but in addition to new colonial commitments, there were thousands of newly unemployed officers who now received half pay. These arguments eventually forced the estimates through, although with a relatively slim majority of seventy. Tangible evidence that the government was looking to save money had helped sway the uncertain. For example, Wellington had always been careful to pay his army's way during the Peninsular War, and he kept up the practice in the Waterloo campaign. Ministers ordered him to start requisitioning food and forage, which cut his expenses by a third.[18]

The 1816 Navy Estimates were the third major budgetary battle that year in Parliament. The debate was in many ways similar to that on the Army Estimates, but the Whigs, grown overconfident by their victory over the income tax, made some basic errors. There were good reasons for them to be aggressive in attacking the estimates, as public opinion seemed to be on their side: one observer claimed to be "perfectly astounded" by the "extravagances" ministers were asking the country to support.[19] Led by George Tierney, the Whigs contrasted recent wartime estimates with the new peace estimates and showed that they had dramatically increased. How could the government promise "oeconomy" while simultaneously *increasing* spending on the navy? In the Commons, Castlereagh fretted, concerned that there was no obvious response to this attack. The government appeared to be on the cusp of another dramatic defeat. Castlereagh turned to Croker to ask what could be done. After frantically sending a messenger to the Admiralty to retrieve a box of key papers, Croker made two points. First, Tierney had made an embarrassing blunder. There were in fact two Navy Estimates each year: an ordinary estimate and a sea service estimate. The sea service estimate was also called the "vote of seamen" and appeared to reflect the number of men serving in the navy. In fact, it did no such thing—it was actually a financial abstraction that paid for the active operations of the navy.

Meanwhile, the ordinary estimate covered the navy's civil administration and the cost of keeping ships in reserve. What Tierney had missed was that the sea service estimate had plummeted, as sailors and ships were discharged and decommissioned, while the ordinary estimate had grown to cover the cost of demobilizing and maintaining the enormous fleet. Tierney's embarrassment was compounded since, as a former treasurer of the navy, he should have known all this.

Once the messenger returned, Croker pressed home his victory by citing the historical precedents for the 1816 estimates. The messenger brought with him a list of the last war and first peace ordinary estimates for every war since 1697. The first peace ordinary estimate always exceeded the last war estimate, Croker showed. Faced with these simple facts, the opposition crumbled. Croker later boasted, "I certainly never saw in Parliament so sudden and complete turning of the tide of victory."[20] The government used historical precedents to justify its transition spending in other areas as well, providing lists of the size of the army and navy in every year in the eighteenth century and other historical data to demonstrate that its policies were in keeping with the normal operations of the fiscal-military state. Indeed, the government's response to peace in 1815 looked like its response to all previous peacetimes since the Glorious Revolution. All that was different was the income tax.[21]

It is important to note, however, that nowhere in the debate over the Navy Estimates did Croker attempt to defend naval spending as stimulative or necessary for defense. He scored a tactical victory in the debate, which provided a temporary reprieve for the navy, but the political winds were blowing in only one direction: austerity. Thus the patterns established in the 1816 debates continued for the rest of the decade, with the only change being that transition costs steadily dropped. Palmerston introduced the Army Estimates each year and made sure to pivot immediately to pointing out the measures that the government had taken to save money. "The detail of [the Army Estimates] was so dry," Palmerston is reported to have said on March 2, 1818, "that the House must, he presumed, feel desirous to have it brought within the shortest possible compass. . . . He should therefore confine himself to that which he hoped would be satisfactory to the House, namely, a statement of the reduction of expense." He then presented a chart showing the difference between the 1817 and 1818 estimates, with the savings of £188,027 19s 3d precisely tabulated for the MPs to see.[22] Despite the government's best efforts at getting ahead of calls for reductions, the opposition often still questioned whether the cuts had gone far enough, at which point the government had to defend even the barest minimum of spending. William Wilberforce, the abolitionist, went so far as to call for the army to be reduced almost to nothing. After all, he asked, why did Britain need an army when her naval supremacy guaranteed the safety of her colonies?[23]

Such attitudes naturally alarmed military and naval men, and these severe budget cuts meant that British military and naval power after 1815 was not as great as most observers assumed it to be. Fret as they might, however, it was not as if the services had much choice in the matter. If there was any doubt about the prevailing opinion on the value of military and naval spending, it was quickly dispelled in March 1816. A large and politically influential group of both army and navy officers had banded together to form the United Service Club. The idea was to get a suitably grand building in central London to serve as a social hub for the many half-pay officers with little else to do. Although the club had the support of Wellington, Liverpool refused to lease the club crown land and told it to make its own arrangements. A petition against the club proved Liverpool's political instincts to be correct: there was simply no support for military spending beyond the barest necessities.[24]

The administrative effects of the cuts were significant, as both services sought to root out what critics called "old corruption": the lingering vestiges of the medieval state. Palmerston was particularly aggressive in the War Office. Some positions that seemed both humble and practical, like the paymaster of widows' pensions, were in fact sinecures in which the officeholder collected a large salary while a deputy did all the work. He worked hard to eliminate such positions. Despite the critics' cries, sinecures were in fact increasingly rare, but Palmerston kept with the spirit of reform by extending working hours, standardizing overtime pay, and eliminating redundancies. The bigger problem was that when he had taken over the War Office in 1809, he had found forty thousand accounts that had not been cleared, some dating back to 1783. By 1817, he had settled all accounts through 1797, and he had instituted policies that prevented the number of uncleared accounts from growing. One biographer estimates that he saved the government more than £100,000, and he did so while still reducing the staff: there were 170 employees in the War Office in 1815, and by 1828, there were only 75. His aggressive search for efficiency exemplified the postwar political climate.[25]

By 1818, the naval budget stabilized at around £6.6 million, while the army and ordnance accounted for about £10 million. Put another way, those budgets were 30 percent of the navy's peak in wartime and 20 percent of the army's. The effects of these cuts are the heart of this book, and it is not necessary here to trace all of them. But it should be noted that the distress and discontent of the postwar period spurred the government into some action that fed back into the military services. The army's budgetary fortunes, for example, improved slightly in response to domestic unrest. While introducing the Army Estimates for 1818, Palmerston suggested that a larger standing army might be necessary—not that people should be governed by the sword, he said, but simply that "the experience of the last few years" demonstrated that the people had been "brought into such a state of fermentation, as to render life and property unsafe, without the protection of a large military force."[26] After Peterloo, the government increased the number of troops designated for service at home by ten thousand, and in the spring of 1820, called out half of the militia for training and exercise in a deliberate attempt to put civilians under military discipline. It marked the postwar peak of expenditure on the militia and indicated how seriously ministers took the threat of revolution in those years.[27]

While the Army and Navy Estimates were the most consequential budgetary issues taken up by Parliament in these years, they were not the only levers of power available to Liverpool and his ministers. To calm the "state of fermentation," Parliament turned to its 1790s playbook, suspending habeas corpus in 1817 and passing the Seditious Meetings Act. The latter prevented clubs and societies from holding meetings without approval from the local authorities. Sidmouth used his power to imprison forty-four printers and leaders of Radical societies for a year, and he harassed others into exile. After Peterloo, the Six Acts strengthened the powers of magistrates, prohibited drilling and the gathering of arms, reinforced the Seditious Meetings Act, and increased the severity of punishments for libel.[28]

Another reason ministers looked to the repressive 1790s for guidance is that many had good reasons to fear for their own personal safety. Lieutenant David Davies suffered a severe breakdown, cut off his penis, and tried to claim a pension as a maimed officer. When he was refused, he attempted to assassinate Palmerston in the staircase of the War Office on April 8, 1818. His pistol shot just missed. Davies was arrested, declared insane, and sent to Bedlam. Three years later, he sent Palmerston a detailed apology and asked to be released on full pay. Palmerston simply noted in the margin, "!!!"[29] While Palmerston's would-be assassin was acting alone, others were not. The prince regent's carriage was attacked in 1817, and when Wellington gave a friend a ride in his carriage along Pall Mall, and he made sure to lock all the doors and give his friend some basic instructions on defending it from attack: "By leaning back you may fight a window better than a parapet wall."[30]

The greatest danger of all came from the Cato Street conspirators in the aftermath of Peterloo. On the evening of February 23, 1820, twenty men met in the hayloft of a stable in Cato Street off the Edgeware Road in London. They had been spurred to action by what they saw as the government's tyrannical response at Peterloo, and they had spent the last few months preparing to assassinate members of the cabinet. Sidmouth and Castlereagh were their priority targets, and after Christmas the conspirators had begun monitoring the ministers' homes to see if they could spot patterns in their behavior to ambush one and then the other. But this night they had received the fortuitous news that the entire cabinet was meeting at Lord Harrowby's house in Grosvenor Square. They resolved to take the opportunity to kill as many of them as possible, parade their heads around London, capture Mansion House and the Bank of England, and declare a provisional government. Before they could do so, however, the Bow Street Runners—a proto–police force acting as constables on the authority of a magistrate—arrived and stormed the hayloft. The Runners had expected support from a detachment of the Coldstream Guards, but the soldiers were late. By the time they arrived, one of the Runners had been killed, and the soldiers had to sweep the surrounding streets in the dark to locate all the conspirators. Eleven men were arrested in all; one went to prison; five were transported to Australia for life; and five were hanged, decapitated, and buried in unmarked graves. The reason the Bow Street Runners had known to storm the hayloft is that the intelligence about the cabinet's dinner had in fact been a ruse planted by an agent provocateur named George Edwards (code name "Windsor"). Sidmouth's Home Office showed no hesitation in using its power to infiltrate Radical organizations.[31]

More positively, Wellington and Palmerston tried to combat the forces of revolution by organizing loyal petitioning meetings in Hampshire after Peterloo. The government also sponsored friendly newspapers, and ceremonies like the coronation of George IV proved to be surprisingly successful demonstrations of loyalist feeling. Liverpool and his ministers also took some of the British government's first hesitant steps toward addressing social ills. We should not celebrate their accomplishments on this front—in fact, they did far too little, far too late—but that they felt compelled to act indicates the extent of the misery. What worried them most of all, and what spurred them to act, was a Malthusian doom spiral of a growing, dependent poor population coupled with a collapsing food supply leading to mass starvation or possibly revolution. There were warning signs in the winter of 1816, as the cost of poor relief rose from an average of £6 million per year in the last years of the wars to £7.8 million. The Poor Employment Act, passed in June 1817, tried to remedy this situation. It gave a total of £1.75 million in loans to individuals, corporations, and vestries to build public works like canals and roads.[32]

The other area in which the government sought to improve the lot of the poor was veterans' benefits. Over the course of the wars, as the manpower crisis deepened, both services took steps to improve the financial and emotional lives of their servicemen and their families. The Royal Military Asylum educated more than two thousand children of soldiers by the end of the wars, and if a soldier died, his family gained the ability to petition the War Office for his effects. From 1795, the navy allowed sailors to remit half of their pay to their families. Both services developed and expanded pension schemes through Chelsea and Greenwich Hospitals. But the services undertook these initiatives because they aided recruitment and retention—helping servicemen and veterans was actually a secondary consideration. That is not to ignore the paternalist instincts of Liverpool and his ministers, but on a macroeconomic level, they were not inclined to address mass unemployment. The return of hundreds of thousands of soldiers and sailors into a depressed labor market was seen as an inevitable consequence of the end of a war.[33]

Responsibility for handling mass poverty remained, as it had for centuries, at the local level. By 1815, most parishes operated what was known as the Speenhamland system, after the town in Berkshire where it was designed in 1795. It used taxes on the wealthy (at the Poor Law rate) to subsidize rural wages by setting a minimum wage indexed to the price of bread and the size of the worker's family. Only those who worked received the wages, in contrast to those who were supported in their local parishes by the Poor Laws. Other support came from charity, often raised by subscription but again handled at the local level. Civic leaders in Glasgow set up a soup kitchen in August 1816, but the weavers who were supposed to benefit from it rioted: they wanted employment, not soup. A local historian in Newcastle, writing in 1827, recorded that in early 1817, "At this time of general distress, a liberal subscription was raised in Newcastle, for the purpose of giving employment to the industrious and unengaged poor."[34]

The scale of the postwar depression overwhelmed local efforts at relief. Demobilized soldiers and sailors entered an economy suffering from a severe lack of demand as the wartime contracts were cancelled. Major centers of employment like the dockyards laid off not only sailmakers and carpenters but also women employed making signal colors. Cuts to the navy's shore establishments had far-reaching effects. For example, from 1814 to 1822, an assistant clerk in the navy pay office named John Dickens found himself steadily reassigned from Portsmouth to London to Sheerness to Chatham and then back to London as the navy reconfigured its operations for peace. All these moves, combined with his growing family, did nothing to help his improvidence, and in 1824, he was committed to the Marshalsea debtors' prison for a few months. Shortly after being released, he retired from the pay office and began collecting a small pension. In the meantime, however, his twelve-year-old son Charles had been forced to seek work sticking labels on jars of shoe polish.[35]

The Thames shipyards took a double hit. First came the ending of the East India Company's monopoly on trade with India in 1813, causing the company to order fewer ships, and then came the cancelation of the Navy Board's contracts. Of 1,474 shipwrights employed on the Thames in 1813, just 657 still had a job in 1814. The Ordnance Office was as aggressive as the Navy Board, halting all orders for new muskets for a decade from 1817. Birmingham's armaments industry collapsed, and thousands of workers became unemployed. Despite an aggressive petitioning campaign, all officials could promise them was that in the event of a new war, the Ordnance Office would once again rely heavily on private industry to supply arms. Similarly, during the wars, Marc Brunel, father of the famous engineer Isambard Kingdom Brunel, had developed a process for using steam power to produce blocks for the navy. He invested the profits in a boot factory, and by the end of the wars it was producing more than four hundred pairs per day for the army. The cancellation of his contracts left him with a surplus of thirty thousand pairs, which the War Office refused to pay for. By 1821, he was bankrupt and in debtors' prison, before Wellington eventually intervened to get the government to defray some of his debts. The collapse of military spending after Waterloo was dramatic and had effects not only on the services themselves but on the industries that supplied them and on the workers they employed.[36]

There was worse news on the agricultural front. Graham Moore, comfortably ensconced in his country estate, surveyed the state of the country in his diary in April 1816: "The great and sudden effects of the change occasioned everywhere by a Universal Peace throughout Europe have been severely felt by almost every class in this Country. Numerous Bankruptcies among the commercial People in the great trading towns and a terrible falling off in the Rents among the Land holders." He estimated that he was "between two and three thousand pounds poorer" than he was three years earlier.[37] He was one of the lucky members of the elite, as was Brunel. Most soldiers and sailors could not afford to lose thousands and did not have friends in high places.

The government did not respond adequately to these problems because it did not believe that it had the capacity to effect change, as Liverpool explained to Canning: "The Restoration of Publick Credit, the Rise of the Funds, and the consequent Fall of the Interest of Money will afford more Relief to the existing Distresses of the Country, than any other Measure which could be adopted."[38] He and his ministers embarked on a mission of slashing budgets much as doctors often proscribed bleeding for their patients. When the economic patient failed to respond, they concluded that they simply needed to bleed it more. As a result, public spending per capita fell steadily from 1815 until it reached its absolute nadir in modern British history in 1834. Well into the 1840s it was still generally assumed that the central government should play a limited role in stimulating the economy, much less remedying the plight of the poor. Liverpool's postwar austerity measures and the return to the gold standard caused acute deflation, which ministers welcomed as a relief from the drunken high prices of the wartime years. In fact, we now know, it had the perverse effect of exacerbating the problems of poor relief and unemployment.[39, i]

To be fair to Liverpool and his ministers, the tools of modern Keynesian economics were unavailable to them, and it is not as if they simply sat on their hands while the country burned. On the contrary, they were increasingly active in passing legislation, even if few of those laws helped employ demobilized soldiers and sailors. In 1818, Liverpool worked closely with bishops of the Church of England to fund the construction of no fewer than six hundred new churches. The primary purpose was to address overcrowding in London, where, for example, the parish of St. Pancras had fifty thousand inhabitants and space for two hundred of them in pews. But the funds were also aimed at defending the established church against the growth of other Protestant sects. In this, it was less successful, as in the ten years from 1810 alone 15,601 non-Anglican churches were built, adapted, or licensed. Similarly, an 1819 bill banning the employment of children under nine years old looks superficially like a step toward an interventionist government. However, it only passed the Lords on the condition that the cotton mills at which it was aimed were a special case and that further interference with private industry was not forthcoming. None of these bills addressed the root problems of slack demand, tight money, and poor harvests, but they do indicate a willingness on the part of the government to take a slightly more

---

i   Economic historians have argued about whether wages rose slightly or fell slightly during the early Industrial Revolution, but there is no evidence that they rose substantially. In other words, they did not keep up with wartime inflation, so workers were generally paid less in real terms by the postwar years than they had been before the wars. See Harley and Crafts, "Simulating the Two Views of the British Industrial Revolution," and Clark, "Condition of the Working-Class."

active role in the country's economic and religious life than had previously been the case.[40]

When we examine what happened when soldiers and sailors came home, we need to understand that they came home amidst an economic crisis that was normal, but on a grander scale. The British fiscal-military state had faced economic crises at the end of every war, but never before had it had to grapple with a depression so deep and long-lasting, or one that took place in the shadow of the second-largest volcanic eruption in human history. The transition from war to peace was always problematic for soldiers and sailors, but there was no precedent for or expectation of relief for working people. Ministers believed that the country simply had to endure the wartime hangover and that the best policy was to slash spending and taxes to limit the government's role in the economic life of the country. The military *was* the budget in 1815, which meant that it was the army and navy that suffered the cuts. Some postwar cuts were undoubtedly necessary, but by rapidly demobilizing, Liverpool's government jeopardized the spoils of its victory. Worse, by cracking down aggressively on dissent and not providing any safety net to the soldiers and sailors who had won that victory, the government threw thousands of unemployed men into a cauldron of unrest and rebellion.

CHAPTER 9

The Experience of Demobilization

Uncovering what it felt like to live through the chaos of 1814 and 1815 appears to be a simple exercise. After all, hundreds of soldiers and sailors wrote memoirs about their experience of the Napoleonic Wars, so all that is needed is to survey those memoirs. Yet doing so raises two problems, one obvious and one subtle. The obvious problem is that memoirists often ignored the process of demobilization. They clearly saw it as a milestone in their lives, but much like contemporary military and naval historians, they used the end of the wars as an excuse to end their memoirs. It is common to find memoirs that end just after Waterloo. They assumed that their readers were not interested in how they reintegrated or how they felt about that process. This chapter, more or less by necessity, privileges the experience of those soldiers and sailors who described the experience of demobilization over those who did not.

The subtle problem is that memoirs are tricky sources. They are processed records of experiences, written by fallible people often decades after the experiences in question. In those intervening decades, the culture and politics in which they lived shaped how they processed their experiences, and the words available to them constrained the language they used to express those experiences. Memoirs have a literary tradition that authors were either consciously or unconsciously participating in, and memoirists wrote in a particular time and place for a particular audience. There was a vibrant market for military memoirs from the 1820s onward. All those factors need to shape how we handle memoirs as sources.[1]

More prosaically, soldiers and sailors were practiced storytellers. Military and naval life lent itself to storytelling: life in the barracks or on board a ship was generally dull, and those who could break the boredom gained social cachet. They honed their techniques, learned from the best, and brought home sea stories and tall tales of their adventures. It seems safe to assume that those who were inclined to be storytellers while on active service were more likely to put their stories in writing after the wars. The telling of them was a way for those who lived through the wars and their aftermath to make sense of their experience. Even if they are littered with exaggeration and sensational claims, they are still useful windows into the words and emotions of the participants.[2,i]

Enough throat clearing. What was it like to be demobilized? The process began with rumors of peace, although that was nothing new. Rumors of peace had spread periodically throughout the Great Wars, and only once before had they been true. Peace was a frequent subject of soldiers' and sailors' letters home because, as sailor James Whitworth wrote to his wife in 1812, "If you hear of a Peace . . . that is the only chance of my seeing you again."[3] Rumors operated independently of the strategic reality. Two months later, just weeks before the beginning of the War of 1812 and Napoleon's invasion of Russia, Whitworth reported, "Here is great talk of Peace."[4] After so many years of false hopes, many took to attributing peace to God's will alone: "I am of opinion that it must come unexpectedly when it does come for paying off, God is the Judge," wrote one sailor to his parents. "God send a peace," wrote another to his wife.[5] Most ordinary soldiers and sailors felt helpless in the face of the great movements of fleets and armies and in the political maneuverings of grandees in far-off London, Paris, and Vienna.

---

i   This disclaimer is insufficient, as Matilda Greig has recently pointed out: "Few [his-
    torians] have engaged critically with how to approach memoirs as sources, mostly
    including a disclaimer on the books' potential unreliability before proceeding to rely
    on quotes from their content regardless." See Greig, *Dead Men Telling Tales,* 7. Her
    point is well taken, but historians should always approach their sources critically and
    look for alternative sources to corroborate claims. I have endeavored to do that in the
    analysis that follows.

When peace finally did arrive, the news was too good to be true. John Wetherell had been captured in 1804 following a shipwreck on the French coast and had spent the next ten years as a prisoner of war. On April 11, 1814, he was one of 339 prisoners being marched through France when he heard peasants crying, "Vive Louis dix huit!" Surprised, he asked a passing farmer what had happened. The farmer responded, "Come my friends, drink, long live Louis the 18th. You are no longer Prisoners. You are our friends and brothers!" But after a decade's captivity, Wetherell and his fellow prisoners were understandably skeptical. Not until they saw a Bourbon flag flying and received white ribbons for their hats from an elderly woman did they believe that peace had arrived: "We were no longer Prisoners! Our captive chains were bust asunder that Moment Louis was proclaim'd king."[6]

Toulouse also burst into celebrations, as at least four memoirs from soldiers fighting there in Wellington's army attest.[7] As the troops marched into town, colors flying, the band played a song called "The Downfall of Paris." Every church bell rang, creating a discordant but celebratory jangling. In a deafening atmosphere that would have seemed familiar to an Allied soldier liberating France in the Second World War, the citizens of Toulouse came out to meet the troops. One soldier recalled that they were "shouting their vivas; men, women, maidens and youths vying with each other who first should have the honor of serving *Monsieur l'Anglaise* with *eau-de-vie* and prime wine." Women came to the balconies and waved white handkerchiefs. They grabbed flowers out of their window boxes and threw them in front of the soldiers, while others rushed up to them "with bottle or flagon in hand . . . urging the brimming glasses into the hands of those who had already partaken of more than was conducive to soldier-like appearance."[8] Another recalled that "joy beamed on every face, and made every tongue eloquent. We sung and drank that whole night, and talked of home."[9]

Elsewhere, however, peace arrived hesitantly. Perhaps no account better summarizes servicemen's desperation for peace, and its promises and uncertainties, than a letter from William Long, a marine stationed in the Scheldt estuary, to his mother, written on April 13, 1814, shortly after Napoleon's first abdication. While the army celebrated in Toulouse, in the Low Countries, the war still raged: "Don't know the minute when we shall die, day or night. They will not believe that Bonaparte is beat. Dear mother I hope they will soon be convinced that he is beat. I have prayed for it for a long time." He reassured his mother that if he did come home, he was not going to bring any surprises: "Believe I shan't bring wife home with me. I am in my prime thank god for it but I dare say they won't look at a poor soldier but I hope the almighty god will give me use of my hands and I shan't know what it is to want a bit of bread if I can get work." But most of all, the peace still seemed unbelievable, so he asked his mother to confirm it: "Please to let me know all the news as you can for we do not know the truth." His attention now turned to returning home, for good, and leaving the military, for good: "I hope we shall be called home to England never to go abroad any more from home. I shall walk my way home for I shan't like to come home with my red jacket as pay is very small for a soldier."[10]

Long was undoubtedly writing while particularly distressed, but we should take his account of the tumultuous weeks in the spring of 1814 seriously. It reflects the ambiguity of this new world and the persistence of the wars. Most soldiers who participated in the fall of France in 1814 did not relish the thought of being sent to another war across the Atlantic, but surprisingly few seem to have anticipated that it was likely. Perhaps the scale of the accomplishment of having finally brought about Napoleon's abdication prevented them from taking a more dispassionate view of British global commitments. Some heard rumors of foreign service, destination unknown, when they returned to Plymouth and Portsmouth, but the true destination did not become clear until they were at sea.[11] John Jones recalled, "We had been on board several days and were going at a swift rate before a fine stiff breeze; but still no land greeted our anxious gaze— no sweet home appeared in view: and having, at length, ascertained that our course was not England-ward, we justly concluded that we were bound on some distant foreign service; but whither no one knew; save, perhaps, the officers."[12] John Spencer Cooper was three weeks short of his discharge date when he heard the bad news that his regiment was to be embarked, but he held out hope up to the last minute that the destination was Cork, where he hoped to get his discharge. Two months later he was fighting at New Orleans.[13]

Such helplessness in the face of the military's demands will reso- nate with all who have ever put on a uniform. Indeed, most soldiers seem to have gotten over their disappointment quickly. They had more mundane concerns, in any case: as several Peninsular War memoirists recall, their uniforms and equipment were falling to pieces, and even a brief pause in their deployment provided a vital opportunity to repair and replenish.[14] They could now turn their attention to their new enemy with confidence. Private William Wheeler, writing in July 1814, guessed that "the Yankees will find some rum customers to deal with, for the troops that [have] been employed under Lord Wellington from long practice are become fire proof."[15] Years later, the American sailor James Durand remembered similar boasts. Serving in a British ship off Bordeaux in June 1814, he recalled that British soldiers embarking for North America said that "since they had whipped Napoleon, they would have no trouble in subduing the U. States. If they had known that Gen. And. Jackson was awaiting them, they would have laughed another way."[16]

The return to the status quo ante bellum at the end of the War of 1812 failed to resolve these questions, but they were temporarily forgotten in the face of Napoleon's return from Elba. Units returning from the defeat at New Orleans heard the news while at sea. Cooper, who had survived New Orleans, recalled that they met a French ship out of La Rochelle in midocean: "'What news have you?' 'Buonaparte has escaped from Elba, and got to Paris, where he has 200,000 men in arms!' My stars, what a sensation!! The news flew like wild fire along the decks. 'We're in for it again!' said some. Others said, 'You seven years men will not get off now.'"[17] Sailor Samuel Leech also heard about Napoleon's return while at sea, and he noticed that officers and men responded differently. Officers celebrated because they had avoided half pay and war "inspired them with hopes of promotion."[18] Or, as one soldier put it, war "again set honour, glory, and promotion, once more before the eyes of their imagination."[19] Meanwhile, Leech's fellow sailors "longed for peace, since war only brought them hard usage, wounds, and death. While, therefore, the officers were rejoicing, they were muttering curses and oaths, wishing Bonaparte and his army at perdition."[20]

In 1815 as in 1814, unexpected deployments threw soldiers off-balance. At Cork, a soldier in the Seventy-First Regiment was just weeks short of the end of his enlistment. Tempted to desert, he decided against it when he learned they were to be embarked for Deal: "My heart bounded with joy: 'Freedom, freedom!'—I would not have taken a thousand pounds to stay,—I would have left the army without a shirt. I was oppressed all the time I was on board; my mind dwelt on nothing but home." A few days later he landed at Antwerp, not Deal, and a few weeks later he was at Waterloo.[21] Cooper was luckier: his regiment returned from New Orleans to the Isle of Wight on May 31, 1815, but as his time was up, he and "all the seven years men were discharged: we got our papers and were free." Meanwhile his regiment was immediately ordered to Ostend, although it arrived just a few days too late to take part in the battle.[22]

Reshuffling the army's deployments to meet the challenges of 1814 and 1815 required putting thousands of soldiers on board transports. Nobody enjoyed that experience. The first challenge was getting soldiers to the ships. The cavalry attached to Wellington's army at Toulouse had the privilege of marching all the way through France to the Channel coast, after having sent their baggage and "other useless encumbrances" to Bordeaux for transport.[23] Parading through enemy country as part of a conquering army was an enjoyable experience, but most soldiers had a more difficult time. Sergeant Thomas Morris and Private Wheeler were among those troops marched to the Channel coast in December 1815, and they recorded it as one of the coldest marches they had experienced. On reaching the coast, regiments began shedding hangers-on. Faced with a crowded transport, many animals had to be sold, but nobody could get a fair price since the French knew full well it was a buyer's market. Officers' servants who were not British frequently deserted, and soldiers who had married or promised to marry French or Spanish women began the difficult process of negotiating the next steps. Some petitioned their officers to allow their wives to accompany them to Britain, with some success; others used it as an excuse to part ways.[24]

The voyage itself was frequently memorable. Small transports were poor sailing vessels in addition to being crowded. "To a person not acquainted with a transport, I feel it would be almost impossible to represent the thing," wrote one young officer. "I became deadly sick, the smell of rum, ropes, tar, and bilgewater, added to that unaccountable way that so many are afflicted by sea-sickness."[25] Ships of the line converted into transports were not spacious either. Cooper estimated that his regiment added about six hundred people to the crew of one such vessel: "The sailors had hammocks, but we had only the deck, therefore at night we lay like a flock of sheep on a common. Consequently, when the ship rolled, as every one knows ships do, in the Bay of Biscay, there was sad squeezing."[26] But seasickness and crowding were the least of soldiers' worries. Most soldiers' memoirs that discuss demobilization mention a storm at sea, often on the voyage home. That may reflect reality, as we will see, but it also reflects their inexperience, as landlubbers exaggerated relatively normal weather patterns into great gales.[ii] A third possibility is that it is a (conscious or unconscious) literary device, in which the storm that they endure marks the transition from their deployment to their homecoming, or perhaps the state of the country to which they were returning.

The Fifty-Ninth Regiment was among the more battle-scarred regiments in the army. The first battalion had taken part in the capture of Mauritius and Java in the Indian Ocean, and the second had been with Wellington in Spain from 1812 through the invasion of France. The second battalion was in the process of returning from Belgium in late January 1816 (it had just missed Waterloo), and its 800 men were divided between two transports: 300 on the *Seahorse* and 500 on the *Lord Melville*. A huge storm rolled in from the North Atlantic, and in heavy seas off Ireland, the mate of the *Seahorse* most familiar with the dangerous coast fell from the rigging and was killed. The resulting wreck was a catastrophe in which only 24 passengers were saved. Nearby, the *Lord Melville* also wrecked, with only 116 survivors. A third transport, the *Boadicea*, also wrecked near Kinsale, and there were only 85 survivors from 283 embarked, most of them from the Eighty-Second Regiment. All told, the 858 British men and women killed on the night of January 30, 1816, rival the casualty figures for some of the most significant battles of the Peninsular War. It is true that on aggregate, most soldiers made it home safely thanks to the laudable efforts of the Transport Board and the navy, but there were at least half a dozen other major wrecks of troop transports from the beginning of large-scale demobilization in 1814.[27]

Soldiers who survived bad storms in transports remembered the experience for the rest of their lives. Ensign Foster Fyans felt entirely

---

ii Further evidence of their inexperience at sea: Cooper claims that one sailor received 150 lashes for refusing to swallow a pint of salt water after the ship crossed the Tropic, which seems unlikely. See Cooper, *Rough Notes of Seven Campaigns*, 134.

out of place on board because he and his fellow soldiers did not understand any of the signal guns and flags or the shipboard vocabulary: "The night was exceedingly dark, the confusion terrific, gun after gun from the Commodore, repeated with blue light signals from all the men of war in the fleet; the master of our own ship bawling loud for Boy Bill, Signal Book, 'Port your helm, you lubber.'" Being part of a group of transports could be reassuring but also dangerous: "Half a dozen ships were about us, carrying away our rigging, and leaving some of theirs on board of ours, bawling, cursing roaring through speaking trumpets, not to be understood. It was now blowing a hurricane, and expecting every minute to be run down by some vessel . . . we were scudding up Channel, guns and signals of blue lights every five minutes, Signal make port, any port."[28]

Disembarking from a transport was often a soldier's first step in the next phase of demobilization: separating from his unit. The unit that mattered most was the mess, as chapter 2 discussed briefly. The shared experience of war—not just combat but the daily grind of marching, working, surviving—forged relationships that rivaled, and in some ways exceeded, those of marriage and family. In the navy, most men were able to choose their own messmates, and the daily rituals of breaking bread (well, hardtack) around a table slung between the guns provided opportunities to support each other through the hardships of life at sea while sharing food and drink. Smaller ships often meant smaller messes, but the usual mess was between four and eight men. The army issued new tents in March 1813 that could house up to one hundred men, but they were so heavy that they needed to be transported on mules. That took up the space that had previously been occupied by heavy kettles that fed ten men, so Wellington had lighter tin kettles made that the soldiers could carry. They served six men, which modern research has shown is coincidentally the "approximate size of the smallest functional combat unit."[29]

Separating from messmates proved difficult for nearly everyone. These were the men they had fought with, and more importantly, fought for. By sharing the risk and providing mutual reinforcement during difficult times, messmates bolstered each other's morale. If a mess's bonds were strong, soldiers and sailors could endure shocking conditions, from starvation to marathon marches to shipwrecks to combat. "It was the breaking up of a large family," wrote one soldier of the dismantling of his regiment. "It was impossible to witness, without feelings of regret, this thorough dispersion of regiments and of individuals so long known to each other."[30]

Their willingness to sacrifice for each other meant that enduring suffering while separated from each other was (in some cases) a fate worse than death. Rifleman Benjamin Harris contracted Walcheren fever on that ill-fated expedition. A combination of malaria, typhus, and typhoid fever, the disease lingered for years. He complained, "I was utterly tired of the hospital life I had altogether so long led. 'For Heaven's sake,' I said, 'let me go and die with my own regiment!'"[31] Along similar lines, Private Wheeler, wounded in the foot, wrote in January 1814 that while he wanted to go home, he missed his regiment more: "As much as I desire to see my dear native land, my home and all my dear relations, old playmates and neighbours, I would much rather rejoin my Regiment again and take my chance with it." Then, if he survived, he would "have the proud satisfaction of landing on my native shores with many a brave and gallant comrade, with whom I have braved the dangers of many a hard fought battle."[32]

That sentiment even extended to Allied soldiers. Rifleman William Surtees recalled watching the Portuguese troops march back home in June 1814. The British gave them three cheers: "Many were the heavy hearts in both armies on this occasion; for it is not easy to conceive how the circumstance of passing through scenes of hardship, trial, and danger together, endeared the soldiers of the two armies to each other."[33] Surtees's opinion was not universally shared, as other members of Wellington's army preferred the Spanish as allies. Nevertheless, parting from allies who had shared the ebbs and flows of the Peninsular War generated surprisingly strong emotions.[34]

How men felt about leaving the army or navy was to a large degree a product of their morale, and mess relationships shaped morale more than any other factor. When sailor Richard Greenhalgh was turned over repeatedly from one ship to another, he registered few complaints in his letters home because his messmates were with him. But when the company of his ship of the line was broken up to man a handful of sloops, they were separated, and his morale crashed. After repeatedly writing home asking for information about his friends, he decided to take matters into his own hands by deserting his ship at Naples. That he would take such a drastic step, and at such an inconvenient port (Greenhalgh was from Scotland, which he eventually reached via merchant ships stopping in Boston and New-foundland) reinforces the importance of messmate relationships for morale.[35]

While we can see broad similarities across soldiers' and sailors' experiences of leaving their messmates, how they felt about leaving military service varied. One common refrain contrasted the difficulty of leaving messmates with the relief of finally being freed from mil-itary service and coming home: "I left my comrades with regret; but the service with joy," remembered one soldier.[36] Others seem to have harbored more positive feelings toward both military service and their units. Private Wheeler wrote from the hospital: "This is the first time of my being absent from my Regiment since I entered into it and I hope it will not be long before I should hear the sound of its soul stirring bugles again."[37] In an oft-quoted passage, Thomas Morris recalled the breakup of the second battalion of his regiment in 1817. The major formed them into a square and "after a very impressive speech, in reference to our past services, the order for disbandment was read, the colours, under which we had fought so often, were taken from their staff (the men presenting arms during the cere-mony) and carefully placed in a box, and afterwards forwarded to London. There was scarcely a man among us, who did not shed a tear at the separation."[38]

Morris's account is likely exaggerated, evidence of what other his-torians have identified as the lingering "age of sensibility" among vet-erans of the Napoleonic Wars.[39] But it is nevertheless worth taking his description of the tears seriously if not literally as an indication of the potential strength of regimental loyalties. Eighty percent of soldiers served in only one regiment, providing ample time to form attach-ments to a regiment's history, tradition, and uniforms. Regiments deliberately constructed these loyalties as well, encouraging the cele-bration of the regiment's battle honors and fostering an atmosphere in which officers felt a paternal obligation to their men. One histo-rian has argued that regiment building "started below and was com-pleted above" as officers organized sporting events, built libraries and regimental schools, and even helped soldiers save money through regimental banks. The men reciprocated because they served the best years of their lives in the regiment, and regiments provided the kind of social and even familial relationships that sustained them, in addition to the nuclear relationship with their messmates.[40]

There was no naval equivalent to regimental loyalties. Ships decay rapidly in salt water, and, as the wars entered their third decade, no sailor could expect to be attached to the same ship for more than two or three years before being turned over to another while it underwent major repairs. What mattered in both services, but especially in the navy, were relationships with people rather than with units. Often this meant connections between officers and men. In the middle of the previous century, it had been common for sailors to be recruited by officers known to them in other contexts—for example, an officer from a mercantile family in Cornwall might be able to recruit effectively from Cornish merchant sailors. As the navy centralized its recruiting in the Impress Service and turned men over from one ship to another with increasing frequency during the Great Wars, these kinds of bonds weakened and became less common. Nevertheless, if a sailor and his messmates felt that they had found a captain who was lucky in prizes or who treated them fairly, they might try to follow him from ship to ship, and officers had some ability to influence those decisions. Demobilization might mean separating from a happy ship, by which sailors usually meant a trained and contented crew led by well-liked officers.[41]

But not all ships were happy, and not all soldiers were attached to their regiments. For some, military life was the opposite of family life. The army imposed what one historian has called a "social death" on its recruits to cause them to create new families in the service, but it did not always take. For these men, many of whom were married or responsible for supporting relatives financially, the regiment was the problem to be escaped rather than the family to be embraced.[42] Examining how men felt when they left their unit reveals the variety of experiences of military service and especially of demobilization. While messes provided the best opportunity to develop the strongest bonds, it is difficult to predict how an individual soldier or sailor might feel about larger units. What we find in studying demobilization, then, is a spectrum of attachment. At one extreme were men who, like William Long and Richard Greenhalgh, became isolated not only from their units but also their mess. Their morale cratered, and they were more likely to desert without waiting for demobilization. Leaving the service for them was like leaving prison—a comparison they made regularly.[iii] Greenhalgh told his parents after he had been separated from his messmates that he considered naval service to be a "floating Imprisonment."[43] Another sailor saw British warships as "gloomy dismal prisons," and one soldier referred to the end of his enlistment period as his "liberation."[44] Although most demoralized men remained in service until the end of the wars, they sought the swiftest possible route out of the army or navy. Even if they lacked prospects in civilian life, demobilization was a relief.

As we move along the spectrum, we find many men who formed strong bonds with their messmates but not with their units. For them, separation from military service was bittersweet because they left their mess but not because they held any particular affinity for their regiment or ship. Most of them did not consider life in the army or navy to be like prison, but they certainly looked forward to the freedom (a word they used frequently) that returning to civilian life afforded them. Given the variety of experiences it is dangerous to make sweeping claims, but from the evidence presented in memoirs, this group seems to have been the largest, especially as most sailors were in this group. They were eager (but not desperate) to go home; they were sad to leave their messmates; they were glad that the wars were over.

At the other extreme were men who formed strong bonds not only with their messmates but also with their units. For these men, many of whom were soldiers, leaving military service left them adrift, cut off from the community that had sustained them. Every aspect of leaving service, from their decision to leave through its consequences, was fraught. William Dawes's 1847 memoir *Jottings from My Sabretasch* described how he became "morose, moody, and discontented" as he contemplated his departure. He worried that if he did not leave, he would be "doomed to serve till all my energies became wasted, my constitution shattered, if not entirely broken, sent to the right-about

---

iii The comparison was most famously made by the lexicographer Dr. Samuel Johnson: "No man will be a sailor who has contrivance enough to get himself into a jail; for being in a ship is being in a jail, with the chance of being drowned." Boswell, *Life of Samuel Johnson*, 1:367–68. Elsewhere, however, Johnson demonstrated a better understanding of why men might volunteer for military service: it was exciting, he said, and it had the "dignity of danger." He also understood the importance of unit cohesion: "Soldiers consider themselves only as parts of a great machine." Boswell, *Dr. Johnson's Table Talk*, 126–27.

[discharged], as others had been, unfit for aught but to be stuck in a chimney corner [to] spin campaigning yarns." He decided he had to leave, although his officers tried halfheartedly to convince him to stay: "What, Sergeant-Major, is this true, you are going to leave us?" However, when the fateful day came, "I very soon became like a fish out of water, and sighed for activity. . . . *Ennui* was beginning to creep in, accompanied by a threatened attack of the 'blues.'" He returned to his hometown, but the war would not leave him. Every field and stream he crossed reminded him of "the identical spot on which a battle had been fought."[45]

To give himself a purpose, Dawes decided to get rid of the roots of a dead oak tree. He took advantage of his military training to shorten the job: he procured some explosives and tried to blow up the stump. His experience as a cavalryman proved to be less helpful with handling ordnance than he had hoped, and he bungled the job. When it exploded before he was ready, he adopted the position "resorted to when a shell is expected to explode near your carcass. . . . I believe the explosion gave rise to strange impressions amongst the village gossips and the unsophisticated; tongues wagged, and whisperings enunciated doubts as to the sanity of the person 'just returned from the army.'" Eventually he dug up the roots, but victory in the Battle of the Oak Stump left him once again adrift. He decided to visit his old regiment, and he immediately "felt more at home the few hours I remained inside the barrack walls than I had since I had left the service."[46]

Dawes's recollections are a useful example of attachment to military life, but we should not assume that his description of his emotions was representative of a large body of men. His memoir is also among the most processed of all those cited so far, and it is easy to read the story of the oak stump as an allegory for his struggle to leave his military service behind. Note also that his memoir was written twenty years after he left the army and more than thirty years after the wars ended. Modern readers undoubtedly see evidence of post–traumatic stress disorder (PTSD) in how he managed the emotions of departing from his regiment. Such a diagnosis was unavailable to him, so we should not retrospectively apply it; instead, he would have likely described how he was feeling as a form of nostalgia—a desire to rejoin his surrogate home—perhaps mixed with melancholia. Both were common diagnoses in the aftermath of the Napoleonic Wars. Nostalgia derives from the Greek *nostos*, which means homecoming. It is what Odysseus, the archetypal veteran, seeks throughout *The Odyssey*. Dawes's feeling of homelessness—he is at home only with his regiment—was and is another common condition of veteranhood. Not all who were nostalgic suffered from PTSD, but his recollections display an overwrought version of the competing emotional pressures that all soldiers and sailors experienced to some degree as they demobilized.[47]

Dawes's strong connection to his unit caused him to suffer from nostalgia, but the opposite was also possible. The anonymous soldier of the Seventy-First Foot certainly had no desire to remain with his regiment when he left in 1815—recall his claim that he would not have stayed in the army for a thousand pounds before he was shipped off to Belgium. After finally securing his discharge after Waterloo, his morale soared. But then he saw Scotland for the first time in years: "A sigh escaped me; recollections crowded upon me,—painful recollections." His parents had harbored dreams of him becoming a clergyman or a writer, but instead he had enlisted impulsively in 1806. When he screwed up enough courage to walk to Edinburgh to see his mother, he recalled: "Everything was strange to me, so many alterations had taken place; yet I was afraid to look any person in the face, lest he should recognize me. I was suffering as keenly, at this moment, as when I went away: I felt my face burning with shame." He found nobody he knew at his mother's last known address, but eventually they were reunited. Three years later, he wrote to a friend, still unsettled: "These three months, I can find nothing to do. I am a burden on Jeanie [his sister] and her husband. I wish I was a soldier again"—a shocking reversal of his feelings toward the army. Unable to find even laboring work, he decided to leave Scotland, perhaps for Spain or South America, to find some purpose.[48]

The act of separating from his unit, the experience of the journey home, and his situation upon arrival—all these factors shaped how a veteran felt about the coming peace, and every man's formula was slightly different. Wounded soldiers, for example, endured a different experience of demobilization than their comrades. In being separated from their units on the battlefield or in a hospital, they lost the control that they had hoped to exercise over the process of separation. The journey home was often especially uncomfortable. John Lowe had taken grape shot under his ribs at Waterloo and had been left for dead on the field for the entire night and day after the battle before being rescued by two Hanoverians. He rode a cart to a hospital in Brussels, then bounced along the road to the coast, followed by a Channel crossing and a ride in another bumpy cart to his regiment's depot.[49]

Similarly, Sergeant Thomas Jackson of the Coldstream Guards had lost his leg in the failed assault on Bergen-op-Zoom. He was carried on stretchers into the hold of a transport, where, along with a "gallant band of legless, armless, and others something else less, about a hundred in number," he endured a gale on the journey home. To complete the indignity, the ship's cook accidentally dumped hot water down the hatch and onto him. Eventually his band of wounded brothers traveled up the Thames to London by barge, and Jackson guessed how it might have looked:

> What a woful [*sic*] and miserable spectacle must we, the occupants of the barge, have presented to the view of the lookers on, from either sides of the river: some laying this way, and some that; some sitting; some lounging in any form to find small ease from their pains; many of them exhibiting the bandages, like mine, of their stump legs; others with their bandaged arms, off by the shoulders; others of body wounds, having their coats slung by the neck; and again, others, to whom the shot had no respect, with their faces or heads strapped in crossings of sticking plaster. This, I thought, must have been an appalling sight indeed, to the kind hearted and sensitive Londoners.[50]

Passing under London Bridge, the bargemaster told them to give three cheers: "The men, all struck with amazement, turned their eyes to look, but their only response was a low, surly growl."[51] Thus did British soldiers greet the horrible peace.

CHAPTER 10

Soldiers and Sailors at Home

It is difficult to overstate the severity of the climate and economic crisis of the years between Waterloo and Peterloo. On the same 1816 trip in which Mary Shelley wrote *Frankenstein*, Lord Byron wrote "Darkness": "I had a dream, which was not at all a dream," it begins. The sun was extinguished, men burned their houses for firewood, and the only people who were happy lived "within the eye / Of the volcanos." The irony of this line was lost on Byron because Europeans did not know that Tambora was the cause, but its effects were clear, as the poem continues:

> And War, which for a moment was no more,
> Did glut himself again: a meal was bought
> With blood, and each sate sullenly apart
> Gorging himself in gloom: no love was left;
> All earth was but one thought—and that was death
> Immediate and inglorious; and the pang
> Of famine fed upon all entrails—men
> Died, and their bones were tombless as their flesh;

"Ships sailorless lay rotting on the sea," it concludes. "And the clouds perish'd; Darkness had no need / Of aid from them—She was the Universe."[1]

Byron focused on the darkness caused by the volcanic ash, but that was just one aspect of the postwar malaise. Demobilization combined with the climate catastrophe to cause widespread unemployment, scarcity, famine, and, in Ireland, a typhus epidemic. In Britain, one observer noted in 1816 that "many military have returned to us of late, who have necessarily increased the want of labour."[2] A circular from the Board of Agriculture that year asked landowners to assess the "state of the labouring poor" in their counties. The vast majority of respondents—237 out of 273—described high unemployment, and more than a hundred used phrases like "extreme distress" and "great misery and wretchedness." The collapse in postwar prices caused agricultural communities to suffer major disruptions. Farmers in some areas laid off workers even in summertime, which was normally the time of greatest employment opportunities.[3]

The homecomings described in the previous chapter took place in that context, but that chapter only scratched the surface of what it was like to return home from the wars. This chapter extends the story. Not only did returning veterans have to overcome the challenges of the postwar depression, but they also had to navigate the military bureaucracy to secure pensions and prize money. In some ways, they were fortunate in that they had access to support that civilians did not, but that is not to say that the military's support for veterans was generous.

The first question facing many men on their homecoming was whether their loved ones were alive. William Long worried that his mother's failure to respond to his letters indicated that she was dead: "Dear mother I am sorry to think you have forgot me now it's peace. I have sent you three letters and no answer from you. I never was disappointed before. I hope you are not dead. I expected to have been dead before."[4] Edward Costello related a story of a sergeant who arrived in Portsmouth after eleven years away to find that his wife, operating under the assumption that he was dead, had married a carpenter and had several children. The eldest, ten years old, was the spitting image of the sergeant, so he presented the girl with a guinea, demanded sixpence from the carpenter, and went to the pub, "[strutting] up the street as if nothing whatever had annoyed him."[5] Costello's story reads like a tall tale, and indeed it slots nicely into a particular genre of story that circulated toward the end of the wars.

The Naval Chronicle passed on a story of a sailor who had remitted half of his pay to his wife for four years, but when the pay stopped coming, the wife assumed he had died, so she remarried. After her second husband died, she was penniless and had to give up her son to the workhouse. In August 1814, she went to a pub to beg, where she met her first husband, who claimed he had been looking for her. After a tearful reunion, they recovered their son from the workhouse and began to piece their lives back together.[6] The particular veracity of these stories is irrelevant—they reflect instead broader concerns on the part of both men and women that their spouses had run off with someone else. It had been a long war.

About a quarter of all soldiers and sailors were married. Correspondence between spouses reveals that both sides worried about the other, particularly as women assumed substantially greater household responsibilities while their husbands were away. Among the officer class, women became responsible for paying rent and taxes, handling repairs and moving expenses, sending children to school, paying servants, and sometimes sending washing and clothing to their deployed husbands. Lower down the social scale, women existed in what one historian has called a "shadowy underworld," most notably in port towns, where they struggled to make ends meet. They might take in washing or help with the harvest or buy and sell common household goods to try to eke out enough to feed their families. It was not uncommon to find sailors' wives moving from parish to parish seeking poor relief and in some cases resorting to prostitution.[7]

As mentioned earlier, the military undertook several initiatives aimed at alleviating the plight of soldiers' and sailors' families while they were serving. The army educated two thousand children of soldiers at the Royal Military Asylum from 1803 to 1815. While undoubtedly helpful for those children and their families, it was never large enough to make more than a marginal difference. In contrast, a 1795 Act of Parliament allowed noncommissioned officers, private soldiers, and seamen to send and receive single letters for one penny. Although initially only those stationed in the British Isles were eligible, the post office extended the penny post concession first in 1806 and then again in 1811 to anywhere that the official packet service operated, which in practice meant everywhere except India. The concession was a real saving—in 1813, it would otherwise have cost 10 pence to send a letter from London to Liverpool—and literacy rates were high. The most recent estimate is that 62 percent of all sailors were literate, and those who were not often asked their literate messmates to act as their scribes. Also in 1795, Parliament passed the Seamen's Family Act, which allowed sailors to remit half of their pay to designated relatives. Slightly more than one in five sailors took advantage, on average, which when combined with the regularity by which they wrote home suggests that many sailors were committed family men. By the end of the wars, soldiers and sailors were in more regular contact with their wives, mothers, and other relatives back home than ever before.[8]

A ship arriving into port was one of the great sights of the age of sail. It was also common: compared with soldiers, sailors had been coming back to Britain regularly throughout the wars, and the demobilization period simply accelerated the regular pattern of worn-out ships returning to Plymouth, Portsmouth, and the dockyards of the Thames and Medway. During the wars, if the ship was due to be sent back to the fleet, or if the crew were to be turned over to another ship ready to sail, the sight of the ship returning was the cue for that "shadowy underworld" to come into the sunlight. Swarms of "bumboats" would come alongside to offer sailors food, tobacco, clothing, trinkets, and prostitutes. The extent to which the prostitutes or wives were allowed on board, or the men allowed shore leave, varied based on the command styles of the officers and the circumstances of the arrival in port, but it was universally remarked that the gun deck of a ship of the line in port was no place for the innocent. A day or two before the ship sailed again, the crew would be paid, and they would settle their debts with the prostitutes and boatmen.[9]

When ships were paid off, as was the case for most of the ships returning to port in 1814 and 1815, the same scenes took place ashore. In lieu of coins, the men were usually given a ticket to collect their pay from a nearby pay office. It was usually in the family's best interest for the sailor's wife or mother to be there to meet him. Even if a fifth of all sailors had been remitting half their pay home, in general, sailors had a well-earned reputation for profligacy. Substantial portions of the economy of a port town were devoted to separating them from their money. Sailors' pay tickets and prize money could be sold at a discount for ready cash, and many men were eager to

feel the weight of metal in their pockets as they sought out the pleasures of life outside the navy. An 1824 pamphlet estimated that there
were twenty thousand prostitutes in Portsmouth (population sixty
thousand), and while that was an exaggeration, the census shows that
there were almost five thousand more women than men in Portsmouth and Portsea in the postwar period.[10]

The return of the fleet and the army was soon followed by outbreaks of venereal disease and eventually an increase in abandoned
children. It was also followed by an increase in crime. The addition of
the climate calamity of 1816 to the usual end-of-war turmoil resulted
in a larger crime wave than normal. According to a parliamentary
study, across Britain, 4,025 trials resulted in convictions and prison
sentences in 1814; in 1817, the number of convictions had more than
doubled to 9,056, and it was even higher in 1819. A typical example
of the relationship between demobilization and crime can be found
in the 1816 case of Ann Jones, who traveled to London to collect
prize money for her dead husband. By the time she arrived, she had
only one penny in her pocket, so she decided to steal two sheets and a
coat from John Wilson Croker, the secretary to the Admiralty.[11]

Crimes of poverty and necessity were the most common, but
assaults also spiked in the postwar period. One modern study looked
at the pattern of demobilization across the eighteenth century in
Portsmouth and found an increase in spousal violence during every
demobilization. The authors concluded that the spike in marital violence could be attributed to "husbands brutalized by war and by their
officers."[12] That seems to be a reasonable conclusion, and clearly soldiers and sailors faced challenges in adjusting to civilian life. On the
other hand, another recent account suggests that we should be surprised that demobilized soldiers and sailors were not more violent,
particularly because the army had a culture of "ostentatious woman-
izing."[13] Whether crime was higher or lower than our expectations,
it was certainly higher than the normal early nineteenth-century
baseline, and contemporaries noticed.

Many homecoming stories had happy endings, however. Robert
Hay had run away to sea at age fourteen, and when he finally returned
home eight years later, he planned his homecoming with a kind of
naïve enthusiasm that stands in contrast to stories of theft and spousal
abuse. Instead of going straight home when he arrived in his village,

he took a room in the pub. The next morning, he woke up early and went to his mother's house, as he later recalled: "I stood some time at the end of the street, and feasted my eyes with scenes that youthful familiarity had rendered dear to me." Still he did not go in but instead returned to the pub to write a letter to his brother, explaining what was happening and asking him to pretend not to know who he was. Then he went to his mother's house and claimed to be a friend of Robert Hay. He gave her the letter, but she was on to him: "Natural affection had begun to work on her from the moment she first saw me." Yet even when his mother accused him of being her son, he continued to play dumb, and when his brother tried to hold up his end of the practical joke, it only made matters worse. Eventually Hay found himself trying to convince his brother that he was who he said he was, all while his mother had seen right through his ploy.[14]

Hay's farce was soon forgotten, and he "indulged freely in those exquisite joys that are experienced in near and dear relations after a long separation." But like many other veterans, once the initial burst of homecoming excitement subsided, he struggled to figure out the next steps. He recalled, "After being so long accustomed to an active life, I could not think of applying myself again to the sedentary business of the loom"—the family business from which he had run away in the first place. Hay had volunteered for the navy as a landsman, but now he was an experienced sailor. Like many others whom the navy had trained for the sea, he decided that his peacetime career would also be maritime. What was unusual about Hay is that while many of his fellow sailors looked for work in merchant ships, he chose to go to school to learn navigation. His mother agreed to help him because she thought it was preferable to letting him go back to sea again. Soon Hay was a steersman on the Androssan Canal, and then he became clerk and storekeeper for the canal company. He married in June 1816 and wrote the narrative of his adventures at sea in 1821 for the benefit of his children.[15]

At the same time Hay was writing his memoir, John Nicol was struggling to find enough food to eat on the streets of Edinburgh. Nicol had spent twenty-five years at sea across the American and French Revolutionary Wars, and his story reveals how sailors might have felt about leaving naval service and the challenges they faced on setting up a new life. When his ship was paid off during the Peace of Amiens, he journeyed to London for "a few days of enjoyment," before putting all that he had saved in a chest except for nine guineas, "which I kept upon my person to provide for squalls"—not all sailors were profligate.[16] Nicol admitted that he felt the need to make the most of his freedom: "I was once more my own master, and felt so happy I was like one bewildered. Did those on shore only experience half the sensations of a sailor at perfect liberty after being seven years on board ship without a will of his own, they would not blame his eccentricities but wonder he was not more foolish." Soon, however, his "cooler reason" took over, and he began to plan life after the navy. He arrived back in Edinburgh, which he had visited only twice in the twenty-five years since he had gone to sea. As a result, he recalled, "Everything was new to me." He knew nobody and it made him miserable: "I felt myself, for a few weeks after my arrival, not so very happy. As I had anticipated, there was scarcely a friend I had left that I knew again. The old were dead, the young had grown up to manhood and many were in foreign climes. . . . I could not settle to work but wandered up and down."[17]

When the wars began again in 1803, Nicol moved inland to escape the press gangs. He married his cousin and got a job on an estate, and all seemed to be going well. But when his wife died, he learned that she had spent more than they had taken in, and he was forced to sell all his property except for one small room (in his memoir, he does not provide the details of what happened). In 1818, his cousin gave him enough money to go to London so that he could ask the government for a pension. When he arrived, he learned that his old captain had died just six weeks prior. With no support, he was at the mercy of the naval bureaucracy: "I left [the captain's] house, my spirits sunk with grief for his death and my own disappointment, as my chief dependence was upon his aid." At Somerset House, he presented the Navy Board with certificates of his service in the American and French Revolutionary Wars, but they sent him to the Admiralty. The clerk there told him he had waited too long to apply, so he went to Greenwich Hospital: "I was not acquainted with him, but I knew the Governor of Greenwich would be a distressed seaman's friend." The governor was not home, nor was another officer whose son's life he had saved. Dispirited, he returned to Scotland.[18]

There in the winter of 1822 he came to the attention of the polymath and publisher John Howell. Howell took pity on him and encouraged him to dictate his memoir. Nicol described his daily diet at that time as leftover bread from the bakers, a few potatoes, and occasionally some tobacco. He perceived pensions as the last resort before throwing himself at the mercy of his parish: "Could I have obtained a small pension for my past services, I should then have reached my utmost earthly wish and the approach of utter helplessness would not haunt me as it at present does in my solitary home. . . . I can look to my death bed with resignation but to the poor's house I cannot look with composure." Nicol's story had a happy ending because Howell's publication of the memoir sold well enough that Nicol was able to leave £30 to his relatives on his death in 1825.[19]

Not all sailors could publish memoirs to make ends meet, however, so of interest for this chapter is Nicol's interaction with the postwar military and naval administration. What to do about old soldiers and sailors was a common topic of discussion as the wars wound down. *The Naval Chronicle* published an editorial on demobilization in the spring of 1814, noting that "thousands of veteran seamen will be discharged, with, perhaps, very slender resources, and no prospects of immediate employ." It argued that such men should be employed for national security reasons. Recalling the experience of men like Nicol who had been discharged in 1802, the editorial claimed that "thousands of those valuable men, abandoned by an ungrateful country, were driven by want to seek their bread in America; and, it is to be feared, they pointed the guns that caused the flag of the United States to float above that of Britain." The solution, it argued, was to make sure that the hundreds of ships that were being put into ordinary should be cared for by able seamen rather than the usual assortment of casual laborers and watermen drawn from near the dockyards. That way valuable sailors would have gainful employment in the peace and be available to serve again in the event of another war.[20]

As we know, the Admiralty did not adopt any such scheme, nor does there seem to be any significant connection between the demobilization of 1802 and the emergence of the U.S. Navy as an effective fighting force in 1812—but when have facts ever stood in the way of a good editorial? The underlying issue that the *Chronicle* identified was important: what was the state's responsibility to the thousands of men who had helped it win the war? It was not a new question. The first military pensions in Britain date from the early seventeenth century, when the Poor Laws provided for small quarterly pensions of a few pence per week for disabled veteran soldiers and sailors. Charles II founded the Royal Hospital, Chelsea, in 1682 to house 472 veteran soldiers and provide pensions of five pence per day for out-pensioners—that is, nonresident veteran soldiers. William III established Greenwich Hospital in 1694 to support naval seamen who "by reason of Age, Wounds or other disabilities shall be uncapable of further Service at Sea," per the Royal Warrant. It also operated with a small number of resident pensioners—a few hundred in the early years—and a larger number of out-pensioners. Both hospitals were explicitly created to aid military recruitment and retention. Across the long eighteenth century, then, the state's answer to the question was that it had a responsibility to provide some support for those who had served in its military forces and become disabled, but it did so primarily so that others would be willing to make the same sacrifices. Pensions survived in a political climate that had no interest in providing handouts to the poor because they had a clearly defined military purpose.[21] Veterans were therefore a class of "deserving poor."[22]

Well, not all veterans. Greenwich gave pensions only to disabled sailors—that is, men who were no longer able to serve because of wounds or illnesses received in the line of duty. There were exceptions right from the start, as some merchant sailors and dockyard workers received pensions in the early eighteenth century, but in general, naval pensions required proof of service and proof that the service had worn the sailor out. That applied to a smaller percentage of sailors than it did to soldiers, not because one service was more difficult, but because of the fluid nature of naval service. Most sailors were young men in their early twenties, and they moved between merchant and naval ships as conditions, pay, and press gangs allowed. They joined or were pressed into the navy for the duration of the war, and they had rare but periodic opportunities to escape naval service as their ships were paid off. Sailors had a marketable skill and no commitment to the navy after the wars ended.[23]

Soldiers, on the other hand, enlisted for life and became eligible for pensions after a period of time served, usually twenty-one years.

Even the wartime expedient "short-service" men who enlisted for defined periods (usually seven years) were eligible for a pension if they continued in the army for fourteen years. There were also credits toward time served applicable to those who had deployed to the East or West Indies and those who were present at Waterloo. Even including discounts, it was common for soldiers to spend twenty and or even thirty years in the army. Those who survived the rigors of campaigns and the perils of disease left the army when they were invalided out by a medical board, by which time they were middle-aged and more likely to have suffered some sort of debilitating wound or illness. As a result, pensions were more common for soldiers than sailors.[24]

The numbers bear this out. Greenwich Hospital added 21,260 new out-pensioners from 1814 to 1820, which grew the total number of out-pensioners to about 30,000 in 1820. In addition, there were 2,700 resident pensioners in 1815. A recent estimate is that 240,000 men served in the navy during the Great Wars, which suggests that Greenwich served less than 15 percent of all sailors. In contrast, Chelsea Hospital was responsible for 80,000 out-pensioners in 1823, growing to 86,000 by 1828.[25]

In addition to the differences in soldiers' and sailors' career patterns, two other factors depressed pension numbers. For the army, a good service record was essential: a study of Chelsea pensioners from the first half of the eighteenth century found zero cases of flogging among twenty-five thousand successful pension applications. On the naval side, each pension was decided individually by a medical board. One might get £12 per year for a lost leg, another might get nothing, and a third might be one of the lucky few to be given a place as a resident pensioner—but there was no way of knowing in advance. Not until 1831 were out-pensions granted at Greenwich according to a set schedule to all comers for any wounds or illnesses that caused them to be discharged from naval service. As a result, most of the sailors who came home from service in the Napoleonic Wars did not receive a pension.[26]

Nevertheless, it is worthwhile to trace the experiences of both soldiers and sailors as they did battle with the military bureaucracy to secure their pay, prize money, and, in some cases, a pension. Winning such battles required persistence and good record keeping. Men like Nicol who had lost contact with the vital patronage networks that oiled the system's gears were at a particular disadvantage. The first challenge for a sailor was getting the pay and prize money due to him. The former was relatively straightforward, so long as he could avoid the temptations of port and make his way to the pay office with his ticket; the latter, however, was often a fraught and drawn-out process. Not only did any prizes captured have to wind their way through the courts, but unscrupulous officers and agents might take advantage of their familiarity with the system to rip off unsuspecting sailors. Jacob Nagle, for example, was cheated out of prize money by one of his former lieutenants and was forced to sue to get it back: he won the case but spent all his prize money on lawyers.[27]

Soldiers received prize money as well, and while the process in the army was also subject to delays, there were (generally speaking) fewer legal uncertainties. Instead, soldiers fixated on questions of fairness. In January 1814 Parliament awarded £800,000 to be distributed to the troops who had served in the Peninsular War, which was divided into six periods. The more periods in which a soldier had served, the more he received, but higher ranks took much larger shares; at the top, the Duke of Wellington received 1,716 shares, or £50,000. John Jones of the Thirty-Ninth Regiment thought this was absurd, particularly as the rumor he heard was that the duke was entitled to much more than that: "Whether the good people of England considered the Field Marshal's life worth 10,000 private soldiers' lives, I know not." In the end, the average payout to the rank and file was about £6, at least according to Jones, who received compensation for four periods of the war.[28]

Records of service and good conduct were essential ammunition for the bureaucratic battles. Service records were preprinted forms that included dates served, in the case of the navy, and additional information about regimental accounts, in the case of the army. They also might include a description of the man's appearance. Careful, literate soldiers like Thomas Jackson made sure to check their discharge papers for discrepancies before they signed them. He noticed that his was missing accounts of back pay and clothing allowances that he was owed (he had kept his own accounts). He refused to sign it, which created annoying administrative friction but saved him from losing the money. It was common for soldiers like Jackson to supplement their discharge papers with attestations of their good conduct from an officer in the regiment. Sailor James Durand's discharge papers included the ships on which he had served, the relevant dates, and a closing recommendation: "during which time he conducted himself with sobriety and attention and was always obedient to commands."[29]

Durand never did receive a pension for his wounds, although that had more to do with the fact that he was an American than with his paperwork or his conduct. He had been pressed out of a merchant ship in 1809; six years later he was discharged, but even though the fleet was no longer engaged in active operations, he thought the threat of being pressed again was so high that he chose to go to the American consul in London to get an updated protection from the press rather than to Greenwich to get his pension. Since his protection had failed to work the first time, he decided it was best not to linger. He hustled to join a ship sailing for New York, and he left in such a hurry that he was forced to abandon £20 (perhaps half a year's pay) in Plymouth. Other impediments to receiving pensions, besides being an American, included ever having run from a ship or being unable to produce letters of support from a captain. William Thorpe had been listed as run in the muster books of the *Unicorn*, so he was denied a pension. His very legitimate excuse was that he had been attending his father's funeral, but it failed to sway the board.[30]

It was common to see disabled seamen around port towns and London. Billy Waters, a Black American who had lost his leg falling from the tops of the *Ganymede* in 1812, became well-known as a fiddler and busker, but eventually he ended up dying in a workhouse in 1823. Joseph Johnson was another Black sailor who, as one 1817 description of him was quick to note, had not served in the navy and was therefore disqualified from the full benefits of a Greenwich pension. He carved out a home on London's streets by singing ballads. He was best-known for a ballad about a ship in a storm, which he sang while wearing a model of a ship, called the *Nelson*, on his head. Ex-sailors like Johnson and Waters were famous and distinctive, but like the rest of the urban poor, they had to rely on the usual sources of parish relief and their own wits. It should be emphasized, however, that most sailors did not receive pensions after 1815 simply because they did not apply for one. The average Greenwich pensioner was fifty-six years old and had spent just under twenty years in the navy. Contrast that profile with Robert

Hay, who served for eight years and left the navy at age twenty-two: it was not worth his time to apply for a pension. Not only was he unlikely to get one, but also, he was unlikely to need one.[31]

Soldiers usually did apply. A common experience for soldiers was to be invalided home while serving abroad. Their regimental surgeon deemed them unfit, or perhaps when their enlistment periods expired, they chose not to reenlist. In such cases, they would receive a free voyage home plus two weeks' pay to reach their hometown (Scottish and Irish soldiers received a month's pay). On their journey, most made sure to stop in London to apply for a pension. The Commissioners of Chelsea Hospital met regularly, usually once or twice per month. After presenting his discharge papers to the board, an agent from his regiment had to verify the handwriting of the officer who had signed the papers. The soldier was then examined by the hospital's own surgeon to confirm the regimental surgeon's opinion that he was unfit for future service.[32]

At the heart of much of the postwar administrative angst were questions of entitlement. Soldiers saw pensions as their right, to provide for a secure livelihood as a reward for services rendered. In contrast, the War Office saw them, as Palmerston put it, as "a retaining fee for future services."[33] We met Rifleman Benjamin Harris in the last chapter, who suffered from Walcheren fever. He learned of the strings attached to pensions the hard way. After being discharged from a veteran battalion following peace in 1814, he received a pension of sixpence per day. He recalled, "Before, however, my pension became due, I was again called upon to attend, together with others, in consequence of the escape of Bonaparte from Elba; but I was then in so miserable a plight with the remains of the fever and ague, which still attacked me every other day, that I did not answer the call, whereby I lost my pension."[34]

In his memoir, Harris also described what it was like to be in Chelsea in 1814: "We met thousands of soldiers lining the streets, and lounging about before the different public-houses, with every description of wound and casualty incident to modern warfare. There hobbled the maimed light-infantry man, the heavy dragoon, the hussar, the artillery-man, the fusilier, and specimens from every regiment in the service. . . . Such were Chelsea and Pimlico in 1814."[35] Some were there to pick up their quarterly pension payments; others were hoping to go before the Board of Commissioners of the Hospital to get out-pensions or, even better, status as a resident pensioner. When Sergeant Robert Butler arrived back at Chelsea in August 1814 after seven years deployed to India, he recalled that it was "completely crowded with invalids from the Continent, besides those from India. . . . This promised very badly with regard to pensions, and upon the 14th of September, the day on which I passed, there were several hundreds who did not get a penny." Butler got ninepence per day, which did not impress him much: it was "but a small recompense for all my hardships, and their bad effects upon my constitution."[36]

The two hospitals saw all types of soldiers and sailors, but the evidence from memoirs suggests that few who "passed the board," as it was called, emerged happy with the result. John Lowe survived his bumpy journey home after being wounded at Waterloo. He was discharged after eleven years and four months in the Rifles, but since he had been at Waterloo, he received two bonus years. Sir David Dundas, the governor of Chelsea Hospital, remarked in his hearing that Lowe was "a more than usually healthy looking invalid," even though Lowe had recently been left for dead on the field. Lowe later blamed his relatively strong appearance for the meagerness of his pension, and he enlisted the help of a clergyman to write an elaborate pamphlet pleading his case for a more generous entitlement.[37]

Pensions ranged from a minimum of about fivepence per day (£7 12s 1d per year) to a maximum of two shillings per day (£36 10s per year), with most receiving between sixpence and a shilling per day (roughly £9 to £18 per year). Only the most generous pensions would have been sufficient to live on: a merchant seaman in this period could expect to earn about £40 per year, and an agricultural laborer might get by on £31 annually. (Officers, it need hardly be said, received substantially greater pensions: Lieutenants James Henry Garrety and William Bateman Dashwood were both awarded £200 annually for losing their arms.) Pensions were distributed quarterly, usually at the nearest excise office in a medium-sized town. Discharged soldiers had the right to work anywhere in the country, and receiving an out-pension did not disqualify them from receiving other forms of relief, although for poor relief, they had to return to their parish of settlement. Parishes could collect pensions on their behalf, which meant some ex-soldiers used their parishes as a kind of bank. It was also another reason why many soldiers returned to their hometowns. One study of Scottish pensioners found that most returned to the district where they had enlisted, usually an urban area, and only 17 percent subsequently moved. If they did, they were required to inform the hospital of their change of address.[38]

Despite soldiers' expectations, the pension scheme was not intended to provide a replacement for a soldier's income but rather just enough to keep him from becoming a pauper and therefore a burden on the Poor Laws.[39] This compromise suited few soldiers. Edward Costello was so unhappy with his pension of sixpence per day that he put on his uniform and accosted Dundas at his official house. Dundas was unimpressed: he "coolly handed the note over his shoulders to me, remarking at the same moment, that he dared say the Lords Commissioners of Chelsea had given me what they thought I deserved." Costello concluded that Dundas was too much of a Spartan to act generously: "Like the two survivors of Thermopilae [sic], he thought my return to England highly inglorious, and unbefitting a soldier; since it had made me a sixpenny burthen on the country I had served." Costello next applied to the Patriotic Fund, which awarded single payments for wounded soldiers. But here again he was rebuffed by the secretary: "Damn it, Sir! Did you expect to fight with puddings or Norfolk dumplings? If men go to battle, what else can they expect but wounds!" Concluding that "begging was out of the question—a *soldier* could not beg," he found a stick and vowed to use it to rob the first person he saw. That person turned out to be an old soldier from his regiment, who instead put him up for the night. He later visited another old officer who fed him and wrote a letter on his behalf to increase the chances that he would find either employment or better luck with the pension boards.[40]

Pensions were particularly valuable for wounded soldiers who were incapable of work. When Butler returned home, he recalled: "I tried my old occupation of working at the loom; but I was compelled to leave it off, as this employment would not agree with my constitution, being much afflicted with a pain in the breast, and a giddiness in my head; which were truly distressing."[41] Jackson's leg continued to bother him for years after the wars. He received a knee crutch free of charge—he referred to it as "this new appendage of Chelsea"—and admitted that he should feel more grateful for his "trophy of war, which I had won by my deeds of arms." But he was embarrassed and disgusted with his appearance while wearing it and considered himself an outcast in society. He resented those who were still able to "dash through the forest jungle" because now he was "cut down in his bloom; humbled, dejected, dispirited; logged by the leg for life to an ugly, odious piece of timber." Eventually he decided he had no choice but to make the best of it, so he returned home to Staffordshire, optimistic that he could make ends meet for himself, his aged parents, and his wife on a shilling per day. The economic crisis intervened, however, and for much of 1816 and 1817 he was unemployed and suffering "with provisions ranging very high at that time." His skill with accounting eventually saved him—remember Jackson was the soldier who questioned the accounts on his discharge paperwork—and he got a job through his cousin as a clerk of a merchant in the coal business. "I had been used a good deal to military books, with all their intricacies," he claimed, so the accounts of a merchant were comparatively simple. His new salary of two shillings seven pence per day, plus his pension and free fuel from his boss, finally gave him some financial security.[42]

What mattered as much as, and sometimes more than, the absolute amount of a pension was its perceived fairness. Just as Jones complained about Wellington's share of Peninsular prize money, the wonderfully named Alexander Alexander, a Scottish artilleryman, complained about his pension before he had even received it. He expected to get one shilling per day but said that even that would be less than some men he had served with, some of whom had been flogged more than once: "After four years more service, to get just the same pension as these privates I could not think equal justice." In the end he received only ninepence per day, which further damaged his morale, but of course ninepence was better than nothing: "I had nothing to look to until the first of July [1815], when I would draw my once despised pension of ninepence per day. In my extreme distress I had applied in vain for its augmentation. I was now literally starving. Day after day my diet was sour ammunition bread, bought at the Tower, and coffee without either sugar or milk; a halfpenny worth of radishes was many a day all the dinner I had."[43]

Further examples of soldiers embittered and impoverished by their meager pensions are not necessary to make the point that many soldiers complained about both the relative and absolute amount of their pensions, and they sought redress, usually unsuccessfully. It is important not to carry the argument too far because the memoirs from which these stories are drawn are more likely to include complaints than celebrations of the bounty issued by Greenwich and Chelsea. Many of the memoirs were written expressly to secure a better pension or to sell well enough to compensate for their meager pensions, as we saw with John Nicol and John Lowe. There are also hints in the memoir literature that some veterans were generally pleased with their pensions, or at least they treated their pension as it was designed, as a supplement to an otherwise stable income. Benjamin Miller returned to his hometown after his discharge in 1815, and it was reported that for the next fifty years until his death in 1865, "he and other old soldiers, drawing pensions, used to hire a cart and drive to Yeovil once a quarter to receive their money. They always returned in merry condition."[44] William Surtees extended a special thanks to Palmerston in his memoir, because Palmerston had introduced a bill in 1826 that allowed quartermasters like himself to retire with full pay after twenty, rather than thirty, years. Surtees happily took up the offer and as a result enjoyed a relatively comfortable retirement.[45]

Nevertheless, the prevailing sentiment expressed by the men who experienced demobilization and came home was one of mismatched expectations. We can see stark evidence of this in Thomas Jackson's memoir, in which he juxtaposed a popular song with the reality of his new life. Called "Jolly Old Farmer" or "The Wounded Soldier," for Jackson it showed what homecoming should have been like. It tells the story of a farmer who sees a lame old soldier walking by his farm. The farmer offers him food and drink and encourages him to tell his war stories. Here is the last verse:

> Now the soldier refreshed, once more he revives,
> And begins of those days o'er to tell;
> How many brave comrades of his lost their lives,
> And how they all gloriously fell.
> "Huzza!" said the farmer, "it ne'er shall be said,
> My heart don't with feeling expand;
> This brave fellow shall ne'er want a morsel of bread,
> For he is one who has guarded our land."[46]

The last line is the refrain—for he is one who has guarded our land. Jackson contrasted the farmer's hospitality with the ways in which the "unwashed" in his hometown gaped at him and his stump: "'Ho's he?' Another answered, 'Why don't yo know him? He's young Jackson, as went into the militia, and then he must volunteer to go and see war, and they'n sarved him out for it.' 'Serves him right,' says another, 'he had no business there.'"[47] Jackson's dismissive classism aside, he shows us that one of the primary challenges for veterans was coming to terms with their lofty expectations for peace and the grim reality of postwar Britain. The particular accuracy of his account (the dialogue is suspiciously on the nose) matters less than his sense that he was perceived as an outcast.

We saw in the last chapter how many soldiers and sailors longed for peace to see their loved ones, to escape military service, or to start a new life. When peace finally came, for many men, it did not live up to its billing, and the false start of 1814 made matters significantly worse. Amid the chaos of redeployments and a war on two fronts, veterans struggled to locate loved ones, adjust to a new life at home, and transition to a world outside the military. Since pensions were designed only to keep them from begging, they did not enter the depressed postwar labor market with much financial security. Many (although not all) responded by fighting for better pensions: they drew on their network of military and social contacts as best they could, they petitioned the hospitals, and they sought charitable support. Mostly, they were unsuccessful. Demobilization proved to be one of the most important and one of the most challenging periods of their lives.

Indeed, Jackson's favorite song painted an unusually rosy picture of postwar Britain. More common were ballads like "A New Song Composed by the Wounded Tars," from 1801: "All you that relieve us the Lord will you bless / For relieving poor sailors in times of distress." Another along similar lines was called "The Seaflower," and it too expressed thanks to those who provided charity to begging sailors: "But by hard fortune you plainly see / We lost our limbs on the raging sea. / All you who extend your charity, / The Lord preserve your family." A song called "The British Tars" took a slightly different tack, warning men not to go to sea in the first place: "For I have ploughed the raging main this twenty years or more, / But now I'm turned adrift to starve upon my native shore."[48] The last line was the refrain, and it reflects the widespread disappointment felt by soldiers and sailors when they came home.

And yet, it is also not altogether accurate. Soldiers were not turned adrift, and in fact they received more direct support from the government than any other group of working poor. It is true that pensions were meager, but it is also true that they were better than nothing at all. That is not to accuse the soldiers quoted in these two chapters of being ungrateful, but we do need to keep in mind that in the context of Britain in 1815, soldiers were among the rare group of "deserving poor." Sailors were turned adrift more so than soldiers, since naval pensions were less common, but on the other hand, sailors had a marketable skill. They did not need to starve if they could find work at sea. Whether they would be able to do so is the subject of the next chapter.

CHAPTER 11

Sailors on Strike

Demobilized sailors possessed a marketable skill, but was there a market for that skill after 1815? Or, put another way, what was the state of the merchant shipping industry during and after the wars?

There were three broad categories of merchant shipping: the coastal trade, including fishing vessels and colliers; the foreign trade; and whalers. About 40 percent of all vessels in 1790 were owned by an owner of multiple vessels, and that number was increasing over time as shipping companies consolidated. But compared to today, what stands out is the small scale of most merchant shipping operations and the wide variation in the size of ships. Vessels engaged in foreign trade were surprisingly small, usually less than 150 tons, and a seventy-ton vessel running to and from Portugal might have a crew of just six. At the other end of the spectrum, an early nineteenth-century East Indiaman would carry a few hundred crew and passengers in a hull displacing slightly more than a thousand tons (for comparison, the forty-four-gun frigate USS *Constitution* displaces just over two thousand tons). Many vessels specialized in a particular trade and ran regular routes, with lifespans of about ten to twelve years.[1]

Men were hired by the voyage. In coastal trades, sailors were generally discharged at the end of one leg so that owners did not have to pay labor costs in port, but often they would remain near the ship in the hopes of being employed on the return leg. In deep-sea trades, the crew would likely continue to be paid in port when abroad but discharged when home. One local historian in Hull complained of fifteen hundred men and boys raising a ruckus during the winter of 1788, "in open violation of decency, good order, and morality," before departing on whaling voyages in the spring.[2] Jacob Nagle was typical of many deep-sea sailors in that he returned from a lengthy overseas voyage and spent four months with his family and friends before wanderlust set in and he found his way to the nearest port to look for his next voyage. Another factor determining patterns of employment was simply whether the sailor had run out of money.[3]

Sailing was a young man's profession. A common career arc in merchant service was to learn the ropes—literally—in coasting vessels as a teenager before "graduating" to deep-sea sailing. Doing so made the sailor a prime target for the navy as well as merchant captains, so pay was highest for this group. It was also a dangerous and physically taxing existence. Careers for able seamen were short—usually ten years or so—both in the navy and merchant service, and unless the sailor learned a complementary trade like carpentry, it was common to see sailors beginning to settle down by the time they turned thirty. They might look to get married and start a family while transitioning back to coasters or to other maritime employment as boatmen, wherrymen, or (with training) shipwrights.[4]

The casual and episodic nature of merchant employment left sailors vulnerable to predators in port. Even Nagle, with more than three decades of experience, fell victim to a crimp who tried to con him into signing over power of attorney while preparing to join the crew of an East Indiaman in 1806. Crimps often ran sailors' boarding houses in port towns, and they liaised with shipowners to provide men for an agreed-upon fee. Sailors were often paid in advance to allow them to equip themselves for long voyages or to provide for their families, and crimps offered to ease the difficulty of finding a ship by guaranteeing sailors employment in exchange for some or all of their advance. In that sense, crimps were important middlemen in the maritime labor market, but unscrupulous crimps were commonly the subject of complaints from sailors. Crimping was not outlawed until 1880, which meant that negotiating the fluid labor market required a certain degree of paranoia and a good knowledge of the qualities of crimps, masters, and shipowners. Sailors voted with their feet and looked for voyages that suited their needs and experience, but during demobilization, they had fewer choices and had to make compromises (whether in wages, voyages, or otherwise) to gain employment.[5]

Men could be paid in one of three ways: at a fixed rate for the voyage, which was most common in coasters; with a share of the earnings, which was most common in whalers; or by the month, which was most common in long deep-sea voyages. Wartime wages were always substantially higher than peacetime wages because the labor market was tight. The onset of naval demobilization in 1814 caused wages to fall until they settled at an average rate of about forty-five to fifty shillings per month for an able seaman and thirty to thirty-five per month for an ordinary seaman. Those rates were comparable to prewar rates even though consumer prices kept falling at an annual rate of about 3 percent from 1813 to 1825—a product of the government's cuts. The likely explanation for the stickiness of merchant seamen's wages is that established conventions helped keep wages from completely collapsing. Those sailors lucky enough to find work were employed "at the going rate." There is no evidence that the spate of postwar strikes made much impact because, as we will see, shipowners were quick to cut wages back once the disturbance had passed.[6]

More than any other factor, the patterns of war and peace shaped the size of the labor pool and therefore the availability of jobs. During the Napoleonic Wars, the navy employed on average almost exactly the same number of men per year as merchant vessels. From 1803 to 1815, there were 122,396 men per year in merchant vessels and 123,622 per year across the same period in the navy. From 1816 to 1828, however, naval employment cratered to an annual average of 26,124, while merchant employment remained nearly static at 124,463. While such a calculation overlooks the important fluctuations of mobilization and demobilization, it allows us to calculate the navy's impact on the labor market. The merchant fleet did not grow rapidly enough to accommodate the influx of sailors. There were nearly 100,000 fewer jobs per year at sea in the decade following 1815 than there were in the decade before.[7]

Conditions on board merchant ships create two problems for historians: first, they defy easy characterization because they varied widely and depended on whether Britain was at war, the nature of the voyage, the state of the ship, the master, and the shipowner, among other factors; second, they are often compared to conditions in the navy and used to advance an argument about the relative evilness of impressment. If conditions in the navy were worse than conditions in merchant vessels, then impressment was even more evil than we thought; if conditions in the navy were better than conditions on merchant vessels, then impressment was an attack on sailors' liberty but perhaps not equivalent to a prison sentence with a chance of drowning.[8]

The onset of peace, however, allows us to set impressment aside because the practice was legal only in wartime. Speaking in general terms, sailors in the navy got better food, more regular pay, and opportunities for bounties and prize money. The workload in the navy was spread more widely because there were far more sailors per ship ton than in sparsely manned merchant ships; at the same time, naval officers were more likely to create work to keep men busy than merchant captains were. Naval vessels had surgeons, unlike most small merchant vessels, although naval service also came with a small chance of being killed in action. The major drawback of naval service was the lack of freedom, not only in wartime press gangs but also in the practice of turning men over from one ship to the next. Merchant sailors were better paid in both peace and war, but they lost portions of their pay to crimps and to penny-pinching shipowners who charged them for victuals and any damage to the cargo. Naturally merchant sailors had more freedom to choose their employers, but if they wanted to guarantee employment, they sacrificed much of that freedom to crimps. Merchant sailors also had some opportunities to earn money on the side, and while being allotted a small portion of the cargo for personal trading was not likely to yield the kinds of spectacular windfalls that made prize money so desirable, it was a way for merchant sailors to recoup some of the losses through friction with shipowners.[9]

All that matters because sailors understood these differences and made choices about where to seek employment based on personal preferences, but the market constrained the choices available to them. Although naval employment collapsed beginning in 1814, the navy remained the largest single employer in maritime Britain. It was also an all-volunteer force, and it was by no means out of the question for a sailor who was otherwise averse to naval service in wartime to consider a berth in the peacetime navy to be a particularly advantageous situation because it provided a regular source of wages. Another sailor might still find naval discipline and low pay not to his liking and decide instead to take his chances getting a berth in a collier.

In general, however, the navy's role in the postwar maritime labor market was to exacerbate the unemployment problem. In response to the navy's vacuuming up of qualified sailors during wartime, merchant captains had turned to foreigners as replacements or relied on men unfit for the navy such as old men and boys. They had also employed what one historian has called a "rag-bag of apprentices" with little seagoing experience, like the future Radical leader Samuel Bamford, who answered an advertisement in Manchester during the wars.[10] These groups regularly clashed when wars ended, and in anticipation, Parliament had passed a bill in 1794 stating that foreign sailors were to be excluded from employment in British merchant ships when the war ended. The problem was that the wars never seemed to end, and by 1815, there was a new group competing in the market that exacerbated the problem: landsmen who volunteered for naval service and had been trained by the navy to become experienced deep-sea sailors. These were men like Robert Hay, who, upon being demobilized, refused to return to the loom and instead sought employment afloat.[11]

To answer the question at the beginning of this chapter, then: there was not much of a market for sailors after the wars. Sailors expected as much because that had been true of all eighteenth-century wars, but the unemployment problem in 1815 was worse than ever before. The question facing sailors was what they should do about it.

In the middle of August 1815, a group of sailors on Tyneside petitioned the mayor of Newcastle asking him to prevent the employment of foreign sailors in the collier fleet while local sailors were out of work. The sailors cited the 1794 precedent and pointed out that the wars were over, yet there were still foreign sailors being employed.[12] They argued that any foreign sailor who could not produce evidence of having served in the navy should be prohibited from being employed in the collier fleet.[i] What they were demanding, in

---

i   They do not seem to have been discerning in their complaint because they considered any sailor not from the northeast to be a "foreigner," but there were undoubtedly both actual foreign nationals and men from elsewhere in Britain being employed in the collier fleet. On the significance of foreigners, see Caputo, "Towards a Transnational History."

short, were veterans' benefits. They also made explicit the role that demobilization had played in creating the unemployment crisis, as well as the international nature of the maritime labor market: "The majority of your petitioners have been discharged from His Majesty's Navy and after a long servitude on their return to their Homes cannot find employment to enable them to provide for themselves and families by which means your petitioners are reduced to great distress and will be under the necessity of emigrating unless some provision should be made for our encouragement in this country."[13]

The mayor told the sailors that he did not have the power to enforce the 1794 act, but he agreed to pass on their petition to the Admiralty. When he did so, he asked the Admiralty to send out a warship to help keep the peace in case the sailors transitioned from petitioning to more aggressive forms of protest. The Admiralty responded that they did not have a vessel handy as the fleet was in the process of demobilizing, but they offered instead to reopen the Impress Service in Newcastle, led by Captain James Caulfield. Sailors would be able to volunteer for naval service, and the Admiralty granted them special dispensation to choose the vessel on which they would initially serve. The mayor admitted that this might help, but he also reminded the Admiralty that they had stationed a frigate in the harbor during the demobilization of 1801 and that it had been helpful in keeping the peace. The Admiralty, its resources stretched, refused to be budged.[14]

Over the next two weeks, it became clear that the navy's actions had not solved the problem. Sailors' complaints grew: not only were shipowners employing foreigners, but they were taking advantage of widespread unemployment to drive wages down. A committee of sailors presented owners with their demands. In addition to banning foreign seamen, owners were to increase wages to £5 per voyage to London (in wartime, wages had been as high as £8 or £9 per voyage) and set a fixed ratio of manning to tonnage. Owners were always looking for ways to decrease crew sizes, but many of the sailors had served on transports during the wars, and the Transport Service had operated with just the kind of fixed scale that the men were demanding. On September 4, the sailors shut down the port, prohibiting all sailings except those licensed by their committee (licensed ships had to satisfy the manning demands and contribute to the strike funds). Five days later, after initially hesitating, the owners agreed to the flat

£5 wage and to employ only those sailors with local connections; but they rejected the manning-to-tonnage ratio, arguing that it would disadvantage British trade and cause it to fall into the hands of foreign shipowners, thereby exacerbating the unemployment problem.[15]

While the sailors continued to petition Caulfield, the owners asked the Newcastle magistrates to open the port by force, citing the "very alarming and riotous Behaviour of the Seamen."[16] In fact, Caulfield reported, the sailors petitioned him "most respectfully" and continued to "conduct themselves in an orderly manner." They even maintained their discipline "as about 6,000 of them walked thro' the town this day, and quietly dispersed."[17] Major General Phineas Riall did order three troops of the Fifth Dragoon Guards to move into the area, but neither he nor the Admiralty wanted to be involved in the violent suppression of the sailors. Public opinion seemed to shade in favor of the sailors, particularly after the owners offered to let insurance companies determine the manning-to-tonnage ratio, which was a tacit admission that their ships were undermanned. The Admiralty finally agreed to send a sloop on September 27, but it ordered the captain not to use force against the strikers—in any case, it seemed unlikely that the crew would follow such orders. The next day, the strikers marched again, demonstrating their ability to keep order by blackening the faces and reversing the jackets of those in their midst who had broken their rules. They further demonstrated their discipline and organization when they prevented a ship from sailing by force on October 2, and on October 7, after an attempt at mediation by the magistrates had failed, they demonstrated their naval prowess by maneuvering large formations of boats in the harbor in response to flag signals.[18]

The Home Office and the Admiralty were becoming increasingly alarmed, worried that the strike would spread. It had already reached Wearside, and there were hints that it might spread further. The mayor asked Sidmouth to send infantry and to ask the Admiralty to send marines, "who are evidently more to be relied on in such a contest, than the seamen yet serving in the ships of war." Sidmouth's chosen representative reported back that the mayor was correct to worry: the forces arrayed against the strikers were clearly inadequate because the veteran sailors, "who have faced death in all its terrors," treated the yeomanry cavalry mustered by the mayor with "derision."

In any case, the representative told Sidmouth that the sailors had a point: most ships sailed undermanned. Sidmouth blamed demobilization for the slow military response, but by the middle of October, as the strike entered its third month, he and the military commanders felt they were strong enough to act. Even if the sailors had a point, the port needed to be reopened. On October 20, the sailors were ordered to accept the owners' offer. When they refused, early the next morning naval seamen and marines seized boats in the harbor and the troops sealed off the landward approaches. Surprisingly, there were no casualties. The sailors, defeated, called off the strike. It was a remarkable way for Newcastle to celebrate the tenth anniversary of the Battle of Trafalgar.[19]

Despite the defeat, the story of striking sailors on Tyneside demonstrates that veterans were not passive victims of the postwar malaise but active participants who gave voice to their complaints and took steps to improve their situations. In general, they were unsuccessful, but their attempts laid the groundwork for later political movements, from trade unionism to parliamentary reform and Chartism. Some historians have waved their hands at demobilized sailors, assuming that they could return to their former employment as merchant sailors or fishermen with little trouble. We should challenge that assumption. Tracing how demobilized sailors navigated the postwar maritime labor market reveals the lasting effects of the enormous manpower demands of the Napoleonic Wars as well as the ways in which sailors were a distinct category of worker whose experiences in peacetime transcended the immediate problems of demobilization in 1815.[20]

Sailors have been organizing themselves since at least the medieval period, forming associations for mutual support. Often connected to particular shipping routes, these guilds or corporations provided religious support and welfare for members. The early seventeenth century saw the emergence of insurance boxes funded out of dues paid each time a sailor left port, which helped families who had lost loved ones or sailors who lost limbs. All such organizations reflected the hazardous nature of life at sea, but they also created structures through which sailors could address grievances about pay, food, or working conditions. That is not to say that sailors' associations organized strikes and mutinies—in general, they did not, and in fact the failure of such associations to address sailors' concerns meant that sailors had to turn to more aggressive measures. Instead, sailors' associations provided templates for future organizing.[21]

The nature of life at sea meant that sailors lived and worked in a separate world from landlubbers. They dressed differently, in long trousers and blue jackets, and they sported tattoos and pigtails. They spoke differently, using a strange ship-based vocabulary. They walked differently, rolling along the streets of the "sailortowns" where they lived. At the same time, they traveled widely and encountered sailors in other port towns. They heard about strikes and mutinies from such connections, and the insularity of their community created fruitful conditions for organizing industrial action. All strikes require solidarity on the part of the strikers, and the maritime subculture provided an important glue that helped bind sailors together when they took on shipowners or the navy.[22]

In 1768, nearly five hundred sailors had marched from North Shields to Sunderland carrying flags and banners demanding better wages. They had struck the yards of the ships in the harbor to the decks to prevent them from sailing, which gave the world the term "strike."[ii] While each strike had its own unique character, in general, sailors' strikes were like we know them to be today: the sailors withheld their labor, prevented the smooth operation of their employers' activities, and organized protest marches to raise awareness of their grievances. Often, they presented petitions to authority figures, as we saw in the 1815 Tyneside example. On the other hand, not all of the petitioners and strikers were currently employed, and in fact the lack of employment opportunities was often a precipitating cause of the strike—in that sense, sailors' strikes in this period differ from contemporary strikes.[23]

When naval sailors took such actions, they were technically engaging in mutiny. In many cases, it was generally understood by both officers and men that the goal was not to take control of the ship and dispose of the officers (as happened on the *Bounty* and *Hermione*) but rather to withhold labor until certain demands relating to pay, food, or conditions were met. Naval authorities tended to treat

---

ii There is some dispute about whether the term "strike" originated in the northeast or with Thames River workers, who took a similar action in the same year. See Frykman, *Bloody Flag*, 6.

such mutinies as strikes, but it is difficult to draw general conclusions: much depended on the timing of the strike or mutiny, the context in which it happened, and whether the relationship between the strikers and the authorities was strong enough for the latter to recognize the legitimacy of the former's complaints.[24]

The history of naval mutinies during the wars informed sailors' approaches to strikes as well as the authorities' responses. We can see the influence of naval service in the ways in which strikers maintained discipline. Organizing maneuvers in the harbor in response to flag signals was one obvious manifestation of naval service during the Tyneside strikes, and one shipowner later commented, "I think I never saw more decorum among men than there were at that time; quite a military organization among themselves."[25] The firmness with which the strikers took control of the harbor and prevented sailings is also reminiscent of naval actions.

The 1815 Tyneside strike came in the middle of almost a century of regular strikes in the northeast ports. One historian has found strikes in 1768, 1775, 1777, 1785, 1790, 1792, 1796, 1815, 1819, 1822, 1824, 1825, 1831, 1843, 1844, 1851, and 1854, to which should be added a Wearside strike in 1816, threatened strikes in 1816 and 1818, and numerous other "disturbances," particularly during the wars, that went unreported. For all these reasons, this chapter, like much of the existing scholarship on sailors' experiences, spends much of its time in the northeast. It is true that the Tyneside strikes were not wholly representative of the British maritime world because there were circumstances in the northeast that made strikes more likely to occur there than elsewhere. The coal trade was governed by a cartel called the Limitation of the Vends, in which each colliery agreed to an annual output. That meant that colliers often waited in Newcastle for long periods until the combination of the best available coals and highest prices in London guaranteed the maximum profit. Long wait times provided more opportunities for sailors to discuss employment issues and organize. They also had a ready example of another group known for its willingness to down tools (i.e., go on strike). Keelmen were highly skilled boatmen who worked the sailing barges that brought coal downstream from the mines. In May 1803, the regulating captain in Newcastle had made the mistake of pressing fifty-three keelmen, and the resulting strike shut down the port until the keelmen gained the protections they felt they deserved. Such strikes, particularly against overeager press gangs, were regular occurrences in the northeast. Yet we should not dismiss the Tyneside strikes as entirely unrepresentative: while conditions there made strikes more likely, many of those conditions existed elsewhere, and strikes occurred in other port towns in the postwar years; 1815 alone saw strikes on the Clyde, at Leith, Hull, Yarmouth, and Lyme Regis, as well as in London.[26]

Striking yards to the deck featured in many episodes, but that was usually just the beginning. For locals, sailors' strikes could be disorienting. Strange looking men who spent most of their time away from the community returned to take control of it, overturning social hierarchies and disrupting regularly scheduled programming. Given that many sailors' strikes derived from meetings organized in pubs, many bystanders expected drunken rioting and often sent panicked reports to magistrates claiming that the sailors had been violent. In fact, calmer observers regularly commented on the rigorous discipline enforced by sailors on strike. Drawing on their shipboard experience, both strikers and mutineers usually organized themselves into watches. In some cases, they appointed officers who oversaw divisions responsible for various aspects of the strike such as preventing ships from leaving port, shipboard maintenance, and husbanding resources. Sailors were often equally disciplined ashore, enforcing curfews and punishing those who disobeyed the rules of the strikers' association. The first example of a sailors' strike committee dates from the 1815 Tyneside strike, but ad hoc groups of men who took on the responsibility of sorting the demands and creating the petitions can be found in most strikes. The benefit associations mentioned earlier provided a model for sailors to think of themselves as part of a collective. Authorities were quick to target ringleaders, so a common practice among strikers was to present petitions using a round robin—at the bottom of the petition, sailors signed their names or made their marks in a circle so that authorities could not tell who had signed it first. The earliest example of such a document dates from 1657.[27]

Historians have generally assumed that all collective action by sailors in this period took place in the shadow of the Great Mutinies of 1797. In the spring of that year, sailors in the Channel Fleet and then the North Sea Fleet had mutinied for higher pay and against poor leadership. While the navy had initially listened to the sailors' complaints, the episode ended with twenty-nine sailors hanging from yardarms. The most recent interpretation sees the Great Mutinies as a turning point in the labor history of sailors because the government's response was so severe that it "finally crushed the lower deck's insurrectionary spirit for good."[28] The events of 1797 shook the foundations of the maritime nation by threatening the country's security, and they threw into question the relationship between officers and men that made the naval machine work. Yet as is often the case with naval history, focusing primarily on wartime events has blinded historians to the broader scope of sailors' stories. The regularity and enthusiasm with which sailors went on strike in large numbers after 1815 demonstrate that sailors' spirits had not been crushed. Also, the methods of the Tyneside strikers—controlling sailings, submitting petitions, and maintaining discipline—echo that of the Spithead mutineers of April 1797. This suggests that, while the Great Mutinies were undoubtedly seminal events in the history of the lower deck, and while they took place in circumstances particular to the navy, they did not mark a break in the tradition of sailors' strikes.[29]

The other event that looms over all postwar protest is the Peterloo Massacre. It is worth asking why the Tyneside strikes of 1815 did not end in violence. After all, the situation in Newcastle on October 21, 1815, bore some striking similarities with that of Manchester on August 16, 1819. In both cities, tension had been building for weeks, with mass protests, marches, and public spats in the newspapers. Local authorities decided it was time to restore order, and the central government provided the military forces necessary to give them the courage to take action. The protestors had been trained in military service and had used that experience to increase their discipline. Yet in Manchester, the result was a cavalry charge into a crowd and mass casualties, while in Newcastle, the strikers went back to work.

The next chapter explores Peterloo in much greater detail, but for now, we can see a few reasons why bloodshed was averted in October 1815. The first is timing. The political situation in 1815 was unsettled following the Corn Law riots in the spring and the chaotic second demobilization after Waterloo. It was not, however, the fourth year in a row in which major protests in Britain's cities seemed to be harbingers of revolution, as 1819 was. Strikes on Tyneside were so normal that the mayor of Newcastle's first letter to the Admiralty reminded them that in the last demobilization, they had stationed a frigate in the harbor to keep the peace. There was little reason for Sidmouth to think that anything out of the ordinary was happening in the northeast. When the authorities did decide to act, moreover, they did so decisively and with a well-planned operation.

Helpfully, strikes on Tyneside in the immediate aftermath of Peterloo provide a natural experiment in the different ways in which the government handled protests in 1815 versus 1819. At the end of September 1819, the keelmen went on strike to protest the recent introduction of coal-loading machinery that threatened to take their jobs. The Home Office received reports that iron workers at nearby Winlaton, who had suffered severely from the cancellation of wartime contracts, were practicing military-style drills in the fields and planning to join the keelmen in a protest march. Shipowners worried that sailors would join as well, and so under threat of a strike, they increased wages on the Tyne. Two days later, on October 11, a demonstration in favor of parliamentary reform brought forty thousand people to Newcastle, of whom twelve thousand were marching in regular order. The hustings were draped in black cloth in memory of the Peterloo victims, but the day passed without incident. Meanwhile the keelmen were still on strike, so the mayor decided to take action on October 14 by gathering up a squad of marines and heading for the keelmen's headquarters. Unlike in 1815, this time the suppression of the strike was poorly planned, and in the resulting riot, the marines fired shots into the crowd, killing one and wounding others. The mayor fled to a pub and had to be smuggled out the back door while the Sixth Dragoon Guards arrived to clear the streets and patrol the town for the next few days.[30]

In addition to the botched response, the other major difference in 1819 was that the keelmen's strike was coincidental with and possibly connected to Radical protests. There had been no Radical involvement in the 1815 strikes which meant the authorities had some experience with their likely course and outcome. But in 1819 it was difficult for the Home Office to separate the serious but commonplace keelmen's strike from seditious activities (as it saw them). In fact, Radical leaders were relatively slow to recognize the

potential political power of the keelmen and sailors, but the Home
Office did not know that. Not until the establishment of one of the
first trade unions in British history did Radical politics and sailors'
organizations fully link up. The Combination Acts of 1799 and 1800
prohibited trade unions, but in 1824, Parliament loosened some of
the restrictions. In October of that year, the Seamen's Loyal Standard
Association (SLSA) was founded on Tyneside, and across 1825, it
organized a series of strikes because wages for London collier voyages
once again had dropped below £5. In February, it shut down sailings
out of Scarborough; in April, it shut down sailings out of Newcastle;
and in August, it attempted to shut down sailings out of Sunderland.
The Admiralty and the Home Office responded by steadily escalat-
ing pressure, first bringing a sloop to anchor in the Tyne following
the April strike, and then in August, sending a magistrate out into
the harbor in a steam-powered vessel to confront sailors attempting
to prevent sailings. Soldiers from the Third Light Dragoons, whom
we met in chapter 7 engaged in counterinsurgency operations in
Ireland, were onboard with the magistrate. They fired indiscriminately into an unruly crowd watching from shore, killing five. The
strike ended only when the owners agreed to add one man to each
ship in the collier fleet to ease unemployment, and sporadic violence
erupted in Sunderland for the rest of the year and into the next.[31]

While much of the postwar unrest occurred in the northeast, all
British sailors confronted the fundamental problems of low wages,
a depressed economy, and a market flooded with more skilled sailors than ever before. Strikes were common, but rarely did they win
long-term successes. After securing a wage increase in 1815, Tyneside
sailors had to threaten to strike again in 1818. Shipowners lowered
wages soon after anyways, as we saw, sparking the SLSA's strikes in
1825. That did not last either, as even though the SLSA grew to
twenty-five hundred members, it soon collapsed amid recriminations
about how much money it was disbursing to members. This was the
unhealthy environment in which sailors sought work. It is true that
they had more marketable skills than soldiers, but that did little to
insulate them from the postwar malaise.[32]

The plight of sailors was a common point of discussion among the
chattering classes. The *Morning Post* printed a few letters in August

1815 debating whether the government should mandate manning-to-tonnage ratios to improve employment prospects.[33] A month later a correspondent to the *Morning Chronicle* argued that the navy should abolish flogging to improve naval recruitment and retention.[34] Well into the peace, concerns about sailors continued to appear regularly in newspapers. In May 1817, the *Liverpool Mercury* reported on a typhus outbreak among seamen in a barrack house in the city center.[35]

But the most well-publicized effort to alleviate sailors' suffering occurred in January 1818 when William Wilberforce chaired a "most respectable" meeting of merchants, shipowners, and other gentlemen in the City of London Tavern for the purpose of "affording relief to unemployed and distressed Seamen."[36] He set the agenda for the meeting by pointing out that "very great distress existed among these gallant men, who had so honorably acquitted themselves in the hour of danger, and fought the battles of their country. That that distress ought to be alleviated in some manner was unquestionable." Thanks to their service, sailors were members of the "deserving poor." Attendees at this inaugural meeting of the Society for the Aid of Destitute Seamen provided examples of their own interactions with starving sailors, including a secondhand report from the coroner of London stating that he had recently seen many veterans who had died of starvation.

The question was what to do about it. In 1816, the lord mayor of London had acquired a vessel and stationed it in the river to act as a receiving ship for vagrant sailors. Magistrates rounded them up and brought them to the vessel where they were examined by naval officers and, if deemed worthy, given clothes to look more presentable when seeking employment. The effort had not been sustained beyond that year, so the members of the society resolved to bring it back. It was clear that one vessel would not meet the scale of the problem, so one of the society's founders, the abolitionist lawyer James Stephen, said that he had applied to Melville and Croker for assistance, and they had promised to do their best to help. But Croker was quick to point out in a letter to Stephen that providing a naval vessel for the purpose would be impossible because the sailors who came on board would not be entered into the navy and therefore not subject to naval discipline—the budget cuts strike again.

Croker's rather weak excuse sparked a characteristic outburst from the Radical politician and naval officer Thomas, Lord Cochrane. He asked why Croker and Melville were not in attendance (perhaps because they knew he would be there?). He dismissed one vessel as wholly inadequate and likely to continue to drive sailors to seek employment abroad (as he was to do later that year—see chapter 15). Cochrane also asked the attendees whether they had ever seen soldiers begging, implying that the government cared more about their welfare than the welfare of veteran sailors'. Stephen did not allow Cochrane's rant to stand unchallenged, saying that "he could say he had seen one [soldier] who had been obliged to beg in consequence of the reduction of the army. He was sure there was no want of attention on the part of the Government to both soldiers and sailors." At the same time, the Society agreed that sailors who had served in the navy should be a lower priority for charitable relief than those who had not because ex-naval sailors were eligible for pensions—in theory at least. There were still tens of thousands of sailors ineligible for relief.[iii] Stephen also admitted that Cochrane was right to doubt the Admiralty's enthusiasm: because of the restrictions put on the Admiralty by tight budgets and how public money could be used, "there was no hope of Government doing any thing, or interfering, until probably after a great number of these poor wretches had perished."[37]

The debate among the members of the Society for the Aid of Destitute Seamen echoes many debates today about charity and welfare. Simply giving sailors money was not even proposed, and instead attendees spent a good deal of energy proscribing the nature of the charity and preventing fraud, real or imagined. The point of the receiving ship was to put naval officers and pursers in charge of identifying true "deserving" sailors and exposing those who were "imposters." Yet even among sailors, there were three subgroups deemed unworthy: foreigners, Black sailors, and sailors over the age of forty-five. Foreigners were to be sent to their respective consuls, who generally refused to deal with them because they considered

---

iii   Merchant seamen were also eligible for small pensions from the Merchant Seamen's Fund, which deducted 6d per month from sailors' wages from its founding in 1747 until its collapse in 1851. The pensions paid out were tiny, however: usually £4 per year or less. See Press, "Collapse of a Contributory Pension Scheme."

them to have become naturalized British citizens.[iv] Black sailors were to be "sent either to Africa, or stationed in some of His Majesty's Colonies abroad." How this was to be done was not explained. Older sailors were not as employable as younger sailors, and because of the mobile nature of their profession, Wilberforce pointed out, sailors were often extraparochial. Separating them out on the receiving ship meant they could become someone else's problem: specifically, they would be sent back to their home parishes where they were eligible for poor relief, even though Stephen admitted that the rates were inadequate.

All that is not to say that we should condemn the charitable instincts of that group of gentlemen based on our own standards, but rather to illustrate some continuities in the ways in which elites think about charity. In 1818, the government, and specifically the navy, was not seen as a viable source of relief, and indeed the navy was quick to point out that it was not a charity. Like most who give charitably, the gentlemen at the meeting were concerned that their resources were aimed in a particular direction. The celebrities who attended the meeting raised its profile, but it was also part of a broader movement aimed at alleviating the plight of sailors. Wilberforce claimed at the beginning of the meeting that he was unqualified to chair it, but in fact, seamen's welfare and abolitionism were parallel movements. Many reformers connected the abolition of impressment and flogging with the abolition of slavery as part of a broader concern with the conditions of the working poor. They supported operations against slavers, and they encouraged debates about discipline and humanitarian reform in the navy. Wilberforce was a perfectly appropriate chairman, and his efforts in 1817 and 1818 raised nearly £8,000 to support the provision of clothing (and later, lodging) for 250 sailors in London. He was also involved in setting up the Seamen's Hospital Society in 1821.[38]

Evangelicals were prominent members of these reform movements. The presence of demobilized sailors begging on the streets raised evangelical interest in their welfare, but as one naval officer at the 1818 meeting summarized, the evangelical diagnosis of the root

---

iv   6 Ann. c. 37 had made all foreigners who served in the navy for two years naturalized citizens, although the fluidity of citizenship across this period means we should not take that law entirely at face value.

causes of poverty among sailors transcended the particular distress of that winter: "The cause, in a great measure of their ruin, might be attributed to their being catched when they came on shore, by a set of petty agents, who laid in wait to entrap them, and their then going to houses of debauchery, where they were stript of their all, and left to wretchedness and woe."[39] Many of those involved in sailors' welfare held two slightly contradictory ideas in their heads at the same time. Sailors were victims of crimps and prostitutes, as above; they were also naturally sinful ashore and needed special attention to turn them to the path of clean living.[40]

To provide that attention, evangelicals helped establish more than one hundred seamen's missionary societies in Britain and Ireland from 1815 to 1914. At the heart of this movement in its first decades was the prolific preacher and writer, the Reverend George Charles Smith of Penzance, known as Bo'sun Smith. He had been pressed into the navy in the French Revolutionary Wars, and that experience, combined with his tireless work ethic and enthusiasm, made him uniquely well qualified to minister to sailors. He helped establish evangelicalism among merchant crews on the Thames after the wars, which soon led to the creation of at least sixty Bethel Societies in just the years 1818–23. Ships would fly the blue and white Bethel flag when they were holding services, indicating that the ship was a place of worship without being formally consecrated ground. Soon the societies began acquiring decommissioned ships from the navy and converting them into floating chapels, complete with pews and pulpits. Smith traveled widely around maritime Britain, and by the end of the 1820s, there were floating chapels off Wapping and in Hull, Leith, Greenock, and even Calcutta. He also published a dizzying array of magazines and newspapers aimed at sailors, with titles like *The Pilot*, *The Sailors' Magazine and Naval Miscellany*, *The Chart and Compass*, and the *New Sailors' Magazine*.[41]

The other major line of effort concerned sailors' homes. Bethel Societies adhered to a version of evangelicalism that, not coincidentally, promoted behavior precisely the opposite of that for which sailors were well-known: missionary zeal for the Bible as the sole authority on matters of faith and life, and sobriety. To encourage this behavior, Bo'sun Smith targeted sailors when they were at their most vulnerable to temptation, ashore between voyages. The Bethel Union published a list of respectable boarding houses generally safe from prostitution and unscrupulous crimps in 1820, and the next year, the London chapter established a sailors' boarding house. It provided cheap accommodation, encouraged sailors to attend church services, and helped them manage their money. While all of Smith's efforts were undermined by his comprehensive inability to manage his own money, he managed to generate enough momentum that by the early 1830s, there were sailors' homes in many ports and mariners' churches funded by evangelicals.[42]

Much of the funding and some of the administration of these kinds of institutions came from naval officers. In 1835, evangelical naval officers established the Dock Street Sailors' Home in London and ran it on naval lines; it soon became the model for sailors' homes around the country. Evangelicals saw sinful sailors as a challenge, and their motivations were as much patriotic and practical as humanitarian. By improving the lot of sailors through discipline and moral teaching, they were simultaneously strengthening British naval power.[43] Yet to pick up again on a theme that has run through this book, the nature of the laissez-faire state meant that evangelical naval officers pursued these goals separate from the formal structures of the navy. The navy was slow to recognize that it could play a useful role in the preservation of its own manpower resources by improving the conditions of working sailors.

Before the 1830s, there is little evidence that any actively serving naval administrators believed that the manning system needed reform. Even if continuing to claim the right to impress guaranteed war with the United States, the system had demonstrated that it could grow the navy to its largest-ever size and that it was more effective in doing so than any system implemented by Britain's rivals. Furthermore, whenever the topic of impressment arose, the navy had to cede the moral high ground. Better, from the navy's perspective, to let the sleeping dog lie. Yet while the dog slept, it was becoming increasingly common for sailors to spend most of their careers either in merchant or naval service, but not to move as freely between the two as before. One driver for this trend may have been the dearth of berths in the navy—with so few available spots, men were less likely to give them up once they had secured them. Another driver was the increasing complexity of naval gunnery. HMS *Excellent* was established as a gunnery training school at Portsmouth in 1830, and one historian has argued that the progress in naval gunnery from 1815 to 1852 "rivalled the progress from blunderbuss to rifle."[44]

As the navy became steadily more aware of the need for trained men, and as sailors' careers became more specialized, administrators began attempting to figure out how many sailors there were in Britain and how many of them would be fit for service in the event of a war. This classic Victorian data-driven approach resulted in a series of Acts of Parliament targeted at merchant and naval sailors, including two attempts to measure more accurately the number and size of British merchant vessels (in 1825 and 1833), two revisions to pension schemes (in 1834 and 1851), and two attempts to create a Register of Seamen (in 1835 and 1844). Each of these efforts struggled to achieve its goals because the machinery of the state was not capable of keeping track of the nearly two hundred thousand sailors in British vessels. They do, however, indicate a shift in the government's approach to working sailors, which culminated in the establishment of the Royal Naval Reserve and the creation of continuous service careers for the lower deck in the 1850s.[45]

Meanwhile, beginning in 1838, the Chartist movement became the "first organized mass movement of British Radicalism in the modern sense."[46] We can see echoes in Chartism of some of the goals that sailors' trade unions had set out to achieve in the 1820s. But that is a different story for a different book. As this chapter has shown, the state stayed out of the market for seafarers in the aftermath of the Napoleonic Wars. For more than a decade, sailors were left to fend for themselves, which they did, although lasting victories eluded them. Charitable initiatives helped at the margins, but the scale of the problem overwhelmed even the most well-connected efforts. Many sailors struggled to find work in the aftermath of demobilization, as the usual postwar malaise was exacerbated by the introduction of tens of thousands of naval-trained sailors.

CHAPTER 12

────

Soldiers versus Veterans

On January 2, 1813, a special commission convened at York. It was an unusual time of year for a judicial proceeding, but the chaos of the previous year had forced the local authorities to act. Men calling themselves Luddites had destroyed textile machinery, started deadly riots, and sworn secret oaths that suggested the beginnings of a more expansive insurrection. In his opening statement to the jury, the judge described the "acts of outrage on the property and persons of individuals" that had lasted "nearly the whole of the year." The goal of the rioters, the judge said, was "the destruction of machinery, which by diminishing the quantity of human labour in our manu-factures, was by them conceived to be inimical to the interests of the labouring classes." The judge made it clear that he did not expect empathy from the jury: "A more fallacious and ill-founded argument cannot be conceived. It is to machinery that we probably owe the existence, certainly the excellence and extent of our manufacturers." This was a show trial, and the verdicts were not in doubt. In March of the previous year, amid the riots, Parliament had passed the Frame-Breaking Act, which made the destruction of textile machinery a capital offense. The special commission at York put it into effect, hanging dozens of convicted Luddites.[1]

The execution of the Luddites was made possible by the presence of the armed forces of the Crown. Soldiers were the most reliable means for suppressing domestic unrest, and indeed before the establishment of the regular police forces, they were often the only means of doing so. In 1812 and 1813, however, most of the army was deployed abroad: the disposal force was in Iberia with Wellington, and there were tens of thousands of troops in other theaters from Canada to South Africa to India. Thus the troops deployed to suppress the Luddites were mainly militiamen and other troops that were not legally allowed to be sent overseas.[2] But over the next decade, as the Luddite riots were joined by disturbances around the country and the end of the wars freed up the disposal force, the army's presence on British soil grew.

The role of soldiers in suppressing disturbances has not been sufficiently appreciated, however. Labor historians have naturally gravitated to the postwar turmoil, and their work, building on the foundational text by E. P. Thompson, has dominated our understanding of it. Yet as others have noticed, labor historians have paid little attention to soldiers despite their potential as a well-catalogued group of working-class men.[3] Instead, the military appears vaguely and seemingly randomly. We read that Radical meetings were occasionally "invaded by the military"[4] and that the Pentrich Rising was dispersed by a magistrate at the "head of a party of hussars." After the Spa Fields riots, "by nightfall the troops had restored order in the City."[5] In none of these cases is it explained where the soldiers came from or why they were (from the government's perspective) in the right place at the right time. Some military historians have noticed the domestic presence of the army in this period, but they tend either to downplay its significance or speak only in broad terms about its deployments.[6]

When faced with social unrest, the most readily available tool was the military, and as a result, soldiers found themselves ensnared in the postwar tumult. But soldiers returning on active duty are only half the story. Facing them in many of the postwar riots were discharged soldiers and sailors—their former comrades. This chapter looks at the early years of the horrible peace to uncover the double importance of soldiers as both perpetrators and suppressors of riots.

Law enforcement in Britain in this period began with members of the landed classes. Lord lieutenants controlled the selection of justices of the peace, who were often Anglican clergy. There were property and income requirements, and they had the authority to issue warrants for arrest. For all matters of enforcement, from property crimes to individual violent crimes to mass unrest, they relied on support from local amateur volunteers. Common law dictated that all citizens were required to act in the event of a riot, although of course this rarely happened in practice. Many were willing, however, to serve as informants for magistrates, warning them about approaching mobs or passing on hearsay about plots. Yet even well-organized communities with attentive magistrates had to resort to calling on military force in extreme—but not uncommon—circumstances.[7]

The larger the crowd, the more likely that this ad hoc system of self-policing would be insufficient. When confronted with a mob, a magistrate's first move was often to read the Riot Act of 1714, which gave crowds one hour to disperse peacefully before arrests would be made.[i] Sometimes, that was enough. If it did not have the desired effect, the next escalatory step was to raise a competing but respectable mob. During riots in East Anglia in 1816, for example, the mayor of Cambridge raised a preventative mob of three hundred men, whom he swore in as special constables.[8]

Few magistrates had such foresight or sufficient time to get ahead of the mob, so they frequently had to react to rapidly changing circumstances by calling the militia or yeomanry. The militia were disembodied at the end of the wars, leaving the yeomanry as the primary amateur military force available during the postwar riots. Boasting about twenty thousand members around the country, the yeomanry was locally organized and usually drawn from the middle ranks of society. A troop consisted of about fifty or sixty mounted men, and they had to pay for most of their equipment and horses. The infamous Manchester and Salford Yeomanry, who charged at Peterloo, were mainly shopkeepers and merchants. In general, the yeomanry sought to preserve the status quo. They were an antirevolutionary organization initially designed to respond to a French invasion, but their respectability and ability to suppress popular protest made them, at least initially, an attractive rapid-response team for postwar magistrates.[9]

---

i   The Riot Act baffled one French visitor to London in 1815. All it did, he said, was to give the rioters more time to riot: "The damage is done when the remedy arrives" ("Le mal est fait quand le remède arrive"). Defauconpret, *Quinze Jours à Londres*, 203.

There are plenty of examples of the militia or yeomanry successfully suppressing riots, but there are also plenty of examples of failures. Peterloo is the most famous of the failures, but it was exceptional in its scale and legacy. More common in the postwar years were smaller clashes between yeomanry and citizens. Most ended much less decisively than Peterloo, as well. When workers went on strike at the Merthyr Tydfil ironworks in Wales in October 1816, the Cardiff yeomanry successfully dispersed a crowd using the flats of their blades. That same year, the yeomanry in East Anglia were less successful when confronted with a crowd demanding the release of a recently captured gang of poachers. The magistrates held their nerve, but neither they nor the yeomanry could prevent the crowd from diverting to the nearest pub, which it destroyed while consuming most of its beer.[10]

When the yeomanry failed, or if the yeomanry was in danger of failing, magistrates called the army. There were plenty of soldiers available, increasingly quartered in barracks. While they had previously been built mostly in coastal areas with invasion defense in mind, they began appearing inland. Demand signals came from mayors, lord lieutenants, and other local officials, who wrote regularly to the Home Office demanding more troops and ships to use in suppressing dissent. William Surtees was one of the eleven thousand troops moved into the northern areas after Peterloo in 1819. He was in no doubt about why they were there: "The Radical war called us to the north."[11] But it was not just in the north. There were also troops available when trouble appeared in East Anglia in 1816 and in the Home Counties in 1820. During the clashes over the funeral procession of Queen Caroline, half of all the troops in Britain—nearly ten thousand—were stationed near London. As E. P. Thompson summarized, "In 1816 the English people were held down by force."[12]

The army was called out repeatedly in the postwar years, but it could act in domestic affairs only on orders from the civil power. During the anti-Catholic Gordon Riots of 1780, London had burned for several days because civil authorities had hesitated to call in the army. In the aftermath, some argued that soldiers had held too firmly to the legal requirement and should, in the future, be set loose on the mob.[13] This history combined with the ready availability of troops during and after the wars to encourage magistrates to call the army to their assistance with increasing frequency. The army, for its part, began to develop tactics for dealing with crowds. This is not to say that there was a doctrine, or that troops drilled for these eventualities—no soldier was comfortable in front of a riot. Rather, the goal here is to trace some common techniques that soldiers deployed.[14]

Step 1 was simply to show up. Soldiers' red coats, tall shakos, bright buttons, and weapons made them instantly recognizable. They might parade in formation, or form lines in front of the mob. Disciplined troops are intimidating, and often simply being present defused the situation. Officers might feel compelled to give speeches, saying that they did not want to fight their own countrymen. But if simply being present did not disperse the crowd, the soldiers usually then deployed to guard key civic buildings. This tactic was the most challenging for the soldiers because standing guard made them tempting targets for both insults and stones. From the crowd's perspective, nothing had changed: the soldiers were still simply present rather than taking active measures to suppress the crowd. This tactic rarely lasted a long time, and almost never proved sufficient to quell the riot.[15]

The most common tactic came next: limited offensive measures. In the Boston Massacre of 1770, the soldiers who had been guarding the custom house fired a ragged volley into the crowd that had been pressing around them for hours. But direct fire was rare. Instead, soldiers could fire blank cartridges, or fire balls over the crowd's heads. That was the most effective tactic in dispersing a crowd, but it also often resulted in casualties. A more disciplined approach was for the infantry to advance against the mob, using the stocks of their muskets as weapons. If cavalry were available, they would wade into the crowd, theoretically using the flats of their blades. It is remarkable that wounds from blades were relatively rare, with the notable exception of Peterloo.

These tactics developed over time, as the examples from the middle of the previous century show. They were not fixed nor were they always followed, but they do give a general sense of how troops might approach their constabulary tasks. We can see how they played out in practice in the postwar years.

Sometimes step 1—showing up—was more difficult than we might think. Despite the construction of inland barracks in the north after 1815, detachments of soldiers often had to travel long distances.

Technically, magistrates could call out local troops only, but that could still mean troops a day's march away or more. While the Cardiff yeomanry were dealing with the striking ironworkers, for example, a troop of dragoons was making its way over the Brecon Beacons by forced march. Upon arriving in an area disturbed by rioting, troops could be concentrated or dispersed. Opinion was divided about the best practice. Military officers preferred to concentrate to maintain discipline. During the Luddite riots, for example, Lieutenant General Sir Thomas Maitland kept his troops concentrated, despite pleas from magistrates to make them more available to civil authorities. Eventually he agreed, with the result that in Huddersfield, a thousand troops were quartered in thirty-three pubs. In the aftermath of Peterloo, however, officers in command of the troops in Scotland made a point of separating soldiers from civilians to insulate them from revolutionary influences.[16]

Dispersing troops made it more likely that they would be on hand when trouble erupted, and that clearly had some value even if it made it more difficult for officers to maintain discipline within their units. "There is nothing to fear from the rioters," wrote one officer to *Bell's Weekly Register* in 1816. "They have no plan, no arms, and flee at the sight of a soldier."[17] Well, sometimes. During the hustings for the 1818 Westminster election, supporters of Captain Sir Murray Maxwell, RN, dressed in patriotic clothing and built a boat on wheels. Their opponents, supporters of the Radical Sir Francis Burdett, ambushed them, captured the boat, and broke it into pieces for use as weapons in their assault on Maxwell's headquarters near Covent Garden. They used the cart that had held the boat as a battering ram. Eventually, the magistrate read the Riot Act and called out some nearby dragoons. When the soldiers arrived, the crowd pelted them with whatever was at hand, mainly cabbages from Covent Garden vegetable carts.[18]

Sergeant Thomas Morris also ran into the problem of how to deal with a crowd that was not intimidated by the arrival of soldiers. His regiment, the Seventy-Third Foot, returned from the Waterloo campaign in December 1815 and was almost immediately deployed to Birmingham to deal with riots in the manufacturing districts. As in Westminster, troops showing up did nothing, and in fact further enraged the crowd. The high constable read the Riot Act, to which the crowd responded by throwing bricks and stones at the soldiers. Morris claims his captain proceeded to skip a few steps. Impatient under the assault from the crowd, he never attempted the limited offensive measures that might have been effective. Instead, he ordered the company to load and fire into the mob. The constable acted quickly to intervene, scolding the captain: "Sir, you are called on to aid and assist the civil power, and if you fire on the people, without my permission, and death ensues, you will be guilty of murder." Morris claimed that his captain "seemed nettled at the circumstance, but consoled himself with the thought, that we should even yet have the privilege of killing a few people."[19] In the end, the captain never got his bloodthirsty wish, but it was a narrow escape.[ii]

During major riots in East Anglia in 1816, there were several examples of more effective management of riotous crowds. After a crowd in Norwich threw "fire balls" during a riot in May, the First Royal Dragoons arrived in the market square. Even though the crowd reacted much as it had in Birmingham, in this case, the dragoons were able to chase the crowd away. They "galloped up stone steps, rode over posts and rails, and followed wherever the ill-disposed thought themselves most secure." Later, at Littleport, two privates from the same regiment of dragoons were so enthusiastic about chasing rioters that they forded a river holding their pistols over their heads. But this was not some lark—the rioters during that summer in East Anglia were deadly serious. A man named John Hassett assaulted a soldier by grabbing his sword and yelling, "Damn your Eyes I have got your sword and will fight any of you you Bugger."[20]

Among the more extreme cases of soldiers clashing with protesters came in March 1815 during the Corn Law riots. Sidmouth ordered more than a thousand troops to London to deal with the crisis, and for three days, the capital was governed by the military and the yeomanry. The Life Guards were called in to defend the Houses of Parliament, and at the height of the protests, they charged the crowd with drawn sabers. A bystander who happened to be a midshipman was killed by gunshot in the ensuing fracas, and it could have been worse. At one point, an officer drew his cutlass in the hopes of slowing the advance of a mob of about a hundred; he later claimed that if he had

---

ii   Morris's description of the tactics used is perhaps more reliable than his description of his captain. He set out in his memoir explicitly to counter the more traditional narratives of high-ranking officers receiving all the glory. See Daly, "British Soldiers and the Legend of Napoleon."

been able to find a magistrate, he would have ordered his men to fire into the crowd.[21]

The Corn Law rioting was not random: protestors targeted those known to be supporters of the bill, such as the Honorable Frederick John Robinson (a future prime minister, as Viscount Goderich). But since Robinson and his fellow MPs were busy in Parliament, it was his servants that bore the brunt of the assault. A mob besieged his house, launching multiple assaults that his servants tried desperately to repel. One servant was a carpenter and was able to board up some of the windows and doors, but nevertheless, the mob broke in, smashed furniture, and threatened to kill every servant if they did not tell them where Robinson was. (Presumably they were more comfortable attacking a private residence than taking on the Life Guards in front of Parliament.) The next morning, the servants managed to get six privates and a corporal from one of the Life Guards regiments into the house to help with the defense. Someone in the crowd drew a picture of Robinson hanging from the gallows, and the fighting intensified, particularly once the crowd realized that the soldiers were only firing blank cartridges. The soldiers naturally reloaded with shot. Jane Watson, a widow, was mortally wounded, and eventually the arrival of more troops on the street outside dispersed the crowd.

The next month, four of the soldiers who had been in the house stood trial for Watson's murder. One, James Ripley, pleaded his case by noting that he "had nothing to do with the Corn Law. We were ordered to defend a house." He argued that his life had been in danger and he was acting in self-defense. His story was corroborated by the servants who had been present, as well as Mr. Robinson himself: they all felt that they had been in mortal danger for multiple days. As Ripley's lawyers put it, the violent defense of property by soldiers was necessary to protect "the peaceable and well-disposed men of society," who otherwise would be "at all times at the mercy of a furious and enraged populace." Unsurprisingly, given the political context and the personal testimony of an MP, the soldiers were found not guilty.[22] Soldiers in such situations were certainly in difficult positions, but the casualties resulting from the Corn Law riots nevertheless reinforced the reputation of the Life Guards as poor constables: they had also killed a man during a riot in 1810, for which they earned the moniker "Piccadilly Butchers."[23]

That, then, is how peace was enforced in Britain in the turbulent aftermath of the Napoleonic Wars: with violence carried out by veterans of those wars. Soldiers had no formal training in crowd control, they possessed no nonlethal weapons, and they were under the orders of panicked magistrates. They were in a tough spot. If they obeyed orders and fired into or above crowds, they might be accused of murder; if they disobeyed orders, they might be accused of mutiny. Usually, they followed orders, with the result that British civilians were killed with remarkable regularity by British troops in the postwar years. This was state-sanctioned violence.[24]

To be fair, as a few historians have pointed out, fewer civilians were killed than we might expect, given how frequently the army clashed with rioters. Nevertheless, the government was forced to admit that soldiers made poor policemen and what was needed was a trained regular police force. The initial purpose of the police was not solving crimes but rather protecting property by suppressing rioting. Not surprisingly, the first regular armed police force came in a colonial counterinsurgency setting—as chapter 7 discussed, Peel established the Royal Irish Constabulary in 1822. The Metropolitan Police was established in London in 1829. These forces were designed to support the maintenance of existing power structures, and they modeled themselves on local initiatives such as the Bow Street Runners and the Marine Police, the latter of which had been created and funded by West India merchants to protect their dock at Wapping in 1798. There were also postwar daytime police forces in some provincial cities like Leeds, Bath, Birmingham, Macclesfield, Manchester, and Cheltenham.[25]

Not all riots were the same. Some had particular targets in mind: the Luddites targeted threshing machines; the protestors outside Robinson's house targeted his vote. Others grew out of a more general frustration with unemployment or poverty or unfairness; some of these were led by charismatic figures, like Jeremiah Brandreth in Derbyshire in 1817. Some riots were little more than excuses to smash up pubs and drink beer; others were peaceful movements with coherent political agendas that nevertheless found themselves fighting with soldiers. Some were combinations of multiple types, as when rebels declared a provisional government in western Scotland in 1820, called for a general strike, and then collapsed into sporadic violence when they failed to gain sufficient support. Despite the variety of reasons to riot and ways of rioting, veterans emerge in the postwar period as a common thread across all of them. What set veterans apart, or, from our perspective, what allows us to connect the varieties of riots was that veteran soldiers used the skills learned in the army to increase the effectiveness of the rioters. The exception, perhaps, is drunken assaults on pubs, but in most other cases, veterans made rioters more disciplined and more effective.

In nearly every postwar riot and plot, veterans can be found, which is hardly surprising given the scale of the mobilization effort of the wars. William Turner, veteran of the Egyptian campaign, was executed following Brandreth's failed rebellion. Andrew Hardie and Robert Baird were veterans and also leaders of the Scottish weavers' attempted insurrection at Bonnymuir, part of the Radical War of 1820. Of the Cato Street conspirators, at least four had seen military service; Arthur Thistlewood, the leader, had been in the militia.[26]

Veterans influenced all aspects of popular unrest, from organization to tactics. During the East Anglian riots of 1816, an "ensign" took charge of one group, taking it into the fields in the early morning hours for target practice. In the subsequent trials, a witness recalled that when a handful of veteran soldiers had come "into action," they had organized the rioters into three ranks. The first was armed with pitchforks and was to take a knee "with the Fork Irons upwards to meet the cavalry," while the second rank stood behind them. The third rank rested "Long Duck guns" on the shoulders of the second rank and prepared to fire at the soldiers.[27]

Veterans used their military experience to organize protests in Glasgow. The protestors appointed a general and a central committee of delegates ("a House of Lords," according to one ex-rifleman), and the city was organized into sixteen regiments. Each sent a representative to the committee, and each also coordinated a street-by-street rapid response plan, "so that in case of a turn-out they could parade . . . 'just as we did in the towns of Spain and France,'" said the rifleman.[28] During a spinners' strike in Manchester in 1818, a government informant marveled at their organization: each factory nominated a commander, who formed the workers into ranks, and whom they obeyed "as Strickly as the armey do their Colonel and as Little Talking as in a Regiment."[29]

The consistency with which authorities reported on veteran activities betrays their fear that the uncoordinated unrest would cohere into a viable national rebellion. Nowhere was this more apparent than at Peterloo. For weeks before the meeting, men had gone out onto the moors to practice marching in ranks and columns. It was the only place they could meet, since many towns were cracking down on indoor meetings and withholding permission to use central squares.[30] Summoned by buglers at dawn and under the instruction of former drill sergeants, they gathered in the cool mists to learn how to halt and to turn and to march in lock step with commanders positioned along the column. They used sticks in place of muskets and clapping in place of firing. Samuel Bamford remembered, "Our drill masters were generally old soldiers of the line. . . . They put the lads through their facings [turning in unison] in quick time, and soon learned them to march with a steadiness and regularity which would not have disgraced a regiment on parade."[31]

To authorities like Major General John Byng, in command of the northern district, this behavior betrayed the sinister nature of the planned protest: "The peaceable demeanour of so many thousand unemployed men is not natural."[32] Thomas Grenville was even more explicit. Not only was it unnatural, it was so dangerous that the government could not allow "this rebel army" to exist: "If it once be permitted that under the pretence of discussing Parliamentary Reform, large bodies of men may learn the military exercise, may march with seditious banners, & with all the emblems & tunes of the French revolution, & may take undisturbed possession of the city of Manchester, . . . there is an end of all existing law & government, & the population of this country must be set loose to frame a new order of society through the same bloody practices which have attended the French Revolution."[33]

In fact, the French Revolution was at the forefront of some of the marchers' minds, but not in the way Grenville assumed. The Manchester Female Reformers had called on all women from the "Higher and Middling Classes of Society" to join the march, which they saw as calling for change that was intimately connected to the wars and their effects. They wanted not just parliamentary reform but also economic relief from the wars' hangover. The wars had been unpopular, said their advertisement for the march, and they had been fought "for the purpose of placing upon the Throne of France, contrary to the people's interest and inclination, the present contemptible Louis, . . . this war, to reinstate this man, has tended . . . to load our beloved country with such an insurmountable burden of Taxation, that is too intolerable to endure longer; it has nearly annihilated our once flourishing trade and commerce, and is now driving our merchants and manufacturers to poverty and degradation."[34]

Whether or not this was the beginning of another revolution, what mattered to both sides is that the protest maintained discipline. The day of the meeting, the marchers arrived "in a kind of military array," as one constable put it. With "military precision, [the column] stepped off with as much regularity as a Regiment of Infantry."[35] In fact there were dozens of separate columns, each from a different Lancashire district. At the head of each were two rows of six of the best-dressed young men, followed by the rest of the marchers in rows of four or five. For every hundred marchers, there was a leader with a sprig of laurel in his hat; just as in Glasgow, each of these reported to a higher rank, and eventually to the leader of the district's delegation. The leader marched at the head of the column and was accompanied by a bugler. The marchers displayed banners with the town's name or symbols, both for reasons of pride and for the practical matter of helping to keep neighbors together. Bamford recalled, "I re-joined my comrades, and forming about a thousand of them into file, we set off to the sound of fife and drum, with our only banner waving."[36]

Yet borrowing military organizational schemes did not make the marchers a military organization. Admittedly, Henry Hunt later estimated that one-third of the protestors had served either in the militia or in the regular army, but women and children, dressed in their Sunday best, were also prominent in the crowds. Women wore white to demonstrate their respectability: they were not participating in the political process as disgraceful members of an unruly mob but rather as decent Englishwomen petitioning for reasonable change. The presence of so many women made the march more like a festival procession than a regiment. It was common for Lancashire villages to hold annual rush-bearing processions, which brought fresh rushes to cover the cold stone floor of the parish church. The march to

Peterloo was, in many ways, a rush-bearing procession that happened to terminate in St. Peter's Fields rather than the parish church. The drummers, buglers, and fifers on the march to Peterloo were the same drummers, buglers, and fifers who would have marched to the parish church.[37]

The Crown saw the procession differently. In making their case after the massacre, the prosecution argued that sixty thousand people had arrived in Manchester "in a formidable and menacing manner and in military procession and array with Clubs, Sticks and other offensive Weapons and instruments and with diverse Seditious and inflammatory inscriptions and devices to the great alarm and terror of the peaceably disposed subjects of . . . the King."[38] The fundamental misunderstanding that led to the tragedy is visible here: were the marchers peacefully mimicking a village festival, or an army sent to overthrow the established order? The presence of veterans among the crowd, and their role in organizing and equipping the marchers, exacerbated this misunderstanding. That is not to blame the veterans for the subsequent tragedy but simply to point out that the military rituals they brought to Manchester helped maintain order among the marchers while simultaneously making it more likely that the magistrates and the military would act stupidly out of fear.

The Manchester magistrates committed the original sin: they did not communicate their intentions clearly, and then they panicked, creating a crisis out of a peaceful meeting. The leaders, including the orator Hunt, had been told that they would not be arrested at the meeting. Yet when the magistrates saw the scale and regimented organization of the crowd, they changed their minds and ordered the yeomanry to arrest Hunt. St. Peter's Fields is only about three acres in size: the crowd of nearly fifty thousand (not sixty thousand as the government claimed) overwhelmed its capacity, and mounted men stood little chance of penetrating to Hunt at the center without causing a deadly crush.

Nevertheless, the yeomanry waded into the crowd. From horseback, they could see ahead to Hunt, but from the middle of the crowd, confusion prevailed. First, a murmur of concern, then a jostle, then a cry of alarm, then a wave of panic, and finally, a crush. The first casualties occurred at this point. From the yeomanry's perspective, the failure of the crowd to make way for their members' horses must have been frustrating. That does not excuse their subsequent actions. It is difficult to untangle the web of motives that caused them to use their blades indiscriminately in the subsequent melee. Some have argued it was deliberate class warfare; others, that poor training and horsemanship were to blame; still others, that the crowd was armed and dangerous; and recently, that the yeomanry were "spoiling for a fight, in order to show the Radicals who was in charge."[39]

Whatever their motivations, the yeomanry was soon trapped in the middle of the crowd. As had happened at other public meetings, the regular troops, which included twelve companies drawn from the Thirty-First, Seventy-First, and Eighty-Eighth Foot as well as nine troops of the Fifteenth Hussars and two six-pound cannon, had been kept out of sight as a reserve. Now they entered the fray to rescue the yeomanry, at which point the melee became a massacre. The yeomanry lashed out, capturing banners from the crowd and treating them like enemy standards. The only shots fired likely came from the yeomanry, as the Hussars and the infantry relied on blades. The regulars did a better job of maintaining their discipline, but that had the perverse effect of worsening the massacre when they blocked off exit routes for the crowd with their bayonets.[40]

For the young officer William Jolliffe of the Fifteenth Hussars, the casualties were unfortunate: "The Hussars drove the people forward with the flats of their swords, but sometimes, as is almost inevitably the case when men are placed in such situations, the edge was used." He thought most injuries, however, were caused by "the pressure of the routed multitude."[41] The Radical perspective was substantially different—it truly was a massacre. The Hussars killed women and children indiscriminately, and the field was strewn with the dead, dying, and injured. Indeed, that perspective—that it was a battlefield—was shared by some of the military participants, but not because they sympathized with the Radical cause. Major Dyneley of the Royal Horse Artillery described the "Battle of Manchester" as ending in "the complete discomfiture of the Enemy. . . . I had the pleasure of seeing Hunt &c. scoured & sent off, the Colors & Cap of liberty in the hands of our troops, the hustings torn to pieces, & I must not say the *pleasure* of seeing the field of Battle covered with Hats, Sticks, Shoes, Laurel Branches, Drum Heads &c &c in short the field was as complete as I had ever seen one after an action."[42]

Percy Shelley's version is evocative: "Let the horsemen's scimitars / Wheel and flash, like sphereless stars / Thirsting to eclipse their burning / In a sea of death and mourning."[43] Eighteen people were killed, which, out of a crowd of tens of thousands suggests Shelley might have overstated his case. Yet the injury tally was staggering, and fully worthy of his evocative imagery. One recent account has it at 736 injuries suffered by 602 people, of which 200 were cut by sabers and about the same number were trampled by horses or crowd pressure. Women were more likely to be injured than men among the crowd, while in addition, 67 soldiers and 20 horses were injured. Postwar riots regularly resulted in casualties, but nothing matched the scale of Peterloo.[44]

Nor was the action confined to the crush in St. Peter's Fields. In the chaotic aftermath, the Hussars demonstrated the standard crowd control techniques—the same techniques the yeomanry had failed to use. After the massacre, the Hussars spent a few hours patrolling the streets, which were by that point mostly empty. That evening, two troops of horses and some infantry (from the Eighty-Eighth Foot) were ordered to set up a picket. Immediately after they had done so, a crowd gathered around them. The crowd grew increasingly agitated as darkness fell, throwing stones at the soldiers. Jolliffe described the soldiers' attempts to use nonlethal force: "The Hussars many times cleared the ground by driving the mob up the streets leading from the New Cross." Here we can see the usual pattern of escalation: show up, guard something, suffer stones from the crowd, and then advance against them without firing. It did not work. Locals used their knowledge of the narrow passages between streets to re-form and launch another attack. For nearly an hour and a half, the soldiers endured the assault, "being more and more pressed upon," as Jolliffe put it. A magistrate showed up to read the Riot Act, to no avail. Having exhausted the nonlethal options, the officer in charge, with the approval of the magistrate, "ordered the 88th to fire (which they did by platoon firing) down three of the streets. The firing lasted only a few minutes; perhaps not more than thirty shots were fired; but these had a magical effect; the mob ran away and dispersed forthwith, leaving three or four persons on the ground with gunshot wounds."[45]

No postwar riot matched the significance of Peterloo. With the support of leading members of the government, including Wellington, the cabinet drafted an official letter of thanks to the magistrates.

The prince regent also praised the yeomanry, and while some cabinet members were privately appalled, publicly, all expressed support. How could they not? To admit that the yeomanry and troops had made mistakes was to implicate the magistrates and the army, and the government's system of order depended on the support of both. Wellington, for one, believed wholeheartedly in the necessity of repression, telling Sidmouth to enforce the Six Acts as strictly as possible. The next spring, Hunt and his colleagues were convicted of unlawful and seditious assembling for the purpose of exciting discontent, with prison sentences ranging from one to two and a half years. The troops involved escaped legal action, even though they were at the center of the post-Peterloo debate.[46]

There were many extenuating circumstances that explain some of their actions, and Peterloo has to be seen in the context of the riotous postwar period. Other riots had been dispersed much more effectively, sometimes even by the same chain of command. Byng had effectively suppressed riots in Manchester in 1817, and in February 1819 in Stockport, troops had endured much worse from the crowd and yet resisted putting it down by force.[47] Fundamentally, however, soldiers made poor policemen, and they knew it. Byng, veteran of Waterloo, wrote to Sidmouth with concern on Christmas Day 1816: "[I am] always afraid my zeal may outrun my prudence, how can a man who has been *making war* nearly all his life, know anything about *preserving the peace?*"[48] Another soldier claimed, "Of all the services which a soldier is called upon to perform, there is none so unpalatable to him as that of waging war against a domestic enemy."[49]

The military's high-profile failure to act with restraint at Peterloo, attacking a peaceful assembly, fundamentally changed the political dynamic of postwar Britain. Veterans were at the heart of that change. The Fifteenth Hussars had been with Wellington in the Peninsular War and at Waterloo, and many were wearing their Waterloo medals that day. On the other side, veteran soldiers had helped organize the march to Manchester, drilling in the fields before dawn and adopting a military organizational structure. John Lees, a Waterloo veteran and one of those who had attended the meeting, died three weeks after Peterloo of a brain hemorrhage or possibly blood poisoning resulting from internal bleeding and fractures sustained during the chaos.[50]

That veterans were on both sides of these protests suggests that Radical leaders missed an opportunity. If soldiers on active duty could have been convinced to join their former comrades on the other side of the barricades, perhaps the postwar turmoil would not have fizzled out. This is not an anachronistic suggestion. A French visitor to London in 1820 saw the Radicals attempting to do exactly that "because they know they would become formidable if the soldier declared himself for them."[51] Shelley was also aware of the possibilities, as his post-Peterloo poem "England in 1819" suggests: "An army, whom liberticide and prey / Makes as a two-edged sword to all who wield."[52] In other words, although the army kills liberty, it may also be the undoing of the tyrants. In William Cobbett's 1816 address "To the Journeymen and Labourers of England, Wales, Scotland, and Ireland," he made the obvious but important point that none of Britain's great victories in the wars would have been possible without ordinary soldiers and sailors: "Titles and immense sums of money have been bestowed upon numerous naval and military commanders. Without calling the justice of these into question, we may assert that the victories were obtained by *you*." Now was their chance to be recognized for their contribution to Britain's victory by being given the vote. If Radicals could connect military service to full citizenship, they might be able to mobilize a powerful coalition for reform.[53]

Thanks in part to Cobbett's clear statement of intent, both the government and its opponents were aware of the importance of monitoring soldiers' loyalties—recall the banner at the Spa Fields meeting. The Cato Street conspirators hoped to encourage soldiers to overthrow the regime, coincidental with their assassination of the cabinet. They missed their chance by just a few months, as in June 1820, some of the Life Guards regiments in London mutinied. It seems that the mutiny stemmed less from political dissatisfaction than from more mundane complaints about their accommodation and onerous duties; furthermore, the mutiny was inconsistently executed. Still, the risk of defection was such that Sidmouth left a dinner party near Piccadilly and personally oversaw the dispersal of a crowd by a troop of the Second Life Guards, which had not mutinied.[54] The next day, York immediately ordered the troublesome regiments to march to Portsmouth, where they were reviewed by Wellington on the fifth anniversary of Waterloo. He later wrote to Liverpool, "In one of the most crucial moments that ever occurred in this country, we and the public have reason to doubt the fidelity of the troops. The sergeants and corporals of the Guards are certainly excellent soldiers . . . but it must be observed that they are taken from the ranks, and of the class of the people, and liable to be influenced by the views and sentiments of the people."[55]

In general, however, the Radical opponents of Liverpool's regime failed to capitalize on the opportunity presented by the uncertain loyalties of soldiers. Not until the second half of the nineteenth century, according to the most recent leading account, were men able to demand full citizenship rights in exchange for military service.[56] Cobbett's call to action was not followed up with a consistent campaign aimed at the military, and indeed his address spent most of its energy arguing that excessive government spending was the root cause of the country's misery in 1816. In making that argument, Cobbett backed himself into the uncomfortable rhetorical corner of attacking spending on soldiers: "As to the money subscribed by *Regiments of Soldiers*, whose pay arises from taxes, in part paid by you, though it is the most shocking spectacle to behold, I do not think so much of it. The soldiers are your fathers, brothers, and sons."[57] In Shelley's "The Masque of Anarchy," written in 1819, he lists the occupations of those who should stand against the tyrants: those who use the "Loom, and plough, and sword, and spade." Perhaps ordinary soldiers, men of the sword, may be allies in the fight for revolutionary change. Yet elsewhere in that poem, he is clear that soldiers are in fact "hired murderers," "the Tyrant's crew," who greet the cabinet (represented as the Four Horsemen of the Apocalypse) "with pomp," singing their praises and indicating their willingness to kill for them.[58]

In addition to mixed messaging from the Radicals, soldiers remained generally loyal because loyalism retained much of its power despite the postwar unrest. It was patriotic loyalism, not Radicalism, that many soldiers perceived as a more effective path to broader citizenship.[59] Following Peterloo, ministers redoubled their efforts to promote loyalist newspapers, and exiling key Radical figures proved to be an effective means of muzzling them. As chapter 8 discussed, they embodied the militia for the first time since the wars and increased the army's domestic deployments. Rumors about mutinous regiments rarely had any truth in them, and separating the army from the government proved too difficult for Radicals to undertake a serious effort.[60]

Furthermore, many soldiers had been gone from Britain too long to feel a sense of solidarity with the communities they were policing. When Captain Harry Smith and his men returned from the Army of Occupation in 1818, Smith recalled, "We heard of nothing but 'the French are coming over.'" They had been gone for so long that British soldiers were now, as Smith put it, a "*them.*" As they traversed the countryside, they looked around nervously, expecting the enemy to take advantage of their scattered deployments: "Although I repeated to myself a hundred times daily, 'You are in England,' the thought would arise, 'You are in the power of your enemy.'" Smith and his soldiers were still fully militarized when they deployed to Glasgow to deal with riots in the manufacturing districts. They saw the country through the eyes of veteran campaigners. It was, they thought, a difficult country to make war in, and Smith recalled conversations among his men: "'I say, Bill, look at that wood on the hill there and those hedgerows before it. I think we could keep that ourselves against half Soult's Army. Ah, I had rather keep it than attack it! But Lord, the war's all over now.'" These were men used to following orders, used to preparing for combat, and used to viewing the world as perpetually in a state of war—as it had been for most of their lives. One of Smith's superiors said he was "proud . . . to see one of his old Battalions in peace the same ready soldiers they were in war." We should perhaps not be surprised, then, that when confronted with an unruly crowd, they were ready to put their training and experience to use. When stones started flying, it did not matter if they were flying from the hands of fellow countrymen.[61]

Suppressing rioting was "very laborious and irksome," Smith recalled decades later, and he "never had more arduous duties than on this occasion"—this from a veteran of campaigns on four continents. "We had neither enemy nor friends: a sort of *Bellum in Pace,* which we old campaigners did not understand." Smith did claim to understand the importance of deferring to the civil authority, however. When he and his men were sent to arrest some Radicals, they were confronted by a mob. He ordered his men to use the flats of their swords to "make the heads of some ache, while brickbrats, stones, etc. were flying among us half as bad as grapeshot." The magistrates were worried he would order his men to fire, but as he later explained to his commanding officer, "I did not desire to bring upon my head either the blood of my foolish and misguided countrymen, or the odium of the Manchester magistrates."[62]

CHAPTER 13

Officers at Home

Shortly before Christmas 1815, just as the London social season was beginning, Captain Rees Howell Gronow of the First Battalion of the First Regiment of Grenadier Guards was invited to dine at Sir James Bland Burges's house in Mayfair. Burges was the father of one of Gronow's friends in the guards, and he had invited several interesting dinner guests that night. Walter Scott "was quite delightful," Gronow later recalled. "He appeared full of fire and animation." John Wilson Croker "was also agreeable, notwithstanding his bitter and sarcastic remarks on everything and everybody. The sneering, ill-natured expression on his face, struck me as an impressive contrast to the frank and benevolent countenance of Walter Scott." Lord Byron was handsome and added plenty of value to any dinner party, but he was also "all show-off and affection."[i] Gronow had never met these illustrious men before, but he did not feel out of place. Born into a landed family in Wales, he had been close friends with Percy Shelley at Eton. Instead of going to Oxford, he had purchased his commission in one of the most elite regiments in the British army in 1812 and spent the next two years in the Peninsular War.[1]

---

i   From context, it is likely Gronow used "affection" in the now-rare sense of "affecting or assuming artificiality." *Oxford English Dictionary*, s.v. "affection, n.2."

For Gronow, demobilization provided an opportunity to enjoy the vibrant social scene in London, at the center of which were clubs like Almack's. In 1814, while "enjoying the fame of our Spanish campaign," Gronow and his fellow guardsmen schemed to gain entrance. "One can hardly conceive the importance which was attached to getting admission to Almack's, the seventh heaven of the fashionable world . . . this exclusive temple of the *beau monde;* the gates of which were guarded by lady patronesses, whose smiles or frowns consigned men and women to happiness or despair." Lady Cowper, later Lady Palmerston, was the most popular of the ruling clique, which included Viscountess Castlereagh, the Countess of Jersey, and the Countess de Lieven, wife of the Russian ambassador. They turned away even Wellington when he failed to meet their exacting dress code. Regency London was full of military and naval officers willing to risk their fortunes for a chance to breathe such rarefied airs. Led by fashionistas like Beau Brummell (himself the owner of a commission in the Tenth Hussars, the Prince of Wales's Own), they were members of Almack's and other clubs like White's (for Tories) and Brookes's (for Whigs). They drank heavily late into the night, frittering away their fortunes gambling enormous sums. Brummell's brief reign ended in bankruptcy and disgraceful exile; Gronow himself declared bankruptcy in 1823.[2]

That was a relatively minor setback, however, as bankruptcies among clubgoers were common. Lieutenant Samuel Walters, in contrast, did not have a similar financial cushion. He spent the last two years of the wars on the far side of the world, in command of a transport to New South Wales. When he returned in September 1815, his transport was released from service and he was placed on half pay. With no family fortune, his meager income kept him far away from the club scene. He may have spent a year at sea in a merchant ship, but since commissioned officers had to apply to the Admiralty for permission to do so and there is no record of his having applied, we cannot be sure. In May 1819, he wrote some lines of verse in which he asked whether being rich made someone happy—a sure sign of poverty. To his credit, he concluded it was hard to tell from the outside: "Though clothed with grandeur, enriched with wealth, and heaped with honours, who can tell what the mind sustains?" He never again was employed at sea, and in 1834, while visiting some relatives who had emigrated to Canada, he died of cholera, age fifty-six.[3]

Both Gronow and Walters were officers, yet their experience of demobilization could hardly have been more different. Broadly speaking, there were two kinds of officers: a small elite and a much larger group of officers from middling backgrounds with limited social prospects. Elite officers were often high ranking because their pay, prestige, and prize money helped them move in elevated social circles, but for a junior officer like Gronow, family fortunes could serve the same purpose. Elite officers could live profligate lives in the prince regent's circle or establish themselves as comfortable landowners in the countryside. Most officers, however, did not come from money. They relied on their active duty pay to sustain their appearances as gentlemen of the sword. Demobilization and the collapse in employment prospects, especially in the navy, threw thousands of officers into financial difficulties. This chapter examines what happened when both kinds of officers came home.

For elite officers, the arrival of the first peace in 1814 was the starting gun of a mad scramble for rewards. The most coveted was a peerage because it was permanent, passed down through male heirs indefinitely, and because it was exclusive. The British aristocracy was tiny by European standards, with just two hundred families in 1780 compared to hundreds of thousands in France. Since the French Revolution, however, the British aristocracy had grown marginally less exclusive as its members sought to forestall revolution at home by rewarding those who had served the state. The long wars had provided more opportunities for senior officers to stake claims to peerages than any generation before them. The government often rewarded the victor of a major battle with a peerage, as, for example, Duncan after Camperdown, Nelson after the Nile, and Wellington after Talavera. Sustained periods of excellence in charge of large armies or naval stations also could qualify, so in 1814, Pellew became Baron Exmouth following a decade of service in the East Indies and the Mediterranean on top of a glittering career as a frigate captain.[4]

The result of the growth of this service elite was peerage inflation: for every successful candidate, half a dozen others claimed that they were equally deserving. Take Sir James Saumarez, who transformed a defeat into victory at Algeciras in 1801, after which he made it clear that he felt he deserved a barony for it. But Nelson had recently been given a barony for his victory at the Nile that had involved about twice as many ships, so ministers decided that Saumarez would have to be content with receiving the Order of the Bath. Similarly, in 1814, after his important tenure in the Baltic had come to an end, Saumarez watched jealously as Pellew received a peerage for being the successful commander in chief of a diplomatically sensitive theater, while he had to settle for an honorary doctorate from Oxford. Saumarez wrote to Liverpool begging for a peerage, but he was refused. He resigned himself to a quiet life on Guernsey until Earl Grey's Whig government in 1831 sought to stack the House of Lords with friendly peers, at which point he finally became Baron de Saumarez.[5]

An authoritative list of the military and naval officers raised to the peerage for their service in the wars is difficult to produce because peerage creation was, by its very nature, political. There are eighteen strong candidates who meet the criteria, twelve naval and six military: Hood, Bridport, Barham, St. Vincent, Duncan, Nelson, Collingwood, Keith, Gardner, Gambier, Exmouth, and Saumarez; and Wellington, Lake, Lynedoch, Combermere, Hill, and Beresford, respectively. The two-to-one ratio of naval to military officers reflects the navy's longer record of high-profile successes combined with the higher likelihood that army officers would already be members of the aristocracy when they received their rewards. After Waterloo, for example, no fewer than twenty-one peerages were created, but every single creation was for an officer who already held a peerage. The classic example is the Earl of Uxbridge who was created the Marquess of Anglesey.[6]

Men like Saumarez and especially Exmouth used their service records to catapult themselves from middling backgrounds to the highest ranks of British society, but still they looked up at an even more exclusive group. Just as in the United States today, objectively wealthy families can feel comparatively poor. The wealthiest 1 percent own roughly as much wealth as the next 9 percent put together, and the same was likely true for the United Kingdom in 1820. Wellington stood at the pinnacle of the postwar reward system. He received sizeable grants to support his rise through the ranks of the aristocracy, capped by £400,000 voted for his dukedom and a further £200,000 for the victory at Waterloo. His wealth was astonishing but not unparalleled, as Keith made perhaps £500,000 in prize money during the wars. In contrast, not all the military and naval officers who received peerages for their wartime service became true grandees.

The Exmouth and Hood families owned fewer than three thousand acres by the end of the nineteenth century, which put them in the bottom ranks of the landed elite.[7]

An officer did not have to be a peer to be a member of the elite, however. A more common, but still exclusive, reward was to be inducted into the chivalric Order of the Bath. The order had been founded in 1725 specifically to reward victory in European wars, and membership was restricted to just thirty-five companions before 1815. Nelson had declined a baronetcy after his spectacular performance at the Battle of Cape St. Vincent in 1797 in favor of the Bath because of its reputation as the preserve of military heroes. It also came with a bright red sash and a star embroidered on the officer's uniforms, which suited Nelson's public image. In 1815, however, the government decided to expand the order dramatically to defuse some of the tension among senior officers who felt their services had been unfairly overlooked. The revised version of the order had three classes, in descending order of precedence: Knights Grand Cross (GCB), Knights Commander (KCB), and Companions (CB). It also now encompassed more than two thousand officers. There were 115 GCBs, 338 KCBs, and 1,815 CBs created in 1815; after Waterloo, a further 101 CBs were added, which accounted for about 20 percent of all the staff and field officers present at the great battle.[8]

Despite this explosion of postwar CBs, the British were generally in agreement that continental officers were over-generaled and over-decorated. Croker told his wife that "on *an average*, every man in Paris would have *two* crosses. I saw one man yesterday with 6, twenty with 4 or 5, and hundreds with 3 different orders at their button hole. . . . In fact, the greatest distinction our people have here is that they are without them."[9] Perhaps, but the reality was that British officers were as eager for rewards as any Prussian. They gleefully collected foreign honors, like the Austrian Order of Maria Theresa, and Wellington recommended many of his Peninsular War officers for the Spanish Order of St. Ferdinand. George IV and William IV both took advantage of their status as Electors of Hanover to sidestep the relatively constrained British reward system to induct favored officers into the Royal Guelphic (or Hanoverian) Order.[10]

Nor was the scramble for status restricted to chivalric orders. Officers sought medals for individual battles. "We are to have the medals for the last action," Collingwood wrote to his wife with satisfaction after Trafalgar, "and I do not despair of getting another soon: I am the only officer in the Service with three."[11, ii] The navy struck medals after six major fleet actions and twelve individual actions, and the army after many of the great Peninsular War battles including Talavera, Badajoz, and Orthez.[12] Only senior officers received these medals, and there did not seem to be consistent criteria for which battles were worthy. That all changed when Wellington asked for a medal to be struck and given to every participant at Waterloo. Campaign medals were not unknown—there was a Peninsular campaign medal for senior officers—but the Waterloo medal marked an important turning point in the commemoration of ordinary British soldiers. It was the first campaign or battle medal issued to all soldiers regardless of rank, the first campaign medal given to the next of kin of those killed, and the first medal with the recipient's name, rank, and regiment impressed on it. At least thirty-six thousand one-ounce silver medals were struck using a new machine process at the Royal Mint. On one side was the prince regent in profile, and on the other, winged Victory with "WELLINGTON," "WATERLOO," and "JUNE 18, 1815."[13]

In the aftermath of the creation of the Waterloo medal, inflation struck again: Exmouth asked for a medal after Algiers. It was not an unreasonable request, as the government had thought the victory worthy of elevating him from a baron to a viscount. (Apparently George IV was terrified of the strong and energetic admiral, which may have helped his case.[14]) But Croker, whose support would have been essential to create an Algiers medal, disabused him: "Why should that be done for five thousand men who were at Algiers, which has not been done for the million of men who have served in so many glorious actions since 1793? You will say that the soldiers of Waterloo have had medals, but surely it is impossible to compare Waterloo with any other battle. The soldiers of Salamanca, Talavera, Vittoria, Toulouse, and the Pyrenees, have no medals."[15] Here Croker made a

---

ii   Collingwood well knew how fraught the politics of battle medals could be. He had participated at the Glorious First of June, but he was maliciously left off the list of captains to receive a medal. Only after he had distinguished himself at the Battle of Cape St. Vincent was he able to force the Admiralty to rectify the error and give him medals for both actions.

strong case, accidentally, for the Naval and Military General Service Medals, which were introduced in 1847 for surviving veterans of the Great Wars. This three-decade delay (during which tens of thousands of veterans died, unmedaled) requires some explanation. Some have blamed Wellington, arguing that he sought to elevate Waterloo above all other victories and so squashed attempts to create a Peninsular campaign medal.[16] But as Croker's letter suggests, it was not just Wellington who saw Waterloo as distinct from all other achievements. He concluded to Exmouth, "In short, my dear Lord, . . . I should be sorry to see anything done for [Algiers], which should seem to throw a shade over the 1st June, Camperdown, St. Vincent's, the Nile, and Trafalgar."[17]

Everything about the rewards system in this period was calibrated, contested, and compared, and the Waterloo medal was no exception. Even within regiments, it caused problems, as Edward Costello remembered when he received his medal at Cambrai in February 1816: "I am sorry to say this caused many dissensions among the men, particularly some of the old veterans of the Peninsular campaigns. One named Wheatley, as brave a man as any in the service, was unfortunately in hospital at Brussels during the action, and was not honoured with this mark of bravery; whenever he met with badges on what he termed recruits, he would instantly tear them off, and frequently throw them away."[18] Sergeant John Lowe was frustrated to receive a medal impressed "Corporal John Lowe." He pleaded, "As I expect to have little to leave to my Children beyond my medal, I don't wish them, and those who may come after them, to be deceived as to the station I held in so decisive a battle."[19] The haphazard distribution of the medal exacerbated veterans' resentments, created a black market for counterfeits, and provided opportunities for those who had not been present to claim otherwise—an early example of what today is called "stolen valor."[20]

All military men, but especially officers, guarded their status jealously and did not hesitate to ask for more. Major John Slessor's unit had been peripheral to the major action on June 18, but he did receive a medal, which he accepted "with satisfaction and pleasure."[21] But what he most desired was to be made a CB, although his petitions to that effect failed. Sir William Dillon had been made a CB, but he wanted to be at least a KCB. His petition to the prince regent also failed. Naturally this grasping attitude extended to questions of cash rewards. Every general officer at Waterloo received £1,274 and there was a descending scale from there, but many officers wrote to Wellington to make sure their claim was not overlooked. During the wars, prize money sloshed around the coffers of admirals and post-captains, and they made sure as little spilled out as possible by continuing to work with their prize agents well into the peace to guard their shares as old cases wound their way through the courts.[22]

The government managed the reward system deliberately. Croker, for example, relied on historical precedents to inform his positions on the validity of various rewards. In his papers is a study of all the examples in which military commanders had been empowered by the Crown to create knighthoods from 1509 to 1640, presumably because returning to that practice had been suggested as one way to tamp down on the jealous squabbling.[23] In general, Croker and his colleagues were successful. The 1815 expansion of the Order of the Bath particularly helped the government achieve its goal of reward-ing its senior officers for their service, thereby relieving some of the pressure they felt from this influential group. That is not to say that everyone was pleased, of course. St. Vincent thought the expansion of the Bath devalued his own membership (which dated from 1782), and for the rest of his life he refused to wear his star or sash except in the presence of the sovereign.[24]

Sir William Hoste exemplifies the prickly elite officer. As soon as his haul of postwar honors seemed to have been fully gathered, he took the common step of having his portrait painted—having saved about £12,000 in prize money, he could afford it. Joseph Farington visited him while he was sitting for his portrait and asked him to explain his honors. He was proud of his KCB and the Order of Maria Theresa, he said, "but what He most valued was the medal given to Him for the action in the *Adriatic* in which He commanded [the victory at Lissa]. That was for Specific Service while on the contrary there were many to whom the rank of Knight Commander was given, Men who never saw a shot fired in real service: they obtained this Honor by *interest*, which being known, it lowered its value." Hoste was frustrated because the KCB regulations stated that the recipient had to return any medals for service, so he petitioned the prince regent for the right to continue to wear it. He was also annoyed that the star of the Order of the Bath could only be worn by flag and general officers: "Thus, He observed, an officer is precluded from wearing that distinction probably during that period of His life when He [would] most feel the advantage of it."[25]

Hoste's modern biographer describes his new postwar grandiosity: "He could call himself Captain Sir William Hoste, Bart., RN, KCB, KMT, and augment his family's arms with an arm protruding from a naval crown to grasp a flag enscribed 'Cattaro' [celebrating his successful siege of that town in late 1813]."[26] Elite officers expended enormous emotional energy and political capital on status symbols in 1815 because they knew that peace likely would put an end to their opportunities for advancement. They lived in a status-obsessed society, and the end of the wars was their last chance to make major changes to their status. Jane Austen's *Persuasion* appeared just two years after Hoste sat for his portrait, and the opening lines paint a vivid picture of this world: "Sir Walter Elliot, of Kellynch Hall, in Somersetshire, was a man who, for his own amusement, never took up any book but the Baronetage. . . . He considered the blessing of beauty as inferior only to the blessing of a baronetcy; and the Sir Walter Elliot, who united these gifts, was the constant object of his warmest respect and devotion."[27, iii]

Officers who succeeded in securing sufficient funds and making useful social connections settled into lives as country gentlemen. They managed their large houses and estates from which they drew rents, they visited and dined with their neighbors, they attended balls, they hunted, and they patronized charitable societies. Many took advantage of the opening of the Continent to embark on belated grand tours. Admiral Sir Philip Broke, his first biographer reported, cared about two things in his retirement: augmenting his family arms and corresponding with fellow officers. He "cherished to his last hour . . . private and personal congratulations and tokens of regard."[28] Sir Pulteney Malcolm also tried to remain connected to his naval networks, especially in Scotland—Keith was his wife's uncle and Melville had been his patron. But when no postwar command was forthcoming, Malcolm threw himself into family life, dividing

---

iii *Burke's Peerage*, the most popular and enduring of the genealogical surveys of the elite, was founded in 1826.

his time between Scotland and his in-law's home outside of London. From November to April, he and his family rented a house in Marylebone for the social season.[29]

Some officers also became involved in national politics, and not always on the government's side. There were reform-minded MPs from both services like Sir George De Lacy Evans and Lord Cochrane. Equally, however, there are examples of officers who got involved on the front lines of domestic politics by attacking signs of Radicalism. The army officers and MPs Charles John Brandling and Matthew Bell led yeomanry detachments to suppress striking keelmen on the Tyne in 1822 and 1823. But the average military or naval MP was a quiet, dependable vote for the government—better, many calculated, not to bite the hand that fed them. When officers did speak, the results were occasionally surprising and colorful. The Whig army officer Thomas Davies distinguished himself from his colleagues by not only speaking frequently but by regularly calling for a reduction in military spending. James Wemyss's speeches were described as those of "a jolly mariner, rough, homespun, full of a sort of ready raillery, blunt, off-hand and ready witted."[30] The most common military and naval speakers, however, had more straightforward agendas. For example, Sir George Cockburn's position on the Admiralty Board required him to explain the Navy Estimates annually. The army was roughly twice as large as the navy, but the tendency of army officers to come from wealthier backgrounds than naval officers meant that the army was overrepresented in Parliament. From 1790 to 1820 there were four times as many army MPs as naval MPs; from 1820 to 1832, there were nearly five times as many.[31]

The different social makeup of the two services caused some annoyances during the negotiations about setting up the United Service Club. Some naval officers, including St. Vincent and Captain Francis Beaufort, complained about the high cost of membership. Their objections were overruled, however, and there was enough interest in the club to fund the rental of a large house on Albemarle Street. Over the course of the next decade, the thousand-plus members (field grade officers in the army and commanders and above in the navy, alongside other high-ranking officeholders) raised funds for a more permanent home in a John Nash–designed clubhouse on Pall Mall in 1828.[32]

Despite naval officers' complaints, in general the story of elite officers in the postwar period is one of insulation from the turmoil. General William Dyott complained in his diary that the 1816 Lichfield races lacked the usual ostentatious displays from the leading families in the area. He was saddened that there was no longer a tacit competition for the most decorated carriage pulled by the most horses, but that was the extent of his concern with the postwar depression. Unrest in 1819 before and after Peterloo stirred him to attend some loyalist meetings, which passed a few resolutions expressing "the abhorrence they felt at the proceedings."[33] Certainly veteran officers who were currently serving in the government could not afford to be so passive, but a large portion of elite officers established a comfortable retirement after 1815.

Junior officers engaged in a similarly mad scramble for promotions at the end of the wars. In expectation of a long peace, many recognized that their window for advancement was rapidly closing. Army promotions were notoriously slow even in wartime because they depended on vacant commissions, so the end of the wars and the concurrent decrease in officer mortality made the problem worse. It could take decades to reach higher ranks: one captain served through the Peninsular War but was still a captain in 1836. One way to sidestep the slow churn of regimental advancements was a brevet promotion, in which an officer was advanced to a higher rank in the army than in his regiment. A month after Waterloo, the War Office announced brevet promotions for fifty-two majors to lieutenant colonels and thirty-five captains to major, but that still left many on the shelf. Two further rounds of brevet promotions followed in 1817 and 1819, and Wellington and York regularly received petitions for more.[34]

Army officers did have more opportunities than naval officers in the postwar period to distinguish themselves in action (or hope to survive a sickly season). An officer with otherwise poor prospects could exchange into a regiment destined for imperial service.[35] But there was still a sizeable contingent left with no hope for employment and no income beyond their half pay. Palmerston explained to the Commons in 1817 that half-pay officers were making "an infinite variety of applications" for employment. "He was sure the House would sympathize with what he might call the distresses of many of those most deserving individuals."[36] In 1820, military and naval officers' half pay was one of the single largest items in the budget at £1.8 million. The situation had not improved even by 1831, when there were 9,404 army officers on half pay but only 6,768 on full pay. Palmerston spent those years working to standardize practices, especially with regards to officers' widows making claims for pensions. Many junior officers, however, ended up in financial difficulties. Creditors came to the Horse Guards hoping to get their loans repaid, which Palmerston admitted was only natural as people used to employment in the army were always likely to struggle to adjust to the "scanty" half pay of an ensign or lieutenant.[37]

A survey of some postwar careers of junior army officers illustrates these challenges. Charles Adams Walsh was a lieutenant in the Third Foot through the Peninsular War, and he remained with the regiment when it joined the Army of Occupation. The reductions of 1818, however, forced him onto half pay. He got married in his native Ireland and remained unemployed except for one brief stint as an officer in charge of fortifications from 1830 to 1834. He died penniless in County Tipperary in 1846.[38] Ensign William Thain avoided half pay but struggled to advance, despite being promoted to lieutenant after being wounded at Waterloo. It took him ten years to make the next step to captain in the Thirty-Third Foot in the West Indies, at which point he exchanged into the Twenty-First Fusiliers so he could try his luck in India. He was killed in action in the Afghan War in 1842.[39]

Henry Acton's career was characterized by instability. After obtaining an ensigncy in the Twenty-Seventh Foot in 1812, he had had to resign his commission because of poor health the next year. By 1814 he felt well enough to return to the army, this time as a cornet in the Thirteenth Light Dragoons. He purchased a commission as a lieutenant in that regiment in 1815, but by July 1816 he had been placed on half pay. Seeking active employment, he exchanged into the Twelfth Light Dragoons and returned to full pay in the Army of Occupation. He got married in the ambassador's chapel in Paris in September 1817, but by the end of the year, the beginning of the breakup of the Army of Occupation forced him back onto half pay. He spent the next decade in Edinburgh, unemployed with two children. By the time he answered a War Office circular in 1828, he had been on full pay for just four of his fifteen years as an officer. Nevertheless, he expressed a desire to return to active service.[40]

Going on half pay after many years on active service could be a jarring emotional experience. It may have contributed to the mental health crisis of Lieutenant Davies, the officer who tried to assassinate Palmerston. Major John Slessor kept a diary throughout the wars, but the last entry was the day he went on half pay: "Having disposed of my military garments, appointments etc, I mounted my horse and started for Dublin, not certainly under the most pleasant reflections, for I felt like a fish out of water, and as if a full stop was put to my professional advancement. In point of pecuniary emoluments, a great loser, but my own Master."[41] Slessor used the same language as Troop Sergeant William Dawes: both were "fish out of water" when they left the military. (Neither was a sailor, ironically.) Transitioning to civilian life was difficult for all ranks.

Family money made it easier, of course. Half pay for rich officers provided flexibility. James Penman Gairdner wrote to his father in February 1819 after he learned he had been returned to full pay in the Rifles: "I confess I felt no very great delight at this as during this time there is so little to be done that I had rather be on half pay, master of my own time to go where I please than be confined to a listless regimental quarter."[42] Eventually he decided to sell his commission, which provided a handy lump sum with which to embark on his postarmy life. An officer in the Rifles expressed a similar sentiment: "I feel no particular *penchant* for passing the remainder of my days in marching off guards, going grand rounds and visiting rounds, and performing other dull, monotonous, and uninteresting duties of the kind on which such great stress is laid, and to which such vast importance is attached, in various stiff-starched garrisons; but, on the contrary, prefer to range, henceforth, free and unfettered by my military trammels, wherever my fancy leads."[43]

Conditions improved for both services in the middle of the 1820s as funding and deployments both increased. In 1825, the Horse Guards also finally allowed officers on half pay to sell their commissions, so long as they were younger than sixty, had purchased their commissions, and served a minimum number of years (twelve for ensigns, fifteen for lieutenants, and twenty for captains and above). Nearly four hundred officers chose to take this step immediately. Such was the backlog of promotions that some full-pay captains bought half-pay majorities.[44]

Naval promotions differed from army promotions in two essential characteristics: they could not be purchased directly, and they could be made regardless of vacancies or ships to command. From the time a young officer was commissioned as a lieutenant, he could theoretically move rapidly to commander and then post-captain. From there, the tempo slowed as promotion to rear-admiral proceeded by seniority. Being made post as early as possible was highly desirable because the officer knew that if he lived long enough, he would eventually be promoted to rear-admiral, even if he had little chance of being employed at that rank. William Farington explained this to his uncle Joseph after he made post. It was "essential to His future happiness. . . . Had He remained a *Commander* only He should never have become truly happy, & that He fully believed it would have shortened His life." Since he had been, however, he claimed to have "nothing more to wish for, & whether He might or not be employed again in the public services would sit easy on his mind, as he had many resources, viz: reading, writing, drawing, the love of a Country life, and pleasures in attending to domestic concerns."[45]

It was highly unlikely that Farington could look forward to going back to sea in any case. The navy's employment crisis dwarfed the army's and indeed was "the greatest employment crisis in all its long history."[46] In January 1815, the unemployment rate for commissioned officers was 66 percent; a year later, 83 percent; and a year after that it stabilized at nearly 90 percent. By 1832, the rate had "improved" to 82 percent. There were several causes of this crisis, but fundamentally it was a question of supply and demand. On the supply side, there were already too many officers, even during the wars. In July 1813, when the navy was at its largest, there were more than two lieutenants for every position and more than three commanders and post-captains for every ship. A career in the navy was seen as respectable and potentially lucrative for upwardly mobile members of the middling sort, and the navy's stellar reputation, particularly early in the wars, meant that more young gentlemen sought naval careers than the Admiralty could hope to employ. Furthermore, the Admiralty had little control over officer entry. Families approached captains and asked them to take their sons on board so they could gain sufficient sea time and experience to pass the lieutenants' exam. The exam was often the first that the Admiralty officially learned of the existence of an officer, despite various attempts during the wars to erode captains' prerogatives.[47]

Dramatically shrinking the number of deployed ships in 1814 and 1815 created an insurmountable demand problem on top of the supply problem. Amid postwar budget cuts, there simply were not enough ships to keep the officer corps busy. Instead, the Admiralty sought to remedy the supply side. The Admiralty finally realized its long-term goal of taking control of officer entry away from captains, ensuring that only Admiralty-approved young gentlemen could be put on a path toward a commission. In 1816 and again in 1830, the Admiralty offered superannuation (literally "being overtaken by years") schemes to lieutenants over the age of fifty: if they accepted a nominal but honorable promotion to commander on the understanding that they would never be employed, the navy would reduce the number of officers seeking ships and clear out space for a younger generation. Yet only 7 percent of officers had taken up the offer by January 1832. The fundamental reason was that officers valued the social status of an active commission with the possibility of employment. Half pay was not lucrative, but it was steady, and there were plenty of examples of men put ashore for more than a decade who managed to get back to sea. At sea, there was always a chance of distinction or money, even in peacetime. Why would any officer voluntarily deprive himself of that chance?[48]

The Admiralty also made its own problem worse. As the wars wound down, senior officers scrambled to secure commissions for their young followers and promotions for their lieutenants and commanders. Sir Philip Durham wrapped up operations against Bonapartists in the West Indies in August 1815, and as was customary, he asked the Admiralty to promote his followers, although this time the approach of peace meant there was even more urgency. The Admiralty agreed to promote two of his lieutenants to commander, but neither was ever employed at that rank. The Admiralty also recognized that the difference between being an unemployed midshipman and an unemployed lieutenant was significant: the former got nothing while the latter at least got half pay. In 1815, they approved commissions for about one thousand new lieutenants.[49]

Two years later, in 1817, the Admiralty made only nineteen lieutenants. While that pattern did not hold throughout the postwar decade (by the 1820s the average rate was about ninety per year), it indicates the scale of the oversupply problem. Not until 1832 were a quarter of all lieutenants employed. Commanders were in an even worse position because it had long been common for a long-serving lieutenant to be promoted to commander with no expectation of command but to make his retirement more comfortable. Many of the 1815 promotions fell into this category, with the result that an average of just 6–8 percent of commanders were employed from 1818 to 1824. Post-captains fared slightly better, with an employment rate in those years of 10–15 percent. Promotion from post-captain to rear-admiral proceeded, as it always had, by seniority, but whereas the generation that had made post just before the wars could expect to see their flag about nineteen years later, the generation after the wars spent thirty years as captains. The result was that by 1843, the youngest full admiral (who might be expected to take up a major command in the event of a war) was seventy-six.[50]

From a strategic perspective, the benefit of massive unemployment was that the Admiralty could be very selective when a command came open; the downside was that many senior officers lacked any experience with major commands. The unemployment crisis also forced the Admiralty to justify its selections, and it seems clear that they increasingly drew from the social elite. The Admiralty explicitly selected officer candidates based on their family backgrounds, and an increasing percentage came from landed or titled backgrounds as a result. From 1818, the optimal path was to be placed on the Admiralty's own list of midshipmen to receive priority placements, including at the Royal Naval College. The navy's increasing exclusivity is not surprising as all navies in the age of sail became harder to join in their austere peacetime structures. But it also meant that the aggression that characterized the British approach to war at sea was steadily replaced by caution. Officers lucky enough to be employed at sea had to worry more about the consequences of minor mistakes, since there were dozens of candidates waiting eagerly for their chance.[51]

Connections, either to the social and political elite or to powerful naval officers, mattered more than they had during the wars. All told, a service that had been remarkably open to ambitious young men from indifferent backgrounds began to close itself off.[52] The generation of officers who came of age in the decade after 1815 was dominated by sons of the service. Admiral Sir David Milne took his son Alexander to sea as an Admiralty-approved Volunteer First Class on board his flagship *Leander* in 1817, and Alexander managed to stay afloat until 1823, at which point he was appointed to a harbor-service ship while spending most of his time ashore in school.[53] Midshipman E. A. Noel joined the navy at the height of the demobilization crisis, and yet, thanks in large part to being the grandson of a First Lord, he managed to get a berth to the East Indies on the *Liverpool*.[54] John Harvey Boteler was commissioned as a lieutenant in September 1815 while stationed in the Leeward Islands, but he knew that was unlikely to be his last promotion: his uncle was the commander in chief, his cousin was the flag lieutenant, and his brother was the first lieutenant.[55]

That is not to say that it was nepotism all the way down, nor was nepotism necessarily inefficient.[56] The reciprocity of the patronage system meant that officers still spoke in terms of merit as one of the criteria for promotion because recommending a connected but incompetent subordinate did not reflect well on the patron. A captain on the west coast of South America explained to Byam Martin in 1824 that he had recommended that a young gentleman be confirmed as a lieutenant. "He is related to Sir Watkin W. Wynn," but "his own merits induced me to name him to Sir Thomas [Hardy]," the commander in chief of the station.[57] Nevertheless, it is clear that naval connections were by far the best way to get ahead in the postwar austerity.[58]

Sir George Cockburn served on the Board of Admiralty from 1818 to 1830, and much of his day-to-day work consisted of correspondence with officers regarding employment prospects. He had to balance a range of considerations: not just political connections but also service qualifications, wartime records, age, and experience. There was no rubric, which gave him flexibility, but at the same time, there were so few appointments to make that most applicants were bound to come away disappointed. Cockburn also worked to balance the need to keep as many ships in service as possible (and therefore as many officers on full pay as possible) with the danger of not equipping the ships properly so that officers and men could keep up their skills. A guardship that served as nothing more than a floating hulk was of little use; better, Cockburn argued, to spend the money to equip the guardships properly so they could be used as training establishments.

Here we see the strategic downside of massive unemployment: it was no use to be able to pick from a large pool of qualified officers if those officers were steadily losing their qualifications.[59]

For the unlucky officer on the beach without naval friends, the experience of the postwar decade depended to a large degree on whether he needed his half pay to make ends meet. Elite officers flourished; officers without independent incomes struggled. Half pay remained static from 1815 to 1832, and it provided a tidy supplement for senior officers. A rear-admiral received about £450 per year, and post-captains' pay ranged from about £250 to £180, depending on seniority. But lieutenants were expected to subsist on about £84 per year, which often meant they had to make difficult choices about rent, food, and medical bills.[60] On the other hand, it was not unheard of for an officer to request to be superseded. Lieutenant William Bowers decided in July 1816 that he had "sufficient of the sinews of war to carry it on for some time. Having seen the lions of London, I essayed the air of Cheltenham, then took a trip to Brighton, and hence crossed over to Paris, the pleasures of which detained me five months."[61]

Some half-pay officers not only vacationed on the Continent but stayed there, where the cost of living was lower. After transporting troops back and forth across the Atlantic in 1817, Commander Daniel Roberts's ship was paid off. By 1820 he was in Lausanne, where he met William Wordsworth, his wife, and his sister. Through a friend, he was soon introduced to the other Romantic poets, and he relocated to Italy. Using his naval expertise, he designed the schooner *Don Juan* for Percy Shelley and the yacht *Bolivar* for Lord Byron. Roberts was not on board the *Don Juan* on the stormy night of July 8, 1822, when Shelley drowned, but he was on the *Bolivar* the next day, searching for survivors. Eventually he recovered the wreckage of the *Don Juan* and repaired the vessel, but his relationship with Byron could not be similarly fixed. He chose to remain in Italy instead of joining Byron's doomed adventure in Greece.[62]

Most officers had more mundane experiences of half pay. Some used the modest freedom it afforded to embark on new careers, often in naval-adjacent professions. Captain Edward Pelham Brenton was appointed to be a flag captain in 1815 but decided instead to resign his command and become a historian, publishing *The Naval History of Great Britain from the Year 1783 to 1822* in 1823, followed by a biography of his patron St. Vincent. Lieutenant John Marshall published a multivolume biographical dictionary of naval officers. Gunner William Richardson was superannuated in 1819 and spent the remainder of his life sailing around the Solent, even slinging a hammock in his bedroom after his wife died. Unlike most army officers, naval officers had marketable skills. Master Luke Brokenshaw opened a nautical school in Cornwall in 1825, teaching among other subjects astronomy, land surveying, geometry, trigonometry, and navigation. Many other officers requested Admiralty permission to serve in merchant ships. It was risky to do so, since in the event of war they would have to report to the Admiralty within six months, but it helped keep their skills sharp.[63]

Overall, however, the story of officers in the peace is a story of unemployment. Of ten commissioned and warrant officers from one recent study, only two saw significant active service in the decade after Algiers. The socially elite among this group became patrons of benevolent societies, got their portraits painted, and became involved in local politics. Those less fortunate remained connected to the sea, working in fishing and coastal trades, or just trying to make ends meet on half pay.[64] Many officers entered the peace with regret, immediately missing the comradery of shipboard life. William Stanhope Lovell described his wartime service as "the best years of my life," but he also held out hope, years later, that his naval services had ended only "for the present."[65] Sir William Dillon could count on relationships with four royal brothers, and he maintained a steady stream of correspondence with the Admiralty seeking employment. Yet he had no luck, and for sixteen unhappy years, his skills declined while he sat on the beach. He was only thirty-nine years old when his exile began. He "ceased to be a naval officer at all, . . . wasting his life in more or less complete idleness."[66]

CHAPTER 14

Commerce and Empire

One of the defining characteristics of empires is that they often operate with different systems of government in the metropole and the periphery. Democracy, or at least a claim to it, at home is often paired with administrative rule abroad. In the early nineteenth-century British Empire, soldiers played a role in upholding the legitimacy of both the elected government in the British Isles and its imperial authority abroad. The difference between the metropole and the periphery, for soldiers, was simply who was in charge. In Britain, soldiers reported to civil authorities, but in the empire, soldiers often were the civil authority. This chapter is about the soldiers and sailors who remained in military service after the wars and their experience maintaining and extending Britain's imperial authority. Despite the unemployment crisis, especially in the navy, both services deployed thousands of men, most of them veterans of the wars, in dozens of ships and in garrisons stretched across six continents.

They encountered a world transformed. No longer was Europe the center of military gravity, and no longer did peer competitors pose the greatest threat. Instead, the army and navy had to shift their priorities toward protecting the spoils of Britain's victory. This was not new, in the sense that the peacetime maintenance of empire in the 1820s was not fundamentally different from the peacetime maintenance of empire in the 1780s and 1760s. But for most officers and men, it was their first experience with an extended peace. Some preferred the clarity of wartime, when the enemy was identifiable, and the size of the armed forces spread responsibilities more evenly. Others grew frustrated with the lack of opportunities for distinction, while a select few took advantage of the new types of operations to make a name for themselves. It is essential to incorporate all these veterans into the history of demobilization, and not just because their stories round out the book. Some of the imperial campaigns had legacies that lasted through the rest of the nineteenth century, and veterans drew on their experience of the Napoleonic Wars to conduct those campaigns.

Britain's massive effort in the Napoleonic Wars had won it command of the ocean, but the navy was in no shape to realize the fruits of that victory in the decade after 1815. With the seas no longer patrolled by battlefleets, a new paradigm emerged, one that would be very familiar to any sailor today. Just as in the aftermath of the Cold War the world's navies have increasingly had to turn their attention to the prevention of illegal fishing, human trafficking, and environmental crimes, so too did the post-1815 British navy have to grapple with problems that looked very different from French ships of the line. Despite its constrained budgets, the navy found itself responsible for maintaining good order at sea.[1] This took the form of campaigns against smuggling and slave trading, the management of fisheries disputes, and hydrographic and exploratory missions designed to increase human knowledge of the world's oceans and improve the safety of mariners.

In its peak years in the eighteenth century, smuggling accounted for perhaps a quarter of all of England's overseas trade and employed more than forty thousand people in Kent and Sussex alone. Luxury items were the most popular, and there was also a vibrant market for spices, coffee, playing cards, and French brandy. Even bulk cargoes like tea and tobacco were staples of smuggling gangs' incomes, often passing through the ports with false papers. The navy had little role to play in enforcing those laws, but it did have a role to play in combating cross-Channel smuggling during and after the Napoleonic Wars. Smugglers were fiendishly difficult to catch, as they used long slender galleys to dash across to the other shore at night. The fastest oared vessels could get from Dunkirk to Deal in five hours with a favorable tide. The larger smuggling gangs had armed vessels of up to two hundred tons with crews of up to fifty. Intimately familiar with both coasts, the gangs used their knowledge to load and unload their cargo in secret using light signals, covering their faces, and using nicknames. Ashore, men guarded the cargo and kept watch, and then moved the goods to market. Former master Luke Broken-shaw, for example, seems to have been in league with smugglers in Cornwall: he was responsible for getting the authorities drunk while the goods passed through secret passageways under his house.[2]

Napoleon had encouraged smuggling by providing havens for smugglers in Dunkirk and Gravelines from 1810 to 1814. He was rewarded with at least 299 French officers who violated their parole as prisoners of war and, more importantly, enormous quantities of British gold. In the first nine months of 1811 alone, smugglers delivered 1.8 million guineas to Napoleon's coffers. The end of the wars removed French state support, but it also added thousands of demobilized sailors into an unforgiving labor market. Given that a laborer in Sussex made about a shilling and a half per day, but a smuggler could take home up to seven shillings in a night, the incentives were clear. Many men participated part time, but there were also well-organized gangs that used blackmail, extortion, and murder to maintain control of the trade. George Ransley's gang effectively ran Kent in 1820: he had foreign suppliers, the backing of wealthy bankers in the City, and seamen and laborers on retainer. He even employed a surgeon to deal with wounds sustained in clashes with the authorities.[3]

The Preventive Water Guard had been established in 1809, but it was underfunded and underequipped, with only thirty-nine revenue cutters and sixty-two boats to cover the entire coastline of England and Wales. The end of the wars provided an opportunity to refocus the government's efforts. The impetus for what became known as the coast blockade came from Captain William McCulloch of the frigate *Ganymede*. He had been deployed to the Channel in the winter of 1815, and unlike his peers, he took his duties seriously. Rather than capturing the odd smuggling vessel here and there, often by accident, he sought to reorganize the entire coastline under naval command. The Admiralty took over command of revenue cutters and assigned them to the nearest port admiral in April 1816, but McCulloch recognized that capturing smugglers at sea was difficult.

The real problem came from the organization of the smuggling rings ashore. After trials of his system in 1816 and 1817, he convinced the Admiralty to extend the blockade all along the Channel. By 1818, he had 1,200 officers and men under his command, growing to 2,784 by 1824. They were organized into divisions commanded by naval lieutenants and supported by a surgeon, a few assistant surgeons, a purser, and some clerks. The men were stationed in Martello Towers or old signal stations that had been built every two or three miles along the coast during the wars to warn about a French invasion. The stations used Popham's new telegraph system to communicate, and the men received training in firearms and seamanship. Each detachment embarked on nightly patrols, both ashore and in small boats.[4]

It was not an accident that McCulloch used the term *blockade* to describe his method: he clearly saw that his duty, and the navy's duty, was to wage war on Britain's own coastal communities. As in any war, there were casualties. When smugglers attacked men from the *Severn* operating ashore, one sailor was shot and killed. The murderer was identified, but the mayor of Deal refused to issue an arrest warrant because the whole town was caught up in the smuggling business. The Admiralty forwarded reports to Liverpool that in Deal, "so great a population have not only separated themselves from the law of the country, but treat it with contempt and derision."[5] Nor were the clashes limited to the Channel coast. The Admiralty gave stern instructions to the commanders in chief at Leith and Cork to prevent smuggling in Scotland and Ireland. As on the Channel, the coastguard in Ireland utilized the signal stations that had been built to watch for French fleets. It was also led by naval officers, and by 1822 it had grown to encompass 160 stations manned by two thousand men.[6]

Despite the glut of demobilized sailors available, it proved surprisingly difficult to recruit both officers and men for this service. Few relished nightly patrols, and when gangs and patrols clashed, it was usually the naval men who were outnumbered and surprised. The service naturally sought to recruit skilled seamen with naval experience, but in practice, many coastal stations were manned by unskilled men with few other employment options. To aid recruitment, from 1821 the Admiralty offered fifteen thousand Greenwich outpensioners who were capable of further service the chance to keep their pensions while earning full pay. Two years later, to reward the men doing most of the work, the Admiralty also increased the share of prize money allocated to petty officers on this service.[7]

But the prevention of smuggling was undesirable work. A disproportionate number of men serving on the Channel coast seem to have been Irish landsmen, which at least had the benefit from the navy's perspective of ensuring that they were less likely to be coopted by local gangs. That was certainly not the case in Ireland, where Sir Benjamin Hallowell, commander in chief at Cork, tried to break up a smuggling ring led by the O'Sullivan family. Morley O'Sullivan was known to pose as an agent of Lloyd's to evade customs duties on large shipments, but Hallowell could do little to stop the practice. In 1816, the signal station on Dursey Island in Bearhaven Harbour was ordered to be closed. The midshipman in charge was an O'Sullivan, who stole the stores at the station, brought them to his family, deserted, and then marooned the lieutenant sent to sort out the situation on the island. When Hallowell dispatched a second lieutenant to help, he contacted the local magistrate, none other than Morley O'Sullivan.[8]

Officers worried that accepting an offer to serve on the coast blockade would prevent them from obtaining a more prestigious appointment. They could earn prize money, but it does not appear to have been a lucrative posting, partially because the Admiralty wanted them to focus on capturing smugglers rather than their contraband. Nevertheless, officers on this service were at least active: they could keep up their seagoing skills, to a point, and they received full rather than half pay. There are also examples of officers who spent time on antismuggling duty who went on to successful careers. David Peat joined the coast blockade as a midshipman in 1817, and his enthusiasm propelled him all the way to commander. John Windham Dalling had been at Trafalgar as a midshipman; promoted to commander in 1814, he was one of the few lucky enough to be employed at that rank. Commanding *Nimrod* on the Leith station, he spent two years patrolling for smuggling from Fife to Eyemouth. Three of the captains of revenue cutters under his command gave him a silver cup when he paid off his ship in 1819. For the next seven years he was on half pay, but he received another command in 1826 and made post in 1828.[9]

The coast blockade was rolled into the coast guard in 1831, bringing an end to the navy's prominent role in combating smuggling. Smuggling is of course with us today, so no campaign can be said to have been wholly successful. Nevertheless, the navy's efforts in the 1820s did make a difference, even if the most important blow to smugglers came in the 1830s when Parliament lowered customs duties.[10] It is remarkable, however, the extent to which those who participated in the coast blockade saw their efforts in terms of their wartime experience. Lieutenant William Bowers was employed in the North Sea in 1816 cruising against smugglers. He reported that his captain was particularly aggressive because he "had made but little prize-money during the war." The captain gave Bowers command of a galley, and his orders were "rigorously to blockade the port" of Flushing. He recalled being in the same spot during the wars on board a ship of the line, watching for the Dutch fleet. Yet antismuggling duty was worse: "The most arduous period of the war, when surrounded with enemies, and the strictest vigilance was necessary, was nothing to this harassing service. Day and night there was no rest for a soul on board; every floating thing was taken for a smuggler and chased, boarded, submitted to the most rigorous search."[11]

Smuggling patrols sometimes went hand in hand with other responsibilities. Every year until 1824, the Admiralty sent a lieutenant to the coast of Scotland "for the purpose of preserving order among the persons employed in the Herring Fishery."[12] While he was in and among the herring busses, he was also ordered to keep a sharp eye out for smugglers. The reason the navy had to be involved in this business was that since the end of the American Revolutionary War, the government had subsidized deep-sea fisheries. The idea was to maintain a nursery of seamen while simultaneously promoting economic development in poor regions.[13, i] The lieutenant in charge of the fleet examined the busses, certified their eligibility for the subsidies and bounties, and ensured that they were employing sufficient men. He was also tasked with "protecting them and their vessels against enemies" while ensuring that they obeyed the fishing regulations.[14] These orders would be familiar to many naval and coast guard officers today.[15]

The navy's other effort to maintain good order at sea was the slave patrol. The navy has long boasted of its proud tradition of combating

---

i   Adam Smith famously criticized the policy, but subsidies and other direct support continued well into the nineteenth century. See Rieser, "The Herring Enlightenment."

slavery following the abolition of the slave trade by the Act of 1807, but in recent years historians have chipped away at this mythology. Demobilization provides more chisels for this effort. The navy never prioritized the West Africa squadron, and demobilization did not cause administrators to reconsider. On the contrary, the decade after 1815 was among the most fallow periods of the West Africa squadron's entire existence. There was one ship on station in September 1815, and none through the winter. The next spring, Sir James Yeo, who had spent the War of 1812 building fleets and fighting the Americans on the Great Lakes, arrived in command of a frigate. He captured a few slaving vessels that summer, but when he sailed home in September 1816, once again the station was left without any British ships. It happened again in 1818, and while the Admiralty soon expanded the West Africa squadron to six vessels, in general the postwar years were characterized by neglect and insufficiency. Nor did the story change much after that: in 1831, there were seven vessels on station.[16]

The ships most needed on the west coast of Africa were fifth-rate frigates. They were fast enough to have a chance to catch elusive slavers and powerful enough to fight all comers on station, but the navy sent 168 of them to the breakers in 1814 and 1815 amid demobilization's budget cuts. Meanwhile, slavers began turning to Baltimore clippers—very fast two-masted schooners—which had been built during the War of 1812. They had little cargo space, but slavers, by definition, cared not for their cargo. What mattered was that Baltimore clippers could be concealed easily in coastal areas, and they could run away from most ships sent to chase them. Based simply on the balance of forces, therefore, the navy in this period could not be more than "sporadically effective."[17]

And it was not just the balance of forces that favored the slavers. Mosquito-borne diseases posed a grave danger to the sailors on station, and not until the widespread introduction of quinine in the 1850s was there an effective countermeasure. Yet mortality rates in the West Africa squadron were always the highest in the navy. These risks were theoretically offset by the opportunities to earn "head money" for successful interdictions. From 1807 to 1817, crews received £60 for every man rescued, £30 for every woman, and £10 for every child. It was steadily reduced in the following years so that by 1830 the treasury was agreeing to pay only £5 per person rescued, but the nominal value of a captured vessel remained high. An 1818 capture of a slaver with seventy-two men, forty-four women, and eighteen children should have netted £5,820. In fact, the crew saw about a third of that after agents, courts, and other stakeholders got involved, and most captures were even less lucrative. One historian has concluded that any enthusiasm shown by officers and men on station "was the result of personal commitment and evangelical zeal rather than the lure of prize money."[18]

The West Africa squadron's goal was to intercept slavers before the Middle Passage, but there were serious legal challenges. An 1816 High Court of Admiralty decision prevented the navy from stopping and searching foreign ships in peacetime. It was therefore simple enough for an American or British slaving vessel to reflag for the convenience of avoiding British searches. That forced Castlereagh to seek bilateral agreements with every possible slave trading power to allow the British navy to search their ships. Shortly after the wars, he convinced the Portuguese to abolish the trade and to allow British naval ships to search Portuguese-flagged vessels, but only north of the equator—and the bulk of Portugal's slave trading happened in the South Atlantic. Similarly, an 1817 agreement with Spain secured the abolition of the slave trade in its dominions by 1820, but Spanish authorities looked the other way when the Cubans continued to deal in enslaved people well after that date. Eventually agreements with Sweden, Brazil, France, Denmark, Sardinia, the Hanse, and Naples followed from 1824 to 1831, but the first ten years after the wars were characterized by international resistance to Britain's efforts.[19]

For officers, service in the West Africa squadron was maddeningly complex. The first problem was often keeping recaptured people alive. In March 1819, Lieutenant Digby Marsh captured a Portuguese slaver and rescued two men weighing sixty-four and eighty-one pounds, while others on board were too sick to be weighed at all. Tragically, deaths following recapture were common.[20] Even successful recaptures often landed officers in legal or financial quagmires following disputed captures. Officers could only condemn them as prizes if they found "clear and undeniable proof" of slaving.[21] That restriction was eased in 1822, but the burden of proof was on the British in the early years. Yeo's orders ran to fourteen pages in the Admiralty minutes because he had to be given clear instructions on topics ranging from the intricacies of head money to the diplomatic implications of the service.[22]

The suppression of the slave trade, in one account, "helped to define and underpin Victorian Britain's sense of national and moral supremacy."[23] Yet the foundation on which that moral supremacy rested was surprisingly shaky. Britons continued to trade enslaved people after abolition, and in the West Indies, plantation owners found plenty of loopholes to exploit. Sir Alexander Cochrane was the commander in chief of the Jamaica and Leeward Islands station when the abolition of the slave trade came into effect. Since he owned a plantation on Trinidad, he found himself in the strange position of enforcing a law that undermined his own financial position. Along with the governor of Trinidad, Sir Ralph Woodward, he worked to ensure that the enforcement of the anti-slave-trade laws was spotty at best. Even when Cochrane captured a slave trader, he was reported to have forced its human cargo into fourteen-year-long "apprentice-ships" on his plantation, and he and other owners continued to flog such unfortunate refugees as if they were enslaved. Nor was he the only naval officer closely connected to slavery: Byam Martin's older brother was a slaveowner on Antigua who lobbied against emancipation in Parliament.[24]

All of this is not to disparage the efforts of the officers and men on the slave patrol, nor is it to discount the importance of Britain leading the world in eradicating the practice. Rather it is to point out that in the decade after 1815, British progress against the slave trade was limited. There is no basis for the triumphalist claims of imperial cheerleaders, such as "If the British wished to abolish the slave trade, they simply sent the navy."[25] In fact, they rarely sent the navy, and when they did, it was underequipped and diplomatically constrained. What successes it achieved derived from that evangelical zeal mentioned earlier. Many officers sent to West Africa were connected to abolitionist establishments like the African Institution, while others became more enthusiastic about abolition after they had experienced the horrors of the trade firsthand. In some cases, the suppression of the slave trade was so morally important that it justified disregarding orders. The deeply religious Captain William Fitzwilliam Owen took the city of Mombasa under British protection in exchange for a promise by the city's leader to abolish slavery in

1824. Owen had no authority to do so, but since Mombasa was a key port for the internal Omani slave trade, he felt that it was his duty to take action to disrupt the trade. While the protectorate did not last much past London becoming aware of it—it was disowned in 1826—Owen's actions indicate the ways in which some officers saw the antislavery campaign as a crusade.[26]

Owen found himself in Mombasa because of the navy's third major line of effort in seeking to maintain good order at sea: hydrography and exploration. Owen had first made his name as a surveyor in the Great Lakes, but his efforts from 1821 to 1826 were on an entirely grander scale. He and his team covered about five thousand miles of the coastline of East Africa. It was one of dozens of such expeditions undertaken in the aftermath of the wars. The Hydrographic Office, established in 1795 under the authority of the secretary to the Admiralty, coordinated these surveys, liaising with the Admiralty to equip, man, and officer the ships and with the Royal Society and later Royal Geographic Society to set goals and report discoveries. Some surveys were natural by-products of other missions. After dropping off Amherst's embassy to the Jiaqing Emperor at Hong Kong in July 1816, Captain Murray Maxwell took his frigate *Alceste* along with the East India Company's *Discovery* on a surveying mission all along the coast of China to the mouth of the Yalu River.[27]

More common were missions designed solely with hydrography in mind. While no corner of the globe was seen as unworthy of a chart, we can identify some patterns in where expeditions were sent. In 1817, for example, whalers reported that the Greenland Sea was surprisingly free of ice, so Thomas Hurd, the hydrographer of the navy, organized a series of expeditions aimed at charting the Arctic and searching for a northwest passage to the Pacific. William Parry, John Franklin, John and James Ross, and others soon embarked on perilous journeys into the ice. When Parry became hydrographer following Hurd's death in 1823, he placed a particular emphasis on polar exploration, which helped generate momentum for an endeavor that sustained public and private attention for the next century.[28]

The key figure at the Admiralty for these efforts was Sir John Barrow, the second secretary from 1807 to 1845. It was his publication of the accounts of the Greenland Sea being free of ice that had inspired the first polar expeditions, and his enthusiasm that sustained the expeditions despite their repeated failures to find the Northwest Passage. At the end of his life, he claimed that the expeditions had been launched "for the acquisition of knowledge, not for England alone, but for the general benefit of mankind."[29] Here we can see echoes of Britain's self-congratulatory framing of the slave patrol, but in this case, there is more to recommend Barrow's claim. Britain really did lead the world in the creation of nautical charts and instruments. When the Russian expedition to the Antarctic departed in 1819, its first stop was London to equip itself with the best quality chronometers, sextants, gravimeters, densitometers, and thermometers, as well as the best charts. The Admiralty could have used its competitive advantage and kept the results of its hydrographic expeditions secret, since a detailed knowledge of the world's coastlines was clearly useful in war.[30] Instead, however, they chose to sell the charts to the public. An 1830 notice in *The Navy List* explained that the Admiralty was "desirous to extend the benefit of marine surveys which have been made for the use of H.M. Navy more generally among the Mercantile Shipping of the empire."[31]

That is not to say that British charting was entirely altruistic, of course. Phillip Parker King led four voyages to Australia between 1817 and 1822 to discover whether there were any navigable rivers that would allow Britain to exploit the interior. The empire grew as explorers named and claimed as they went. As with all European exploration, many "discoveries" were new only to Europeans, but our inheritance of these missions can be seen in place names from the Thousand Islands in Canada, where Owen named many of them after recent notable battles and people (Talavera, Badajoz, Salamanca, Vitoria, Popham, Melville, Croker, etc.), to the poles, where Parry, the Rosses, James Weddell, and other British naval officers' names can still be found. The Admiralty Chart set the global standard for chart making and established conventions that benefitted British interests. Better charts meant it was easier and safer for merchant ships to navigate, which in turn made it more likely that Britain, with the world's largest merchant marine, would be best placed to capitalize on them.[32]

South America was seen as particularly ripe for exploration and exploitation in the aftermath of the revolutions there. The 1826 exploratory voyage of the *Beagle* surveyed the southern part of the

Continent with the goal of opening the Strait of Magellan to trade. But the challenging conditions and the vast scope of the under-taking contributed to the suicide of the officer in charge. He was replaced by Robert FitzRoy, then serving as the flag lieutenant to the commander in chief of the South American station. The failure of that first expedition led to the creation of the second in 1831, when FitzRoy was famously accompanied by the naturalist Charles Darwin.[33]

Hydrography and exploration therefore served both British inter-ests and the world's. One of the Hydrographic Office's most import-ant contributions was improving knowledge of British home waters. Surprisingly, as Hurd told Croker in 1814, "the most remarkable of our deficiencies for a great Maritime Nation is our want of a compe-tent knowledge of the contour and real geographic situation of many parts of our own shores."[34] At no point, however, was the scale of this effort particularly large. In 1823, when Hurd died, there were four surveys operating in home waters and eight on foreign service. The Hydrographic Office's budget was not immune from the postwar cuts, dropping from five thousand pounds in 1814 to a low of fifteen hundred pounds in 1817.[35] Barrow thought even this small effort was valuable, however, as he wrote in 1816: "To what purpose could a por-tion of our naval force be, at any time, but more especially in a time of profound peace, more honourably or more usefully employed than in completing those details of geographical and hydrographical science of which the grand outlines have been boldly and broadly sketched by Cook, Vancouver and Flinders, and others of our own countrymen?"[36]

The other motivation often cited was simply to employ officers, as Hurd explained to Croker: hydrography and exploration "would help to keep alive the services of many meritorious Officers whose abilities should not be permitted to lie dormant."[37] Officers received special pay rates from 1817 of twenty shillings per day for commanders and fifteen shillings per day for lieutenants and masters, in addition to their regular active duty pay for their rank and vessel. But it did not seem likely to lead to promotion, and there were simply not enough surveying ships to go around. It was also brutally difficult duty. In a small vessel of two or three hundred tons, with a crew of forty to eighty, officers were expected to perform intricate calculations in extreme climates. Polar explorers endured shocking conditions in the ice, while expeditions in the tropics suffered from diseases.

Before the *Congo* had sailed two hundred miles up the river of the same name in 1816, all her officers and most of her crew were dead.[38]

To endure such conditions while still meeting the lofty standards of an Admiralty Chart required a particular breed of officer, and none more fully exemplified that breed than Sir Francis Beaufort. In 1816, he published a travelogue and navigation guide to the southern coast of Turkey, which he had surveyed during the wars. Despite being widely admired for his "priggishly precise" measurements, Beaufort spent the first fourteen years of peace on half pay. Eventually he became the hydrographer of the navy following Parry, and he increased the tempo of chart production. Parry had introduced the Admiralty's *Sailing Directions* in 1828, which gave written descriptions of maritime phenomena that could not be presented graphically on the charts. Beaufort continued that effort, organizing the publication of numerous nautical almanacs and notices to mariners. His time at the Hydrographic Office also saw the official adoption of the Beaufort wind force scale, still in use in modified form today.[39]

The army's equivalent of the navy's campaigns to maintain good order at sea was the garrisoning of the empire. The logic of imperialism constantly generated the need to fight frontier wars, which meant that there was plenty of action to be found for those eager to find it. India in particular attracted men who sought distinction and promotion, and campaigns against the Marathas, *pindaris*, Gurkhas, Kandians, and Burmese provided ample opportunities. When regiments rotated in and out of India and its environs, it was common for men to volunteer to transfer into the regiment newly arriving. The Sixteenth Light Dragoons received more than four hundred volunteers from the Eighth and Seventeenth Light Dragoons when it arrived at Cawnpore in 1822; the opposite was true for the Fifty-Third Foot, which lost a similar number when it finally returned to England in 1823 after nearly two decades in India.[40]

Other areas were less exciting, however. Garrison life on Mediterranean islands lent itself to amateur sociology and anthropology, but rather less so to the development of professional military skills. Nevertheless, many men found no compelling reason to return to England, and they had become accustomed to imperial deployments. Some had married or had established themselves in a comfortable domestic arrangement. George Calladine of the Nineteenth Foot, for example, found himself stuck in Ceylon for ten months past the end of his seven-year enlistment period, so he decided to commit to army life and reenlist for unlimited service. When he finally did return home, he wrote in his diary that what he missed most of all was the (possibly enslaved) woman he had been with during his time in the garrison.[41]

In the decade after Waterloo, veteran soldiers spent far more time in forts with little to do than they did on campaign. Fort is a misleading term, as regiments garrisoned a wide variety of structures from castles to monasteries to log cabins to mud huts. No matter the structure, however, they were overcrowded, poorly ventilated, and unhygienic. Until 1827, soldiers in the West Indies received twenty-three inches of sleeping space and less than three hundred cubic feet of air—prisoners got at least twice as much. The day began with muster, followed by drill. To achieve the "uniformed automation" desired by its officers, a regiment would repeat the five parts of drill endlessly: the rote movements of firing and bayonet, volley firing, turning in unison, combinations of volley firing, and maneuvering in close order. It lasted between one and two hours, all before breakfast. In hot climates, soldiers spent the rest of the day sheltering from the heat, performing guard duty, or maintaining their impractically heavy uniforms.[42]

Discipline was maintained by the lash, although more humane officers sought to break up the monotony of garrison life by organizing games, plays, and other activities. Private Wheeler reported that on Sundays on Corfu, where he was stationed in 1823, the troops marched to the church, piled up their weapons, went to services, and then engaged in field exercises or sham fights afterward. They were also employed making roads on the island, which was a particularly unwelcome duty. As for the barracks, he wrote, "Our Barracks are anything but comfortable, by day they're tolerable, but at night there's no rest, the wall, the floor and beds are alive with bugs, fleas, and mosquitoes." Particularly annoying was a lizard that the soldiers called a wood slave. "It is said," wrote Wheeler, "if one of them should run over your leg or arm you instantly loose the use of the member, nay, it is farther affermed they are fond of peeing on people, and so poisonous is there water that the part becomes an incurable ulser."[43]

St. Ann's Fort in Barbados had the most handsome parade ground in the West Indies, but it flooded whenever it rained, which in turn made it a breeding ground for mosquitos. A pioneering 1837 study found that mortality among British troops for the previous two decades ranged from 17 deaths per 1,000 men in the British Isles to 78.5 per 1,000 in the Leeward Islands and a shocking 143 per 1,000 in Jamaica. Harry Smith managed to survive his deployment to Jamaica, but his regiment buried 22 officers and 668 soldiers in just the first six weeks it was there.[44]

In the West Indies, soldiers who survived the diseases and the monotony of garrison life periodically were called to enforce the British slave regime. In other words, while the navy half-heartedly interdicted the slave trade on the African side of the Atlantic, the army made sure the institution thrived on the American side. In April 1816 on Barbados, white troops from the Fifteenth Foot and Black troops from the First West India Regiment brutally suppressed a rising of five thousand enslaved people known as Bussa's Rebellion. The troops killed fifty enslaved people in the fighting, at the cost of just two casualties. In the aftermath, the colonial government executed 214 people in reprisal and sold 170 more off the island. A similar conflagration came to Demerara (modern Guyana) in 1823. The abolition of the slave trade had made the lives of enslaved workers on the sugar plantations worse because it caused owners to drive them even harder; it also caused rumors to spread periodically that emancipation had been passed by Parliament in London but had been blocked by local officials (that had been one of the precipitating causes of Bussa's Rebellion as well). There were approximately seventy-seven thousand enslaved people in Demerara in 1823, and they outnumbered the whites by approximately sixty to one. Thirteen thousand rose up on August 18, seizing the firearms at the Plantation Success and taking all the whites hostage in the hopes that they could negotiate better conditions. The governor declared martial law and sent in the army and other military forces, resulting in the death of at least 250 enslaved people. As at Barbados, the state used executions to deter future rebellions, hanging some by chains outside of plantations and nailing the heads of others to posts.[45]

The experience of veteran soldiers and sailors who remained in service after 1815 shared some similarities with their service during the wars. Disease was the major killer in both cases. Garrison duty was boring in war and peace, and the slave economy needed military force behind it to function throughout its existence. Smuggling formed a large part of the shadow economy during the wars and continued to do so after them; sailors participated in that economy and also suppressed it. At the same time, the postwar world threw up new challenges. Except for the army's domestic policing duties and the navy's coast blockade, military and naval activity in general moved away from Britain's shores to the empire's periphery. In many (although certainly not all) cases, operations were small scale and low intensity.

This shift presented a mixed bag of employment options. None of the navy's postwar attempts to maintain good order at sea was particularly attractive. Antislavery and antismuggling patrols were unpopular and unlikely to lead to advancement. Some polar expeditions made officers into heroes, but many other aspects of hydrographic work were an unappetizing combination of dull and dangerous. The army offered opportunities for distinction in combat, but it meant risking death from disease and being willing to leave Britain for many years at a time. Given these options, many veterans of the Napoleonic Wars chose to seek their fortunes elsewhere.

CHAPTER 15

Veterans Abroad

In 1823, a French army crossed the Pyrenees to rescue Ferdinand VII from liberal reformers in Madrid. Liverpool and his ministers worried that it presaged the restoration of unified Bourbon control over the Iberian Peninsula, but Wellington explained to Canning that even if the British government wanted to intervene, it could not: "We have not men to perform the necessary duties in England nor a battalion nor even a company to relieve or reinforce a post."[1] Sir Robert Wilson, MP, agreed with Canning that the British should intervene and decided to take matters into his own hands.[i] In doing so, Wilson ignored the Foreign Enlistment Act of 1819. As Bathurst had explained during the debate over the bill, it was passed "to prevent his majesty's subjects from engaging in foreign service, from fitting out, equipping, or arming vessels for warlike operations against countries at peace with his majesty, without license."[2] The Spanish had asked the British to pass that law, for reasons that will shortly become clear. But Wilson had opposed its passage and determined, using a logic all his own, that therefore it did not apply to him. He organized a steam vessel, ironically named the *Royal George*, and landed at Vigo with a small party in July.[3]

---

i   Despite Britain's limited capacities, the liberals in Spain seem to have missed an opportunity to encourage British intervention. They also underestimated their leverage in negotiations about the slave trade. See Prida, "From Hope to Defensiveness," and Royle, "Winning the War and Losing the Peace."

Wilson's aggression had periodically served him well as an army officer, but it had been less helpful as a diplomat and politician. He was known in Parliament for speaking at great length about subjects about which he knew little. A Radical, he had supported Queen Caroline in her divorce proceedings with George IV, but when she died in 1820, he made the mistake of dressing in civilian clothes and serving as one of the attendants to her funeral procession. The government had wanted the procession to move quickly and quietly out of the country and to the queen's native Brunswick, but Radicals saw an opportunity to embarrass the government by redirecting the procession through the City of London using barricades. When soldiers clashed with protestors, Wilson rushed headfirst into the fray in an apparent attempt to defuse the situation. The opposite happened, and in the aftermath of the riot, the government blamed him. He was censured, and the Duke of York dismissed him from the army. Thus, when Wilson headed off to Spain in 1823, he was hoping to restore his reputation.[4]

He did not. he was wounded early in the campaign, but even worse, liberal Spanish generals deserted the rebellion to join the French army supporting Ferdinand. Wilson fled from one catastrophe after another until he found himself in command of the defenses of Cadiz. When the city fell, he returned to Britain in disgrace, along with several of his fellow veterans who had become involved in the campaign.[5] John Harley, paymaster of the Forty-Seventh Foot, had followed Wilson to Spain, but after witnessing the sorry end of the rebellion including the execution of seven men, he decided his adventuring days were over. "I now determined to return to my native country," he later wrote, "for the purpose of spending the remainder of my life . . . in domestic retirement."[6]

Harley had agreed to go to Spain because the peace had been unkind to him. He had tried to set up an agency to handle half pay and widow's pensions for his fellow army officers, but he was quickly frustrated: "It is evident that no persons but those in distress, who resided in London, would employ us; but we did not consider this in time; we were eternally employed in making advances to such people, so that our funds soon became exhausted, and then the half-pay officers, after leaving us minus, employed other agents."[7] He lost three hundred pounds, and then his half pay was suspended because his accounts were discovered to be out of order. Spain was an opportunity to recoup some of those losses, he hoped. Other officers made similar calculations. George Aytoun was one of the thousand lieutenants made by the Admiralty in 1815, and he knew there was no chance of employment. He decided to try his luck in Sweden, where there were rumors that Bernadotte, soon to be King Charles XIV John, was hiring foreign officers to improve the Swedish navy.[8]

Alexander Alexander's frustration with his meager pension and lack of prospects spurred him to book passage on a West Indiaman in September 1815. His journey was fueled by vague rumors of opportunities, but he had no definite idea of what he was going to do when he arrived. En route, he decided to lie about his background, claiming to be an officer on half pay. He was ashamed of having been "only one step above a private soldier" despite spending fourteen years in the artillery. He immediately regretted his lie when he disembarked in Barbados because he had to hide from an old artilleryman he knew. His new life in the West Indies proved to be anything but adventurous. He was employed as an overseer on a slave plantation in Demerara, but every time he encountered the forces of the crown, he had to be careful not to be recognized: "So much for my unfortunate soldiering," he later wrote. "Go where I would, it felt as a brand upon my forehead."[9]

Alexander was one of thousands of Britons who headed west for new lives after 1815, although few chose slave plantations as their destination. More common were the armies and navies of Símon Bolívar and José de San Martín. The revolutions in South America seemed to provide exactly the kind of opportunities that young single men needed to break through the peacetime doldrums. William Bowers went to Chile in 1818 because, he later reported, peacetime was causing him to "once more to feel the irksome influence of *ennui*." There he met Martin Guise, who had purchased an eighteen-gun brig the previous year with the intention of contributing to the revolutions. The two men apparently shared a similar sentiment: Guise was "tired of an idle life, and not meeting with that encouragement which his zeal, services, and rank, as a commander in the British navy entitled him to look for."[10]

As one veteran claimed, it did not matter whether they were fighting for Britain: "When a British subject is put into uniform, and placed in the ranks, with a firelock in his hand, before an enemy, he requires no stimulant nor patriotic impulse to urge him in attacking those opposed to him; neither can I see why a British subject should be ridiculed or prevented from (what he terms) 'earning an honest livelihood;' nor why if he prefers being knocked on the head in serving a Foreign Power, he should be termed a mercenary and a murderer."[11] About sixty-five hundred men crossed the Atlantic between 1817 and 1819 with the goal of joining the revolutions. Few of them seem to have known quite what they were getting into, as the British public had a limited understanding of the challenges of South America. Nevertheless, the end of the Napoleonic Wars infused both men and arms (no longer needed by demobilizing European armies and navies) into the revolutionary struggles.[12]

They did not go completely uninvited: both the Spanish and the revolutionary governments sent representatives to London to recruit. The Spanish legation in London reached out to the unfortunately named Colonel Fucker to establish an Anglo-Spanish Legion of demobilized soldiers. On the other side, John Harley met one of Bolívar's recruiters, the Irishman John Devereaux, and Harley was impressed to learn that Devereaux was paid £175 per soldier raised. Recruiters promised land, cash bounties, and adventure, and they had some success. Among those enticed to South America was Gustavus Mathias Hippisley, who had risen to the rank of major in the Ninth Light Dragoons over the course of sixteen years of service during the wars, mainly spent in Ireland and at the Cape. He founded and commanded the First Venezuelan Hussars, and he signed a contract with Bolívar's representative to receive a commission as a colonel in Bolívar's army, provided he raised his own men. James Rooke came from an army family and first saw action in 1793 in Flanders as a captain in the Eighth Foot. To avoid being shipped to Ceylon with that regiment, he sold his commission and bought a majority in the Queen's Light Dragoons. He became addicted to gambling, however, and in 1802 he used the occasion of the peace to go to France to flee his creditors. The resumption of war saw him imprisoned in Verdun, where he remained for ten years until he escaped and joined Wellington's army. He was wounded at Waterloo, but he recovered the next year and sailed to visit his sister, who was married to the British governor of St. Kitts. He heard that Bolívar was offering commissions to European veterans and decided to jump at the opportunity. He rose to command Bolívar's guard of honor.[13]

The problem was quality control. What the revolutionary armies needed were combat veterans; what they got were unemployed laborers. James Rooke was the exception, not the rule: in fact, a substantial majority of officer adventurers had no military experience, and a generous estimate is that a third of the soldiers had ever handled a musket before. It is unlikely that Britain's contribution to the Spanish American revolutions was to improve military discipline, especially on land. There are several reasons why veterans were outnumbered among these adventurers. For an army officer hoping to see action, transferring to a regiment on colonial service served that purpose; there was no need to act precipitously by selling a commission. For the men, many discharged soldiers were discharged because they were unfit for overseas service—a transatlantic journey to a new war was beyond their physical capabilities. Finally, the kind of person who uprooted his life to join a revolutionary army on an unfamiliar continent often skewed toward the colorful end of the spectrum. Captain Peter Alexander Grant likely deserted from his regiment, joined Alexander Alexander as a slavedriver, and then volunteered with Bolívar. He was, according to Alexander, a "specimen of eccentricity," and he was by no means the only one.[14]

It should not be surprising, then, that the most high profile of all the adventurers in the postwar period was both an eccentric and a naval officer with no prospects. Thomas Cochrane had been a dashing frigate captain during the wars whose naval career had come to a standstill after he had accused Admiral Lord Gambier of failing to follow up on an opportunity to destroy the French fleet at anchor off Rochefort. It was neither the first nor the last time he clashed with his superiors. After being found guilty of stock exchange fraud in 1814, Cochrane was fined, imprisoned, stripped of his knighthood, and struck off the navy list. That freed him to accept, in 1817, the offer of the Chilean government to organize and command their fleet in the war against the Spanish. Although he negotiated an astonishing salary of £2,000 per year (about three times Gambier's salary as commander in chief of the Channel Fleet), he was soon bickering with San Martín's naval minister over issues of prize money.[15]

There were only a handful of ships available to the rebels, but the government set about purchasing decommissioned warships and merchantmen to grow the fleet over the course of 1818. By the end of the next year, the British commander in chief of the South American station reported that Chile's navy had become "tolerably respectable and decidedly superior to the Spanish naval force in the southern Pacific."[16] By training and equipping his squadron, the Chilean government provided Cochrane with the tools to clear the Pacific of Spanish ships over the course of 1819 and 1820. Cochrane also escorted an army of invasion to Peru, captured Valdivia, and otherwise burnished his reputation as an enterprising, aggressive commander. He made an important contribution to the independence of Chile, and he is still celebrated today as Chile's first naval hero.[17]

Cochrane's success was not his alone. The Chileans shouldered most of the work of their own independence, of course, but Cochrane was also not the only British naval officer or sailor to join them. By the end of 1818, about half of the two thousand sailors and marines and most of the officers of Cochrane's fleet were North American or British. Some had followed Cochrane, who remained a charismatic figure in naval circles despite his imprisonment, while others had come for the same reasons we have seen elsewhere in this chapter. Robert Forster had entered the British navy in 1795 but had not been promoted past lieutenant despite two decades of operational opportunities. He joined the Chilean navy to improve his prospects, even though the Foreign Enlistment Act caused him to be struck off the navy list in 1819. Martin Guise, having arrived before Cochrane, made important contributions to the early Chilean campaigns, but he soon found Cochrane's volatility to be too much to bear. He resigned his commission in the Chilean navy and join the Peruvian navy instead. He died in combat in 1829 as a vice-admiral, having risen far higher in South America than he ever could have expected to have done in Britain.[18]

Cochrane also soon left Chile to join the Brazilian war of independence in late 1822. Here again there were other British officers, led by Lieutenant John Taylor. Despite being one of the few lieutenants lucky enough to be employed—in his case, on the flagship of Sir Thomas Hardy, commander in chief of the South American station—he saw the writing on the wall and guessed that it would be his last active appointment. He jumped at the chance to become a captain-of-frigate in the new Brazilian navy. Both Hardy and the Admiralty were alarmed at this precedent, so they refused to allow Taylor to resign his commission and marked him as a deserter, to discourage the others. Taylor left anyways, so the Admiralty enlisted Foreign Office help to secure his return. Eighteen months later, "remorseless British diplomatic pressure secured Taylor's discharge, but by that time he was a national hero."[19]

The reason was that Taylor had taken full advantage of his chance. Commanding the frigate *Niterói*, he had cleverly followed a Portuguese convoy back from Salvador to Portugal, where he proceeded to capture seventeen prizes in just four months of cruising off Lisbon. Whenever he encountered a threatening ship, he would send his Brazilian sailors below decks and fly British colors. His cruise made his name, and his forced discharge robbed Cochrane of one of his best officers. There were others, however: John Pascoe Grenfell was another standout who had been with Cochrane in Chile and had followed him to Brazil. Cochrane gave him command of the eighteen-gun brig *Maranhão* and ordered him to suppress a rebellion in Pará. The rebels did not know where Cochrane's squadron was, so Grenfell behaved as if Cochrane was just over the horizon to intimidate the Portuguese authorities. Cochrane meanwhile was blockading the Portuguese army, capturing Portuguese ships, and otherwise waging an effective campaign over the course of 1823. He returned to Rio in triumph that fall and was made Marquis of Maranhão.[20]

The Brazilian navy's success owed much to its recruiting efforts. Major General Felisberto Caldeira Brant Pontes, a significant landowner in Bahia, had spent 1823 organizing a network of recruiters in Liverpool and London. Unsurprisingly, Brant calibrated the pay rates to be just higher than the pay offered by the British navy. Able seamen could earn £2 12s per month, and while lieutenants' full pay was low at just £8 per month, it was nevertheless marginally higher than British half pay. Officers signed on for five-year terms, at which point they were promised a 50 percent pay increase if they continued or Brazilian half pay for life if they left. Passage to Brazil was free, and they were paid from the date they embarked. To get around the Foreign Enlistment Act, all involved maintained the fiction that they were settlers emigrating to Brazil to seek "honest occupations" on land: in this scheme, sailors were laborers and officers were their overseers. Brant initially raised about 450 men and a dozen officers, nearly all of them British naval veterans. It transpired in early 1824 that some of the sailors recruited in Liverpool had been promised pay twice as high as that delivered, and a hundred returned to Britain in protest. To replace them, a second recruiting campaign that year increased the pay rate offered to £3 per month for able seamen, and that convinced four hundred more men to sign up. All told, British officers commanded many of Cochrane's Brazilian ships, and British sailors provided essential experience and skill for his crews.[21]

The presence of former British naval officers and men in such numbers in South America exacerbated the challenge for the current British naval officers charged with protecting British interests in the region. The British had been closely involved in South America since the failed expedition to Buenos Aires in 1806 and the evacuation of the Portuguese royal family in 1807, but the postwar decade presented new challenges. Not only were British forces on station shrunk to the minimum size, but naval commanders had to juggle a range of duties: they had, as one account helpfully summarizes, "to act as consuls and diplomats; to protect British interests, at a time when British trade was establishing its first direct and legitimate contacts with South America; to report on the progress of the revolutions; to serve as intermediaries between British subjects and the old or newly constituted authorities in Spanish America, and sometimes also between patriots and loyalists; and, incidentally, to transport immense quantities of specie to England on behalf of the British merchants."[22] None of these duties allowed them to use force, as one captain reminded Hardy in 1820: "[I have acted] in pursuance of your orders directing me to use every means, short of actual force, for the protection of British commerce in these seas."[23]

To observe but not interfere was in keeping with the broader British postwar strategy of avoiding war at all costs, but Cochrane's reputation made many of his former colleagues nervous that he might undermine that strategy. Sir William Bowles, Hardy's predecessor as commander in chief, reported to Croker in 1818 that he expected foreign officers were "as likely to use their power and influence for the gratification of their private interests or feelings as for the advantage of the country which employs them. Their Lordships will judge what sort of conduct may be expected from Lord Cochrane."[24] Bowles also reported that Cochrane had brought his prize agent with him and was determined "to keep everything in his own hands and to distribute the proceeds of all captures himself."[25] Soon, however, Cochrane's operational successes eased some of Bowles's concerns, and Cochrane seems to have recognized the value in at least pretending to be acting in Britain's interests. Cochrane was reported to have said "that although he had left England he had not forgotten he was an Englishman, and that the commercial interest of Great Britain was as dear to him as ever."[26] That would have been a strange thing for a Scot to have said, but it was not the only example. Bowers met Cochrane when he first arrived, and he claimed that Cochrane told him "his heart and feelings ever would remain English."[27] Cochrane told British officers in 1824 that his blockade of the northern coast of Brazil had been enormously beneficial to British trade and, in fact, he had kept such factors in mind when conducting the operation. There were indeed plenty of British interests in the region. When Cochrane threatened to bombard Recife in 1824, one British captain told him that he would be personally responsible for £500,000 worth of British property in the city. The presence of hundreds of British merchant ships arriving into Rio ever year meant that there were constantly tensions between Cochrane's desire for British sailors and fear on the part of merchants and the navy that Cochrane would attract recruits and deserters.[28]

For the veterans serving in the South American armies and navies, opportunities for advancement and fame were balanced by frustrations with the revolutionary governments. Some of their frustrations were legitimate, even if there was little that anyone could have done about them. Pay was often late to arrive, if it ever did, because the governments struggled to collect taxes. Prize money moved slowly through the courts, and many cases were dismissed. On the other hand, some British complaints were unreasonable and betrayed an ignorance of the situation on the Continent. Cochrane demanded prize money equal to the Brazilian navy's entire operating budget for a year. Few British soldiers and sailors understood the consequences of the Spanish withdrawal and the economic chaos that it left behind. But it was not just financial frustrations. Mercenary soldiers complained about poor or nonexistent medical care, and few adventurers seem to have grasped the physical geography of the Continent before they arrived. They were surprised at both the widespread poverty and the endemic violence that plagued many regions. Of the sixty-five hundred soldier adventurers who arrived between 1817 and 1819, three thousand died of fever or in combat, and another thousand took one look and returned home immediately.[29]

Some did manage to make successful careers out of their time in South America. Less than 8 percent of the soldier adventurers settled permanently, but of the fifty-nine British officers who served in the Brazilian navy, forty-seven remained in service following independence in 1825. John Taylor was reinstated and died in old age at his coffee plantation, having reached the rank of vice-admiral. Others saw service in the subsequent war with Argentina over Uruguay. In fact, the navies on both sides of that war were commanded by and manned substantially with British sailors. Grenfell lost an arm in the Argentinian war, saw more action in the 1830s and 1840s, and died an admiral. His last posting had been as Brazilian consul-general in Liverpool, which had given him the opportunity to attend Cochrane's funeral in Westminster Abbey in 1860. Cochrane's fortunes were not improved by his post-Brazilian adventure in Greece, but the return of the Whigs to power in the 1830s restored his rank and privileges and earned him a pardon for the stock exchange fraud. He was also restored to the navy list and served as the commander in chief of North America and the West Indies from 1848 to 1851. He volunteered for Crimea, age seventy-nine, but was refused. He died still convinced that he was owed £200,000 by Brazil and Chile.[30]

The Napoleonic Wars shaped how these veterans experienced their time in South America. When Taylor had been deployed against Portuguese loyalists in Pernambuco in 1824, the city's leaders had circulated a pamphlet that showed how all these men were operating in the shadow of the Napoleonic Wars: "Who is this John Taylor, this second Nelson? A ridiculous officer of the British Navy who deserted the flag of his nation."[31] Men like Taylor sought the glory and fame that had eluded them during the wars. Cochrane saw a kindred spirit in Wilson, and he invited him to join him in Chile "to leave behind the insuperable evils of the old corrupt and still degenerating world. . . . South America presents a sufficient field for more than one Quixote. . . . The transfer of intellect, spirit of enterprise and indignant feeling will electrify the western hemisphere with a Promethean fire."[32]

Veterans also drew on the networks that they had developed during the Napoleonic Wars. In some cases, these were personal connections, as when Harley helped a former messmate find medical care in London.[33] But in other cases, simply being a veteran was sufficient to establish trust. Alexander Alexander survived his miserable experience in Demerara because he was taken in by a former sergeant in the Foot Guards: "My being 'an army fellow,' was my passport with him; for the good old man was a soldier every inch of him, and never was so happy as when recounting his feats in Holland with the good Duke of York. His wife was an old campaigner, and loved a soldier as well as her husband. He was the only out-and-out British patriot I ever conversed with in the colony; his house was always a home to me during my stay." The sergeant also helped him get an interview with Major General John Murray, the governor, in the hopes of getting a commission in a West Indian regiment. Nothing came of it, so Alexander turned to Bolívar's army as the next best thing.[34]

In Canada, veteran networks pervaded the colony's administration. Discharged soldiers who emigrated to Canada frequently requested to be settled alongside other military men from their own regiments. They did so because military networks provided legal support, job opportunities, and letters of recommendation. Private letters between veterans regularly used veteran status as currency because it established a shared experience and bond of trust.[ii]

Veterans moved to Canada in large numbers after the wars as part of a settlement scheme. It was not the first such scheme—Halifax had been settled by discharged soldiers in 1748, for example—but the quantity of demobilized soldiers and sailors available after 1815 caused it to operate on an even larger scale. Veterans were seen as more likely to be loyal than settlers born in the United States or Canada, and in the atmosphere of tension with the United States in the postwar years, loyalty was a significant consideration. Their mil-

---

ii   Although as one recent study has found, veterans tended to downplay that currency in public. Instead, they joined organizations like the Freemasons that allowed them to transfer some of their martial spirit into civilian channels. Smith, "Forgotten Settlers," 11–17, 108–16.

itary service also made them perhaps more likely to be capable of defending the frontier from American aggression. The basic structure of settlement plans was that a veteran would receive a set amount of land for free, along with tools and some rations. In exchange, the veteran promised to build a home, maintain a road, and remain on the property for a fixed amount of time. The size of the grant depended on rank, so that a lieutenant colonel received twelve hundred acres while a private received just one hundred. A naval settlement on the Ottawa River from 1819 made one hundred acres available to any seaman who had served for three years on the Great Lakes.[35]

Despite the free land, it was not an easy life. The soil was poor in Lower Canada, and there was no guarantee that a former soldier was any good at farming. Here was another reason to cluster together in regimental groups: mutual support in a challenging environment. Two thousand Chelsea out-pensioners moved to Canada from 1815 to 1857, but they were not evenly distributed. Most were in Upper Canada, but more specifically, there were towns like Perth (north of Kingston) in 1819 where seventeen of the twenty-nine residents were half-pay officers. Free land grants to veterans were available in Canada from 1815 to 1834.[36]

New South Wales had a similar scheme that operated until 1831, and there were other initiatives to attract veterans as well. One used an existing structure, Royal Veteran units, and combined it with a land grant scheme. In 1825, the army created Royal Veteran companies for service in New South Wales. The men were to be less than fifty years old, and after a two-year enlistment period, they would be eligible to claim forty to one hundred acres plus equipment. The scheme failed because, in Australia as in Canada, colonial authorities erroneously assumed soldiers would make good settlers. The Royal Veteran companies tended to be full of ill-disciplined troops led by men more interested in more lucrative civil posts. Only about a quarter of all veterans who received land grants were still on their land by 1847.[37]

The specific failure of the Veteran Company scheme should not obscure some success stories. After all, some soldiers did make good settlers. All these veteran land grant schemes seemed to solve two problems: there were too many old soldiers in Britain and too few settlers in Canada and Australia. Thomas Spicer, for example, enlisted in the First Life Guards and served through the Peninsular War and at Waterloo. He transferred to the Third (Buffs) Regiment because he wanted to follow it to New South Wales. He was discharged from that regiment a year later but found a home in a Royal Veteran company. After they were disbanded, he turned his one hundred acres into a more substantial farm of 660 acres. Similarly, Thomas Budd was a Peninsular War veteran who enlisted with the Royal Veteran companies. When he received his one hundred acres, he named his farm Tallivera Grove; another veteran of the rifles named his farm Rifle Farm. Military service formed a core part of their identities.[38]

One reason for the popularity of veteran land grants is that the governors of colonies in both Australia and Canada were frequently themselves veterans. From 1820 to 1850, military men were even more prominent than normal in the empire, with at least thirty governors boasting experience in the Peninsular War alone. That criterion applied to either the governor or lieutenant governor of New South Wales for twenty-five of those years. Men like Sir Colin Campbell (Tobago, Nova Scotia, and Ceylon), Sir William Gomm (Jamaica, Mauritius, India), and Sir Frederick Adam (Malta, Ionian Islands, and Madras) brought their military experience to colonial administration, with the result that veterans tended to have opportunities for advancement under their leadership. They especially favored veterans as magistrates, which provided plenty of incentives for officers to consider resigning their commissions and trying their luck in the empire.[39]

Not all colonies were equally appealing, of course, but a recent study of New South Wales illustrates the calculations that officers used when making these decisions. Some officers had direct experience of the colony, having been stationed there as part of the empire's regimental rotations. It had a reputation for a healthy climate with cheap land, although that was balanced by its violence. Even as it transitioned from primarily a penal colony to a settler colony, the frontier remained relatively lawless. Nevertheless, for an officer willing to take on some risk, there were clearly opportunities for advancement. Those with technical skills like surveying, mapmaking, and engineering knew that they could put those skills to use. Thomas Mitchell, for example, commissioned into the Rifles and then worked for Sir George Murray's Quartermaster-General's Department during the wars. When he arrived in Sydney in 1827, he took up a post as deputy surveyor general of New South Wales. He used his campaign experience when roughing it in the outback, and when he planned the streets of Wagga Wagga, he named them after his former comrades in the Rifles. He ended his career with a knighthood and enormous landholdings. Here was the promise of the empire.[40]

Hundreds of veteran officers arrived in New South Wales following another military grant initiative in 1826 specifically targeted at officers. All officers ranked captain or higher received free grants until 1831, and following that, length of service provided land at discounted rates. The scheme extended to Canada and the Cape of Good Hope, but the impetus for the grants in New South Wales came from paranoia about French intentions on the west coast—better, Bathurst thought, to seed the countryside with military men before the French got any ideas. The grants required officers to be resident for seven years. Some had to sell their commissions to raise the funds they needed to meet the capital requirements of the grant scheme, but in many cases, it was worth it. Networks of fellow veterans and former commanding officers often provided them with opportunities that they would not otherwise have had—and not just as a magistrate, as some became commissioners for crown lands or even justices of the peace.[41]

In the West Indies, the postwar settlement schemes were complicated by racism. Between 1817 and 1825, the West India Regiments were steadily broken up. The white planters refused to allow Black veterans to settle on any of the British islands in the region except for Trinidad. There, a few hundred men established themselves and received small pensions of between five and eight pence per day. They were joined by freed Black Americans, many of them veterans of the War of 1812, who settled "company towns." The result was that by 1862, one-eighth of Trinidad consisted of discharged soldiers and their descendants. Creole veterans were allowed to remain in the islands, but African-born veterans were shipped either to Honduras or to Sierra Leone. The latter received the largest group, as more than two thousand veterans arrived in Freetown from 1817 to 1819. Given small land grants, pensions, and rations, they settled towns named Waterloo, Gibraltar Town, Wellington, York, and Hastings.[42]

Emigration is always best understood in a push-pull framework, so it is important to recognize that it was not just opportunities that

pulled officers and men into the empire after 1815. Edward Close of
the Forty-Eighth Foot described in his diary what it was like to arrive
back in Britain after the Peninsular War: "From very few uniforms
being amongst us we were taken for Frenchmen during the entire
route to Northampton. Whether this proceeded from the above
cause—our sun burnt countenances, or our habit of communicating
our remarks in Portuguese—certain it is we were not acknowledged
for countrymen."[43] Close was not alone in his sense of dislocation.
The wars had transformed him into someone who no longer felt comfortable in Britain. By 1817 he was in New South Wales. He married
in 1821 and sold his commission in 1822 so that he could settle in
the Hunter Valley. He chose his allotment deliberately because it was
within sight of the homes of two officers from his former regiment,
Val Blomfield and Francis Allman.[44]

One way to interpret the story of these three officers is to connect
it to the theme of veteran networks in this chapter. Another, complementary interpretation is that Close, Blomfield, and Allman were
seeking to keep the best of their military experience while leaving
behind the worst. The friendships forged on campaign were strong
enough to last for decades after the wars on the far side of the world.
There, they could leave behind all that was frustrating about military
life while removing themselves from the society that no longer recognized them. There were no more orders. "I am now my own master
and intend to keep so, and have very little to do with any person,"
wrote Blomfield to his sister in 1829.[45] They were still the king's subjects, of course, so they did not go as far as some. But in the release of
veteran soldiers and sailors into and beyond the empire, we can see
how the war's effects spilled over into the peace.

CONCLUSION

Too often, historians and political scientists have used "Britain in 1815" as shorthand for a globe-spanning superpower. That is misleading. In fact, Britain was exhausted by war and eager to retreat from its Continental entanglements for the decade that followed the victory at Waterloo. It is true that it was relatively better off than most of Europe, and that does justify a certain degree of triumphalism when telling the story of the Napoleonic Wars. It had won command of the ocean and defeated Europe's greatest general on the battlefield. But what this book has shown is that Britain exercised restraint in the postwar decade because it had few other choices.

Britain's military and naval weakness was a product of its domestic turmoil. The debt overwhelmed the budget, and Liverpool's government failed to convince the voting public of the need to continue the wartime taxation regime. Economy was the order of the day, and since the bulk of the government's budget concerned the army and the navy, they bore the brunt of the cuts. As a result, the navy, Britain's most potent global weapon, was a threat more in theory than reality. It was not a "fleet in being," ready to be deployed to swat away any challengers; it was a "fleet in ordinary," steadily rotting in crowded dockyards. The potential was there to recapitalize it, but not the political will. Naval historians need to be more sensitive to the collapse in postwar readiness. It had implications for how Britain handled turmoil in South America and the threat of war in North America.

The army was at the peak of its reputation, but it was still substantially smaller than many of its European allies. The tsar had more than one hundred fifty thousand battle-hardened troops in Paris in 1814, and the next year, the British struggled to put even forty thousand in the field.[1] After Waterloo, budget cuts shriveled its deployable strength. Garrisoning the empire stretched its capacities to the limit, and so there was no disposal force to deal with hot spots in Canada and Spain. Nevertheless, the empire grew because the logic of imperialism demands constant warfare. Frontier wars were fought with local resources or on shoestring budgets until the middle of the 1820s, when British military and naval power finally began to rebound toward the heights it had reached in the last years of the Napoleonic Wars.

The budget cuts accelerated the process of bringing soldiers and sailors home. Demobilization began properly with the navy in 1814 and lasted through the breakup of the Army of Occupation in 1818. The navy discharged a larger percentage of its sailors than the army did its soldiers, and in general, sailors arrived first. They found darkness, as Lord Byron put it, and not just because of Tambora. Domestically, the chaos of demobilization combined with the prevailing laissez-faire political attitude resulted in a deep and prolonged depression. The government was in no position to help the economy wean itself off wartime contracts, nor did it desire to do so. The arrival of soldiers and sailors exacerbated the unemployment crisis that characterized the period from Waterloo to Peterloo. The Tambora catastrophe could not have come at a more challenging time.

Some veterans, alongside other members of the working class, rejected this new reality. They demanded action, and when they realized that the government was so unrepresentative as to be deaf to their demands, they took to the streets. The fighting did not end at Waterloo. The army deployed throughout the British Isles to enforce the government's version of the peace. It was a violent and turbulent process, and while it did prevent the British equivalent of the storming of the Bastille, it was not wholly successful. Calls for parliamentary reform grew louder, especially after the yeomanry and hussars killed innocent protestors at Peterloo.

Letting veterans drive the story enhances our understanding of British history in the first quarter of the nineteenth century because veterans are a fruitful category of analysis. Centering veterans provides an opportunity to connect domestic and foreign policy, to understand the militancy of the postwar protests, and to grapple with the government's response. Centering veterans also helps historians write across the 1815 barrier. The army's victory at Waterloo and Napoleon's surrender to the navy provide a perfect matched-pair culmination to the Napoleonic Wars, and it is understandable that the years that follow often have been, and likely will always be, fodder for epilogues. Yet stopping the story there comes with costs to our understanding of the wars.

Historians writing about veterans should look beyond the Peninsular War. Many veterans of campaigns elsewhere in the global conflict, including but by no means limited to sailors, wrote prolifically about their experiences, but too often historians have narrowed their study of memoirs to just those who fought "alongside Wellington." While that can be helpful in examining different perspectives on the same events, it also eliminates many hundreds of memoirs that have equally interesting things to say about the wars and their aftermath. The most recent study of military memoirs from the Peninsular War shares just one memoir with this book's bibliography.[2]

Nor are memoirs the only sources available to those interested in veterans. Caches of letters are still regularly discovered in dusty attics, and more could be done to track down such primary sources in regional archives. Veterans also regularly interacted with bureaucracies that asked questions helpful to historians: Who are you? What do you do? What have you done? And so on. This book merely scratched the surface of the pension records available.

Pension schemes themselves are also worthy of further study. While the history of military pensions predates the 1815 demobilization, the scale of the Napoleonic Wars raised new questions and opened new possibilities, both of which resonate today. This book has examined a contradiction between the laissez-faire state that cut government spending to the lowest per capita in British history by the 1830s, and its hesitant forays into centralized welfare provisions via large-scale pension schemes. Veterans exemplified the idea of the "deserving poor" in 1815. Pensions were recruiting tools as well as rewards for service to the state, and it was difficult to make the political case that veterans should not receive some government funds. As a result, pension schemes suggested that the state had the capacity and perhaps even the responsibility to fund welfare as well as warfare.

Veterans' expectations for the country to which they returned seem to have mainly focused on their pensions, although some Radical leaders successfully connected wartime service with a demand for more widespread suffrage. That is an interesting avenue for further research. There are others as well. This book raised some questions about the origins of policing. Soldiers were uncomfortable as policemen. They lacked the training to de-escalate situations because they were trained to do the opposite, to bring overwhelming lethal force to bear on the enemy. Yet they were often the only option available to a magistrate faced with an unruly mob. Regular professional police forces emerged in the postwar period in part to address this problem, but there were other reasons as well. That the first modern police force came in the context of the British colonial occupation of Ireland is not surprising, but there is more that could be done to look at the relationships among soldiers, police, riots, and the state.

Some readers will be disappointed that this book did not look more carefully at the connection between demobilization and the Great Reform Act, or in detail at the security paradigm of the Congress System. Stopping the story circa 1825 imposes limitations that undoubtedly will frustrate some readers interested in Wellington's political career, in Chartism, in the abolition of slavery, and in a thousand other worthy subjects. This book focused mostly on the mechanics of veterans' return, but more research would be helpful on how veterans were perceived by the government and how they understood themselves to be perceived. We also do not have a good understanding of the extent to which veterans picked up political ideas (whether Radical or Tory) during the wartime service. Broadening the story from Britain to look at the international context for the postwar suppression of Radicalism would be another useful future project.

We can give the last word to one of those veterans who gained new perspectives on Britain both during and after his military service. In 1822, our wandering bombardier, Alexander Alexander, saw British shores for the first time since he had left his artillery unit at the end of the wars: "I stood on the quarter-deck in the wildest amaze, overcome by a thousand feelings, over which a sense of utter loneliness prevailed." After tracking down his long-lost mother, he successfully applied to get his pension restarted; he was also partially successful in getting some of the pension funds he had not been able to collect while he was participating in the South American revolutions. But it was not enough, especially after he failed to find any gainful employment in Glasgow. The most significant problem was his health, which had suffered severely in his travels. He had two operations to deal with physical injuries, but he ended up penniless and broken, his pension consumed. Traveling to London in search of work made things worse, not better: "For some weeks I struggled for existence in London, that paradox of society, that centre of want and profligate profusion. . . . O! how my heart yearned after South America, and blushed for my country, at the insults and abuses I endured. Good God! I often exclaimed, am I in Britain? Am I amongst Christian men?"

A long-simmering conflict with his father eventually resulted in Alexander spending four years in jail. There, at least, he had food and lodging (at his father's expense). It also gave him space to reflect on his experience as a veteran abroad: "The man that returns to his native country with riches, no matter how they are obtained, is a gentleman; but he that returns poor, no matter from what cause, is worthless and despised." Following his release, he began writing his memoir: "After it was nearly complete, (and a long and heart-breaking task it was, during which I often threw down my pen and gnashed my teeth in a state of mental distraction,) I knew well, such was the state of my feelings, that it could not appear before the public as it was."[3]

Eventually he connected with an editor, John Howell, who had already shepherded the stories of John Nicol and the anonymous soldier of the Seventy-First Regiment through the publication process. The similarities in tone among the three works suggests Howell wielded a strong editorial pen. Yet even more than Howell's earlier collaborations, Alexander's is over-the-top in its romantic sentimentality and nearly impossible to verify. Nevertheless, its exaggerations evoke the emotions of homecoming, and we should take those emotions seriously even if we question some of his "just-so" stories. Alexander had eagerly welcomed the end of the Napoleonic Wars and the end of his time in the British military, but his postwar experience had not lived up to his expectations. His adventures abroad had not brought him riches, nor had they opened new career horizons. He found himself in 1822 not far off where he had been in 1814: in Glasgow, with no prospects, struggling to make ends meet. His time abroad had given him a new perspective on British society, exposing fault lines that had not previously been visible to him. Not all veterans suffered as he claimed to have suffered after returning home, but loneliness, dislocation, and unemployment were common to many.

Notes

ABBREVIATIONS

BAN	Knight, *Britain against Napoleon*
BDN	Muir, *Britain and the Defeat of Napoleon*
BL	British Library
GMD	Sir Graham Moore: Diaries, Cambridge Univ. Lib., GB 12 MS.Add.9303
INW	Davey, *In Nelson's Wake*
LLA	Cookson, *Lord Liverpool's Administration*
LMA	London Metropolitan Archives
LS	Watt with Hawkins, eds., *Letters of Seamen*
NA	The National Archives, Kew
NAM	National Army Museum
NC	Tracy, ed., *Naval Chronicle*
NIT	Lewis, *Navy in Transition*
NMM	National Maritime Museum
NW	Mikaberidze, *Napoleonic Wars*
ODNB	*Oxford Dictionary of National Biography* (2004)
SSS	Bamford, *Sickness, Suffering, and the Sword*
WSD	Second Duke of Wellington, ed., *Wellington Supplementary Despatches*
WW	Davies, *Wellington's Wars*

PREFACE

1 Haynes, *Our Friends*; Graaf, *Fighting Terror*; Graaf, Haan, and Vick, *Securing Europe*.
2 Department of Defense, "2021 TAP Curriculum: Managing Your Transition," February 1, 2021.
3 Department of Defense, "2021 TAP Curriculum."
4 Dreisbach and Anderson, "Nearly 1 in 5 Defendants in Capitol Riot Cases Served in the Military."

NOTE ON CONVENTIONS

1 Hobhouse, *Recollections*, 2:113.

INTRODUCTION

1 Howell, *A Complete Collection of State Trials*, 32:86.
2 "Spa-Fields Meeting," *Morning Post*, December 3, 1816.
3 "Spa-Fields Meeting."

4 Linda Colley first asked the question in *Britons*, 321.
5 The major exceptions to this assertion are Schroeder, *Transformation*, and Bayly, *Imperial Meridian*. There are a few studies of demobilization and its effects. Despite its age, the most comprehensive study of naval demobilization remains *NIT*. Other studies, not limited to Britain, include the special issue of the *Journal of Military History* 80, no. 1 (2016), and Forrest, Hagemann, and Rowe, *War, Demobilization and Memory*. In general, however, historians have been less interested in the mechanics of demobilization and its effects (the focus of this book) and more interested in military memoirs, commemoration, and other aspects of historical memory. Interested readers might consult Grieg, *Dead Men Telling Tales*; Hopkin, "Storytelling"; Kennedy, *Narratives*; Ramsey, *Military Memoir*; Forrest, Hagemann, and Rendall, *Soldiers, Citizens and Civilians*; Forrest, *Legacy of the French Revolutionary Wars*; Reynolds, "Who Owned Waterloo?"; Milkes, "A Battle's Legacy."
6 The two most important studies, which have each spawned their own subfield, are Thompson, *Making of the English Working Class*, and Colley, *Britons*. Other important works of the political and social history of Britain in the postwar period include but are not limited to Briggs, *Age of Improvement*; White, *Waterloo to Peterloo*; *LLA*; Hilton, *Mad, Bad*; and Chase, *1820*.
7 Editorial, *The Times*, March 27, 1816.
8 Kennedy, *Narratives*, 171–81; Favret, "Everyday War."
9 Rev. John Stonard to Richard Heber, April 15, 1814, in Cholmondeley, *Heber Letters*, 267.
10 Coleridge, *Fears in Solitude*, 86–89, 91–96, 108.
11 From Burke's memorial to Pitt the Elder, as quoted in Colley, *Britons*, 71.
12 O'Brien, "Inseparable Connections," 74–75; Brewer, *Sinews of Power*, 199; *NW*, 627.
13 Franklin to Banks, Passy, July 27, 1783, in Labaree et al., *Papers of Benjamin Franklin*, 40:118, emphasis in original.
14 Paine, *Rights of Man: Part the Second*, 4.
15 Madison, "Political Observations, April 20, 1795," in Hutchinson et al., *Papers of James Madison*, 15:511–34.
16 Kant, *To Perpetual Peace*, 9; Murray and Lacey, *Making of Peace*, vii. See also Howard, *Invention of Peace*, 2–6.
17 Leach, *Rough Sketches*, 367.
18 McNeill, *Mosquito Empires*, 8.
19 Thant Myint-U, *Hidden History*, 12–13.
20 Henry Kissinger's doctoral dissertation looked to 1815 as a model for the post–World War II settlement. See Kissinger, *A World Restored*. Unfortunately, it is common to read less rigorous analyses of the lessons of 1815 by practitioners today. For example, see Campbell and Doshi, "How America Can Shore Up Asian Order."
21 Clausewitz, *On War*, 89.
22 Ikenberry, *After Victory*, 82.
23 Kissinger, *Diplomacy*, 88–91.
24 Buckley, *Napoleonic War Journal*, 283.

CHAPTER 1: THE GOVERNMENT AT THE BEGINNING OF THE END

1 Emsley, *British Society*, 180–81; Colley, *Britons*, 1–9; Innes, "Parliament."
2 Mitchell, *British Historical Statistics*, 9–11, 103; Brunt and Meidell, "How Fast and How Broad."
3 Wilson, "Naval Defence of Ireland."
4 Cookson, *British Armed Nation*, 1–10.

5 French, *British Way*, 116–17.
6 White, *Waterloo to Peterloo*, 8; Hopkins, *American Empire*, 77; Hilton, *Mad, Bad*, 200; *LLA*, 8.
7 Cannadine, *Victorious Century*, 135–36; Hay, *Lord Liverpool*.
8 Thorne, *House of Commons*, 1:235–63; Craig, "Tories and the Language of 'Liberalism' in the 1820s."
9 Evans, *Britain before the Reform Act*, 14; O'Gorman, *Long Eighteenth Century*, 262–63.
10 Hilton, *Mad, Bad*, 275–80.
11 Poole, *Peterloo*, 10.
12 *ODNB*, s.v. "Scott, John, first Earl of Eldon," "Peel, Sir Robert, second baronet," and "Canning, George."
13 Bamford, *Passages*, 2:95.
14 Hilton, *Mad, Bad*, 200–203; Bew, *Castlereagh*.
15 *ODNB*, s.v. "Vansittart, Nicholas, first Baron Bexley."
16 *ODNB*, s.v. "Dundas, Robert Saunders, second Viscount Melville."
17 Barrow, *Autobiographical Memoir*, 323.
18 Jennings, *Croker Papers*, 1:3–23.
19 Knight, "Battle for the Control."
20 Stirling, *Pages & Portraits*, 2:151–61; *ODNB*, s.v. "Frederick, Prince, duke of York and Albany."
21 *LLA*, 8.
22 Bourne, *Palmerston*, 90–92.
23 Brewer, *Sinews of Power*, 40.
24 Pincus and Robinson, "Wars and State-Making," 9–34. They note that 35 percent of British expenditures in the 1720s were for social or economic initiatives "once one excludes debt and loan repayments"—a significant caveat.
25 O'Brien, "Political Economy," 2.
26 Smith, *Wealth of Nations*, 2:338.
27 Dickson, *Financial Revolution*, 11–15.
28 Harling and Mandler, "From 'Fiscal-Military' State," 53.
29 O'Brien, "Impact of the Revolutionary and Napoleonic Wars," 373.
30 Hilton, *Mad, Bad*, 257–62.
31 For example: O'Brien, "Impact of the Revolutionary and Napoleonic Wars"; Rodger, "War as an Economic Activity"; Satia, *Empire of Guns*. For a summary of some counterarguments, see Kedrosky, "All Quiet on the Investment Front."
32 Harling and Mandler, "From 'Fiscal-Military' State"; Evans, *Britain before the Reform Act*, 44–46.

CHAPTER 2: THE ARMY AND THE NAVY AT THE BEGINNING OF THE END

1 *INW*, 231–35; Knight, *Convoys*.
2 French, *British Way*, 110.
3 *INW*, 238, 300–301; James, *Naval History*, 6:152–53; Corbett, "Napoleon and the British Navy," 240–48; Voelcker, *Admiral Saumarez*, 184–96.
4 *INW*, 293–301.
5 Black, *British Seaborne Empire*, 159–60.
6 Byam Martin to Lord Keith, September 21, 1813, in Hamilton, *Byam Martin Papers*, 2:409.
7 Hall, *Wellington's Navy*, 111–31; *INW*, 291–95.
8 Wilson, "Social Background and Promotion Prospects."
9 Wilson, *Social History*, 33–56, 105–29.
10 Byam Martin to Melville, July 8, 1819, in Crimmin, "The Supply of Timber for the Royal Navy," 225–26.

11 Webb, "Construction, Repair and Maintenance," 218.
12 J. A. Worth to Philip Durham, December 21, 1812, in Rubenstein, *Durham Papers*, 307–8.
13 Lord Melville to Lord Keith, September 3, 1813, in Hamilton, *Byam Martin Papers*, 2:368.
14 Rodger, *Command of the Ocean*, 639.
15 Farington, *Farington Diary*, March 22, 1816; Daly, *British Soldier*, 2–3; Linch, *Britain and Wellington's Army*, 34, 114.
16 Dancy, *Myth of the Press Gang*, 42.
17 Dancy, *Myth of the Press Gang*, 49–53; Kennedy, "'True Britons and Real Irish,'" 38–47.
18 Coss, *All for the King's Shilling*, 191–210; Lavery, *Shipboard Life*, 244.
19 *SSS*, 165–68; Linch, *Britain and Wellington's Army*, 144–47.
20 Sixty-one of 103 regiments had second battalions in 1808. See Fremont-Barnes, "The British Army," 130–31.
21 *SSS*, 113–25; MacArthur, "British Army Establishments," 156–64.
22 Wilson, *Social History*, 160–63.
23 Cookson, "Regimental Worlds," 27–29.
24 *WW*, 172; Fremont-Barnes, "The British Army," 130.
25 Linch, "Desertion," 820; MacArthur, "British Army Establishments," 162; Sutcliffe, *British Expeditionary Warfare*, 17.
26 Wellington to Bathurst, August 23, 1813, in Gurwood, *Wellington's Dispatches*, 11:34–35.
27 Gates, "Transformation," 139.
28 Corbett, *Some Principles*, 60–72.
29 *SSS*, 95–96.

CHAPTER 3: VICTORY IN EUROPE, 1812–14

1 Lieven, *Russia against Napoleon*, 78–85.
2 Hall, *British Strategy*, 197–98; French, *British Way*, 114.
3 Hall, *British Strategy*, 198–99; Voelcker, *Admiral Saumarez*, 195–96; Ryan, "An Ambassador Afloat," 254–55.
4 Ross, *Memoirs and Correspondence*, 2:292–97; *NC*, 5:107; *NW*, 539. Reports reached Britain about Napoleon's retreat in early November, but not until January 1813 was the scale of the disaster known. See Hall, *British Strategy*, 199–200.
5 *BDN*, 307–9.
6 *SSS*, 160–65.
7 List Books, 1810–13, NA, ADM 8:99–100; "British First Rate ship of the line 'Victory' (1765)," *Three Decks*, https://threedecks.org/index.php?display_type=show_ship&id=17.
8 *BDN*, 238; Esdaile, *Napoleon's Wars*, 480.
9 *INW*, 259–61.
10 McCranie, *Utmost Gallantry*, 121–25.
11 *NC*, 5:105.
12 Joseph Bute and forty-five others to Durham, February 9, 1814, in Rubinstein, *Durham Papers*, 408–9; Bickham, *Weight of Vengeance*, 152–53; *INW*, 256–57; Dudley, "Flawed British Blockade," 38–39; Lambert, *The Challenge*, 382–84.
13 *NW*, 547–49; *BDN*, 235–36; Linch, "Desertion," 813–18.
14 Dudley, "Flawed British Blockade," 38–40.
15 List Books, 1810–13, NA, ADM 8:99–100; *BAN*, 447–48; Cordingly, *Billy Ruffian*, 226–27; French, *British Way*, 115; *INW*, 251–62; McCranie, *Utmost Gallantry*, 95.
16 *GMD*, 1813–14, 129–31.

17 *INW*, 251–53; Arthur, *How Britain Won*, 91; James, *Naval History*, 6:143–52; Lambert, *The Challenge*, 254–55.

18 Warren to Melville, *San Domingo*, Bermuda, February 19, 1813, as quoted in Arthur, *How Britain Won*, 88.

19 *Cobbett's Weekly Political Register*, 24:73, as quoted in *INW*, 265–74 at 265; Lambert, *The Challenge*, 116, 243; Arthur, *How Britain Won*, 102–3.

20 Monthly disposition of the army, 1803–27, NA, WO 379/6; Admiralty Journals (Board Room), July 1–December 31, 1813, NA, ADM 7/264.

21 *NW*, 498–500.

22 Monthly disposition of the army, 1803–27, NA, WO 379/6; Admiralty Journals (Board Room), July 1–December 31, 1813, NA, ADM 7/264; *SSS*, 42–43.

23 Bickham, *Weight of Vengeance*, 135–36.

24 *BDN*, 238–39.

25 French, *British Way*, 111; *BDN*, 198–99, 203–16; *WW*, 159–69.

26 *WW*, 171–86.

27 *BDN*, 256–71, 284; *NW*, 566–67; *WW*, 189–92.

28 *WW*, 187, 203–6; Hall, *British Strategy*, 199–200.

29 Letters from Captains, Surnames H: 1813, Thomas Heddington to Croker, August 16, 1813, NA, ADM 1/1948; Rogers, "British Impressment and Its Discontents," 52–73.

30 *BAN*, 440–47.

31 GMD, 1813–14, 131–41.

32 *WW*, 202–8.

33 Lambert, *The Challenge*, 382–84; *NC*, 5:173; *NIT*, 67–68; GMD, 1813–14, 286–90.

34 Cobbett, *Regency*, chap. 5, para. 277, as quoted in Uglow, *In These Times*, 606.

CHAPTER 4: DEMOBILIZATION AND THE WAR OF 1812

1 Navy Board, Documents relating to Armaments, 2nd Series, 1806–17, NA, ADM 106/3065.

2 R. B. Vincent to Exmouth, September 14, 1815, NMM, Pellew Papers, PEL/24.

3 Mallinson, *Send It by Semaphore*, 168–69.

4 Navy Board, Documents relating to Armaments, 2nd Series, 1806–17, NA, ADM 106/3065; Navy Board, Abstracts of letters from the Admiralty, 1814–15, NA, ADM 106/2096.

5 Admiralty Journals (Board Room), January 1–June 30, 1814, NA, ADM 7/265; *NC*, 5:228–30.

6 Navy Board, Barrow to the respective Captains, Commanders, and Commanding Officers of His Majesty's Ships and Vessels ordered to be paid off, May 11, 1814, NA, ADM 106/3065.

7 Admiralty Journals (Board Room), July 1–December 31, 1814, NA, ADM 7/266; McCranie, *Utmost Gallantry*, 246.

8 Navy Board, Documents relating to Armaments, 2nd Series, 1806–17, NA, ADM 106/3065.

9 Minutes of General Meetings of Members, March 25, 1814, Lloyd's of London, LMA, MS31570/001.

10 McCranie, *Utmost Gallantry*, 247–52.

11 Cockburn to W. L. C. Barrie, July 16, 1814, William L. Clements Library, Barrie Papers, as quoted in Morriss, *Cockburn*, 294.

12 *NC*, 5:233–34, 264–66; Fagal, "British Responses."

13 *NC*, 5:237.

14 Minutes of General Meetings of Members, September 21, 1814, Lloyd's of London, LMA, MS31570/001.

15 Admiralty Journals (Board Room), July 1–December 31, 1814, NA, ADM 7/266.
16 Admiralty Journals (Board Room), January 1–December 31, 1814, NA, ADM 7/265–66; McCranie, *Utmost Gallantry*, 215–17; Lambert, *The Challenge*, 256–60.
17 Admiralty Journals (Board Room), July 1–December 31, 1814, NA, ADM 7/266; GMD, 1814–19, 12–19; *NC*, 5:263; Dudley, "The Flawed British Blockade," 43–44; McCranie, *Utmost Gallantry*, 243–44; Lambert, *The Challenge*, 258–95, 308.
18 Bickham, *Weight of Vengeance*, 151–52; *BAN*, 447–52; *NW*, 590; Graves, "The Redcoats Are Coming!"
19 *SSS*, 39.
20 Monthly disposition of the army, 1803–27, NA, WO 379/6; Graves, "The Redcoats Are Coming!"
21 Monthly disposition of the army, 1803–27, NA, WO 379/6; Graves, "The Redcoats Are Coming!"; *BAN*, 452.
22 *SSS*, 41; Linch, *Britain and Wellington's Army*, 34; *BAN*, 452; Sutcliffe, *British Expeditionary Warfare*, 229.
23 Linch, "Desertion," 808–28.
24 *NW*, 587.
25 *NW*, 587.
26 *NW*, 587–89; Graves, "'The Finest Army.'"
27 GMD, 1814–19, 4–11.
28 *NW*, 587–89; *BDN*, 332–33; Dudley, "The Flawed British Blockade," 44; Minutes of General Meetings of Members, March 22, 1815, Lloyd's of London, LMA, MS31570/001; Bickham, *Weight of Vengeance*, 13–19. The chairman of Lloyd's later claimed to have played a role in bringing about the settlement as well.
29 *INW*, 274–75.
30 *NW*, 588–89.
31 *INW*, 275–76.
32 Thomas Pierrepont and eleven others to Durham, Barbados, April 3, 1815, in Rubenstein, *Durham Papers*, 439; Dudley, "The Flawed British Blockade," 44; Morriss, *Cockburn*, 119.
33 Admiralty Journals (Board Room), January 1–June 30, 1815, NA, ADM 7/267; Monthly disposition of the army, 1803–27, NA, WO 379/6. See also McCranie, "The War of 1812."
34 Admiralty Journals (Board Room), January 1–June 30, 1816, NA, ADM 7/269; Monthly disposition of the army, 1803–27, NA, WO 379/6.
35 Clausewitz, *On War*, 69, emphasis original.
36 McCranie, *Mahan, Corbett*, 230–31.
37 Sumida, *Decoding Clausewitz*, 20.
38 Bickham, *Weight of Vengeance*, 227.
39 Clausewitz, *On War*, 77–84.

CHAPTER 5: DEMOBILIZATION AND THE HUNDRED DAYS

1 Penrose, *Lives*, 59–60.
2 *INW*, 305–6.
3 *INW*, 305–6.
4 Hayter, *The Backbone*, 284–88; see also GMD, 1813–14, 321–26.
5 Wilson, "The Monster from Elba."
6 *Hansard Parliamentary Debates*, 1st Series (1803–20), 30:545–83.
7 Admiralty Journals (Board Room), January 1–December 31, 1814, NA, ADM 7/265–66.
8 *NC*, 5:285–86.
9 Rodger, *Command of the Ocean*, 574.
10 GMD, 1814–1819, 94–98.

11 Navy Board, Documents relating to Armaments, 1st Series, 1815, NA, ADM 106/3062.
12 Admiralty Journals (Board Room), January 1–December 31, 1815, NA, ADM 7/267–68.
13 Sutcliffe, *British Expeditionary Warfare*, 233; Letters of March 28–April 25, 1815, BL, Martin Papers, Add. MSS 41393.
14 Navy Board, Documents relating to Armaments, 1st Series, 1815, NA, ADM 106/3062; Mallinson, *Send It by Semaphore*, 170–77.
15 Navy Board, Documents relating to Armaments, 1st Series, 1815, NA, ADM 106/3062; Hall, *British Strategy*, 203–5; *INW*, 307.
16 *NW*, 595–607; *BDN*, 345–52; Muir, *Wellington: Waterloo*, 14–30; Glover, *Waterloo*, 16–32; *WW*, 214–15.
17 Castlereagh to Wellington, April 13, 1815, *WSD*, 10:75. I am grateful to Roger Knight for the reference.
18 Glover, *Waterloo*, 32; Muir, *Wellington: Waterloo*, 30.
19 *BDN*, 355; Sutcliffe, *British Expeditionary Warfare*, 233–37.
20 *BAN*, 456–57; Simms, *Longest Afternoon*, 77–79; *NW*, 610.
21 Wellington to Stewart, Brussels, May 8, 1815, Wellington, *Dispatches*, 12:358, as quoted in *WW*, 225.
22 *BDN*, 360–61; *WW*, 237.
23 Cordingly, *Billy Ruffian*, 227–67; McCranie, *Admiral Lord Keith*, 168.
24 Glover, *Waterloo*, 217–27.
25 Letters of June–August 1815, in Rubenstein, *Durham Papers*, 452–70; Weiss, "Mission Command."
26 For the navy, see House of Commons *Parliamentary Papers* (1859), session 1, 6:362 (in *U.K. Parliamentary Papers*, ProQuest, https://parlipapers.proquest.com/ parlipapers); Clowes, *Royal Navy*, 6:190; *NIT*, 67–68; and Rodger, *Command of the Ocean*, 639. For the army, *SSS*, 41; Linch, *Britain and Wellington's Army*, 34; Graves, "'The Finest Army'"; and Graves, "The Redcoats Are Coming!"
27 Other Military Records for France, Germany, the Low Countries and the Waterloo Campaign, 1814–16, University of Southampton Library, WP 9/7/1.
28 Admiralty Journals (Board Room), January 1–December 31, 1815, NA, ADM 7/267–68.
29 Mitchell, *British Historical Statistics*, 587; Hall, *British Strategy*, 203–5.

CHAPTER 6: THE NAVY AFTER NAPOLEON

1 Monteiro, *Theory of Unipolar Politics*, 1–3.
2 Ford, *Europe*, 308; Webster, *Foreign Policy of Castlereagh, 1815–1822*, 47.
3 Bartlett, "Britain and the European Balance," 145.
4 Kissinger, *A World Restored*, 106–7.
5 Richmond, *Statesmen and Sea Power*, 258.
6 Harding, *Seapower and Naval Warfare*, 277–78; Black, *British Seaborne Empire*, 173.
7 Glete, *Navies and Nations*, 421–22.
8 Kennedy, *Rise and Fall of British Naval Mastery*, 156–72.
9 Lambert, *Last Sailing Battlefleet*, 164–66.
10 Ikenberry, *After Victory*, 82.
11 Bartlett, *Great Britain and Sea Power*, 56.
12 Castlereagh to Charles Bagot, November 10, 1817, as quoted in Merk, *Oregon Question*, 17–25. A similar analysis can be found in Middleton, *Administration of British Foreign Policy*, 25–28.
13 Glete, *Navies and Nations*, 549–682; Kennedy, *Rise and Fall of British Naval Mastery*, 156–72; Bourne, *Britain*, 9.
14 *Hansard Parliamentary Debates*, 3rd Series (1830–91), 97:780.

15 Lambert, *Last Sailing Battlefleet*, 16; Brown, *Before the Ironclad*, 26–30; Sondhaus, *Naval Warfare*, 18–20.

16 MacDougall, *Chatham Dockyard*, xvi, 209–10; Lambert, *Last Sailing Battlefleet*, viii, 21–22; Bartlett, *Great Britain and Sea Power*, 21–29.

17 Bourne, *Britain*, 26–27.

18 Glete, *Navies and Nations*, 422, 451, 470; Bartlett, *Great Britain and Sea Power*, 21–34; Grindal, *Opposing the Slavers*, 183; Brown, *Before the Ironclad*, 26–30; Lambert, "Preparing for the Long Peace," 44–45.

19 Bromley, *Manning of the Royal Navy*, 151–72.

20 Madison to James Monroe, November 28, 1818, in Madison and Hunt, *Writings of James Madison*, 8:418.

21 Liverpool to Castlereagh, September 26, 1816, NA, FO 5/119, as quoted in Bourne, *Britain*, 7.

22 Bourne, *Britain*, 7–8; Bickham, *Weight of Vengeance*, 253–61.

23 Bourne, *Britain*, 3–4; Burrows, *Captain Owen*, 55–62.

24 Captain Sir James Yeo to Melville, May 30, 1815, NA, ADM 1/2738.

25 Bourne, *Britain*, 13–17.

26 Sir Robert Hall to Byam Martin, October 1816, BL, Martin Papers, Add. MSS 41400.

27 Croker to Byam Martin, July 6, 1816, BL, Martin Papers, Add. MSS 41400.

28 Bourne, *Britain*, 3–29; Perkins, *Castlereagh and Adams*, 239–44; Hall to Byam Martin, July 31, 1817, BL, Martin Papers, Add. MSS 41400.

29 Bourne, *Britain*, 9–11; Perkins, *Castlereagh and Adams*, 244; Lambert, "Winning without Fighting."

30 Gough, *Britannia's Navy*, 47–58. The Americans had technically sold Fort George to the North West Company, so there was a legitimate argument that it was exempt from the treaty negotiations. See also Gibson and Istomin, *Russian California*.

31 Gough, *Britannia's Navy*, 47.

32 Gough, *Britannia's Navy*, 63.

33 Merk, *Oregon Question*, 17–27; Gough, *Britannia's Navy*, 59–62.

34 Remini, *Andrew Jackson*, 351–76; Bartlett, *Great Britain and Sea Power*, 64–65.

35 Andrew Jackson to John C. Calhoun, May 5, 1818, in Jackson, *Correspondence of Andrew Jackson*, 2:365–68.

36 Remini, *Andrew Jackson*, 351–76.

37 McCarthy, *Privateering*, 14–15, 46–47; Hunter, *Policing the Seas*, 27.

38 McCarthy, *Privateering*, 18–19, 69; Blaufarb, "The Western Question," 742–63; Schroeder, *Transformation*, 630–55.

39 Gough and Borras, *War against the Pirates*, 46–48, 111.

40 McCarthy, *Privateering*, 47–50, 72–74, 158.

41 Gough and Borras, *War against the Pirates*, 85–90.

42 McCarthy, *Privateering*, 159–160; Gough and Borras, *War against the Pirates*, 16, 60–75; Hunter, *Policing the Seas*, 51, 82–83, 197; Armstrong, *Small Boats*, 122–49. On the French navy's actions in this period, see the chapter by Hélène Vencent in Graaf, Vaisset, and Dessberg, *Soldiers in Peace-Making*.

43 McCarthy, *Privateering*, 160.

44 Gough and Borras, *War against the Pirates*, 76–90.

45 Gough, *Pax Britannica*, 109.

46 GMD, 1814–19, September 1816.

47 de Lange, "From Augarten to Algiers." See also Sondhaus, *Naval Warfare*, 6–8; Dull, *American Naval History*, 65; Parkinson, *Edward Pellew*, 426–37; Perkins, *Gunfire in Barbary*, 45–46.

48 GMD, 1814–19, September 1816; Perkins, *Gunfire in Barbary*, 75–77; Letter from Regulating Captain at Tower Hill to Admiralty Secretariat, July 12, 1816, NA, ADM 1/3664.

49 A General Abstract of the Killed and Wounded in the Squadron under Admiral Lord Exmouth's Command in the Attack of Algiers, August 27, 1816, NMM, Pellew Papers, PEL/29; Ryan, "The Price of Legitimacy in Humanitarian Intervention," 232–36; Bartlett, *Great Britain and Sea Power*, 61–64; Lambert, *Last Sailing Battlefleet*, 99; Gale, "Barbary's Slow Death."

50 Bartlett, *Great Britain and Sea Power*, 63.

51 Melville to Bathurst, August 11, 1817, in Bickley, *Report on the Manuscripts of Earl Bathurst*, 436–9.

52 Bartlett, *Great Britain and Sea Power*, 64–65, 78–79.

CHAPTER 7: THE ARMY AFTER NAPOLEON

1 *WW*, 214–15.

2 Strachan, *From Waterloo to Balaclava*, viii.

3 Bayly, *Imperial Meridian*, 248–49.

4 Rodger, *Naval History III*, in preparation. I am grateful to Nicholas Rodger for allowing me to see some chapters in draft form. Published evidence in support of this claim can be found in the Cabinet's Memorandum on the Maritime Peace, December 26, 1813, in Webster, *British Diplomacy, 1813–1815*, 127.

5 Duffy, "British Policy."

6 Commander in Chief, Letters on Reduction of Army to Peace-Time Level, Memorandum of August 28, 1818, NA, WO 1/952.

7 Fortescue, *History of the British Army*, 11:7–8.

8 Fitzpatrick, "Ireland and the Empire," 494–98.

9 Commander in Chief, Letters on Reduction of Army to Peace-Time Level, Comparison of 1792 and 1818 deployments, NA, WO 1/952; Fortescue, *History of the British Army*, 11:50–2; Cannon, *North Devon Regiment of Foot*, 79–83; Cannon, *Queen's Own Regiment of Hussars*, 82–83.

10 Fenning, "Typhus Epidemic in Ireland," 117; Chase, *1820*, 32.

11 Peel to Lord Whitworth, March 8, 1817, BL, Peel Papers, Add. MSS 40292, ff. 174–78, as quoted in *LLA*, 93.

12 Surtees, *Twenty-five Years*, 417; Chase, *1820*, 106.

13 Dawes, *Jottings from My Sabretasch*, 236–40.

14 Fortescue, *History of the British Army*, 11:55.

15 Malcolm, "From Light Infantry to Constabulary."

16 Cannon, *King's Own Regiment of Light Dragoons*, 78–84.

17 Surtees, *Twenty-Five Years*, 417.

18 Reynolds, "Who Owned Waterloo?," 235.

19 Dawes, *Jottings from My Sabretasch*, 236–40.

20 Alexander, *Life of Alexander Alexander*, 1:213.

21 Linch, "Desertion," 817–18; Bayly, *Imperial Meridian*, 127; Chase, *1820*, 32; Bourne, *Palmerston*, 113.

22 Haynes, *Our Friends*, 31–32, 78; Haynes, "Making Peace," 51.

23 *WSD*, 11:202–3.

24 Muir, *Wellington: Waterloo*, 109–10; Graaf, *Fighting Terror*, 8–11.

25 *BAN*, 467; Haynes, *Our Friends*, 45–46; *LLA*, 28–30.

26 Haynes, *Our Friends*, 121–22, 143; Cannon, *King's Own Regiment of Light Dragoons*, 76–77; Cannon, *Queen's Own Regiment of Hussars*, 82–83; Reynolds, "Who Owned Waterloo?," 210.

27 Haynes, *Our Friends*, 79–131.

28 Haynes, *Our Friends*, 162–63, 299; Muir, *Wellington: Waterloo*, 111–18.

29 Haynes, *Our Friends*, 175–82; Muir, *Wellington: Waterloo*, 114–15; Bourne, *Letters of the Third Viscount Palmerston*, October 15, 1818.

30 GMD, 1814–19, 344–83.
31 Commander in Chief, Letters on Reduction of Army to Peace-Time Level, Memorandum of February 22, 1816, NA, WO 1/952.
32 Bayly, *Imperial Meridian*, 197–99.
33 Martin, "Canada from 1815," 525.
34 Commander in Chief, Letters on Reduction of Army to Peace-Time Level, Memorandum of February 22, 1816, NA, WO 1/952.
35 Commander in Chief, Letters on Reduction of Army to Peace-Time Level, Memorandum of February 22, 1816, NA, WO 1/952; Heuman, "The British West Indies," 472–77.
36 Commander in Chief, Letters on Reduction of Army to Peace-Time Level, Memorandum of February 22, 1816, NA, WO 1/952.
37 Bayly, *Imperial Meridian*, 205–7; Denoon with Wyndham, "Australia and the Western Pacific," 548; Commander in Chief, Letters on Reduction of Army to Peace-Time Level, Memorandum of February 22, 1816, NA, WO 1/952. For New South Wales, Bayly cites a population of 8,235 in 1820; Denoon and Wyndham say Sydney and Hobart had fifteen thousand people in 1815.
38 Gough, *Pax Britannica*, 81; Bayly, *Imperial Meridian*, 3–4.
39 Commander in Chief, Letters on Reduction of Army to Peace-Time Level, Memoranda of July 30, August 20, 28, and 29, 1818, NA, WO 1/952.
40 Commander in Chief, Letters on Reduction of Army to Peace-Time Level, Memorandum of February 22, 1816, NA, WO 1/952.
41 Strachan, *Politics of the British Army*, 78–79.
42 Washbrook, "India, 1818–1860," 404–5.
43 Elkins, *Legacy of Violence*, 43–44; Mill, *History of British India*, vii–xxvii.
44 Bayly, *Imperial Meridian*, 186, 214; Peers, "Soldiers," 454; Graham, *Politics of Naval Supremacy*, 42.
45 Copy of Major W. Richards' journal of the attack on the Fort of Jumtee, Military Papers of the Phipps Family, NAM, 1981-08-7; Sheppard, *Short History*, 179–81; Fortescue, *Empire and the Army*, 233.
46 Shipp, *Memoirs*, 166–208.
47 Jasanoff, *Liberty's Exiles*, 339.
48 Vartavarian, "Pacification and Patronage"; Bayly, *Imperial Meridian*, 106.
49 Sheppard, *Short History*, 182–84; Fortescue, *Empire and the Army*, 233–34.
50 Shipp, *Memoirs*, 219.
51 Bayly, *Imperial Meridian*, 185.
52 Vartavarian, "Pacification and Patronage," 1756–66.
53 Bayly, *Imperial Meridian*, 7.
54 Lieutenant Thomas J. Anquetil to Captain P. Phipps, April 5, 1817, Military Papers of the Phipps Family, NAM, 1981-08-7.
55 Malcolm to Wellington, July 8, 1818, University of Southampton Library, WP 1/600.
56 Bayly, *Imperial Meridian*, 191–92; Jayasuria, "Recruiting Africans"; Jones, "Lascorins"; Jones, "The Ceylon Light Dragoons"; Sivasundaram, "Tales of the Land"; Fortescue, *Empire and the Army*, 234–35; Graham, *Politics of Naval Supremacy*, 47–49.
57 Graham, *Politics of Naval Supremacy*, 51–52; Gough, *Pax Britannica*, 118–22.
58 Ramachandra, "The Outbreak of the First Anglo-Burmese War," 66–99; Fortescue, *Empire and the Army*, 235–38.
59 Peers, "War and Public Finance," 638–39; Harrison, "Scurvy on Sea and Land," 12–13; Brown, "Fall of Mrauk U"; Fortescue, *Empire and the Army*, 235–38.
60 Thant Myint-U, *Hidden History*, 14–15; Clement, "Cross-Cultural Encounter."

61 Bell, *Narrative*, 37.
62 Myatt, *The British Infantry*, 106; Fortescue, *History of the British Army*, 11:86–87.

CHAPTER 8: THE POLITICS OF DEMOBILIZATION

1 Mitchell, *British Historical Statistics*, 586–603; Uglow, *In These Times*, 627–39; Cannadine, *Victorious Century*, 107; *LLA*, 33–36.
2 Lambert, "Preparing for the Long Peace," 42; Hilton, *Mad, Bad*, 264–66; Wells, *Wretched Faces*, 39–76, 187–204.
3 O'Brien, "Impact of the Revolutionary and Napoleonic Wars," 357; Hobson, *Dark Days*, 34; O'Gorman, *Long Eighteenth Century*, 241; Wade Martins, *Coke of Norfolk*, 92; Poole, *Peterloo*, 18.
4 Evans, *Britain*, 17; Mackenzie, *Historical Account of Newcastle*, 66–88.
5 Emsley, *British Society*, 165–66; *LLA*, 90; Hilton, *Mad, Bad*, 266–67.
6 *LLA*, 22–27; Thorne, *House of Commons*, 1:388.
7 *LLA*, 59.
8 *The Parliamentary Register*, 43:601; Hopkins, *American Empire*, 58–64; *LLA*, 33–36, 69–70.
9 Gash, "After Waterloo," 145–57.
10 O'Brien, "Impact of the Revolutionary and Napoleonic Wars," 365; Evans, *Britain*, 11; *LLA*, 38–47; Thorne, *House of Commons*, 1:246.
11 GMD, 1814–19, 207–15.
12 Hilton, *Mad, Bad*, 251; *LLA*, 69–70; O'Gorman, *Long Eighteenth Century*, 263.
13 Hopkins, *American Empire*, 58; Harling and Mandler, "From 'Fiscal-Military' State"; Brewer, *Sinews of Power*, 116–19.
14 George IV, *Letters of King George IV*, 2:161, as quoted in *LLA*, 74.
15 O'Brien, "Political Economy," 12–16.
16 Hobson, *Dark Days*, 18; no original source given.
17 *LLA*, 44–51.
18 *LLA*, 23–24, 28.
19 *The Times*, March 26, 1816.
20 Croker to Lord Hatherton, February 1, 1857, in Croker, *Croker Papers*, 1:73–77.
21 For example, see *Parliamentary Papers* (1816), 12:383–401 (in *U.K. Parliamentary Papers*, ProQuest, https://parlipapers.proquest.com/parlipapers).
22 *Hansard Parliamentary Debates*, 1st Series (1803–20), 37:701–10.
23 *LLA*, 51.
24 Hay, *Lord Liverpool*, 180, 187–88.
25 Bell, *Lord Palmerston*, 1:31–34; Bourne, *Palmerston*, 97–112.
26 *Hansard Parliamentary Debates*, 1st Series (1803–20), 37:862–76, as quoted in Bourne, *Palmerston*, 158.
27 Chase, *1820*, 126–27.
28 Navickas, "A Reformer's Wife," 246–47.
29 Bourne, *Palmerston*, 156–61.
30 Phipps, *Memoirs*, 2:31, as quoted in Chase, *1820*, 12–13.
31 McElligott and Conboy, eds., *Cato Street Conspiracy*, 1–11. See also Gatrell, *Conspiracy at Cato Street*.
32 Bourne, *Palmerston*, 158–61; Chase, *1820*, 71; Hilton, *Mad, Bad*, 252–54; *LLA*, 98.
33 Cookson, "Regimental Worlds"; Lin, "Caring for the Nation's Families"; Bickham and Abbey, "The Greatest Encouragement."
34 Mackenzie, *Historical Account of Newcastle*, 66–88; Hobson, *Dark Days*, 40–41.
35 Navy Board to Commissioner Barlow, July 6, 1816, in MacDougall, *Chatham Dockyard*, 214; *ODNB*, s.v. "Dickens, Charles John Huffam."
36 Lincoln, *Trading in War*, 255–56; Satia, *Empire of Guns*, 142–44, 161.

37 GMD, 1814–19, 215–23.
38 *LLA*, 63.
39 Harling and Mandler, "From 'Fiscal-Military' State."
40 O'Gorman, *Long Eighteenth Century*, 295; Hobson, *Dark Days*, 155.

CHAPTER 9: THE EXPERIENCE OF DEMOBILIZATION

1 Scott, "The Evidence of Experience"; Forrest, Hagemann, and Rendall, *Soldiers, Citizens and Civilians*, 4–12; Ramsey, *Military Memoir*.
2 Hopkin, "Storytelling," 186–98.
3 Whitworth to his wife, *Portia*, North Yarmouth, March 29, 1812, in *LS*, A166.
4 Whitworth to his wife, *Portia*, Sheerness, May 29, 1812, in *LS*, A170.
5 Richard Greenhalgh to his parents, *Powerful*, Spithead, September 26, 1797; and John Booth to his wife, *Amazon*, Hamoaze, May 6, 1808 in *LS*, A38, A132.
6 Wetherell, *Adventures of John Wetherell*, 260–61.
7 In addition to the two quoted, see Costello, *Adventures of a Soldier*, 272, and Dawes, *Jottings from My Sabretasch*, 224.
8 Jones, "The Old Halberdier," 211–12.
9 *Journal of a Soldier of the 71st*, 213.
10 Long to his mother, *Bedford*, the Scheldt, Netherlands, April 13, 1814, in *LS*, A189. Long's spelling is so poor as to be unreadable, so I have modernized it.
11 Surtees, *Twenty-Five Years*, 323–24.
12 Jones, "The Old Halberdier," 213–14.
13 Cooper, *Rough Notes*, 129–34.
14 Surtees, *Twenty-Five Years*, 323–24; Costello, *Adventures of a Soldier*, 282–83.
15 Liddell Hart, *Letters of Private Wheeler*, 154–55.
16 Durand, *Life and Adventures*, 74.
17 Cooper, *Rough Notes*, 150–52.
18 Leech, *Thirty Years from Home*, 219–20.
19 Surtees, *Twenty-Five Years*, 406.
20 Leech, *Thirty Years from Home*, 219–20.
21 *Journal of a Soldier of the 71st*, 213–15.
22 Cooper, *Rough Notes*, 150–52.
23 Dawes, *Jottings from My Sabretasch*, 229–31.
24 Liddell Hart, *Letters of Private Wheeler*, 187–94; Morris, *The Napoleonic Wars*, 97–101; Jones, "The Old Halberdier," 213–14; Surtees, *Twenty-Five Years*, 318–21.
25 Diary of Captain Foster Fyans, 1811, 1:28, NAM, 2007-02-69.
26 Cooper, *Rough Notes*, 129–34.
27 Grocott, *Shipwrecks*, 390–98.
28 Diary of Captain Foster Fyans, 1811, 1:29–33, NAM, 2007-02-69.
29 Coss, *All for the King's Shilling*, 3–8, 191–201, 209; Lavery, *Shipboard Life*, 244.
30 Leach, *Rough Sketches*, 405–6.
31 Harris, *Recollections*, 122.
32 Liddell Hart, *Letters of Private Wheeler*, 148.
33 Surtees, *Twenty-Five Years*, 316.
34 Costello, *Adventures of a Soldier*, 276–77.
35 See the series of letters from Greenhalgh to his parents, 1795–1802, in *LS*, A19, A67, A71, and A78.
36 *Journal of a Soldier of the 71st*, 228.
37 Liddell Hart, *Letters of Private Wheeler*, 148.
38 Morris, *The Napoleonic Wars*, 114–15.
39 Dodman, "1814 and the Melancholy of War," 47–49.
40 Cookson, "Regimental Worlds," 33–37; Hurl-Eamon, *Marriage*, 146–47.

41 Rodger, *Wooden World*, 119–24. About sailors' social worlds, see the forthcoming book by Elin Jones, *Naval Masculinity and Shipboard Society, 1756–1815*.
42 Hurl-Eamon, "Husbands."
43 Greenhalgh to his parents, *Powerful*, Portsmouth Harbor, January 1, 1798, in *LS*, A44.
44 Choate, *At Sea under Impressment*, 179–80; Cooper, *Rough Notes*, 129. For a discussion of soldiers' perceptions of their freedom, or lack thereof, see Hurl-Eamon, "Enslaved by the Uniform."
45 Dawes, *Jottings from My Sabretasch*, 280–87.
46 Dawes, *Jottings from My Sabretasch*, 289–90.
47 Dodman, "1814 and the Melancholy of War," 31–55.
48 *Journal of a Soldier of the 71st*, 228–32.
49 Lowe, *Humble Address*, 18.
50 Jackson, *Narrative*, 91.
51 Jackson, *Narrative*, 91–92.

CHAPTER 10: SOLDIERS AND SAILORS AT HOME

1 Byron, "Darkness," *Prisoner of Chillon*, 27–31.
 2 Peacock, *Bread or Blood*, 50–51.
 3 Board of Agriculture, *Agricultural State of the Kingdom*; Peacock, *Bread or Blood*, 39–40.
 4 Long to his mother, *Bedford*, Spithead, June 10, 1814, in *LS*, A190.
 5 Costello, *Adventures of a Soldier*, 278–81.
 6 *NC*, 5:231.
 7 Lincoln, "Impact of Warfare," 71–76; Stark, *Female Tars*, 25–35.
 8 Vale, "The Post Office"; Bickham and Abbey, "The Greatest Encouragement."
 9 For descriptions of a ship's return, see Robinson, *Jack Nastyface*, 87–101; Vernon, *Voyages and Travels*, 10–12.
10 Lincoln, "Impact of Warfare," 78; Stark, *Female Tars*, 29–31; Rodger, *Wooden World*, 130–31.
11 *LLA*, 162; Hobson, *Dark Days*, 131.
12 Warner and Lunny, "Marital Violence in a Martial Town," 269–70.
13 Hurl-Eamon, *Marriage*, 150, 211–13.
14 Hay, *Landsman Hay*, 215–19.
15 Hay, *Landsman Hay*, 215–19. Hay eventually became a printer and editor in Paisley, where he died in 1847, age 58. See Taylor, *Sons of the Waves*, 382.
16 Nicol, *Life and Adventures*, 53–55.
17 Nicol, *Life and Adventures*, 183–92.
18 Nicol, *Life and Adventures*, 183–92.
19 Nicol, *Life and Adventures*, 183–92.
20 *NC*, 5:222.
21 Cox, "Records of the Registrar-General," 168–88; Wilcox, "The 'Poor Decayed Seamen'"; Kennerley, "British Seamen's Missions," 4–6.
22 Lin, "Citizenship." Along similar lines, see the earlier description of the Seamen's Family Act of 1795, drawn from Bickham and Abbey, "The Greatest Encouragement."
23 Wilcox, "The 'Poor Decayed Seamen.'"
24 Cookson, "Alexander Tulloch," 60–82; Cormack, "The Life of a Soldier."
25 Cookson, "Early Nineteenth-Century Scottish Military Pensioners"; Wilcox, "The 'Poor Decayed Seamen'"; Bickham and Abbey, "'The Greatest Encouragement.'"
26 *NIT*, 227–30; Taylor, *Sons of the Waves*, 408; Cormack, "The Life of a Soldier," 20.

27 Nagle, *The Nagle Journal*, 245–46.
28 The discussion of prize money is well covered in a footnote by the editor of Jones's recollections, Eamonn O'Keeffe. Jones, "The Old Halberdier," 146–47.
29 Durand, *Life and Adventures*, 80–86; Choate, *At Sea under Impressment*, 159–60; Jackson, *Narrative*, 98.
30 Durand, *Life and Adventures*, 80–86; Choate, *At Sea under Impressment*, 148–60; Wilcox, "The 'Poor Decayed Seamen.'"
31 Taylor, *Sons of the Waves*, 372–75; Cox Jensen, *Ballad-Singer*, 44–45, 169–89.
32 Cormack, "The Life of a Soldier," 26; Hagist, *Noble Volunteers*, 244–50; Jackson, *Narrative*, 98.
33 Cookson, "Alexander Tulloch," 76–82.
34 Harris, *Recollections*, 124–25; Hagist, *Noble Volunteers*, 252.
35 Harris, *Recollections*, 124–25.
36 Butler, *Narrative*, 276–77.
37 Lowe, *Humble Address*, 18–20.
38 Cookson, "Alexander Tulloch," 60–64; Lindert and Williamson, "Revising England's Social Tables," 401; Cormack, "The Life of a Soldier," 27–9; Hagist, *Noble Volunteers*, 252; Cookson, "Early Nineteenth-Century Scottish Military Pensioners," 327–28; Michals, *Lame Captains*, 207–20.
39 Cookson, "Alexander Tulloch," 64.
40 Costello, *Adventures of a Soldier*, 309–18.
41 Butler, *Narrative*, 288.
42 Jackson, *Narrative*, 99–106.
43 Alexander, *Life of Alexander Alexander*, 1:229–30, 244–46.
44 Miller, "Adventures of Serjeant Benjamin Miller," 9.
45 Surtees, *Twenty-Five Years*, 418–19.
46 Quoted in Jackson, *Narrative*, 101–102. The ballad was widely printed in the 1820s, and broadsides of it can be found at the Bodleian's Broadside Ballads Online (ballads.bodleian.ox.ac.uk). See, e.g., Shelfmark 2806 c.16(267).
47 Jackson, *Narrative*, 103.
48 Firth, *Naval Songs and Ballads*, xcvii, 316.

CHAPTER 11: SAILORS ON STRIKE

1 Davis, *Rise of the English Shipping Industry*, 110–44; Solar, "Late Eighteenth-Century Merchant Ships"; Williams, "British Merchant Shipping," 6–8.
2 Hadley, *History of the Town of Kingston-Upon-Hull*, 424, as quoted in Davis, *Rise of the English Shipping Industry*, 116.
3 Nagle, *The Nagle Journal*, 251–52.
4 Bruijn, "Career Patterns," 27–33; Jones, "Community and Organisation," 49–50.
5 Nagle, *The Nagle Journal*, 262–63; Williams, "British Merchant Shipping," 24–25; Taylor, *Sons of the Waves*, 347–48.
6 Davis, *Rise of the English Shipping Industry*, 133; Press, "Wages in the Merchant Navy"; Armstrong, *The Vital Spark*, 25–26. Another explanation for "stickiness" may be that foreign merchants, especially Americans, continued to pay higher wages in peacetime.
7 Starkey, "Quantifying British Seafarers"; Davis, *Rise of the English Shipping Industry*, 166–67.
8 Compare the descriptions of merchant and naval service in Dancy, *Myth of the Press Gang*, 72–77, with Frykman, *Bloody Flag*, 26–30. On impressment as an attack on liberty, see Brunsman, "Men of War."

9 Press, "Wages in the Merchant Navy," 37–52; Palmer and Williams, "British Sailors"; Starkey, "Private Enterprise," 157–59; Blakemore, "Pieces of Eight, Pieces of Eight."

10 Jones, "Community and Organisation," 65; Bamford, *Passages*, 1:195.

11 Davids, "Seamen's Organizations," 166–67.

12 McCord, "The Seamen's Strike of 1815," 127–28.

13 The Petition of the Seamen of North and South Shields and its Vicinity, September 8, 1815, NA, ADM 1/1669.

14 McCord, "Seamen's Strike of 1815," 127–31

15 Seamens Wages, September 7, 1815, NA, ADM 1/1669; McCord, "Seamen's Strike of 1815," 131–34.

16 McCord, "Seamen's Strike of 1815," 130.

17 Caulfield to Croker, September 8, 10, and 16, 1815, NA, ADM 1/1669.

18 McCord, "Seamen's Strike of 1815," 134–36

19 McCord, "Seamen's Strike of 1815," 136–43.

20 *NIT*, 67–68; Hope, *New History of British Shipping*, 263–64.

21 Davids, "Seamen's Organizations," 146–58; Kennerley, "British Seamen's Missions," 4–6.

22 Pfaff and Hechter, *Genesis of Rebellion*, 249–55; Pietsch, "Ships' Boys and Charity," 196–200; Davids, "Seamen's Organizations," 146–62; Kennerley, "British Seamen's Missions," 7–8.

23 Jones, "Community and Organisation," 42–44.

24 Pfaff and Hechter, *Genesis of Rebellion*, 244–47.

25 *Parliamentary Papers* (1825), 4:87, as quoted in Jones, "Community and Organisation," 55.

26 Jones, "Community and Organisation," 37–43; McCord, "Tyneside Discontents and Peterloo," 94–95; Rowe, "A Trade Union," 81–82; Davids, "Seamen's Organizations," 165–66; McCord, "Seamen's Strike of 1815," 127; Taylor, *Sons of the Waves*, 373–75; Fewster, *Keelmen*, xv–xxviii.

27 Jones, "Community and Organisation," 44–56; Rowe, "A Trade Union," 81; Davids, "Seamen's Organizations," 160–62.

28 Frykman, *Bloody Flag*, 9–10.

29 See also Pfaff and Hechter, *Genesis of Rebellion*, 7.

30 McCord, "Tyneside Discontents and Peterloo," 91–111; Fewster, ed., *Keelmen*, Documents 290–330a.

31 Rowe, "A Trade Union," 81–98; Jones, "Community and Organisation," 48–56; Davids, "Seamen's Organizations," 163–69.

32 Jones, "Community and Organisation," 60.

33 "On the Subject of Sailors," *Morning Post*, August 23 and 29, 1815.

34 "On the Situation of Seamen," *Morning Chronicle*, September 7, 1815.

35 "The Indigent Seamen," *Liverpool Mercury etc.*, May 9, 1817.

36 All accounts of the 1818 meeting derive from "Relief of Distressed Seamen," *Morning Chronicle*, January 6, 1818.

37 "Relief of Distressed Seamen," *Morning Chronicle*, January 6, 1818.

38 Kennerley, "Seamen's Missions," 125; Blake, *Religion in the British Navy*, 10–11; Hobson, *Dark Days*, 51; Taylor, *Sons of the Waves*, 375.

39 "Relief of Distressed Seamen," *Morning Chronicle*, January 6, 1818.

40 Kennerley, "Seamen's Missions," 122; Blake, *Religion in the British Navy*, 1–3.

41 Kennerley, "British Seamen's Missions," 79–81; Blake, *Religion in the British Navy*, 17–27.

42 Kennerley, "British Seamen's Missions," 80–81; Kennerley, "Seamen's Missions," 135–37; Blake, *Religion in the British Navy*, 22–23.

43 Blake, *Religion in the British Navy*, 22–33.
44 The quotation is from Taylor, "Manning the Royal Navy," 304. See also Preston, "Constructing Communities," 19; Palmer and Williams, "British Sailors," 110; Morriss, *Cockburn*, 153, 163.
45 Cox, "Records of the Registrar-General"; Burton, "Counting Seafarers."
46 Cannadine, *Victorious Century*, 181–82.

CHAPTER 12: SOLDIERS VERSUS VETERANS

1 *Historical Account of the Luddites*; 52 Geo III, cap. 16.
2 Linch, *Britain and Wellington's Army*, 4–5.
3 Mansfield, "Military Radicals."
4 Thompson, *Making of the English Working Class*, 610.
5 White, *Waterloo to Peterloo*, 144–45, 172.
6 Beckett, *Amateur Military Tradition*, 126–27; Myatt, *British Infantry*, 110. There are two exceptions—works that take the role of the army in suppressing domestic unrest seriously. Hayter, *Army and the Crowd*, provides an excellent survey of an earlier period. Historians of policing have also discussed the role of the army in riot suppression. See especially Palmer, *Police and Protest*. Political scientists interested in civil-military relations have also tracked the domestic use of the military. As an entry point to the literature, see Cohn, "To Execute the Laws of the Union."
7 White, *Waterloo to Peterloo*, 110.
8 Charles M. Clode, *Confidential Memorandum for the Secretary of State for the War Department*, February 2, 1867, NA, WO 33/18; Palmer, *Police and Protest*, 57–65; White, *Waterloo to Peterloo*, 105–9; Peacock, *Bread or Blood*, 118–19.
9 Hay, *Yeomanry Cavalry*, 2–4, 84–85, 245–47; Beckett, *Amateur Military Tradition*, 132–37; Palmer, *Police and Protest*, 189.
10 Peacock, *Bread or Blood*, 87–89; Hobson, *Dark Days*, 28.
11 Surtees, *Twenty-Five Years*, 415.
12 White, *Waterloo to Peterloo*, 111–12; Palmer, *Police and Protest*, 61–62, 159–62, 172, 180–90; Fewster, *Keelmen*, Documents 290, 291, 295, 297, 303; Thompson, *Making of the English Working Class*, 605.
13 Charles M. Clode, *Confidential Memorandum for the Secretary of State for the War Department*, February 2, 1867, NA, WO 33/18.
14 The tactics described here are modified from Hayter, *Army and the Crowd*, 167–86.
15 On soldiers' constabulary duties and uniforms, see Linch and McCormack, "Defining Soldiers," 146–47, and Myerly, *British Military Spectacle*, 120–38.
16 Hobson, *Dark Days*, 28; Palmer, *Police and Protest*, 181–82; Chase, *1820*, 48–49.
17 Hobson, *Dark Days*, 28.
18 Hobson, *Dark Days*, 63.
19 Morris, *The Napoleonic Wars*, 109–16.
20 Peacock, *Bread or Blood*, 78–84, 107–12.
21 Thompson, *Making of the English Working Class*, 603; Uglow, *In These Times*, 609–15; *The Times*, March 13, 1815.
22 Old Bailey Proceedings Online, www.oldbaileyonline.org, version 8.0, July 18, 2019, April 1815, trial of James Ripley, Robert Herbert, Richard Burton, Richard Mathews (t18150405–13).
23 Palmer, *Police and Protest*, 166–75.
24 Palmer, *Police and Protest*, 65.
25 Lincoln, *Trading in War*, 6, 114, 202–5; Chase, *1820*, 26.
26 Emsley, *British Society*, 176–77
27 Peacock, *Bread or Blood*, 50–51, 98, 101. The Luddites also drilled on the fields. See Navickas, "The Search for 'General Ludd,'" 290–91.

28 Smith, *Autobiography*, 325.

29 Thompson, *Making of the English Working Class*, 681.

30 Navickas, *Protest and the Politics of Space*, 58–67.

31 Poole, *Peterloo*, 231–33.

32 White, *Waterloo to Peterloo*, 182; Poole, "The March to Peterloo," 146–47; Thompson, *Making of the English Working Class*, 682.

33 Grenville to Charles Williams-Wynn, October 1, 1819, National Library of Wales, Coedymaen MSS, as quoted in *LLA*, 181.

34 Sloane, *Uncontrollable Women*, 110–11.

35 Poole, "The March to Peterloo," 146–47.

36 Poole, "The March to Peterloo," 109–16; Thompson, *Making of the English Working Class*, 710.

37 Gash, "After Waterloo," 145–57; Poole, "The March to Peterloo," 117–20.

38 Poole, "The March to Peterloo," 109–10.

39 Thompson, *Making of the English Working Class*, 684; Beckett, *Amateur Military Tradition*, 135–37; Bates, "The Bloody Clash."

40 Thompson, *Making of the English Working Class*, 679; Poole, *Peterloo*, 248–50.

41 Jolliffe, *Charge of the 15th Hussars*, 53. Jolliffe was a cornet at the time.

42 Report of Major Dyneley, August 16, 1819, NA, TS 11/1056, as quoted in Poole, *Peterloo*, 326.

43 Shelley, "The Masque of Anarchy," in Shelley, *Poetical Works*, stanza 78.

44 Poole, *Peterloo*, 374; Beckett, *Amateur Military Tradition*, 135–37.

45 Jolliffe, *Charge of the 15th Hussars*, 56–57.

46 Longford, *Wellington*, 61–62; Bates, "The Bloody Clash."

47 Poole, *Peterloo*, 93–126, 209–11.

48 Byng to Sidmouth, December 25, 1816, NA, HO 40/3/1 f. 707, as quoted in Poole, *Peterloo*, 88.

49 Stocqueler, *British Soldier*, 191, as quoted in Poole, *Peterloo*, 373.

50 Brown, *Scum of the Earth*, 186.

51 Defauconpret, *Londres en Mil Huit Cent Vingt*, 132. "Les radicaux courtisent le militaire, parce qu'ils savent qu'ils deviendraient formidables si le soldat se déclarait pour eux."

52 Shelley, "England in 1819," in Shelley, *Poetical Works*, lines 8–9.

53 Colley, *Britons*, 318; Cobbett and Cobbett, *Selections from Cobbett's Political Works*, 5:1–2.

54 White, *Waterloo to Peterloo*, 143; Palmer, *Police and Protest*, 172; Poole, *Peterloo*, 235–36.

55 Wellington, Memorandum to the Earl of Liverpool Respecting the State of the Guards, June 1820, *WSD*, 1:127–29, as quoted in Chase, *1820*, 148–49.

56 Colley, *Gun*, 7–8; Colley, *Britons*, 371.

57 Cobbett and Cobbett, *Selections from Cobbett's Political Works*, 5:17.

58 Shelley, "The Masque of Anarchy," in Shelley, *Poetical Works*, stanzas 15–16, 41.

59 Colley, *Britons*, 5.

60 Chase, *1820*, 126–27, 168–69.

61 Smith, *Autobiography*, 319–28.

62 Smith, *Autobiography*, 319–28.

CHAPTER 13: OFFICERS AT HOME

1 Gronow, *Reminiscences*, 12–14, 120–21.

2 Gronow, *Reminiscences*, 43–45, 49–50, 58–63.

3 Parkinson, *Samuel Walters*, 110–18.

4 Wilson, *Social History*, 175, 205–17.

5 Ross, *Memoirs and Correspondence*, 2:297–309.

6 The naval officers come from Wilson, *Social History*, 216; the army officers were compiled from their entries in the *ODNB*. For peerage creations after Waterloo, see List of Peers Created after the Battle of Waterloo and the Crimean War, 1919, NA, LCO 2/2566. I am grateful to Luke Reynolds for this reference.

7 Board of Governors of the Federal Reserve System, "Distribution of Household Wealth in the U.S. Since 1989," available at federalreserve.gov; Morrow, *British Flag Officers*, 230–40; Muir, *Wellington: Waterloo*, 10, 90; McCahill and Wasson, "The New Peerage," 16.

8 *ODNB*, s.v. "Nelson, Horatio, Viscount Nelson"; Wilson, *Social History*, 208–13; Elson, *Nelson's Yankee Captain*, 336; Milkes, "A Battle's Legacy," 123–24.

9 Croker to his wife, July 12, 1815, in Jennings, *Croker Papers*, 1:57.

10 Miscellaneous Papers: Returns for Medals, 1815, Wellington Papers, University of Southampton Library, WP 1/489; Heuvel, "Admiral Sir John Wentworth," 154.

11 Collingwood to his wife, *Ocean*, May 22, 1806, in Newnham Collingwood, *Correspondence*, 226–28.

12 Miscellaneous Papers, including Claims for Medals, 1816, Wellington Papers, University of Southampton Library, WP 1/511; Wilson, *Social History*, 206–8.

13 There is some disagreement about the number of medals struck. Milkes, "A Battle's Legacy," 139–46, says 36,000; Reynolds, "Who Owned Waterloo?," chap. 3, says 37,000; and Glover, *Waterloo*, 207–8, says 39,000. See also Brown, *Scum of the Earth*, 134.

14 Stirling, *Pages & Portraits*, 2:256–58.

15 Croker to Exmouth, October 23, 1816, in Jennings, *Croker Papers*, 1:84.

16 James, "The Experience of Demobilization," 68–69.

17 Croker to Exmouth, October 23, 1816, in Jennings, *Croker Papers*, 1:84.

18 Costello, *Adventures of a Soldier*, 300–301.

19 Lowe, *Humble Address*, 55.

20 Glover, *Waterloo*, 207–8. See Monroe, "Stolen Valor."

21 Hayter, *The Backbone*, 327.

22 Dillon, *Narrative*, 2:425–27; Brown, *Scum of the Earth*, 113–14; Pocock, *Remember Nelson*, 240–43.

23 Instances where subjects, holding Military Commands, have been empowered by the Crown to confer the Honour of Knighthood, from 1509 to 1640, after 1819, BL, Croker Papers, Add. MSS 52467, ff. 108–112b.

24 Wilson, *Social History*, 208–13.

25 Farington, *Farington Diary*, August 3, 1816, emphasis original.

26 Pocock, *Remember Nelson*, 238.

27 Austen, *Persuasion*, chap. 1.

28 Brighton, *Admiral Sir P.V.B. Broke*, 337–38.

29 Martinovich, *Sea Is My Element*, 231–38.

30 *Fifeshire Journal*, April 6, 1854, as quoted in Fisher, *House of Commons*, https://www.historyofparliamentonline.org/volume/1820–1832/survey/vi-members.

31 Morrow, *British Flag Officers*, 229–36; McCranie, *Admiral Lord Keith*, 176; Pocock, *Remember Nelson*, 239–42; Strachan, *Politics of the British Army*, 25–30; Thorne, *House of Commons*, 1:306–17; Wilson, *Social History*, 156–65; *The History of Parliament*, https://www.historyofparliamentonline.org/.

32 Farington, *Farington Diary*, March 3 and 10, 1816.

33 Dyott, *Dyott's Diary*, 1:314–15, 326–30.

34 Milkes, "A Battle's Legacy," 126–28; Fortescue, *History of the British Army*, 11:38–41; Muir, *Wellington: Waterloo*, 104.

35 Strachan, *Politics of the British Army*, 24–25. See also Sir H. Taylor's description of this practice in a letter to Sir Thomas Byam Martin, Horse Guards, May 18, 1823, in Hamilton, *Byam Martin Papers*, 3:75–76.

36 *Hansard Parliamentary Debates,* 1st Series (1803–20), 36:516–31.

37 Chase, *1820,* 149–50; Strachan, *Politics of the British Army,* 30; Bourne, *Palmerston,* 151–54.

38 Three documents relating to Ens Charles Adam Walsh, NAM, 2001-11-56.

39 Bamford, *Triumphs and Disasters,* 114–21.

40 Services of Officers (Retired) on Full and Half Pay, Returns to the Circular of October 22, 1828, NA, WO 25/749.

41 Hayter, *The Backbone,* 330.

42 Glover, *American Sharpe,* 202–3.

43 Leach, *Rough Sketches,* 406–7.

44 Fortescue, *History of the British Army,* 11:86–91.

45 Farington, *Farington Diary,* October 8, 1815.

46 *NIT,* 58–60.

47 *NIT,* 58–69; Wilson, *Social History,* 13–43.

48 Wilson, *Social History,* 50–52; Cavell, *Midshipmen and Quarterdeck Boys,* 161–72.

49 Durham to Croker, August 15, 1815, in Rubenstein, *Durham Papers,* 468–70; Cavell, *Midshipmen and Quarterdeck Boys,* 166.

50 Wilcox, "Peaceable Times," 475–76; Wilson, *Social History,* 50–51; *NIT,* 70–88.

51 Cavell, *Midshipmen and Quarterdeck Boys,* 159–91; Dillon, *Narrative,* 2:422; Wilson, "Practicing Aggression," 11–46.

52 On the contrast with wartime promotions, see Wilson, "Social Background and Promotion Prospects."

53 Beeler, *Milne Papers,* x–xiv.

54 Poole, "The Letters of Midshipman E.A. Noel," 330.

55 Boteler, *Recollections,* 55–56.

56 Hamilton, "John Wilson Croker."

57 Captain Brown to Byan Martin, *Tartar,* Valparaiso, February 28, 1824, in Hamilton, *Byam Martin Papers,* 3:76–8.

58 Another network was that of evangelical officers. See Blake, *Religion in the British Navy,* 10–11, and Atkins, "Religion, Politics, and Patronage."

59 Morris, *Cockburn,* 154–64, 174–84.

60 *NIT,* 219–28; Wilcox, "Peaceable Times," 478.

61 Bowers, *Naval Adventures,* in King with Hattendorf, *Every Man Will Do His Duty,* 404–5.

62 Prell, *Biography of Captain Daniel Roberts,* 46–60.

63 Hattendorf, "The Brentons of Newport, Rhode Island," 183–90; Brenton, *Memoir of Captain Edward Pelham Brenton,* 32–33; *NIT,* 92; Taylor, *Sons of the Waves,* 360; Hughes, "Luke Brokenshaw," 203–4; Wilcox, "'Peaceable Times,'" 481–83.

64 Noel-Smith and Campbell, *Hornblower's Historical Shipmates,* 81–154.

65 Lovell, *Personal Narrative of Events,* 180.

66 Dillon, *Narrative,* 2:476–77.

CHAPTER 14: COMMERCE AND EMPIRE

1 Till, *Seapower,* 306–59.

2 Waugh, *Smuggling,* 7–27; Daly, "English Smugglers," 45; Hughes, "Luke Brokenshaw," 206.

3 Waugh, *Smuggling,* 7–27; Daly, "Napoleon and the 'City of Smugglers,'" 333–52.

4 Admiralty Board: Special Minutes, 1816–24, NA, ADM 3/262; Daly, "Napoleon and the 'City of Smugglers,'" 333–52; Philp, *Coast Blockade,* 21–50; Waugh, *Smuggling,* 32–33.

5 Admiralty Board to Liverpool, November 3, 1818, BL, Liverpool Papers, Add. MSS 38274, f. 58, as quoted in Morriss, *Cockburn,* 156.

6 Admiralty Board: Special Minutes, 1816–24, NA, ADM 3/262; Symes, "The Coast-guard in Ireland." On the development of signal stations and coastal defense during the wars, see Wilson, "Naval Defence of Ireland."

7 Philp, *Coast Blockade*, 19–41.

8 Symes, "The Coastguard in Ireland," 201–10; Elson, *Nelson's Yankee Captain*, 350–52.

9 *NIT*, 88–90; Philp, *Coast Blockade*, 33–40; Wood, "Portrait of a Trafalgar Midshipman," 118–21.

10 Waugh, *Smuggling*, 32–34.

11 Bowers, *Naval Adventures*, 1:294–96.

12 Admiralty Board: Special Minutes, 1816–24, NA, ADM 3/262. See also *Additional Instructions for an Officer of the Fishery, Under the Acts 48 Geo. III. Cap. 110. and 55 Geo. III. Cap. 94*. Edinburgh: Sir D. Hunter Blair and J. Bruce, 1815.

13 Gambles, "Free Trade and State Formation."

14 Admiralty Board: Special Minutes, 1816–24, NA, ADM 3/262.

15 Till, *Seapower*, 311–12.

16 Grindal, *Opposing the Slavers*, 183–233; Wilson, *Empire of the Deep*, 472–73.

17 Blyth, "Britain," 78–79; Grindal, *Opposing the Slavers*, 183–86.

18 Blyth, "Britain," 80–81; Grindal, *Opposing the Slavers*, 203; *NIT*, 234–38; Wills, *Envoys of Abolition*, 4, 27, 75–78, 84–87.

19 Grindal, *Opposing the Slavers*, 192–211; Blyth, "Britain," 78–80; Wilson, *Empire of the Deep*, 472–73; Wills, *Envoys of Abolition*, 22. See also Royle, "Winning the War and Losing the Peace."

20 Wills, *Envoys of Abolition*, 98–101.

21 Morriss, "Endeavour, Discovery, and Idealism," 242–45.

22 Admiralty Board: Special Minutes, 1816–24, NA, ADM 3/262.

23 Blyth, "Britain," 78. Similarly, see Wills, "At War with the 'Detestable Traffic,'" 124.

24 Cavell, "Abolition"; Taylor, "British West India Interest," 1478–1511; Wills, *Envoys of Abolition*, 91.

25 Ferguson, *Empire*, 139.

26 Blyth, "Britain," 84–85; Wills, "At War with the 'Detestable Traffic,'" 126–32; Wills, *Envoys of Abolition*, 47–49, 169–70; Morriss, "Endeavour, Discovery, and Idealism," 242–45; Ritchie, *The Admiralty Chart*, 121–23; *ODNB*, s.v. "Owen, William Fitzwilliam."

27 Morriss, "Endeavour, Discovery, and Idealism," 236–37; Burrows, *Captain Owen*, 47–49; Platt, *Imperial Twilight*, 161–66.

28 Day, *Admiralty Hydrographic Service*, 22–34.

29 Barrow, *Auto-biographical Memoir*, 333; Lloyd, *Mr. Barrow of the Admiralty*, 129.

30 Bulkeley, "Bellingshausen in Britain"; Davey, "Advancement of Nautical Knowledge."

31 Day, *Admiralty Hydrographic Service*, 42–43.

32 Burrows, *Captain Owen*, 63–64; Day, *Admiralty Hydrographic Service*, 34; Friendly, *Beaufort of the Admiralty*, 262.

33 Rigby, Van Der Merwe, and Williams, *Pacific Exploration*, 224–33.

34 Day, *Admiralty Hydrographic Service*, 27–29.

35 Day, *Admiralty Hydrographic Service*, 33; Webb, "Expansion," appendix 6. On surveys of home waters, see Walker and Webb, "The Making of Mr George Thomas RN."

36 Lloyd, *Mr. Barrow of the Admiralty*, 112.

37 Burrows, *Captain Owen*, 48–49.

38 Day, *Admiralty Hydrographic Service*, 29–30; Webb, "Expansion," 90–93, appendix 8; Lloyd, *Mr. Barrow of the Admiralty*, 121.

39 Friendly, *Beaufort of the Admiralty*, 218–64.

40 Cannon, *Queen's Regiment of Light Dragoons*, 86–116; Cannon, *Shropshire Regiment of Foot*, 22–25.

41 Ferrar, *Diary of Colour-Sergeant George Calladine*, 74–75.

42 Buckley, *British Army in the West Indies*, 325–52; Burroughs, "An Unreformed Army?" 172–74.

43 Liddell Hart, *Letters of Private Wheeler*, 201–23.

44 Campbell, "St Ann's Fort and the Garrison," 3–16; Buckley, *British Army in the West Indies*, 298–99; Smith, *Autobiography*, 343–46.

45 Colonel Edward Codd to James Leith, April 25, 1816, CO 28/85; Heuman, "The British West Indies," 472–77; Elkins, *Legacy of Violence*, 51–52.

CHAPTER 15: VETERANS ABROAD

1 Glover, *A Very Slippery Fellow*, 180–86; Richmond, *Statesmen and Sea Power*, 259.

2 *Hansard Parliamentary Debates*, 1st Series (1803–20), 40:1377–1416.

3 Brown, *Adventuring through Spanish Colonies*, 13–15; Harley, *The Veteran*, 244–46.

4 Glover, *A Very Slippery Fellow*, 166–74.

5 Glover, *A Very Slippery Fellow*, 180–86.

6 Harley, *The Veteran*, 244–80.

7 Harley, *The Veteran*, 234–35.

8 Farington, *Farington Diary*, 35–36.

9 Alexander, *Life of Alexander Alexander*, 1:249–307.

10 Bowers, *Naval Adventures*, 2:1, 139–41.

11 Costello, *Adventures of a Soldier*, 320–21.

12 Brown, *Adventuring through Spanish Colonies*, 1–21; Gregory, *Brute New World*, 1; Blaufarb, "Arms for Revolutions," 100–13.

13 Blaufarb, "The Western Question," 754; Harley, *The Veteran*, 237–38; Hughes, *Conquer or Die!*, 26–27, 74–76.

14 Hughes, *Conquer or Die!*, 81.

15 *ODNB*, s.v. "Cochrane, Thomas, tenth earl of Dundonald"; Vale, "Lord Cochrane in Chile," 60–61.

16 William Bowles to Thomas Hardy, December 25, 1819, in Graham and Humphreys, *Navy and South America*, 286–87.

17 Cubitt, *Lord Cochrane and the Chilean Navy*, 328.

18 Bowles to Croker, October 31, 1818, in Graham and Humphreys, *Navy and South America*, 250; Vale, "Lord Cochrane in Chile," 61–67.

19 Vale, *Independence or Death!*, 18–22.

20 Vale, *Independence or Death!*, 65–96.

21 Vale, *Independence or Death!*, 24–44, 101, 171.

22 Graham and Humphreys, *Navy and South America*, ix.

23 Searle to Hardy, June 3, 1820, in Graham and Humphreys, *Navy and South America*, 306.

24 Bowles to Croker, December 21, 1818, in Graham and Humphreys, *Navy and South America*, 259.

25 Bowles to Croker, March 15, 1819, in Graham and Humphreys, *Navy and South America*, 263–64.

26 Frederick Hickey to Bowles, May 24, 1819, in Graham and Humphreys, *Navy and South America*, 268–71.

27 Bowers, *Naval Adventures*, 2:32–34.

28 Vale, *Independence or Death!*, 3, 36, 64, 134, 150–51.

29 Vale, *Independence or Death!*, 100–9; Gregory, *Brute New World*, 175–81; Brown, *Adventuring through Spanish Colonies*, 42.

30 Brown, *Adventuring through Spanish Colonies*, 42; Vale, *Independence or Death!*, 170–78.
31 Vale, *Independence or Death!*, 121.
32 Glover, *A Very Slippery Fellow*, 179–80.
33 Harley, *The Veteran*, 240.
34 Alexander, *Life of Alexander Alexander*, 1:287–89.
35 Smith, "Forgotten Settlers," 14–55.
36 Smith, "Forgotten Settlers," 4–9, 111–24.
37 Wright, "Military Settlers," 158–61.
38 Wright, "Military Settlers," 162–72.
39 Wright, *Wellington's Men in Australia*, 46, 117–19, 153–74.
40 Wright, *Wellington's Men in Australia*, 38–39, 61, 93.
41 Wright, *Wellington's Men in Australia*, 18–29, 122–28.
42 Buckley, *Slaves in Red Coats*, 134–39.
43 Wright, *Wellington's Men in Australia*, 14.
44 Wright, *Wellington's Men in Australia*, 55–57.
45 Wright, *Wellington's Men in Australia*, 55.

CONCLUSION

1 Lieven, *Russia against Napoleon*, 521; *BAN*, 456–57.
2 Greig, *Dead Men Telling Tales*.
3 Alexander, *Life of Alexander Alexander*, 2:310–27.

Bibliography

ARCHIVAL SOURCES

The British Library

Martin Papers. Add MS 41346–41475.
Croker Papers (Second Series). Add MS 52465–52472.

Cambridge University Library

Sir Graham Moore: Diaries. GB 12 MS.Add.9303.

London Metropolitan Archives

Records of Lloyd's of London, Marine Insurers. CLC/B/148.

The National Archives, Kew

Admiralty: Correspondence and Papers. ADM 1.
Admiralty: Minutes. ADM 3.
Admiralty: Miscellanea. ADM 7.
Admiralty: List Books. ADM 8.
Colonial Office and Predecessors: Correspondence, Original: Secretary of State. CO 28.
Home Office: Private and Secret Entry Books. HO 79.
Lord Chancellor's Office: House of Lords. LCO 2.
Navy Board: Records. ADM 106.
Office of the Commander-in-Chief and Treasury: Commissariat Department, Ireland: Records. WO 63.
Office of the Commander-in-Chief and War Office: Adjutant General's Office: Disposition and Movement of Regiment, Returns and Papers (Regimental Records). WO 379.
Secretary-at-War: Office of Army Accounts: In-letters relating to Accounts ('A' Papers).WO 41.
Sir James Carmichael Smyth: Papers. PRO 30/35.

Sir Galbraith Lowry Cole: Papers. PRO 30/43.
War Office and predecessors: In-letters and Miscellaneous Papers. WO 1.
War Office and predecessors: Secretary-at-War, Out-letters. WO 4.
War Office and predecessors: Secretary-at-War, Secretary of State for War, and
      Related Bodies, Registers. WO 25.
War Office: Reports, Memoranda and Papers (O and A Series). WO 33.

National Army Museum, Chelsea

A collection of manuscript letters written by Lt William Cowper Coles to his family,
      1816–17. 1968-07-419.
Manuscript Diaries of Lt James Penman Gairdner, 95th Regiment, 1812–16.
      1969-02-5.
Manuscript: Extracts from a Record of Captain H. Hollinsworth's War and Subse-
      quent Services. 1974-08-81.
Papers of Deputy Assistant Commissary General Thomas Marsden, 1811–17.
      1977-01-36.
Collection of Papers of Col Sir Thomas Downman, Royal Artillery, his ancestors and
      sons, 1759–1870. 1980-05-52.
Military Papers of the Phipps Family and others, 1808–1915. 1981-08-7.
Three documents relating to Ens Charles Adam Walsh, 3rd Bn 3rd (The East Kent)
      Regiment of Foot (The Buffs), 1810–18. 2001-11-56.
Bound photocopy of the typescript diary of Captain Foster Fyans. 2007-02-69.

National Maritime Museum, Greenwich

Pellew Papers. PEL.
Markham Family Papers. MRK.

University of Southampton Library

Wellington Papers. MS 61.
Palmerston Papers. MS 62.

PRINTED PRIMARY SOURCES

Alexander, Alexander. *Life of Alexander Alexander: Written by Himself.* Edited by John
      Howell. 2 vols. Edinburgh: William Blackwood, 1830.
Austen, Jane. *Persuasion.* London, 1818.
Bamford, Andrew. *Triumphs and Disasters: Eyewitness Accounts from the Netherlands
      Campaign, 1813–1814.* Barnsley: Frontline Books, 2016.
Bamford, Samuel. *Passages in the Life of a Radical, and Early Days.* London: T. F.
      Unwin, 1905.
Barrow, John. *An Auto-biographical Memoir of Sir John Barrow, Bart., Late of the Admi-
      ralty.* London: John Murray, 1847.
Beeler, John, ed. *The Milne Papers: The Papers of Admiral of the Fleet Sir Alexander
      Milne, Bt., K.C.B. (1806–1896).* Aldershot: Navy Records Society, 2004.
Bell, Henry G. *Narrative of the Late Military and Political Operations in the Birmese
      Empire.* Edinburgh: Constable, 1827.
Bickley, Francis, ed. *Report on the Manuscripts of Earl Bathurst, Preserved at Cirencester
      Park.* London: H. M. Stationery Office, 1923.

Board of Agriculture. *The Agricultural State of the Kingdom, in February, March and April 1816*. London: Charles Clement, 1816.

Boswell, James. *Dr. Johnson's Table Talk*. London: C. Dilly, 1798.

Boswell, James. *The Life of Samuel Johnson, LL.D.* New ed. Edited by John Wilson Croker. Boston: Carter, Hendee, 1832.

Boteler, John Harvey. *Recollections of My Sea Life from 1808 to 1830*. Edited by David Bonner-Smith. London: Navy Records Society, 1942.

Bourne, Kenneth, ed. *The Letters of the Third Viscount Palmerston to Laurence and Elizabeth Sullivan, 1804–1863*. London: Royal Historical Society, 1979.

Bowers, William. *Naval Adventures during Thirty-Five Years' Service*. 2 vols. London: Richard Bentley, 1833.

Brenton, Jahleel. *Memoir of Captain Edward Pelham Brenton, R.N., C.B.* London: J. Nisbet, 1842.

Brighton, J. G., ed. *Admiral Sir P.V.B. Broke, Bart., K.C.B., &c.: A Memoir*. London: Sampson Low, Son, and Marston, 1846.

Bromley, J. S., ed. *The Manning of the Royal Navy: Selected Public Pamphlets, 1693–1873*. London: Navy Records Society, 1974.

Buckley, Roger Norman, ed., *The Napoleonic War Journal of Captain Thomas Henry Browne, 1807–1816*. London: Bodley Head for the Army Records Society, 1987.

Butler, Robert. *Narrative of the Life and Travels of Serjeant B——, Written by Himself*. Edinburgh: David Brown, 1823.

Byron, George Gordon. *The Prisoner of Chillon, and Other Poems*. London: John Murray, 1816.

Cholmondeley, R. H., ed. *The Heber Letters, 1783–1832*. London: Batchworth Press, 1950.

Cobbett, John M., and James P. Cobbett, eds. *Selections from Cobbett's Political Works*. 6 vols. London: Anne Cobbett, 1835.

Cobbett, William. *History of the Regency and Reign of King George the Fourth*. London: William Cobbett, 1830.

Coleridge, Samuel Taylor. *Fears in Solitude*. London: J. Johnson, 1798.

Cooper, John Spencer. *Rough Notes of Seven Campaigns in Portugal, Spain, France, and America, during the years 1809-10-11-12-13-14-15*. 2nd ed. Carlisle: Coward, 1914.

Costello, Edward. *Adventures of a Soldier; Or, Memoirs of Edward Costello, K.S.F.* London: Henry Colburn, 1841.

Crimmin, P. K., ed. "The Supply of Timber for the Royal Navy, c. 1803–c. 1830." In *The Naval Miscellany, Volume VII*, edited by Susan Rose. London: Navy Records Society, 2008.

Croker, John Wilson. *The Croker Papers: The Correspondence and Diaries of the Late Right Honourable John Wilson Croker*. Edited by Louis J. Jennings. 2 vols. New York: Charles Scribner's Sons, 1884.

Dawes, William ("A Chelsea Pensioner"). *Jottings from My Sabretasch*. London: Richard Bentley, 1847.

Defauconpret, Auguste-Jean-Baptiste. *Londres en Mil Huit Cent Vingt*. Paris: Gide, 1821.

Defauconpret, Auguste-Jean-Baptiste. *Quinze Jours à Londres, à la Fin de 1815*. Paris: A. Eymery, 1816.

Department of Defense. "2021 TAP Curriculum: Managing Your Transition." February 1, 2021.

Dillon, William Henry. *A Narrative of My Professional Adventures (1790–1839)*. Edited by Michael Lewis. 2 vols. London: Navy Records Society, 1953–56.

Durand, James R. *The Life and Adventures of James R. Durand*. Sandwich, Mass.: Chapman Billies, 1995.

Dyott, William. *Dyott's Diary, 1781–1845: A Selection from the Journal of William Dyott, Sometime General in the British Army and Aide-de-Camp to His Majesty King George III*. Edited by Reginald W. Jeffery. 2 vols. London: Archibald Constable, 1907.

Farington, Joseph. *The Farington Diary*. Edited by James Grieg. 8 vols. New York: George H. Doran, 1922–28.

Ferrar, M. L., ed., *The Diary of Colour-Sergeant George Calladine, 19th Foot, 1793–1837*. London: E. Fisher, 1922.

Fewster, Joseph M., ed. *The Keelmen of Newcastle upon Tyne, 1638–1852*. Woodbridge, Suffolk: Boydell Press, 2021.

Firth, C. H., ed. *Naval Songs and Ballads*. London: Navy Records Society, 1908.

Franklin, Benjamin. *The Papers of Benjamin Franklin*. Edited by Leonard W. Labaree et al. New Haven: American Philosophical Society and Yale University, 1954–2021.

George IV, *The Letters of King George IV, 1812–1830*. Edited by Arthur Aspinall. 3 vols. Cambridge: Cambridge University Press, 1938.

Glover, Gareth. *The American Sharpe: The Adventures of an American Officer of the 95th Rifles in the Peninsular and Waterloo Campaigns*. Barnsley: Frontline Books, 2016.

Graham, Gerald S. and R. A. Humphreys, eds. *The Navy and South America, 1807–1823: Correspondence of the Commanders-in-Chief on the South American Station*. London: Navy Records Society, 1962.

Gronow, Rees Howell. *The Reminiscences and Recollections of Captain Gronow, Being Anecdotes of the Camp Court, Clubs, & Society, 1810–1860*. Abridged and with an introduction by John Raymond. London: Bodley Head, 1864.

Hadley, George. *A New and Complete History of the Town and County of the Town of Kingston-upon-Hull*. Kingston-upon-Hull: T. Briggs, 1788.

Hamilton, Richard Vesey, ed., *Letters and Papers of Admiral of the Fleet Sir Thomas Byam Martin [Byam Martin Papers]*. 3 vols. London: Navy Records Society, 1898–1902.

Hansard Parliamentary Debates, 1st Series. London: Hansard, 1803–20.

Hansard Parliamentary Debates, 2nd Series. London: Hansard, 1820–30.

Hansard Parliamentary Debates, 3rd Series. London: Hansard, 1830–91.

Harley, John. *The Veteran or 40 Years' Service in the British Army: The Scurrilous Recollections of Paymaster John Harley 47th Foot—1798–1838*. Warwick: Helion, 2018.

Harris, Benjamin. *Recollections of Rifleman Harris as Told to Henry Curling*. Edited by Christopher Hibbert. Hamden: Archon Books, 1970.

Hay, Robert. *Landsman Hay: The Memoirs of Robert Hay*. Edited by Vincent McInerney. Barnsley: Seaforth, 2010.

Hayter, Althea, ed. *The Backbone: Diaries of a Military Family in the Napoleonic Wars*. Edinburgh: Pentland Press, 1993.

An Historical Account of the Luddites of 1811, 1812, and 1813. Huddersfield: J. Cowgill, 1862.

Hobhouse, John Cam. *Recollections of a Long Life*. Edited by Lady Dorchester. 6 vols. New York: Charles Scribner's Sons, 1909–11.

Howell, T. B., ed. *A Complete Collection of State Trials and Proceedings for High Treason and other Crimes and Misdemeanors*. 34 vols. London: Longman, Hurst, 1816–28.

Hutchinson, William T. et al., eds. *The Papers of James Madison.* 1st ser. Vols. 11–17. Charlottesville: University Press of Virginia, 1977–91.

Jackson, Andrew. *Correspondence of Andrew Jackson.* Edited by John Spencer Bassett. 7 vols. Washington, D.C.: Carnegie Institute of Washington, 1926–35.

Jackson, Thomas. *Narrative of the Eventful Life of Thomas Jackson: Militiaman and Cold-stream Sergeant, 1803–15.* Solihull: Helion, 2018.

James, W. M. *The Naval History of Great Britain during the French Revolutionary and Napoleonic Wars.* 6 vols. Mechanicsburg, Penn.: Stackpole, 2002.

Jolliffe, William. *The Charge of the 15th Hussars at Peterloo.* 1845. Reprinted in F. A. Bruton, ed., *Three Accounts of Peterloo.* Manchester: Manchester University Press, 1921.

Jones, John. "The Old Halberdier: From the Pyrenees to Plattsburgh with a Welsh-man of the 39th." Edited by Eamonn O'Keeffe. *Journal of the Society for Army Historical Research* 95, nos. 381–83 (Spring, Summer, Autumn 2017): 17–34, 141–60, 207–26.

Journal of a Soldier of the 71st, or Glasgow Regiment, Highland Light Infantry, from 1806 to 1815. 2nd ed. Edinburgh: Balfour and Clarke, 1819.

Kant, Immanuel. *To Perpetual Peace: A Philosophical Sketch.* Translated and edited by Ted Humphrey. London: Hackett, 2003.

King, Dean, with John B. Hattendorf, eds., *Every Man Will Do His Duty: An Anthology of Firsthand Accounts from the Age of Nelson, 1793–1815.* New York: Henry Holt, 1997.

Lavery, Brian, ed. *Shipboard Life and Organisation, 1731–1815.* Aldershot: Navy Records Society, 1998.

Leach, J. *Rough Sketches of the Life of an Old Soldier.* London: Longman, Rees, 1831.

Leech, Samuel. *Thirty Years from Home, or a Voice from the Main Deck.* 15th ed. Boston: J.M. Whittemore, 1847.

Liddell Hart, B. H., ed. *The Letters of Private Wheeler, 1809–1829.* London: Michael Joseph, 1951.

Lovell, William Stanhope. *Personal Narrative of Events, from 1799 to 1815, with Anec-dotes.* London: William Allen, 1879.

Lowe, John. *The Humble Address of John Lowe.* Arranged and edited by the Rev. F. Newnham. London: Sarah Davis, 1827.

MacDougall, Philip, ed. *Chatham Dockyard, 1815–1865: The Industrial Transformation.* Farnham, Surrey: Navy Records Society, 2009.

Mackenzie, Eneas. *Historical Account of Newcastle-upon-Tyne Including the Borough of Gateshead.* Newcastle-upon-Tyne: Mackenzie and Dent, 1827.

Madison, James, and Gaillard Hunt. *The Writings of James Madison: Comprising His Public Papers and His Private Correspondence.* 9 vols. New York: G. P. Putnam's Sons, 1900–10.

Mill, James. *The History of British India.* 3 vols. London: Baldwin, Craddock, and Joy, 1817.

Miller, Benjamin. "The Adventures of Serjeant Benjamin Miller during his Service in the 4th Battalion, Royal Artillery, from 1796 to 1815." *Journal of the Society of Army Historical Research* 7, no. 1 (January 1928): 9–51.

Morris, Thomas. *The Napoleonic Wars.* Edited by John Selby. London: Longman, 1967.

Nagle, Jacob. *The Nagle Journal: A Diary of the Life of Jacob Nagle, Sailor, from the Year 1775 to 1841.* Edited by John C. Dann. New York: Weidenfeld and Nicolson, 1988.

Newnham Collingwood, G. L., ed., *A Selection from the Public and Private Correspondence of Vice-Admiral Lord Collingwood, Interspersed with Memoirs of His Life.* 4th ed. London: James Ridgway, 1829.

Nicol, John. *Life and Adventures, 1776–1801.* Edited by Tim Flannery. Melbourne: Text Publishing, 1997.

Paine, Thomas. *The Rights of Man: Part the Second, Combining Principle and Practice.* London: J. S. Jordan, 1792.

Paley, William. *The Principles of Moral and Political Philosophy.* London: R. Faulder, 1785.

The Parliamentary Register, or, History of the Proceedings and Debates of the House of Commons [and of the House of Lords] Containing an Account of the Interesting Speeches and Motions ... During the 6th Session of the 17th Parliament of Great Britain. London: J. Debrett, 1796.

Penrose, John. *Lives of Vice-Admiral Sir Charles Vinicombe Penrose and Captain James Trevenen.* London: John Murray, 1850.

Phipps, Edmund, ed. *Memoirs of the Political and Literary Life of Robert Plumer Ward, Esq.* 2 vols. London: John Murray, 1850.

Poole, Eric, ed. "The Letters of Midshipman E.A. Noel, 1818–1822." In *The Naval Miscellany, Volume V,* edited by N. A. M. Rodger. London: Navy Records Society, 1984.

Robinson, William. *Jack Nastyface: Memoirs of a Seaman.* Annapolis, Md.: Naval Institute Press, 1973.

Ross, John. *Memoirs and Correspondence of Admiral Lord de Saumarez.* 2 vols. London: Richard Bentley, 1838.

Rubenstein, Hilary L., ed. *The Durham Papers: Selections from the Papers of Admiral Sir Philip Charles Henderson Calderwood Durham G.C.B. (1763–1845).* London: Navy Records Society, 2019.

Saxo. *A Hasty Sketch of the Origin, Nature, and Progress of the British Constitution.* York: Thomas Wilson and Sons, 1817.

Shelley, Percy Bysshe. *The Poetical Works of Percy Bysshe Shelley.* Edited by Mary Shelley. London: Edward Moxon, 1839.

Shipp, John. *Memoirs of the Extraordinary Military Career of John Shipp, Late a Lieut. in His Majesty's 87th Regiment.* Edited by H. Manners. London: T. Fisher Unwin, 1890.

Smith, Adam. *An Inquiry into the Nature and Causes of the Wealth of Nations.* New ed. 2 vols. Hartford: Oliver D. Cooke, 1804.

Smith, Harry. *The Autobiography of Lieutenant-General Sir Harry Smith, Baronet of Aliwal on the Sutlej.* London: John Murray, 1903.

Stirling, A. M. W. *Pages & Portraits from the Past: Being the Private Papers of Sir William Hotham, G.C.B., Admiral of the Red.* 2 vols. London: Herbert Jenkins, 1919.

Stocqueler, J. H. *The British Soldier: An Anecdotal History of the British Army from Its Earliest Formation to the Present Time.* London: W. S. Orr and Co., 1859.

Surtees, William. *Twenty-Five Years in the Rifle Brigade.* Edinburgh: William Blackwood, 1833.

Tracy, Nicholas, ed. *The Naval Chronicle: The Contemporary Record of the Royal Navy at War.* 5 vols. London: Chatham, 1999.

Vernon, Francis Venables. *Voyages and Travels of a Sea Officer.* London: Printed for the author, 1792.

Watt, Helen, with Anne Hawkins, eds. *Letters of Seamen in the Wars with France, 1793–1815.* Woodbridge: Boydell Press, 2016.

Webster, C. K., ed. *Britain and the Independence of Latin America, 1812–1830: Select Documents from the Foreign Office.* 2 vols. New York: Octagon Books, 1970.

Webster, C. K., ed. *British Diplomacy, 1813–1815: Select Documents Dealing with the Reconstruction of Europe.* London: G. Bell and Sons, 1921.

Wellington, Duke of. *The Dispatches of Field Marshal the Duke of Wellington: During his Various Campaigns in India, Denmark, Portugal, Spain, the Low Countries, and France, from 1799 to 1812.*13 vols. Compiled by John Gurwood. London: John Murray, 1837–44.

Wellington, Second Duke of, ed. *Supplementary Despatches and Memoranda of Field Marshal Arthur, Duke of Wellington.* 15 vols. London: John Murray, 1858–72.

Wetherell, John. *The Adventures of John Wetherell.* Edited by C. S. Forester. London: Michael Joseph, 1954.

SECONDARY SOURCES

Armstrong, Benjamin. *Small Boats and Daring Men: Maritime Raiding, Irregular Warfare, and the Early American Navy.* Norman: University of Oklahoma Press, 2019.

Armstrong, John. *The Vital Spark: The British Coastal Trade, 1700–1930.* St. John's, Newfoundland: International Maritime Economic History Association, 2009.

Arthur, Brian. *How Britain Won the War of 1812: The Royal Navy's Blockades of the United States, 1812–1815.* Woodbridge: Boydell Press, 2011.

Atkins, Gareth. "Religion, Politics, and Patronage in the Late Hanoverian Navy, c. 1780–c. 1820." *Historical Research* 88, no. 240 (2015): 272–90.

Bamford, Andrew. *Sickness, Suffering, and the Sword: The British Regiment on Campaign, 1808–1815.* Norman: University of Oklahoma Press, 2013.

Banerjee, Tarasankar. "The Marathas and the Pindars: A Study in Their Relationship." *Quarterly Review of Historical Studies* 11 (1972): 71–82.

Bartlett, C. J. "Britain and the European Balance, 1815–48." In *Europe's Balance of Power, 1815–1848,* edited by Alan Sked. New York: Barnes and Noble, 1979.

Bartlett, C. J. *Great Britain and Sea Power, 1815–1853.* Oxford: Oxford University Press, 1964.

Barua, Pradeep. "Military Developments in India, 1750–1850." *Journal of Military History* 58 (October 1994): 599–616.

Bates, Stephen. "The Bloody Clash That Changed Britain." *The Guardian,* January 4, 2018.

Bayly, C. A. *Imperial Meridian: The British Empire and the World, 1780–1830.* London and New York: Longman, 1989.

Beckett, Ian F. W. *The Amateur Military Tradition, 1558–1945.* Manchester: Manchester University Press, 1991.

Bell, Herbert C.F. *Lord Palmerston.* 2 vols. Hamden: Archon Books, 1966.

Bew, John. *Castlereagh: A Life.* Oxford: Oxford University Press, 2012.

Bickham, Troy. *The Weight of Vengeance: The United States, the British Empire, and the War of 1812.* Oxford: Oxford University Press, 2012.

Bickham, Troy, and Ian Abbey. "'The Greatest Encouragement to Seamen': Pay, Families, and the State in Britain during the French Wars, 1793–1815." *Journal of Social History* 56, no. 1 (2022): 1–31.

Black, Jeremy. *The British Seaborne Empire.* New Haven and London: Yale University Press, 2004.

Black, Jeremy, and Philip Woodfine, eds. *The British Navy and the Use of Naval Power in the Eighteenth Century.* Leicester: Leicester University Press, 1988.

Blake, Richard. *Religion in the British Navy, 1815–1879: Piety and Professionalism.* Woodbridge: Boydell Press, 2014.

Blakemore, Richard. "Pieces of Eight, Pieces of Eight: Seamen's Earnings and the Venture Economy of Early Modern Seafaring." *Economic History Review* 70, no. 4 (November 2017): 1153–84.

Blaufarb, Rafe. "Arms for Revolutions: Military Demobilization after the Napoleonic Wars and Latin American Independence." In *War, Demobilization and Memory*, edited by Alan Forrest, Karen Hagemann, and Michael Rowe, 100–16. Basingstoke: Palgrave Macmillan, 2016.

Blaufarb, Rafe. "The Western Question: The Geopolitics of Latin American Independence." *American Historical Review* 112, no. 3 (June 2007): 742–63.

Blyth, Robert J. "Britain, the Royal Navy and the Suppression of Slave Trades in the Nineteenth Century." In *Representing Slavery: Art, Artefacts and Archives in the Collections of the National Maritime Museum*, edited by Douglas Hamilton and Robert J. Blyth, 76–91. Aldershot: Lund Humphreys, 2007.

Bourne, Kenneth. *Britain and the Balance of Power in North America, 1815–1908*. Berkeley and Los Angeles: University of California Press, 1967.

Bourne, Kenneth. *Palmerston: The Early Years, 1784–1841*. New York: Macmillan, 1982.

Brewer, John. *The Sinews of Power: War, Money and the English State, 1688–1783*. Cambridge, Mass.: Harvard University Press, 1988.

Briggs, Asa. *The Age of Improvement, 1783–1867*. London: Longman, 2000.

Brown, Anthony. "The Fall of Mrauk U, An Episode in the First Anglo-Burmese War, 1825." *Journal for the Society for Army Historical Research* 97 (2019): 319–37.

Brown, Colin. *The Scum of the Earth: What Happened to the Real British Heroes of Waterloo?* Stroud: Spellmount, 2015.

Brown, D. K. *Before the Ironclad: Development of Ship Design, Propulsion and Armament in the Royal Navy, 1815–60*. Annapolis, Md.: Naval Institute Press, 1990.

Brown, Matthew. *Adventuring through Spanish Colonies: Simón Bolívar, Foreign Mercenaries and the Birth of New Nations*. Liverpool: Liverpool University Press, 2006.

Bruijn, Jaap. "Career Patterns." In *"Those Emblems of Hell"? European Sailors and the Maritime Labour Market, 1570–1870*, edited by Paul van Royen, Jaap Bruijn, and Jan Lucassen, 25–34. St. John's, Newfoundland: International Maritime Economic History Association, 1997.

Brunsman, Denver. "Men of War: British Sailors and the Impressment Paradox." *Journal of Early Modern History* 14 (2010): 9–44.

Buckley, Roger Norman. *The British Army in the West Indies: Society and the Military in the Revolutionary Age*. Gainesville: University Press of Florida, 1998.

Buckley, Roger Norman. *Slaves in Red Coats: The British West India Regiments, 1795–1815*. New Haven and London: Yale University Press, 1979.

Bulkeley, Rip. "Bellingshausen in Britain: Supplying the Russian Antarctic Expedition, 1819." *Mariner's Mirror* 107, no. 1 (2021): 40–53.

Burroughs, Peter. "Crime and Punishment in the British Army, 1815–1870." *English Historical Review* 100, no. 396 (July 1985): 545–71.

Burroughs, Peter. "An Unreformed Army? 1815–1868." In *The Oxford History of the British Army*, edited by David Chandler, 161–86. Oxford: Oxford University Press, 1994.

Burrows, E. H. *Captain Owen of the African Survey*. Rotterdam: A. A. Balkema, 1979.

Burton, V. C. "Counting Seafarers: The Published Records of the Registry of Merchant Seamen, 1849–1913." *Mariner's Mirror* 71, no. 3 (1985): 305–20.

Cain, P. J., and A. G. Hopkins. *British Imperialism, 1688–2015*. 3rd ed. London: Routledge, 2016.

Campbell, Kurt M., and Rush Doshi, "How America Can Shore Up Asian Order: A Strategy for Restoring Balance and Legitimacy." *Foreign Affairs,* January 12, 2021.

Campbell, P. F. "St Ann's Fort and the Garrison." *Journal of the Barbados Museum and Historical Society* 35, no. 1 (March 1975): 3–16.

Cannadine, David. *Victorious Century: The United Kingdom, 1800–1906.* New York: Viking, 2017.

Cannon, Richard. *Historical Record of the Eleventh, or the North Devon Regiment of Foot.* London: Parker, Furnivall & Parker, 1845.

Cannon, Richard. *Historical Record of the Fifteenth, or King's Regiment of Light Dragoons, Hussars.* London: Parker, 1841.

Cannon, Richard. *Historical Record of the Fifty-Third, or the Shropshire Regiment of Foot.* London: Parker, Furnivall & Parker, 1849.

Cannon, Richard. *Historical Record of the Fourteenth, or the King's, Regiment of Light Dragoons.* London: Parker, Furnivall & Parker, 1847.

Cannon, Richard. *Historical Record of the Ninth, or the Queen's Royal Regiment of Light Dragoons; Lancers.* London: Parker, 1841.

Cannon, Richard. *Historical Record of the Seventh, or the Queen's Own Regiment of Hussars.* London: Parker, 1842.

Cannon, Richard. *Historical Record of the Seventy-Third Regiment.* London: Parker, Furnivall & Parker, 1851.

Cannon, Richard. *Historical Record of the Sixteenth, or the Queen's Regiment of Light Dragoons, Lancers.* London: Parker, 1842.

Cannon, Richard. *Historical Record of the Third, or the King's Own Regiment of Light Dragoons.* London: Parker, Furnivall & Parker, 1847.

Cannon, Richard. *Historical Record of the Thirteenth Regiment of Light Dragoons.* London: Parker, 1842.

Caputo, Sara. "Towards a Transnational History of the Eighteenth-Century British Navy," *Annales historiques de la Révolution française* 397, no. 3 (2019): 13–32.

Carter, Thomas, ed. *Historical Record of the Twenty-Sixth, or Cameronian Regiment.* London: W. O. Mitchell, 1867.

Cavell, S. A. "Abolition, the West India Colonies and the Troubling Case of Vice-Admiral Sir Alexander Cochrane, 1807–1823." *Mariner's Mirror* 107, no. 1 (2021): 23–39.

Cavell, S. A. *Midshipmen and Quarterdeck Boys in the British Navy, 1771–1831.* Woodbridge: Boydell Press, 2012.

Chandler, David, ed. *The Oxford History of the British Army.* Oxford: Oxford University Press, 1994.

Chase, Malcolm. *1820: Disorder and Stability in the United Kingdom.* Manchester: Manchester University Press, 2013.

Choate, Jean. *At Sea under Impressment: Accounts of Involuntary Service aboard Navy and Pirate Vessels, 1700–1820.* Jefferson, N.C.: McFarland, 2010.

Clausewitz, Carl von. *On War.* Edited and translated by Michael Howard and Peter Paret. Princeton, N.J.: Princeton University Press, 1976.

Clement, Mark. "A Cross-Cultural Encounter in Pre-Colonial Burma: Henry Gouger's Narrative of Commerce and Captivity, 1822–26." *Journal of Burma Studies* 17, no. 2 (2013): 335–71.

Clowes, William Laird. *The Royal Navy: A History from the Earliest Times to the Present.* 7 vols. London: Marston, Low, 1897–1903.

Cohn, Lindsay P. "To Execute the Laws of the Union: Domestic Use of Federal Military Force in the United States." In *Military Operation and Engagement in the*

Domestic Jurisdiction: Comparative Call-Out Laws, edited by Pauline Collins and Rosalie Arcala-Hall, 57–90. Leiden: Brill Nijhoff, 2022.

Colley, Linda. *Britons: Forging the Nation, 1707–1837*. 2nd ed. New Haven and London: Yale University Press, 2005.

Colley, Linda. *The Gun, the Ship, and the Pen: Warfare, Constitutions, and the Making of the Modern World*. New York: Liveright, 2021.

Cookson, J. E. "Alexander Tulloch and the Chelsea Out-Pensioners, 1838–43: Centralisation in the Early Victorian State." *English Historical Review* 125, no. 512 (February 2010): 60–82.

Cookson, J. E. *The British Armed Nation, 1793–1815*. Oxford: Clarendon Press, 1997.

Cookson, J. E. "Early Nineteenth-Century Scottish Military Pensioners as Homecoming Soldiers." *Historical Journal* 52, no. 2 (2009): 319–41.

Cookson, J. E. *Lord Liverpool's Administration: The Crucial Years, 1815–1822*. Hamden: Archon, 1975.

Cookson, J. E. "Regimental Worlds: Interpreting the Experience of British Soldiers during the Napoleonic Wars." In *Soldiers, Citizens and Civilians: Experiences and Perceptions of the Revolutionary and Napoleonic Wars, 1790–1820*, edited by Alan Forrest, Karen Hagemann, and Jane Rendall, 24–38. Basingstoke: Palgrave Macmillan, 2009.

Corbett, Julian. "Napoleon and the British Navy after Trafalgar." *Quarterly Review* 237 (January and April 1922): 238–55.

Corbett, Julian. *Some Principles of Maritime Strategy*. Annapolis, Md.: Naval Institute Press, 1988.

Cordingly, David. *Billy Ruffian: The* Bellerophon *and the Downfall of Napoleon: The Biography of a Ship of the Line, 1782–1836*. London: Bloomsbury, 2003.

Cormack, Andrew. "The Life of a Soldier before and after Service as Revealed by the Out-Pensioner Records of the Royal Hospital, Chelsea." In *Life in the Red Coat: The British Soldier, 1721–1815*, edited by Andrew Bamford, 17–29. Warwick: Helion, 2020.

Coss, Edward J. *All for the King's Shilling: The British Soldier under Wellington, 1808–1814*. Norman: University of Oklahoma Press, 2010.

Cox Jensen, Oskar. *The Ballad-Singer in Georgian and Victorian London*. Cambridge: Cambridge University Press, 2021.

Cox, Nicholas. "The Records of the Registrar-General of Shipping and Seaman." *Maritime History* 2, no. 2 (September 1972): 168–88.

Craig, David. "Tories and the Language of 'Liberalism' in the 1820s." *English Historical Review* 135, no. 576 (October 2020): 1195–228.

Cubitt, David John. *Lord Cochrane and the Chilean Navy, 1818–1823*. Valparaiso: Corporación Cultural Arturo Prat Chacón, Museo Marítimo Nacional, and Chile + Hoy, 2018.

Daly, Gavin. *The British Soldier in the Peninsular War: Encounters with Spain and Portugal, 1808–1814*. Basingstoke: Palgrave Macmillan, 2013.

Daly, Gavin. "British Soldiers and the Legend of Napoleon." *Historical Journal* 61, no. 1 (March 2018): 131–53.

Daly, Gavin. "English Smugglers, the Channel, and the Napoleonic Wars, 1800–1814." *Journal of British Studies* 46 (January 2007): 30–46.

Daly, Gavin. "Napoleon and the 'City of Smugglers', 1810–1814." *Historical Journal* 50, no. 2 (2007): 333–52.

Dancy, J. Ross. *The Myth of the Press Gang: Volunteers, Impressment and the Naval Manpower Problem in the Late Eighteenth Century*. Woodbridge: Boydell Press, 2015.

Davey, James. "The Advancement of Nautical Knowledge: The Hydrographical Office, the Royal Navy and the Charting of the Baltic Sea, 1795–1815." *Journal for Maritime Research* 13, no. 2 (2011): 81–103.

Davey, James. *In Nelson's Wake: The Navy and the Napoleonic Wars.* New Haven and London: Yale University Press, 2015.

Davids, Karel. "Seamen's Organizations and Social Protest in Europe, c. 1300–1825." *International Review of Social History* 39, no. S1 (1994): 145–69.

Davies, Huw J. *Wellington's Wars: The Making of a Military Genius.* New Haven and London: Yale University Press, 2012.

Davis, Ralph. *The Rise of the English Shipping Industry in the Seventeenth and Eighteenth Centuries.* Newton Abbot: David and Charles, 1962.

Day, Archibald. *The Admiralty Hydrographic Service, 1795–1919.* London: H. M. Stationery Office, 1967.

Denoon, Donald, with Marivic Wyndham. "Australia and the Western Pacific." In *The Nineteenth Century*, edited by Andrew Porter, 546–72. Vol. 3 of *The Oxford History of the British Empire*, edited by William Roger Louis. Oxford: Oxford University Press, 1999.

Dickson, P. G. M. *The Financial Revolution in England: A Study in the Development of Public Credit 1688–1756.* London: Macmillan, 1967.

Dodman, Thomas. "1814 and the Melancholy of War." *Journal of Military History* 80 (January 2016): 31–55.

Dreisbach, Tom, and Meg Anderson, "Nearly 1 in 5 Defendants in Capitol Riot Cases Served in the Military." *NPR*, January 21, 2021. https://www.npr.org /2021/01/21/958915267/ nearly-one-in-five-defendants-in-capitol-riot-cases-served-in-the-military.

Dudley, Wade. "The Flawed British Blockade, 1812–15." In *Naval Blockades and Seapower: Strategies and Counter-Strategies, 1805–2005*, edited by Bruce A. Elleman and S. C. M. Paine, 35–45. London: Routledge, 2006.

Duffy, Michael. "British Policy in the War against Revolutionary France." In *Britain and Revolutionary France: Conflict, Subversion and Propaganda*, edited by Colin Jones, 11–26. Liverpool: Liverpool University Press, 1983.

Dull, Jonathan R. *American Naval History, 1607–1865: Overcoming the Colonial Legacy.* Lincoln: University of Nebraska Press, 2012.

Elkins, Caroline. *Legacy of Violence: A History of the British Empire.* New York: Alfred A. Knopf, 2022.

Elson, Bryan. *Nelson's Yankee Captain: The Life of Boston Loyalist Sir Benjamin Hallowell.* Halifax: Formac Publishing, 2008.

Emsley, Clive. *British Society and the French Wars, 1793–1815.* London and Basingstoke: Macmillan, 1979.

Esdaile, Charles. *Napoleon's Wars: An International History, 1803–1815.* London: Penguin, 2007.

Evans, Eric J. *Britain before the Reform Act: Politics and Society 1815–1832.* 2nd ed. Abingdon: Routledge, 2008.

Fagal, Andrew J.B. "British Responses to the US Steam Frigate *Fulton the First*." *Mariner's Mirror* 107, no. 2 (May 2021): 188–201.

Favret, Mary A. "Everyday War." *ELH* 72, no. 3 (Fall 2005): 605–33.

Fenning, Hugh. "Typhus Epidemic in Ireland, 1817–1819: Priests, Ministers, Doctors." *Collectanea Hibernica* 41 (1999): 117–52.

Ferguson, Niall. *Empire: The Rise and Demise of the British World Order and the Lessons for Global Power.* London: Allen Lane, 2002.

Fisher, D. R., ed. *The House of Commons, 1820–1832.* 7 vols. London: History of Parliament Trust, 2009.

Fitzpatrick, David. "Ireland and the Empire." In *The Nineteenth Century,* edited by Andrew Porter, 495–521. Vol. 3 of *The Oxford History of the British Empire,* edited by William Roger Louis. Oxford: Oxford University Press, 1999.

Ford, Franklin L. *Europe, 1780–1830.* New York: Longman, 1989.

Forrest, Alan. *The Legacy of the French Revolutionary Wars: The Nation-in-Arms in French Republican Memory.* Cambridge: Cambridge University Press, 2009.

Forrest, Alan, Karen Hagemann, and Jane Rendall, eds. *Soldiers, Citizens and Civilians: Experiences and Perceptions of the Revolutionary and Napoleonic Wars, 1790–1820.* Basingstoke: Palgrave Macmillan, 2009.

Forrest, Alan, Karen Hagemann, and Michael Rowe, eds. *War, Demobilization and Memory: The Legacy of War in the Era of Atlantic Revolutions.* Basingstoke: Palgrave Macmillan, 2016.

Fortescue, J. W. *The Empire and the Army.* London: Cassell, 1928.

Fortescue, J. W. *A History of the British Army.* Vol. 11, *1815–1838.* London: Macmillan, 1923.

Fremont-Barnes, Gregory, "The British Army." In *Armies of the Napoleonic Wars,* edited by Gregory Fremont-Barnes, 127–49. Barnsley: Pen and Sword, 2011.

French, David. *The British Way in Warfare, 1688–2000.* New York: Unwin Hyman, 1990.

Friendly, Alfred. *Beaufort of the Admiralty: The Life of Sir Francis Beaufort, 1774–1857.* London: Hutchinson, 1977.

Frykman, Niklas. *The Bloody Flag: Mutiny in the Age of Atlantic Revolution.* Oakland: University of California Press, 2020.

Fury, Cheryl A., ed. *The Social History of English Seamen, 1650–1815.* Woodbridge: Boydell Press, 2017.

Gale, Caitlin M. "Barbary's Slow Death: European Attempts to Eradicate North African Piracy in the Early Nineteenth Century." *Journal for Maritime Research* 18, no. 2 (2016): 139–54.

Gambles, Anna. "Free Trade and State Formation: The Political Economy of Fisheries Policy in Britain and the United Kingdom circa 1780–1850." *Journal of British Studies* 39 (July 2000): 288–316.

Gash, N. "After Waterloo: British Society and the Legacy of the Napoleonic Wars." *Transactions of the Royal Historical Society* 28 (December 1978): 145–57.

Gates, David. *The Napoleonic Wars, 1803–1815.* New York: Edward Arnold, 1997.

Gates, David. "The Transformation of the Army, 1783–1815." In *The Oxford History of the British Army,* edited by David Chandler, 132–60. Oxford: Oxford University Press, 1994.

Gatrell, Vic. *Conspiracy at Cato Street: A Tale of Liberty and Revolution in Regency London.* Cambridge: Cambridge University Press, 2022.

Gibson, James R., and Alexei A. Istomin, eds. *Russian California, 1806–1860: A History in Documents.* 2 vols. London: Hakluyt Society, 2014.

Glete, Jan. *Navies and Nations: Warships, Navies and State Building in Europe and America, 1500–1860.* 2 vols. Stockholm: Almqvist & Wiksell International, 1993.

Glover, Gareth. *Waterloo: Myth and Reality.* Barnsley: Pen and Sword, 2014.

Glover, Michael. *A Very Slippery Fellow: The Life of Sir Robert Wilson, 1777–1849.* Oxford: Oxford University Press, 1978.

Gough, Barry. *Britannia's Navy on the West Coast of North America, 1812–1914.* Victoria: Heritage, 2016.

Gough, Barry. *Pax Britannica: Ruling the Waves and Keeping the Peace before Armageddon*. Basingstoke: Palgrave MacMillan, 2014.

Gough, Barry, and Charles Borras, *The War against the Pirates: British and American Suppression of Caribbean Piracy in the Early Nineteenth Century*. Basingstoke: Palgrave Macmillan, 2018.

Graaf, Beatrice de. *Fighting Terror after Napoleon: How Europe Became Secure after 1815*. Cambridge: Cambridge University Press, 2020.

Graaf, Beatrice de, Frédéric Dessberg, and Thomas Vaisset, eds. *Soldiers in Peace-Making: The Role of the Military at the End of War, 1800–Present*. London: Bloomsbury Academic, 2023.

Graaf, Beatrice de, Ido de Haan, and Brian Vick, eds. *Securing Europe after Napoleon: 1815 and the New European Security Culture*. Cambridge: Cambridge University Press, 2019.

Graham, Gerald S. *The Politics of Naval Supremacy: Studies in British Maritime Ascendancy*. Cambridge: Cambridge University Press, 1965.

Grainger, John D. *The British Navy in the Mediterranean*. Woodbridge: Boydell Press, 2017.

Graves, Donald E. "'The Finest Army Ever to Campaign on American Soil'? The Organization, Strength, Composition, and Losses of British Land Forces during the Plattsburgh Campaign, September 1814." *The War of 1812 Magazine* 24 (November 2015): 1–10.

Graves, Donald E. "The Redcoats Are Coming! British Troop Movements to North America in 1814." *Journal of the War of 1812* 6, no. 3 (2001): 12–18.

Gregory, Desmond. *Brute New World: The Rediscovery of Latin America in the Early Nineteenth Century*. London: British Academic Press, 1992.

Greig, Matilda. *Dead Men Telling Tales: Napoleonic War Veterans and the Military Memoir Industry, 1808–1914*. Oxford: Oxford University Press, 2021.

Grindal, Peter. *Opposing the Slavers: The Royal Navy's Campaign against the Atlantic Slave Trade*. London: I. B. Tauris, 2016.

Grocott, Terence. *Shipwrecks of the Revolutionary and Napoleonic Eras*. London: Chatham, 1997.

Grove, Eric J. *The Royal Navy since 1815: A New Short History*. Basingstoke: Palgrave Macmillan, 2005.

Hagist, Don N. *Noble Volunteers: The British Soldiers Who Fought the American Revolution*. Yardley: Westholme, 2020.

Hall, Christopher D. *British Strategy in the Napoleonic War, 1803–1815*. Manchester: Manchester University Press, 1992.

Hall, Christopher D. *Wellington's Navy: Sea Power and the Peninsular War, 1807–1814*. London: Chatham, 2004.

Hamilton, C. I. "John Wilson Croker: Patronage and Clientage at the Admiralty, 1809–1857." *Historical Journal* 43, no. 1 (March 2000): 49–77.

Harding, Richard. *Seapower and Naval Warfare, 1650–1830*. London: Routledge, 1999.

Harding-Edgar, John. *Next to Wellington: General Sir George Murray*. Warwick: Helion, 2018.

Harley, C. Knick, and N.F.R. Crafts. "Simulating the Two Views of the British Industrial Revolution." *Journal of Economic History* 60, no. 3 (September 2000): 819–41.

Harling, Philip, and Peter Mandler. "From 'Fiscal-Military' State to Laissez-Faire State, 1760–1850." *Journal of British Studies* 32, no. 1 (January 1993): 44–70.

Harrison, Mark. "Scurvy on Sea and Land: Political Economy and Natural History, c. 1780–c. 1850." *Journal for Maritime Research* 15, no. 1 (2013): 7–25.

Hattendorf, John B. "The Brentons of Newport, Rhode Island." In *From Across the Sea: North Americans in Nelson's Navy*, edited by Sean M. Heuvel and John A. Rodgaard, 160–93. Warwick: Helion, 2020.

Hay, George. *The Yeomanry Cavalry and Military Identities in Rural Britain, 1815–1914*. Basingstoke: Palgrave Macmillan, 2017.

Hay, William Anthony. *Lord Liverpool: A Political Life*. Woodbridge: Boydell Press, 2018.

Haynes, Christine. "Making Peace: The Allied Occupation of France, 1815–1818." In *War, Demobilization and Memory: The Legacy of War in the Era of Atlantic Revolutions*, edited by Alan Forrest, Karen Hagemann, and Michael Rowe, 51–67. Basingstoke: Palgrave Macmillan, 2016.

Haynes, Christine. *Our Friends the Enemies: The Occupation of France after Napoleon*. Cambridge, Mass.: Harvard University Press, 2018.

Hayter, Tony. *The Army and the Crowd in Mid-Georgian England*. London: Roman and Littlefield, 1978.

Heuman, Gad. "The British West Indies." In *The Nineteenth Century*, edited by Andrew Porter, 470–94. Vol. 3 of *The Oxford History of the British Empire*, edited by William Roger Louis. Oxford: Oxford University Press, 1999.

Heuvel, Sean M. "Admiral Sir John Wentworth Loring KCB KCH." *Trafalgar Chronicle* 24 (2014): 146–54.

Heuvel, Sean M., and John A. Rodgaard, eds. *From Across the Sea: North Americans in Nelson's Navy*. Warwick: Helion, 2020.

Hilton, Boyd. *A Mad, Bad, and Dangerous People?: England 1783–1846*. Oxford: Oxford University Press, 2008.

Hobson, James. *Dark Days of Georgian Britain: Rethinking the Regency*. Barnsley: Pen and Sword, 2017.

Hope, Ronald. *A New History of British Shipping*. London: John Murray, 1990.

Hopkin, David M. "Storytelling, Fairytales and Autobiography: Some Observations on Eighteenth- and Nineteenth-Century French Soldiers' and Sailors' Memoirs." *Social History* 29, no. 2 (May 2004): 186–98.

Hopkins, A. G. *American Empire: A Global History*. Princeton, N.J.: Princeton University Press, 2018.

Howard, Michael. *The Invention of Peace: Reflections on War and International Order*. New Haven and London: Yale University Press, 2000.

Hughes, Ben. *Conquer or Die! Wellington's Veterans and the Liberation of the New World*. Oxford: Osprey Publishing, 2010.

Hughes, Nigel. "Luke Brokenshaw, Master RN: Part 2." *Trafalgar Chronicle* 23 (2013): 192–212.

Hunter, Mark C. *Policing the Seas: Anglo-American Relations and the Equatorial Atlantic, 1819–1865*. St. John's, Newfoundland: International Maritime Economic History Association, 2008.

Hurl-Eamon, Jennine. "Enslaved by the Uniform: Contemporary Descriptions of Eighteenth-Century Soldiering." *War in History*. Published online July 2022. doi.org/10.1177/09683445221105258.

Hurl-Eamon, Jennine. "Husbands, Sons, Brothers, and Neighbors: Eighteenth-Century Soldiers' Efforts to Maintain Civilian Ties." *Journal of Military History* 86 (April 2022): 299–320.

Hurl-Eamon, Jennine. *Marriage and the British Army in the Long Eighteenth Century*. Oxford: Oxford University Press, 2014.

Ikenberry, G. John. *After Victory: Institutions, Strategic Restraint, and the Rebuilding of Order after Major Wars*. Princeton, N.J.: Princeton University Press, 2001.

Innes, Joanna. "Parliament and the Shaping of Eighteenth-Century English Social Policy." *Transactions of the Royal Historical Society* 40 (1990): 63–92.

James, Leighton S. "The Experience of Demobilization: War Veterans in the Central European Armies and Societies after 1815." In *War, Demobilization and Memory*, edited by Alan Forrest, Karen Hagemann, and Michael Rowe, 68–83. Basingstoke: Palgrave Macmillan, 2016.

Jasanoff, Maya. *Liberty's Exiles: The Loss of America and the Remaking of the British Empire*. London: Harper Press, 2011.

Jayasuria, Shihan de Silva. "Recruiting Africans to the British Regiments in Ceylon: Spillover Effects of Abolition in the Atlantic." *African and Asian Studies* 10 (2011): 15–31.

Jones, Randolph. "The Ceylon Light Dragoons, 1803–32." *Journal of the Society for Army Historical Research* 80 (2002): 313–25.

Jones, Randolph. "The Lascorins of Ceylon in British Service." *Journal of the Society for Army Historical Research* 80 (2002): 1–15.

Jones, Stephen. "Blood Red Roses: The Supply of Merchant Seamen in the Nineteenth Century." *Mariner's Mirror* 58, no. 4 (1972): 429–42.

Jones, Stephen. "Community and Organisation: Early Seamen's Trade Unionism on the North-East Coast, 1768–1844." *Maritime History* 3, no. 1 (April 1973): 35–66.

Kedrosky, Davis. "All Quiet on the Investment Front: Did Britain Sacrifice the Industrial Revolution to Defeat Napoleon?" *Economic History Research*, August 30, 2021. https://daviskedrosky.substack.com/p/all-quiet-on-the-investment-front.

Kennedy, Catriona. *Narratives of the Revolutionary and Napoleonic Wars: Military and Civilian Experience in Britain and Ireland*. Basingstoke: Palgrave Macmillan, 2013.

Kennedy, Catriona. "'True Britons and Real Irish': Irish Catholics in the British Army during the Revolutionary and Napoleonic Wars." In *Soldiering in Britain and Ireland*, edited by Catriona Kennedy and Matthew McCormack, 37–56. Basingstoke: Palgrave Macmillan, 2013.

Kennedy, Catriona, and Matthew McCormack, eds. *Soldiering in Britain and Ireland, 1750–1850: Men of Arms*. Basingstoke: Palgrave Macmillan, 2013.

Kennedy, Paul. *The Rise and Fall of British Naval Mastery*. London: Allen Lane, 1976.

Kennerley, Alston. "British Seamen's Missions in the Nineteenth Century." In *The North Sea: Twelve Essays on Social History of Maritime Labour*, edited by Lewis R. Fischer et al., 79–97. Stavanger: Stavanger Maritime Museum, 1992.

Kennerley, Alston. "Seamen's Missions and Sailors' Homes: Spiritual and Social Welfare Provision for Seafarers in British Ports in the Nineteenth Century, with some Reference to the South West." In *Studies in British Privateering, Trading Enterprise and Seamen's Welfare, 1775–1900*, edited by Stephen Fisher, 121–51. Exeter: University of Exeter Press, 1987.

Kissinger, Henry. *Diplomacy*. New York: Simon and Schuster, 1994.

Kissinger, Henry. *A World Restored: Metternich, Castlereagh and the Problems of Peace, 1812–22*. Boston: Haughton Mifflin, 1957.

Knight, Roger. "The Battle for the Control of the Navy, 1801–1835," *Global Maritime History*. Accessed November 19, 2019. http://globalmaritimehistory.com/the-battle-for-control-of-the-royal-navy-1801-1835/.

Knight, Roger. *Britain against Napoleon: The Organization of Victory, 1793–1815*. London: Penguin, 2013.

Knight, Roger. *Convoys: The British Struggle against Napoleonic Europe and America*. New Haven and London: Yale University Press, 2022.

Lambert, Andrew. *The Challenge: America, Britain and the War of 1812*. London: Faber & Faber, 2012.

Lambert, Andrew. *The Last Sailing Battlefleet: Maintaining Naval Mastery 1815–1850*. London: Conway Maritime Press, 1991.

Lambert, Andrew. "Preparing for the Long Peace: The Reconstruction of the Royal Navy 1815–1830." *Mariner's Mirror* 82, no. 1 (1996): 41–54.

Lambert, Andrew. "Winning without Fighting: British Grand Strategy and Its Application to the United States, 1815–65." In *Strategic Logic and Political Rationality: Essays in Honor of Michael I. Handel*, edited by Bradford A. Lee and Karl F. Walling, 164–95. London: Frank Cass, 2003.

Lange, Erik de. "From Augarten to Algiers: Security and 'Piracy' around the Congress of Vienna." In *Securing Europe after Napoleon: 1815 and the New European Security Culture*, edited by Beatrice de Graaf, Ido de Haan, and Brian Vick, 231–48. Cambridge: Cambridge University Press, 2019.

Lavigne, Franck, et al. "Source of the Great A.D. 1257 Mystery Eruption Unveiled, Samalas Volcano, Rinjani Volcanic Complex, Indonesia." *Proceedings of the National Academy of Sciences* 110, no. 42 (September 2013): 16742–47.

Lewis, Michael. *The Navy in Transition, 1814–1864: A Social History*. London: Hodder and Stoughton, 1965.

Lieven, Dominic. *Russia against Napoleon: The True Story of the Campaigns of "War and Peace."* New York: Viking, 2009.

Lin, Patricia Y. C. E. "Caring for the Nation's Families: British Soldiers' and Sailors' Families and the State, 1793–1815." In *Soldiers, Citizens and Civilians: Experiences and Perceptions of the Revolutionary and Napoleonic Wars, 1790–1820*, edited by Alan Forrest, Karen Hagemann, and Jane Rendall, 99–113. Basingstoke: Palgrave Macmillan, 2009.

Lin, Patricia Y. C. E. "Citizenship, Military Families, and the Creation of a New Definition of 'Deserving Poor' in Britain, 1793–1815." *Social Politics: International Studies in Gender, State and Society* 7, no. 1 (Spring 2000): 5–46.

Linch, Kevin. *Britain and Wellington's Army: Recruitment, Society and Tradition, 1807–15*. Basingstoke: Palgrave Macmillan, 2011.

Linch, Kevin. "Desertion from the British Army during the Napoleonic Wars." *Journal of Social History* 49, no. 4 (2016): 808–28.

Linch, Kevin, and Matthew McCormack. "Defining Soldiers: Britain's Military, c. 1740–1814." *War in History* 20, no. 2 (2013): 144–59.

Linch, Kevin, and Matthew McCormack. "Wellington's Men: The British Soldier of the Napoleonic Wars." *History Compass* 13, no. 6 (2015): 288–96.

Lincoln, Margarette. "The Impact of Warfare on Naval Wives and Women." In *The Social History of English Seamen, 1650–1815*, edited by Cheryl A. Fury, 71–88. Woodbridge: Boydell Press, 2017.

Lincoln, Margarette. *Trading in War: London's Maritime World in the Age of Cook and Nelson*. New Haven and London: Yale University Press, 2018.

Lindert, Peter H., and Jeffery G. Williamson. "Revising England's Social Tables, 1688–1812." *Explorations in Economic History* 19 (1982): 385–408.

Lloyd, Christopher. *Mr. Barrow of the Admiralty: A Life of Sir John Barrow, 1764–1848*. London: Collins, 1970.

Longford, Elizabeth. *Wellington: Pillar of State*. New York: Harper & Row, 1972.

Louis, William Roger, ed. *The Oxford History of the British Empire*. 5 vols. Oxford: Oxford University Press, 1998–2001.

MacArthur, Roderick. "British Army Establishments during the Napoleonic Wars." *Journal of the Society for Army Historical Research* 87, no. 350 (Summer 2009): 150–72.

Malcolm, E. "From Light Infantry to Constabulary: The Military Origins of the Irish Police, 1798–1850." *Irish Sword* 21 (1998): 163–75.

Mallinson, Howard. *Send It by Semaphore: The Old Telegraphs during the Wars with France.* Ramsbury: Crowood Press, 2005.

Mansfield, Nick. "Military Radicals and the Making of Class, 1790–1860." In *Soldiering in Britain and Ireland,* edited by Catriona Kennedy and Matthew McCormack, 57–75. Basingstoke: Palgrave Macmillan, 2013.

Marshall, P. J., ed. *The Eighteenth Century.* Vol. 2 of *The Oxford History of the British Empire,* edited by William Roger Louis. Oxford: Oxford University Press, 1998.

Martin, Ged. "Canada from 1815." In *The Nineteenth Century,* edited by Porter, 522–45. Vol. 3 of *The Oxford History of the British Empire,* edited by William Roger Louis. Oxford: Oxford University Press, 1999.

Martinovich, Paul. *The Sea Is My Element: The Eventful Life of Admiral Sir Pulteney Malcolm, 1768–1838.* Warwick: Helion, 2021.

McCahill, Michael, and Ellis Archer Wasson. "The New Peerage: Recruitment to the House of Lords, 1704–1847." *Historical Journal* 46, no. 1 (2003): 1–38.

McCarthy, Matthew. *Privateering, Piracy and British Policy in Spanish America, 1810–1830.* Woodbridge: Boydell Press, 2013.

McCord, Norman. "The Impress Service in North-East England during the Napoleonic War." *Mariner's Mirror* 54, no. 2 (1968): 163–80.

McCord, Norman. "The Seamen's Strike of 1815 in North-East England." *Economic History Review* 21, no. 1 (April 1968): 127–43.

McCord, Norman. "Tyneside Discontents and Peterloo." *Northern History* 2 (1967): 91–111.

McCranie, Kevin D. *Admiral Lord Keith and the Naval War against Napoleon.* Gainesville: University Press of Florida, 2006.

McCranie, Kevin D. *Mahan, Corbett, and the Foundations of Naval Strategic Thought.* Annapolis, Md.: Naval Institute Press, 2021.

McCranie, Kevin D. *Utmost Gallantry: The U.S. and Royal Navies at Sea in the War of 1812.* Annapolis, Md.: Naval Institute Press, 2011.

McCranie, Kevin D. "The War of 1812 in the Ongoing Napoleonic Wars: The Response of Britain's Royal Navy." *Journal of Military History* 76 (October 2012): 1067–94.

McElligott, Jason, and Martin Conboy, eds. *The Cato Street Conspiracy: Plotting, Counter-Intelligence, and the Revolutionary Tradition in Britain and Ireland.* Manchester: Manchester University Press, 2020.

McNeill, J. R. *Mosquito Empires: Ecology and War in the Greater Caribbean, 1620–1914.* Cambridge: Cambridge University Press, 2010.

Mearsheimer, John J. *The Tragedy of Great Power Politics.* New York: W. W. Norton, 2014.

Merk, Frederick. *The Oregon Question: Essays in Anglo-American Diplomacy and Politics.* Cambridge, Mass.: Harvard University Press, 1967.

Michals, Teresa. *Lame Captains & Left-Handed Admirals: Amputee Officers in Nelson's Navy.* Charlottesville: University of Virginia Press, 2021.

Middleton, Charles Ronald. *The Administration of British Foreign Policy, 1782–1846.* Durham, N.C.: Duke University Press, 1977.

Mikaberidze, Alexander. *The Napoleonic Wars: A Global History.* New York: Oxford University Press, 2020.

Mitchell, B. R. *British Historical Statistics.* Cambridge: Cambridge University Press, 1988.

Monroe, Rachel. "Stolen Valor: Military Impostors, and the People Who Track Them Down." *New Yorker,* October 26, 2020.

Monteiro, Nuno P. *Theory of Unipolar Politics.* New York: Cambridge University Press, 2014.

Morriss, Roger. *Cockburn and the British Navy in Transition: Admiral Sir George Cockburn, 1772–1853.* Columbia: University of South Carolina Press, 1997.

Morriss, Roger. "Endeavour, Discovery, and Idealism, 1760–1895." In *The Oxford Illustrated History of the Royal Navy,* edited by J. R. Hill, 227–49. Oxford: Oxford University Press, 1995.

Morrow, John. *British Flag Officers in the French Wars, 1793–1815: Admirals' Lives.* London: Bloomsbury Academic, 2018.

Muir, Rory. *Britain and the Defeat of Napoleon, 1807–1815.* New Haven and London: Yale University Press, 1996.

Muir, Rory. *Wellington: The Path to Victory, 1769–1814.* New Haven and London: Yale University Press, 2013.

Muir, Rory. *Wellington: Waterloo and the Fortunes of Peace, 1814–1852.* New Haven and London: Yale University Press, 2015.

Murray, Williamson, and Jim Lacey, eds. *The Making of Peace: Rulers, States, and the Aftermath of War.* Cambridge: Cambridge University Press, 2009.

Musteen, Jason R. *Nelson's Refuge: Gibraltar in the Age of Napoleon.* Annapolis, Md.: Naval Institute Press, 2011.

Myatt, Frederick. *The British Infantry, 1660–1945: The Evolution of a Fighting Force.* Dorset: Blandford Press, 1983.

Myerly, Scott Hughes. *British Military Spectacle: From the Napoleonic Wars through the Crimea.* Cambridge, Mass.: Harvard University Press, 1996.

Navickas, Katrina. *Protest and the Politics of Space and Place, 1789–1848.* Manchester: Manchester University Press, 2016.

Navickas, Katrina. "'A Reformer's Wife Ought to Be a Heroine': Gender, Family and English Radicals Imprisoned under the Suspension of Habeas Corpus Act of 1817." *History* 101, no. 345 (April 2016): 246–64.

Navickas, Katrina. "The Search for 'General Ludd': The Mythology of Luddism." *Social History* 30, no. 3 (August 2005): 281–95.

Nielsen, Caroline. "'Continuing to Serve?' Representations of the Elderly Veteran Soldier." In *Men after War,* edited by Stephen McVeigh and Nicola Cooper, 18–35. London: Routledge, 2015.

Noel-Smith, Heather, and Lorna M. Campbell. *Hornblower's Historical Shipmates: The Young Gentlemen of Pellew's Indefatigable.* Woodbridge: Boydell Press, 2016.

O'Brien, Patrick K. "The Impact of the Revolutionary and Napoleonic Wars, 1793–1815, on the Long-Run Growth of the British Economy." *Review (Fernand Braudel Center)* 12, no. 3 (Summer 1989): 335–95.

O'Brien, Patrick K. "Inseparable Connections: Trade, Economy, Fiscal State, and the Expansion of Empire, 1688–1815." In *The Eighteenth Century,* edited by P. J. Marshall, 53–77. Vol. 2 of *The Oxford History of the British Empire,* edited by William Roger Louis. Oxford: Oxford University Press, 1999.

O'Brien, Patrick K. "The Political Economy of British Taxation, 1660–1815." *Economic History Review,* 2nd series, 41, no. 1 (1988): 1–32.

O'Gorman, Frank. *The Long Eighteenth Century: British Political and Social History, 1688–1832.* London: Hodder Arnold, 1997.

Palmer, Sarah, and David M. Williams. "British Sailors, 1775–1870." In *"Those Emblems of Hell"? European Sailors and the Maritime Labour Market, 1570–1870,* edited by Paul van Royen, Jaap Bruijn, and Jan Lucassen, 93–114. St. John's, Newfoundland: International Maritime Economic History Association, 1997.

Palmer, Stanley H. *Police and Protest in England and Ireland, 1780–1850.* Cambridge: Cambridge University Press, 1988.

Parkinson, C. Northcote. *Edward Pellew, Viscount Exmouth, Admiral of the Red.* London: Methuen, 1934.

Parkinson, C. Northcote. *Samuel Walters, Lieutenant, R.N.* Liverpool: Liverpool University Press, 1949.

Peacock, A. J. *Bread or Blood: A Study of the Agrarian Riots in East Anglia in 1816.* London: Victor Gollancz, 1965.

Peers, Douglas M. "Soldiers, Scholars, and the Scottish Enlightenment: Militarism in Early Nineteenth-Century India." *International History Review* 16, no. 3 (August 1994): 441–65.

Peers, Douglas M. "War and Public Finance in Early Nineteenth-Century British India: The First Burma War." *International History Review* 11, no. 4 (November 1989): 628–47.

Perkins, Bradford. *Castlereagh and Adams: England and the United States, 1812–1823.* Berkeley: University of California Press, 1967.

Perkins, Roger. *Gunfire in Barbary.* Havant: Kenneth Mason, 1982.

Pfaff, Steven, and Michael Hechter. *The Genesis of Rebellion: Governance, Grievance and Mutiny in the Age of Sail.* Cambridge: Cambridge University Press, 2020.

Philp, Roy. *The Coast Blockade: The Royal Navy's War on Smuggling in Kent & Sussex, 1817–31.* Horsham: Compton Press, 1999.

Pincus, Steve, and James Robinson. "Wars and State-Making Reconsidered: The Rise of the Developmental State." *Annales HHS (English Edition)* 71, no. 1 (2016): 9–34.

Platt, Stephen R. *Imperial Twilight: The Opium War and the End of China's Last Golden Age.* New York: Alfred A. Knopf, 2018.

Pocock, Tom. *Remember Nelson: The Life of Sir William Hoste.* Barnsley: Pen and Sword, 2005.

Poole, Robert. "French Revolution or Peasants' Revolt? Petitioners and Rebels in England from the Blanketeers to the Chartists." *Labour History Review* 74, no. 1 (April 2009): 6–26.

Poole, Robert. "The March to Peterloo: Politics and Festivity in Late Georgian England." *Past and Present* 192 (August 2006): 109–53.

Poole, Robert. *Peterloo: The English Uprising.* Oxford: Oxford University Press, 2019.

Porter, Andrew, ed. *The Nineteenth Century.* Vol. 3 of *The Oxford History of the British Empire,* edited by William Roger Louis. Oxford: Oxford University Press, 1999.

Prell, Donald. *A Biography of Captain Daniel Roberts.* Palm Springs, Calif.: Strand Publishing, 2010.

Press, Jon. "The Collapse of a Contributory Pension Scheme: The Merchant Seamen's Fund, 1747–1851." *Journal of Transport History* ss-5, no. 2 (September 1979): 91–104.

Press, Jon. "Wages in the Merchant Navy, 1815–54." *Journal of Transport History* 2, no. 2 (September 1981): 37–52.

Prida, Gonzalo Butrón. "From Hope to Defensiveness: The Foreign Policy of a Beleaguered Liberal Spain, 1820–1823." *English Historical Review* 133, no. 562 (June 2018): 567–96.

Ramachandra, G.P. "The Outbreak of the First Anglo-Burmese War." *Journal of the Malaysian Branch of the Royal Asiatic Society* 51, no. 2 (1978): 66–99.

Ramsey, Neil. *The Military Memoir and Romantic Literary Culture, 1780–1835.* Farnham: Ashgate, 2012.

Ramsey, Neil. "'A Real English Soldier': Suffering, Manliness and Class in the Mid-Nineteenth-Century Soldiers' Tale." In *Soldiering in Britain and Ireland*, edited by Catriona Kennedy and Matthew McCormack, 136–55. Basingstoke: Palgrave Macmillan, 2013.

Remini, Robert V. *Andrew Jackson and the Course of American Empire, 1767–1821.* New York: Harper & Row, 1977.

Richmond, Herbert. *Statesmen and Sea Power.* Westport, Conn.: Greenwood Press, 1974

Rieser, Alison. "The Herring Enlightenment: Adam Smith and the Reform of British Fishing Subsidies, 1783–1799." *International Journal of Maritime History* 29, no. 3 (2017): 600–19.

Rigby, Nigel, Pieter Van Der Merwe, and Glyn Williams. *Pacific Exploration: Voyages of Discovery from Captain Cook's Endeavour to the Beagle.* London: Bloomsbury, 2018.

Ritchie, G. S. *The Admiralty Chart: British Naval Hydrography in the Nineteenth Century.* New ed. Edinburgh: Pentland Press, 1995.

Rodger, N. A. M. *The Command of the Ocean: A Naval History of Britain, 1649–1815.* New York: W. W. Norton, 2004.

Rodger, N. A. M. "War as an Economic Activity in the 'Long' Eighteenth Century." *International Journal of Maritime History* 22, no. 2 (December 2010): 1–18.

Rodger, N. A. M. *The Wooden World: An Anatomy of the Georgian Navy.* Annapolis, Md.: Naval Institute Press, 1986.

Rogers, Nicholas. "British Impressment and Its Discontents." *International Journal of Maritime History* 30, no. 1 (2018): 52–73.

Rowe, D. J. "A Trade Union of the North-East Coast Seamen in 1825." *Economic History Review* 25, no. 1 (February 1972): 81–98.

Royle, Dan. "Winning the War and Losing the Peace: Spain and the Congress of Vienna." *International History Review* 44, no. 2 (2021): 1–16.

Ryan, A. N. "An Ambassador Afloat: Vice-Admiral Sir James Saumarez and the Swedish Court, 1808–1812." In *The British Navy and the Use of Naval Power in the Eighteenth Century,* edited by Jeremy Black and Philip Woodfine, 237–58. Leicester: Leicester University Press, 1988.

Ryan, Maeve. "The Price of Legitimacy in Humanitarian Intervention: Britain, the Right of Search, and the Abolition of the West African Slave Trade, 1807–1867." In *Humanitarian Intervention: A History,* edited by Brendan Simms and D. J. B. Trim, 231–56. Cambridge: Cambridge University Press, 2011.

Satia, Priya. *Empire of Guns: The Violent Making of the Industrial Revolution.* New York: Penguin, 2018.

Schroeder, Paul W. *The Transformation of European Politics, 1763–1848.* Oxford: Clarendon Press, 1994.

Scott, Joan W. "The Evidence of Experience." *Critical Inquiry* 17, no. 4 (Summer 1991): 773–97.

Sheppard, Eric William. *A Short History of the British Army.* 4th ed. London: Constable, 1950.

Siemann, Wolfram. *Metternich: Strategist and Visionary.* Translated by Daniel Steuer. Cambridge, Mass.: Harvard University Press, 2019.

Simms, Brendan. *The Longest Afternoon: The 400 Men Who Decided the Battle of Waterloo.* London: Allen Lane, 2014.

Sivasundaram, Sujit. "Tales of the Land: British Geography and Kandyan Resistance in Sri Lanka, c. 1803–1850." *Modern Asian Studies* 41, no. 5 (2007): 925–65.

Sloane, Nan. *Uncontrollable Women: Radicals, Reformers and Revolutionaries.* London: I. B. Tauris, 2022.

Solar, Peter M. "Late Eighteenth-Century Merchant Ships in War and Peace." *International Journal of Maritime History* 28, no. 1 (2016): 36–63.

Sondhaus, Lawrence. *Naval Warfare, 1815–1914.* London: Routledge, 2001.

Sondhaus, Lawrence. *Navies in Modern World History.* London: Reaktion Books, 2004.

Spence, Daniel Owen. *A History of the Royal Navy: Empire and Imperialism.* London: I. B. Tauris, 2015.

Stark, Suzanne J. *Female Tars: Women aboard Ship in the Age of Sail.* Annapolis, Md.: Naval Institute Press, 1996.

Starkey, David J. "Private Enterprise, Public Policy and the Development of Britain's Seafaring Workforce." In *The Social History of English Seamen, 1650–1815,* edited by Cheryl A. Fury, 147–82. Woodbridge: Boydell Press, 2017.

Starkey, David J. "Quantifying British Seafarers, 1789–1828." In *Maritime Labour: Contributions to the History of Work at Sea, 1500–2000,* edited by Richard Gorski, 88–101. Amsterdam: Aksant, 2007.

Strachan, Hew. "The British Army, 1815–1856." *Journal of the Society for Army Historical Research* 63, no. 254 (Summer 1985): 68–79.

Strachan, Hew. *From Waterloo to Balaclava: Tactics, Technology, and the British Army, 1815–1854.* Cambridge: Cambridge University Press, 1985.

Strachan, Hew. *The Politics of the British Army.* Oxford: Clarendon Press, 1997.

Sumida, Jon Testuro. *Decoding Clausewitz: A New Approach to "On War."* Lawrence: University Press of Kansas, 2008.

Sutcliffe, Robert K. *British Expeditionary Warfare and the Defeat of Napoleon, 1793–1815.* Woodbridge: Boydell Press, 2016.

Symes, E. P. "The Coastguard in Ireland." *Irish Sword* 23 (2002): 201–10.

Taylor, Michael. "The British West India Interest and Its Allies, 1823–1833." *English Historical Review* 133, no. 565 (December 2018): 1478–511.

Taylor, R. "Manning the Royal Navy: The Reform of the Recruiting System, 1852–1862." *Mariner's Mirror* 44, no. 4 (1958): 302–13.

Taylor, Stephen. *Sons of the Waves: The Common Seaman in the Heroic Age of Sail.* New Haven and London: Yale University Press, 2020.

Thant Myint-U, *The Hidden History of Burma: Race, Capitalism, and the Crisis of Democracy in the 21st Century.* New York: W. W. Norton, 2021.

Thompson, E. P. *The Making of the English Working Class.* New York: Vintage, 1965.

Thorne, R. G. *The House of Commons, 1790–1820.* 5 vols. London: History of Parliament Trust, 1986.

Till, Geoffrey. *Seapower: A Guide for the Twenty-First Century.* 4th ed. London: Routledge, 2018.

Uglow, Jenny. *In These Times: Living in Britain through Napoleon's Wars, 1793–1815.* London: Faber & Faber, 2014.

Vale, Brian. *Independence or Death! British Sailors and Brazilian Independence, 1822–1825.* London: I. B. Tauris, 1996.

Vale, Brian. "Lord Cochrane in Chile: Heroism, Plots and Paranoia." In *The Age of Sail: The International Annual of the Historic Sailing Ship,* edited by Nicholas Tracy, 1:59–68. London: Conway Maritime, 2002.

Vale, Brian. "The Post Office, The Admiralty and Letters to Sailors in the Napoleonic Wars." *Mariner's Mirror* 105, no. 2 (2019): 148–61.

Van Royen, Paul, Jaap Bruijn, and Jan Lucassen, eds. *"Those Emblems of Hell"? European Sailors and the Maritime Labour Market, 1570–1870.* St. John's, Newfoundland: International Maritime Economic History Association, 1997.

Vartavarian, Mesrob. "Pacification and Patronage in the Maratha Deccan, 1803–1818." *Modern Asian Studies* 50, no. 6 (2016): 1749–91.

Voelcker, Tim. *Admiral Saumarez versus Napoleon: The Baltic, 1807–12.* Woodbridge: Boydell Press, 2008.

Wade Martins, Susanna. *Coke of Norfolk (1754–1842): A Biography.* Woodbridge: Boydell Press, 2009.

Walker, David, and Adrian Webb. "The Making of Mr George Thomas RN, Admiralty Surveyor for Home Waters from 1810." *Mariner's Mirror* 104, no. 2 (2018): 211–24.

Warner, Jessica, and Allyson Lunny. "Marital Violence in a Martial Town: Husbands and Wives in Early Modern Portsmouth, 1653–1781." *Journal of Family History* 28 (2003): 258–76.

Washbrook, D. A. "India, 1818–1860." In *The Nineteenth Century*, edited by Andrew Porter, 395–421. Vol. 3 of *The Oxford History of the British Empire*, edited by William Roger Louis. Oxford: Oxford University Press, 1999.

Waugh, Mary. *Smuggling in Kent and Sussex, 1700–1840.* 2nd ed. Newbury, Berkshire: Countryside Books, 1998.

Webb, Paul. "Construction, Repair and Maintenance in the Battle Fleet of the Royal Navy, 1793–1815." In *The British Navy and the Use of Naval Power in the Eighteenth Century*, edited by Jeremy Black and Philip Woodfine, 207–20. Leicester: Leicester University Press, 1988.

Webster, Charles K. *The Foreign Policy of Castlereagh, 1815–1822: Britain and the European Alliance.* London: G. Bell, 1925.

Webster, Charles K. *The Foreign Policy of Castlereagh, 1812–1815: Britain and the Reconstruction of Europe.* London: G. Bell, 1931.

Wells, Roger A. E. *Wretched Faces: Famine in Wartime England, 1793–1801.* London: Breviary Stuff, 2011.

Weiss, Josh. "Mission Command in the Age of Sail." *Naval War College Review* 75, no. 3 (Summer 2022): 93–127.

White, R. J. *Waterloo to Peterloo.* London: W. Heinemann, 1957.

Wilcox, Martin. "The 'Poor Decayed Seamen' of Greenwich Hospital, 1705–1763." *International Journal of Maritime History* 25, no. 1 (2013): 65–90.

Wilcox, Martin. "'These Peaceable Times Are the Devil': Royal Navy Officers in the Post-War Slump, 1815–1825." *International Journal of Maritime History* 26, no. 3 (2014): 471–88.

Wills, Mary. "At War with the 'Detestable Traffic': The Royal Navy's Anti-Slavery Cause in the Atlantic Ocean." In *The Royal Navy and the British Atlantic World, c. 1750–1820*, edited by John McAleer and Christer Petley, 123–46. London: Palgrave Macmillan, 2016.

Wills, Mary. *Envoys of Abolition: British Naval Officers and the Campaign Against the Slave Trade in West Africa.* Liverpool: Liverpool University Press, 2019.

Wilson, Ben. *Empire of the Deep: The Rise and Fall of the British Navy.* London: Weidenfeld & Nicolson, 2013.

Wilson, Evan. "Britain: Practicing Aggression." In *Eighteenth-Century Naval Officers: A Transnational Perspective*, edited by Evan Wilson, AnnaSara Hammar, and Jakob Seerup, 11–46. Basingstoke: Palgrave Macmillan, 2019.

Wilson, Evan. "The Limits of Naval Power: Britain after 1815." In *Navies in Multipolar Worlds: From the Age of Sail to the Present*, edited by Paul Kennedy and Evan Wilson, 62–81. London: Routledge, 2020.

Wilson, Evan. "The Monster from Elba: Napoleon's Escape Reconsidered." *Mariner's Mirror* 107, no. 3 (2021): 265–79.

Wilson, Evan. "The Naval Defence of Ireland in the French Revolutionary and Napoleonic Wars." *Historical Research* 92, no. 257 (2019): 568–84.

Wilson, Evan. "Social Background and Promotion Prospects in the Royal Navy, 1775–1815." *English Historical Review* 131, no. 550 (2016): 570–95.

Wilson, Evan. *A Social History of British Naval Officers, 1775–1815.* Woodbridge: Boydell Press, 2017.

Wilson, Evan. "Soldiers versus Veterans: Peacemaking in Britain after Napoleon." In *Soldiers in Peace-Making: The Role of the Military at the End of War, 1800–Present,* edited by Beatrice de Graaf, Frédéric Dessberg, and Thomas Vaisset, chapter 11. London: Bloomsbury Academic, 2023.

Wilson, Evan, AnnaSara Hammar, and Jakob Seerup. "The Education and Careers of Naval Officers in the Long Eighteenth Century: An International Perspective." *Journal for Maritime Research* 17, no. 1 (2015): 17–33.

Wood, Stephen. "Portrait of a Trafalgar Midshipman: John Windham Dalling of HMS *Defence.*" *Trafalgar Chronicle* 23 (2013): 103–22.

Wright, Christine. "Military Settlers: The Men of the Royal Veteran Companies and Royal Staff Corps (1825)." *Journal of the Royal Australian Historical Society* 95, no. 2 (June 2009): 158–75.

Wright, Christine. *Wellington's Men in Australia: Peninsular War Veterans and the Making of Empire, c. 1820–1840.* Basingstoke: Palgrave Macmillan, 2011.

UNPUBLISHED DISSERTATIONS AND WORKING PAPERS

Brunt, Liam, and Erik Meidell. "How Fast and How Broad Was British Industrialization?" Economic History Association Working Paper, 2013. EH.net.

Clark, Gregory. "The Condition of the Working-Class in England, 1209–2004." Working Paper, No. 05–39 (2005), University of California, Department of Economics, Davis, CA.

Kennerley, Alston. "British Seamen's Missions and Sailors' Homes, 1815 to 1970: Voluntary Welfare Provision for Serving Seafarers." PhD diss., University of Plymouth, 1989.

Milkes, Elisa Renee. "A Battle's Legacy: Waterloo in Nineteenth-Century Britain." Ph.D. diss., Yale University, 2002.

Pietsch, Roland W. W. "Ships' Boys and Charity in the Mid-Eighteenth Century: The London Marine Society (1756–1772)." PhD diss., Queen Mary University of London, in collaboration with the National Maritime Museum, 2003.

Preston, Virginia. "Constructing Communities: Living and Working in the Royal Navy, c. 1830–1860." PhD diss., University of Greenwich, 2008.

Reynolds, Luke. "Who Owned Waterloo? Wellington's Veterans and the Battle for Relevance." PhD diss., the City University of New York, 2019.

Smith, Shane. "Forgotten Settlers: The Migration, Society and Legacies of British Military Veterans to Upper Canada (Ontario), from 1815–1855." PhD diss., University of Northumbria at Newcastle, 2018.

Webb, Adrian. "The Expansion of British Naval Hydrographic Administration, 1808–1829." PhD diss., University of Exeter, 2010.

Williams, David M. "British Merchant Shipping and Its Labour Force in an Era of Economic Expansion and Social Change, 1790–1914." PhD diss., University of Leicester, 2003.

DATABASES

The British Newspaper Archive. The British Library. https://www.britishnewspaperar-
        chive.co.uk.
Harrison, Cy, et al. *Three Decks: Warships in the Age of Sail*. https://threedecks.org.
Hitchcock, Tim, Robert Shoemaker, Clive Emsley, Sharon Howard, and Jamie
        McLaughlin et al. *The Old Bailey Proceedings Online, 1674–1913*. https://www.
        oldbaileyonline.org, version 8.0.
U.K. Parliamentary Papers. ProQuest. https://parlipapers.proquest.com/parlipapers.

Index